P9-DWJ-931

582 Down-Home Recipes Right at Your Fingertips

"I'VE BEEN a subscriber to *Taste of Home* since it was first introduced, and I find the magazine a refreshing change from other cooking publications," writes Joanne Brookover of Garrettsville, Ohio.

"But since my collection of issues is growing, I often have a hard time finding a recipe I want in all those back issues. I wish you'd gather each year's recipes into a book and index them thoroughly so I could find any recipe I want in a jiffy."

Our test-kitchen staff received so many reader requests like Joanne's that we just had to respond—and you're holding the result in your hands. This *1997 Taste of Home Annual Recipes* book will be the "time-savingest" cookbook in your kitchen for a number of reasons:

1. Its 324 pages are organized into 16 handy chapters for easy reference. Between its covers you have at hand every single *Taste of Home* recipe we published in 1996.
2. Plus we've included *dozens* of bonus recipes never before published in *Taste of Home.* So you'll have a whole group of new down-home recipes to try.
3. We've listed all 582 of these recipes in *three different indexes* to make any of them easy to find—one indexes them by food category, one tells you which issue of *Taste of Home* it originally appeared in, and one designates every recipe that meets diabetic and restricted diet needs. These handy indexes can be found on pages 306-318.
4. The full-color pictures in this cookbook are *bigger* than ever so you can plainly see what many of these dishes will look like before you begin preparing them.
5. We've used larger print for easy reading while cooking. And each recipe is presented "all-on-a-page", so you never have to turn back and forth while cooking.
6. This volume is printed on the highest-quality coated paper to make the foods more attractive and appealing. More importantly, it lets you wipe away spatters easily.
7. The book's spine is "rounded and relaxed" instead of square, so it lies open and *stays open* as you cook. Its durable hard cover will give you *years* of use (you'll never have to worry about dog-earring your magazine collection again).

But the real proof of this volume's value is in the tasting. Your family will *rave* at the results of these recipes, all of which are favorites of other families.

Tight on time? See our "Meals in Minutes" chapter. Its 55 fast-to-fix recipes give you complete meals that you can whip up in 30 minutes or less (including dessert).

On a budget? How would you like to feed your family for 98¢ per plate? You can, if you turn to page 257 for hearty "Chili Burgers" with zesty "Garden Potato Salad" and simmering "Hot Apple Sundaes".

Family picnic? Or need a dish for a potluck or other group gathering? Try one of the 42 "Cooking for a Crowd" recipes and you'll be the "star" of the party.

You're sure to refer to this thoroughly indexed treasury of recipes again and again for years to come. You'll never be at a loss when you're looking to treat your family or friends to a hearty *Taste of Home.*

1997 Taste of Home Annual Recipes

Editors: Julie Schnittka, Geri Truszynski

Art Director: Vicky Marie Moseley

Assistant Art Directors: Linda Dzik, Maribeth Greinke, Thomas Hunt, Ellen Lloyd, Bonnie Ziolecki

Associate Editor: Kristine Krueger

Executive Editor: Kathy Pohl

Food Editor: Mary Beth Jung

Assistant Food Editor: Coleen Martin

Senior Editor: Bob Ottum

Managing Editor: Ann Kaiser

Assistant Managing Editor: Faithann Stoner

Associate Editors: Henry de Fiebre, Kristine Krueger, Sharon Selz

Test Kitchen Home Economists: Karla Spies, Corinne Goshaw

Test Kitchen Assistants: Judith Scholovich, Sherry Smalley

Editorial Assistants: Mary Ann Koebernik, Barb Czysz

Design Director: Jim Sibilski

Art Director: Vicky Marie Moseley

Food Photography: Scott Anderson, Glenn Thiesenhusen

Food Photography Artist: Stephanie Marchese

Photo Studio Coordinator: Anne Schimmel

Production: Ellen Lloyd, Judy Pope

Publisher: Roy Reiman

Taste of Home Books
©1996 Reiman Publications, L.P.
5400 S. 60th St., Greendale WI 53129

International Standard Book Number:
0-89821-176-X

All rights reserved.
Printed in U.S.A.

PICTURED AT RIGHT. Clockwise from lower left: Herbed Pot Roast (p. 71), Raspberry Ribbon Cheesecake (p. 144), Peasant Soup for One, Apple Ham Salad and Sunny Cornmeal Muffins (p. 279), Hot Cross Buns (p. 105), Special Cinnamon Rolls (p. 102), Italian Easter Bread (p. 104) and Orange Knots (p. 98).

Taste of Home 1997
Annual Recipes

PICTURED ON THE FRONT COVER. Clockwise from bottom: Scott's Beef Brisket (p. 78), Plum Pie (p. 132), Sour Cream 'n' Chive Biscuits (p. 98) and Three-Green Salad (p. 170).

PICTURED ON THE BACK COVER. Clockwise from bottom: Vanilla Cream Fruit Tart (p. 135), Blueberry French Toast (p. 90), Super Strawberry Shortcake (p. 138) and Lemon Whirligigs with Raspberries (p. 149).

Photo Contributors: p. 191—The Wright Studio, p. 195—Dennis A. Carney, p. 203—Diane Cattau.

FOR ADDITIONAL COPIES of this book or information on other books, write: *Taste of Home* Books, P.O. Box 990, Greendale WI 53129. **Credit card orders call toll-free 1-800/558-1013.**

Snacks & Beverages

These hearty appetizers, satisfying snacks and refreshing beverages can be whipped up in a hurry.

PICTURED AT LEFT. Clockwise from top right: Low-Fat Bean Dip (p. 13), Hearty Cheese Spread (p. 10), Pretzels with Cheese Dip (p. 9), Crunchy Italian Mix (p. 12), Cajun Popcorn (p. 12) and Blackberry Fizz (p. 9).

VEGGIE CHRISTMAS TREE

(Pictured above)

I've been serving this festive appetizer for years. Everyone comments on how pretty it is. I especially like it because it's so easy to make. —Leola Seltmann
Wichita, Kansas

✓ **This tasty dish uses less sugar, salt and fat. Recipe includes *Diabetic Exchanges*.**

  1 bottle (8 ounces) ranch salad dressing
  4 cups broccoli florets
  1 broccoli stem
  3 to 4 cups cauliflowerets
  4 to 5 cherry tomatoes, quartered
  1 medium carrot, sliced

Cover the bottom of a 13-in. x 9-in. x 2-in. glass dish with dressing. Arrange broccoli in a tree shape, using the stem as the trunk. Place cauliflower around tree. Add tomatoes and carrot slices as ornaments. **Yield:** 20 servings. **Diabetic Exchanges:** One serving (prepared with low-fat dressing) equals 1 vegetable; also, 37 calories, 102 mg sodium, 0 cholesterol, 4 gm carbohydrate, 2 gm protein, 2 gm fat.

CITRUS MINT PUNCH

Mint gives this citrus punch some real spark. I especially like to serve this beverage at bridal and baby showers and during the summer months at luncheons.
—Judith Anglen
Riverton, Wyoming

  1 cup packed fresh mint leaves
Grated peel of 1 orange
Grated peel of 1 lemon
  3 cups boiling water

  1 can (12 ounces) frozen lemonade concentrate, thawed
  1 can (12 ounces) frozen orange juice concentrate, thawed
1-1/2 quarts cold water
Additional mint leaves, optional

Place mint and peels in a heat-resistant pitcher or bowl; add boiling water. Let steep 1 hour; strain. Add concentrates and water; stir well. Chill. Serve over ice; garnish with mint if desired. **Yield:** 18-20 servings (3 quarts).

SALMON PARTY SPREAD

This recipe deliciously showcases our state's flavorful salmon. So whenever we have out-of-state visitors, this spread is sure to appear on the menu.
—Kathy Crow
Cordova, Alaska

  1 package (8 ounces) cream cheese, softened
  1 can (7-1/2 ounces) pink salmon, drained, flaked and cartilage removed
  3 tablespoons chopped fresh parsley
  2 tablespoons finely chopped green pepper
  2 tablespoons finely chopped sweet red pepper
  2 teaspoons grated onion
  1 teaspoon lemon juice
  1 teaspoon prepared horseradish
1/2 teaspoon liquid smoke, optional
Finely chopped pecans *or* additional parsley
Crackers

In a bowl, combine the first nine ingredients; stir until well blended. Cover and chill 2-24 hours. Transfer to a serving bowl; sprinkle with pecans or parsley. Serve with crackers. **Yield:** 2 cups.

HERBED GARLIC TOAST

My wife and I grow over 300 different herbs and sell plants and fresh and dried herbs. Herbs sure make meals more interesting. We use them generously in a variety of recipes...like this. —Bruce Shomler
Paso Robles, California

1/4 cup minced fresh parsley
  3 tablespoons minced fresh basil
  3 tablespoons minced fresh thyme
  1 tablespoon chopped fresh mint
  3 tablespoons olive *or* vegetable oil
  2 tablespoons red wine vinegar

1 tablespoon sugar
2 garlic cloves, minced
1/2 teaspoon salt
1/4 teaspoon pepper
1 loaf (1/2 pound) French bread

In a small bowl, combine the first 10 ingredients; let stand at room temperature for 30 minutes. Cut bread into 12 slices; place in a single layer on an ungreased baking sheet. Bake at 350° for 5 minutes or until lightly browned. Immediately top each slice with 2 teaspoonfuls of herb mixture. Serve hot. **Yield:** about 6 servings.

PICADILLO DIP

Like a hearty hot dip that's both sweet and savory? This recipe with deliciously different ingredients is!
—Lisa Revell
Vernon, New Jersey

1 pound ground beef
1 cup water
1 garlic clove, minced
1/2 teaspoon salt
1/4 teaspoon pepper
1 can (14-1/2 ounces) diced tomatoes, undrained
1 can (6 ounces) tomato paste
1/2 cup raisins
1/2 cup slivered almonds
1/4 cup chopped stuffed olives
1/2 teaspoon sugar
Tortilla chips

In a large saucepan, brown beef. Add water, garlic, salt and pepper. Cover and simmer for 20 minutes; drain. Add the next six ingredients; mix well. Cover and simmer for 45 minutes, stirring occasionally. Serve hot with chips. **Yield:** 4 cups.

BLACKBERRY FIZZ

For a festive beverage with a distinctive berry flavor and a hint of spice, try this recipe. We save it for holidays and special times with family and friends. It's a delightful drink people will remember. *—Andrea Eberly*
Sarasota, Florida

3 quarts fresh *or* frozen blackberries
4 cups water
3 cups sugar
1 tablespoon whole cloves
1 tablespoon whole allspice
2 cinnamon sticks (4 inches), broken
Lemon-lime *or* white soda

Crush the blackberries in a large kettle. Add water and bring to a boil. Reduce heat to medium and cook for 10 minutes. Strain through a jelly bag, reserving juice and discarding pulp. Add water to juice if necessary to equal 2 qts.; pour into a large kettle. Slowly stir in sugar until dissolved. Place spices in a cheesecloth bag; add to juice. Simmer, uncovered, for 30 minutes. Bring to a boil; remove the spice bag and discard. Pour hot into hot jars, leaving 1/4-in. headspace. Adjust caps. Process for 15 minutes in a boiling-water bath. To serve, mix about one-third concentrate with two-thirds soda. **Yield:** about 4 pints concentrate.

PRETZELS WITH CHEESE DIP

These are by far the best soft pretzels I've ever tasted. I make them often to serve as a snack or even as part of a meal. Chewy and golden brown, they're delicious!
—Shannon Cooper
South Gibson, Pennsylvania

1 package (1/4 ounce) active dry yeast
1 cup warm water (110° to 115°)
2 tablespoons butter *or* margarine, softened
1 tablespoon sugar
1/2 teaspoon salt
2-3/4 cups all-purpose flour
4 cups water
2 tablespoons baking soda
Coarse salt
8 ounces process American cheese, cubed
1 package (3 ounces) cream cheese, cubed
1 to 2 tablespoons milk
Prepared mustard

In a large mixing bowl, dissolve yeast in warm water. Add butter, sugar, salt and 2 cups flour; beat until smooth. Add enough remaining flour to form a soft dough. Cover and let rise in a warm place for 20 minutes. Punch dough down. Divide into 12 equal pieces. On a lightly floured board, roll each piece into a 15-in.-long strip; twist into a pretzel shape. In a large non-aluminum kettle, bring water to a boil; add baking soda. Drop two pretzels into water; boil for 1 minute. Remove with a slotted spoon; drain. Place on a greased baking sheet; sprinkle with coarse salt. Repeat for each pretzel. Bake at 475° for 10-12 minutes. Meanwhile, combine cheeses in a microwave-safe bowl. Microwave on high for 2-3 minutes or until melted, stirring occasionally. Stir in milk. Serve the pretzels with the cheese dip and mustard. **Yield:** 1 dozen (1-1/4 cups dip).

SWEET POTATO CHIPS

My husband never cared for sweet potatoes until he married me. I tell him it must be my cooking! He can't resist dipping into a bowl of these crunchy chips. They're a nice change from regular potato chips.
—Janelle Lee
Lake Charles, Louisiana

1 pound sweet potatoes, peeled and thinly sliced
Cooking oil for deep-fat frying
Salt to taste

Soak potatoes in 2 qts. of ice water for 1 hour; drain and pat dry. Heat oil to 375° in an electric skillet or deep-fat fryer. Fry potatoes, seven or eight slices at a time, until golden brown, 1-2 minutes, turning once. Drain on paper towels; sprinkle with salt. Cool. **Yield:** 4-5 servings.

GARLIC-PARMESAN CRISPS

Instead of buying snack mixes that are loaded with preservatives, I like to make my own. People find these tasty crisps irresistible, so I always keep a couple of batches on hand for anytime snacking.
—Kathleen Sowinski
Lompoc, California

1/2 cup butter *or* margarine, softened
2 teaspoons garlic salt
4 pita breads (6 inches)
3 tablespoons grated Parmesan cheese
2 teaspoons dried basil

In a small bowl, mix butter and garlic salt until well blended. Split each pita in half to make two rounds. Spread each with butter mixture. Sprinkle with Parmesan cheese and basil. Cut each round into six wedges; place on an ungreased baking sheet. Bake at 325° for 8-10 minutes or until crisp. **Yield:** 4 dozen.

WHITE CHOCOLATE PARTY MIX

My family has stated that the holidays wouldn't be complete without bowls brimming with this satisfying snack. They can't limit themselves to just one handful of this mouth-watering mix!
—Norene Wright
Manilla, Indiana

1 package (10 ounces) mini pretzels
5 cups Cheerios
5 cups Corn Chex
2 cups salted peanuts

1 pound M&M's
2 packages (12 ounces *each*) vanilla chips
3 tablespoons vegetable oil

In a large bowl, combine first five ingredients; set aside. In a microwave-safe bowl, heat chips and oil on medium-high for 2 minutes, stirring once. Microwave on high for 10 seconds; stir until smooth. Pour over cereal mixture and mix well. Spread onto three waxed paper-lined baking sheets. Cool; break apart. Store in an airtight container. **Yield:** 5 quarts. **Editor's Note:** This recipe was tested using a 700-watt microwave.

PINEAPPLE CREAM CHEESE SPREAD

For a satisfying snack, try this spread, With only two ingredients, it couldn't be easier. I use this on crackers and celery sticks. It has a refreshing pineapple taste.
—Rita Addicks
Weimar, Texas

✓ **This tasty dish uses less sugar, salt and fat. Recipe includes *Diabetic Exchanges*.**

1 package (8 ounces) fat-free cream cheese, softened
1 can (8 ounces) crushed pineapple in juice, drained

In a bowl, combine cream cheese and pineapple. Chill. **Yield:** 1-1/8 cups. **Diabetic Exchanges:** One serving (1 tablespoon) equals a free food; also, 21 calories, 68 mg sodium, 0 cholesterol, 3 gm carbohydrate, 2 gm protein, 0 fat.

HEARTY CHEESE SPREAD

I use the red wax covering from gouda cheese to fashion a festive "poinsettia" bowl in which to serve this treat. I always get compliments! —Vernie Nicolaisen
Cherokee, Iowa

1 gouda cheese round in red wax covering (7 ounces), room temperature
1 package (2-1/2 ounces) smoked sliced beef, finely chopped
1/4 cup sour cream
2 tablespoons sweet pickle relish
2 teaspoons prepared horseradish
Apple slices *or* crackers

Carefully slice through wax and cheese to within 1 in. of the bottom, forming eight pie-shaped wedges. Carefully fold wax back to expose cheese; remove cheese. In a mixing bowl, beat the cheese until creamy. Add the beef, sour cream, relish and horse-radish; mix well. Spoon into wax shell. Chill. Serve with apple slices or crackers. **Yield:** 1-1/2 cups.

HONEY-MUSTARD TURKEY MEATBALLS

I serve this appetizer often during the holidays. These tangy meatballs can be made ahead, so drop-in guests can be treated to a hot snack. —Bonnie Durkin
Nescopeck, Pennsylvania

    1 pound ground turkey
    1 egg, lightly beaten
    3/4 cup crushed butter-flavored crackers
    1/2 cup shredded mozzarella cheese
    1/4 cup chopped onion
    1/2 teaspoon ground ginger
    6 tablespoons Dijon mustard, *divided*
1-1/4 cups unsweetened pineapple juice
    1/4 cup chopped green pepper
    2 tablespoons honey
    1 tablespoon cornstarch
    1/4 teaspoon onion powder

In a bowl, combine turkey, egg, cracker crumbs, cheese, onion, ginger and 3 tablespoons mustard. Form into 30 balls, 1 in. each. Place in a greased 13-in. x 9-in. x 2-in. baking dish. Bake, uncovered, at 350° for 20-25 minutes or until juices run clear. In a saucepan, combine pineapple juice, green pepper, honey, cornstarch and onion powder; bring to a boil, stirring constantly. Cook and stir 2 minutes more; reduce heat. Stir in remaining mustard until smooth. Brush meatballs with about 1/4 cup sauce and return to the oven for 10 minutes. Serve remaining sauce as a dip for meatballs. **Yield:** 2-1/2 dozen.

VEGGIE DILL DIP

I like to keep this good-for-you dip on hand, along with a variety of cut-up vegetables, for an easy snack.
—Hazel Baber
Yuma, Arizona

   ✓ **This tasty dish uses less sugar, salt and fat.**
     Recipe includes *Diabetic Exchanges*.

    1 carton (16 ounces) low-fat cottage cheese
    3 tablespoons skim milk
    3/4 cup fat-free mayonnaise
    1 tablespoon dried minced onion
    1 tablespoon dried parsley flakes
    1 teaspoon dill weed

    1 teaspoon seasoned salt
    1/4 teaspoon garlic powder

In a blender, blend cottage cheese and milk until smooth. Stir in remaining ingredients and mix well. Chill overnight. Serve with raw vegetables. **Yield:** 2-1/2 cups. **Diabetic Exchanges:** One 2-tablespoon serving equals a free food; also, 24 calories, 233 mg sodium, 1 mg cholesterol, 2 gm carbohydrate, 3 gm protein, trace fat.

CUCUMBER DILL SPREAD

For a delightfully different way to serve refreshing cucumbers, try this recipe. This creamy spread is so good with crackers or vegetables. —Doris Heath
Bryson City, North Carolina

   ✓ **This tasty dish uses less sugar, salt and fat.**
     Recipe includes *Diabetic Exchanges*.

    2 packages (8 ounces *each*) cream cheese, softened
    2 teaspoons lemon juice
    2 teaspoons minced onion
    1/2 teaspoon dill weed
    1/4 teaspoon prepared horseradish
Dash hot pepper sauce
    3/4 cup finely diced seeded cucumber

In a mixing bowl, beat cream cheese until smooth. Add lemon juice, onion, dill, horseradish and hot pepper sauce. Fold in cucumber. Cover and chill for at least 1 hour. Serve with crackers or raw vegetables. **Yield:** 2-1/3 cups. **Diabetic Exchanges:** One 2-tablespoon serving (prepared with fat-free cream cheese) equals 1 vegetable, 1/2 very lean meat; also, 45 calories, 240 mg sodium, 0 cholesterol, 4 gm carbohydrate, 7 gm protein, 0 fat.

STRAWBERRY YOGURT DIP

When I was a hostess for our monthly ladies' meeting, I served this light, fluffy dip with a variety of fruit. It was a big hit. —Nancy Johnson
Laverne, Oklahoma

1-1/2 cups frozen whole strawberries, thawed
    1 carton (8 ounces) strawberry yogurt
    1 cup whipped topping
Assorted fruit *or* angel food cake

In a bowl, mash berries. Add yogurt and mix well. Fold in whipped topping. Serve with fruit or cake. **Yield:** 2-3/4 cups.

GOLDEN CHICKEN NUGGETS

I usually serve these baked bites with a sweet-and-sour sauce for dipping. But be creative and also try them with barbecue sauce or honey. —Karen Owen
Rising Sun, Indiana

- 1/2 cup dry bread crumbs
- 1/4 cup grated Parmesan cheese
- 2 teaspoons Italian seasoning
- 1 teaspoon salt
- 6 boneless skinless chicken breast halves, cut into 1-inch cubes
- 1/2 cup butter *or* margarine, melted

Combine the first four ingredients. Dip chicken in butter; roll in crumb mixture. Place in a single layer on an ungreased 15-in. x 10-in. x 1-in. baking pan. Bake at 400° for 12-15 minutes or until juices run clear. **Yield:** about 4 dozen.

CAJUN POPCORN

Authentic Cajun popcorn is actually deep-fried craw-fish tails seasoned with peppery spices. But we like this light, simpler version. —Ruby Williams
Bogalusa, Louisiana

- 1 teaspoon salt
- 1/2 teaspoon ground cumin
- 1/2 teaspoon garlic powder
- 1/2 teaspoon dried basil
- 1/2 teaspoon dried thyme
- 1/2 teaspoon paprika
- 1/4 teaspoon pepper
- 1/8 teaspoon cayenne pepper
- 2 tablespoons vegetable oil
- 3 quarts popped popcorn

In a small bowl, combine the first eight ingredients; set aside. In a small saucepan, heat oil over medium for 1 minute; add seasonings. Cook and stir over low heat for 1 minute. Place the popcorn in a large bowl; add seasoning mixture and toss to coat. Serve immediately. **Yield:** 3 quarts.

APPETIZER MEATBALLS

These tasty meatballs are a perennial favorite at our Christmas parties. But with such wonderful flavor, you'll get requests year-round. —Pat Waymire
Yellow Springs, Ohio

- 1 pound ground beef
- 1 egg, lightly beaten

- 1/2 cup soft bread crumbs
- 1/4 cup milk
- 1/3 cup finely chopped onion
- 1 teaspoon salt
- 1/2 teaspoon Worcestershire sauce

SAUCE:
- 1/2 cup ketchup
- 1/2 cup chopped onion
- 1/3 cup sugar
- 1/3 cup vinegar
- 1 tablespoon Worcestershire sauce
- 1/8 teaspoon pepper

Combine the first seven ingredients; mix well. Shape into 1-in. balls. In a skillet over medium heat, brown meatballs; drain. Place in a 2-1/2-qt. baking dish. Combine sauce ingredients. Pour over meatballs. Bake, uncovered, at 350° for 50-60 minutes or until meatballs are done. **Yield:** about 3 dozen.

CREAMY EGG SPREAD

We like this cool, creamy spread on rye crackers or tiny slices of cocktail rye bread. —Denise Goedeken
Platte Center, Nebraska

- 1/2 cup mayonnaise
- 1-1/2 tablespoons lemon juice
- 2 teaspoons Dijon mustard
- 1 tablespoon finely chopped onion
- 1/4 teaspoon hot pepper sauce
- 6 hard-cooked eggs, quartered
- 1 package (3 ounces) cream cheese, softened
- 1/2 teaspoon seasoned salt

Pinch white pepper
- 2 teaspoons chopped fresh dill, optional

In a blender, combine first five ingredients; process until smooth. Add the egg quarters, one at a time, blending well after each addition. Add the cream cheese, salt and pepper; process until creamy. Stir in dill if desired. **Yield:** 2 cups.

CRUNCHY ITALIAN MIX

We love this mix when we get the munchies in the evening. I started out fixing it for our bridge group and now I also make it just for us. —Sharon Evans
Rockwell, Iowa

- 1/2 cup butter *or* margarine
- 1 tablespoon Worcestershire sauce
- 1 teaspoon Italian seasoning
- 1/2 teaspoon garlic powder

bowl. Use raw vegetables or tortilla chips for dipping. Store in the refrigerator. **Yield:** 1-3/4 cups. **Diabetic Exchanges:** One 2-tablespoon serving (prepared with fat-free mayonnaise and without salt) equals 1 vegetable; also, 28 calories, 149 mg sodium, 0 cholesterol, 5 gm carbohydrate, 2 gm protein, trace fat.

CHUTNEY CRACKER SPREAD

This savory spread on crackers is a delicious alternative to the usual cheese spread. —Carolyn Eastham
South Bend, Washington

- 1 **package (8 ounces) cream cheese, softened**
- 2 **tablespoons sour cream**
- 1 **to 2 teaspoons curry powder**
- 1/2 **cup sliced green onions with tops**
- 1/2 **cup chopped peanuts**
- 1 **bottle (9 ounces) chutney**

In a small mixing bowl, beat the cream cheese, sour cream and curry powder until smooth. Fold in the onions and peanuts. Spread about 1/2 in. thick on a serving plate. Chill. Just before serving, pour chutney over all. Serve with crackers. **Yield:** 1-1/2 cups.

CREAMY TACO DIP

You'll know this snack is a hit at your next gathering when you come home with an empty pan!

—Denise Smith
Lusk, Wyoming

- 2 **packages (8 ounces each) cream cheese, softened**
- 1 **cup (8 ounces) sour cream**
- 1 **jar (8 ounces) taco sauce *or* salsa**
- 2 **teaspoons ground cumin**
- 1 **can (15 ounces) refried beans**
- 1 **cup shredded lettuce**
- 1 **cup (4 ounces) shredded cheddar cheese**
- 1 **medium tomato, diced**
- 1/4 **cup chopped ripe olives**
- 1/4 **cup canned chopped green chilies**
Tortilla chips

In a mixing bowl, beat cream cheese and sour cream until smooth. Stir in taco sauce and cumin; set aside. Spread the refried beans over the bottom of a serving platter or 13-in. x 9-in. x 2-in. dish. Spread cream cheese mixture over the beans, leaving about 1 in. uncovered around the edges. Top with layers of lettuce, cheese, tomato, olives and chilies. Serve with tortilla chips. **Yield:** 16-20 servings.

[top-left recipe partially obscured]

...e first ...s until butter is melted, mix well. In ... combine cereals, pretzels, nuts and Parmesan cheese. Drizzle with butter mixture and mix well. Place in an ungreased 15-in. x 10-in. x ...-in. baking pan. Bake, uncovered, at 250° for 45 minutes, stirring every 15 minutes. **Yield:** ... cups.

SHRIMP AND CHEDDAR SNACKS

If time is short, prepare this spread ahead. When guests arrive, quickly assemble and bake. —Margery Bryan
Royal City, Washington

- 2 **cups (8 ounces) shredded cheddar cheese**
- 1 **cup mayonnaise**
- 1 **can (6 ounces) broken shrimp, rinsed and drained**
- 1 **small onion, finely chopped**
- 1/4 **teaspoon garlic powder**
- 42 **slices snack rye bread, toasted**

Combine cheese, mayonnaise, shrimp, onion and garlic powder; mix well. Spread 1 tablespoon on each slice of bread; place on ungreased baking sheets. Bake at 350° for 7-9 minutes or until bubbly. Serve hot. **Yield:** 3-1/2 dozen.

LOW-FAT BEAN DIP

This creamy dip is great to snack on with raw vegetables or tortilla chips. And it tastes so much better than store-bought bean dips. —Gladys DeBoer
Castleford, Idaho

✓ **This tasty dish uses less sugar, salt and fat. Recipe includes *Diabetic Exchanges*.**

- 3 **tablespoons lemon juice**
- 1 **can (15 ounces) pinto beans, rinsed and drained**
- 3 **tablespoons chopped green onions**
- 2 **tablespoons mayonnaise**
- 1-1/2 **teaspoons seeded minced jalapeno pepper**
- 1 **teaspoon Worcestershire sauce**
- 1/2 **to 3/4 teaspoon salt, optional**
- 1/4 **teaspoon sugar**

Combine all ingredients in a blender or food processor and process until smooth. Transfer to a serving

PRONTO MINI PIZZAS

(Pictured above)

These quick savory pizzas on pita bread crusts are an excellent snack anytime. I also serve them as a light meal on busy days. —Debbi Smith
Crossett, Arkansas

  1 **pound ground beef** *or* **turkey**
  1 **cup sliced fresh mushrooms**
1/2 **cup chopped green pepper**
1/2 **cup chopped onion**
  2 **garlic cloves, minced**
  1 **can (8 ounces) tomato sauce**
  1 **teaspoon fennel seed**
1/2 **teaspoon salt**
1/2 **teaspoon dried oregano**
  4 **pita breads**
  1 **cup (4 ounces) shredded mozzarella cheese**

In a skillet, cook meat, mushrooms, green pepper, onion and garlic until meat is browned and vegetables are tender; drain. Stir in tomato sauce, fennel, salt and oregano. Simmer for 1-2 minutes. Meanwhile, warm pitas in the microwave. Top each with meat mixture; sprinkle with cheese. Microwave or broil until cheese is melted. Cut into quarters. **Yield:** 4 servings.

MULLED GRAPE CIDER

I came up with this recipe one year when I attempted to make grape jelly and ended up with 30 jars of delicious grape syrup instead. I then simmered the syrup with spices to make this beverage. —Sharon Harmon
Orange, Massachusetts

  5 **pounds Concord grapes**
  8 **cups water,** *divided*
1-1/2 **cups sugar**
  8 **whole cloves**
  4 **cinnamon sticks (4 inches)**
Dash ground nutmeg

In a large saucepan or Dutch oven, combine grapes and 2 cups of water; bring to a boil, stirring constantly. Press through a strainer; reserve juice and discard skins and seeds. Pour juice through a double layer of cheesecloth into a slow cooker. Add sugar, cloves, cinnamon sticks, nutmeg and remaining water. Heat on low for 3 hours. Discard cloves and cinnamon sticks before serving. **Yield:** 10-12 servings (2-3/4 quarts).

CREAMY CHICKEN SPREAD

This tasty chicken spread came from a member of the Texas church where my husband served as a pastor. It's a versatile spread that's perfect for lunchtime, dinnertime and snacktime. —Lynn Scheiderer
Bishop, California

1-1/2 **cups chopped cooked chicken**
  1 **package (8 ounces) cream cheese, softened**
1/2 **cup chopped celery**
1/2 **cup mayonnaise**
  2 **tablespoons chopped onion**
  1 **teaspoon onion powder**
1/2 **teaspoon salt**

Place all ingredients in a food processor; process until coarsely chopped. Use as a sandwich spread or serve on crackers. **Yield:** 2-1/2 cups.

SWEET SNACK MIX

Tempt your troops with this twist on caramel corn. Whenever I set out this snack, the bowl empties quickly. —Dee Georgiou
Omaha, Nebraska

14 **cups popped popcorn**
  3 **cups crisp rice cereal**
  2 **cups salted peanuts**
  1 **pound white confectionery coating***
  3 **tablespoons creamy peanut butter**

In a large bowl, combine the popcorn, cereal and peanuts. In the top of a double boiler over simmering water, melt the coating and peanut butter, stirring occasionally. Pour over popcorn mixture; stir to coat. Spread evenly on waxed paper. Allow to set for at least 2 hours. Store in an airtight container. **Yield:** 5-6 quarts. ***Editor's Note:** White confectionery coating is found in the baking section of most grocery stores. It is sometimes labeled "almond bark" or "candy coating" and is often sold in bulk packages of 1 to 1-1/2 pounds.

PECAN-DATE CHEESE BALL

This lightly sweet cheese ball is great to have on hand when we crave something creamy or if company drops by. It's even nice enough for the holidays.

—Sue Broyles
Cherokee, Texas

> 1 teaspoon ground mustard
> 1 teaspoon water
> 2 packages (8 ounces *each*) cream cheese, softened
> 1/4 cup mayonnaise
> 1/4 teaspoon ground nutmeg
> 2 cups (8 ounces) shredded cheddar cheese
> 1 cup chopped dates
> 1 cup chopped pecans

Crackers

In a small bowl, dissolve mustard in water; let stand for 10 minutes. In a mixing bowl, beat cream cheese and mayonnaise until smooth. Add nutmeg and mustard mixture. Stir in cheese and dates. Chill for 15 minutes. Shape into a ball; roll in pecans. Chill. Serve with crackers. **Yield:** 3-1/2 cups (4-inch ball).

TUNA SNACK SPREAD

For a satisfying snack, all you need is this creamy tuna spread and a box of your favorite crackers. Or spread it on bread for a different kind of sandwich.

—Denise Goedeken
Platte Center, Nebraska

> 1 can (6 ounces) tuna, drained and flaked
> 1 package (8 ounces) cream cheese, softened
> 2 to 3 teaspoons lemon juice
> 1 teaspoon onion salt
> 3 to 4 drops hot pepper sauce
> 1/4 cup minced fresh parsley

In a bowl, combine the first five ingredients until well mixed. Shape into a ball and roll in parsley. Chill. Serve with crackers. **Yield:** 1-1/2 cup.

POPCORN SNACKS

We always had popcorn balls at Christmastime when I was growing up. A couple years ago, my mother gave me this recipe for an updated version. *—Vicki Theis*
Shakopee, Minnesota

> 1/2 cup butter *or* margarine
> 1 bag (16 ounces) miniature marshmallows
> 1/2 cup vegetable oil
> 1 teaspoon vanilla extract

> 1/2 teaspoon salt
> 6 quarts popped white popcorn
> 1 bag (16 ounces) M&M's
> 1 jar (16 ounces) lightly salted dry roasted peanuts

In a saucepan over medium heat, cook and stir butter and marshmallows in oil until the marshmallows are melted. Stir in vanilla and salt. In a very large bowl, combine popcorn, M&M's and peanuts. Pour marshmallow mixture over popcorn; mix well. Press into two greased 13-in. x 9-in. x 2-in. pans or two 12-cup molds. Allow to set for at least 2 hours. Remove from pans or molds and slice. Store in an airtight container. **Yield:** 3 to 3-1/2 dozen.

BRAUNSCHWEIGER SPREAD

This spread is so creamy and delicious it's satisfying even to those who think they don't like liver sausage.

—Gayle Lewis
Yucaipa, California

> 1 tube (8 ounces) liver sausage
> 1 package (3 ounces) cream cheese, softened
> 1/3 cup mayonnaise *or* salad dressing
> 2 to 3 tablespoons dill pickle relish
> 2 tablespoons chopped onion
> 1/2 teaspoon Worcestershire sauce
> 1/8 teaspoon garlic powder

Chopped fresh parsley
Assorted crackers

Combine the first seven ingredients; pat into a bowl lined with plastic wrap. Cover with the wrap and chill. Invert onto a serving platter and sprinkle with parsley. Serve with crackers. **Yield:** about 1-1/2 cups.

PEANUT BUTTER PUFFS

With just three ingredients, these satisfying snack bites are no fuss, no mess and ready in a snap. They are tasty and go great with a glass of milk and a good movie.

—Vickie Gray
Kimberly, Wisconsin

> 3 to 4 tablespoons peanut butter
> 20 vanilla wafers
> 80 miniature marshmallows

Spread about 1/2 teaspoon peanut butter on each wafer. Place on a foil-lined baking sheet. Top each with four marshmallows. Broil for 2-3 minutes or until the marshmallows are lightly browned. Serve warm. **Yield:** 20 snacks.

MOZZARELLA PUFFS

(Pictured above)

These savory cheese biscuits go over great at my house. Since they're so quick to make, I can whip up a batch whenever my family asks for them.
—Joan Mousley Dziuba
Waupaca, Wisconsin

  1 tube (7-1/2 ounces) refrigerated
    buttermilk biscuits
  1 teaspoon dried oregano
  1 block (2 to 3 ounces) mozzarella cheese
  2 tablespoons pizza sauce

Make an indentation in the center of each biscuit; sprinkle with oregano. Cut the mozzarella into 10 cubes, 3/4 in. each; place a cube in the center of each biscuit. Pinch dough tightly around cheese to seal. Place seam side down on an ungreased baking sheet. Spread pizza sauce over tops. Bake at 375° for 10-12 minutes or until golden brown. **Yield:** 10 servings.

ZESTY SNACK MIX

This crisp snack mix is a mouth-watering combination of sweet and spicy. I've taken it to numerous gatherings. Why not make a bowlful next time the munchies hit your hungry clan?
—Jeanette Grantstein
Wichita, Kansas

  4 cups Oat Squares *or* Chex cereal
  4 cups corn chips
  1 cup salted peanuts
  1 cup quick-cooking oats
  1/3 cup butter *or* margarine, melted
  3 tablespoons honey

  4 teaspoons chili powder
  1 teaspoon dried oregano
  1 teaspoon onion salt

In a large bowl, combine the cereal, corn chips, peanuts and oats. Combine butter and honey; drizzle over cereal mixture. Sprinkle with chili powder, oregano and salt; toss to coat. Spread evenly on an ungreased 15-in. x 10-in. x 1-in. baking pan. Bake at 350° for 25 minutes, stirring once. Cool. Store in an airtight container. **Yield:** about 10 cups.

LUNCH-BOX APPLE DIP

Apples become an even more "a-peeling" snack when paired with this sweet creamy dip. It's a fun and flavorful way to get kids to eat fruit.   —Shelly Korell
Bayard, Nebraska

  1 package (8 ounces) cream cheese, softened
  1 cup packed brown sugar
  1 teaspoon vanilla extract
  1 teaspoon lemon juice
  3 to 4 apples, cut into wedges

In a mixing bowl, beat the first four ingredients until smooth. Divide into 1/3- to 1/2-cup servings and store in individual containers in the refrigerator. Serve with apples. **Yield:** 3-4 servings.

WADE'S SHRIMP SPREAD

I prefer to prepare main dishes, but I do make desserts once in a while and appetizers for parties. This is a flavorful spread with a bit of zip. I've been making this for the holidays for over 15 years.   —Wade Harmon
Orange, Massachusetts

  2 cans (4-1/4 ounces each) shrimp, rinsed
    and drained
  1 package (3 ounces) cream cheese, softened
  1/4 cup finely chopped green onions
  2 teaspoons sour cream
  2 teaspoons lemon juice
  1 teaspoon Dijon mustard
  1/2 teaspoon hot pepper sauce
Assorted crackers

Finely chop shrimp; place in a bowl. Stir in the next six ingredients until well blended. Cover and refrigerate for 8 hours or overnight. Serve with crackers. **Yield:** 1-1/2 cups.

Enjoy Teatime Anytime!

TEA can be the basis for some delicious hot and cold beverages. Add some fruit juice, spices or other ingredients like those suggested in the recipes here from Lipton Soothing Moments Tea.

ALMOND DREAM

With whipping cream, this rich-tasting, creamy beverage is almost a dessert in itself.

2-1/2 cups boiling water
6 almond herbal tea bags
1/2 cup sugar
1 cup whipping cream
Ground nutmeg, optional

In a teapot, pour boiling water over tea bags; cover and steep for 5 minutes. Remove tea bags. Stir in sugar; cool. In a blender, process cream at high speed for 30 seconds or until thickened. Add tea mixture; process until blended. Pour into glasses. Garnish with nutmeg if desired. **Yield:** 6 servings.

BLACKBERY BREEZE

With its tropical flair, this refreshing drink is perfect for summer sipping. Folks will agree this is a fun twist to traditional tea.

1 cup boiling water
6 blackberry-flavored tea bags
1/2 cup pineapple juice
1 can (8 ounces) crushed pineapple, undrained
1/3 cup sugar
18 ice cubes

In a teapot, pour boiling water over tea bags; cover and steep for 5 minutes. Remove tea bags. Chill tea. In a blender, process the tea, pineapple juice, pineapple and sugar until smooth. Add the ice cubes, one at a time, processing after each addition until blended. **Yield:** 4 servings.

WARM TEA PUNCH

A satisfying spicy drink with lovely color, it's sure to chase the chill on cold mornings. Plus, the orange-red color is so appealing.

1-1/2 cups water
6 orange herbal tea bags
10 whole cloves
2 cinnamon sticks
2 cups cranberry juice
1-1/2 cups white grape juice
1/2 cup packed brown sugar
Orange slices and additional whole cloves, optional

In a medium saucepan, bring water to a boil. Turn off heat; add tea bags, cloves and cinnamon sticks. Cover and steep for 5 minutes. Remove tea bags. Stir in the juices and brown sugar; heat through. Remove spices. Garnish with clove-studded orange slices if desired. **Yield:** 8 servings.

RASPBERRY LEMON SMOOTHIE

A cool thirst-quencher, this hits the spot on a hot day. The raspberry sherbet makes it sweet and creamy.

2 cups boiling water
8 lemon herbal tea bags
2 cups pineapple juice
1 pint raspberry sherbet
Lemon slices, optional

In a teapot, pour boiling water over tea bags; cover and steep for 5 minutes. Remove bags. Chill tea. In a blender, process tea, pineapple juice and sherbet until smooth. Pour into glasses. Garnish with lemon if desired. **Yield:** 4 servings.

CINNAMON APPLE REFRESHER

Here's a crisp, fruity beverage that gets a tasty twist from cranberry juice. It nicely combines two favorite fruit flavors.

4 cups boiling water
5 cinnamon-apple herbal tea bags
1-1/3 cups cranberry juice
2 tablespoons sugar
Apple slices, optional

In a teapot, pour boiling water over tea bags; cover and steep for 5 minutes. Remove bags. Stir in cranberry juice and sugar. Pour into glasses. Garnish with apple slices if desired. **Yield:** 4 servings.

LEMON CRANBERRY CIDER TEA

This lightly sweet drink with robust flavor is great for cooler weather. The natural sweetness from honey shines through splendidly.

2 cups water
6 honey/lemon-flavored tea bags
6 whole cloves
1 cinnamon stick
1 cup cranberry juice
1 cup apple cider
Sugar to taste

In a saucepan, bring water to a boil. Remove from the heat; add tea bags, cloves and cinnamon stick. Cover and steep for 5 minutes. Remove tea bags, cloves and cinnamon stick. Stir in the cranberry juice, cider and sugar; heat through. **Yield:** 4 servings.

Family and friends will be delighted to sit down to a hearty main-dish salad throughout the year. And a medley of fruit or vegetable salads makes any potluck unforgettable.

Partially freeze beef. Slice across the grain into thin strips; set aside. For dressing, combine lime juice, sugar, soy sauce, basil and mint; set aside. In a medium nonstick skillet that has been coated with nonstick cooking spray, saute jalapeno, garlic and ginger for 30 seconds. Add beef; stir-fry until cooked as desired. Remove beef from pan; gently toss with red pepper and cucumber. Place greens in a large bowl or divide among individual bowls or plates; top with beef mixture. Add dressing to pan and bring to a boil; remove from the heat and drizzle over salad. Serve immediately. **Yield:** 4 servings. **Diabetic Exchanges:** One serving (prepared with low-sodium soy sauce) equals 2 very lean meat, 2 vegetable; also, 152 calories, 171 mg sodium, 45 mg cholesterol, 11 gm carbohydrate, 17 gm protein, 5 gm fat.

LETTUCE WITH BUTTERMILK DRESSING

When my garden is brimming with homegrown lettuce, this is the recipe I reach for most often. The delectable dressing lets the fresh flavor come through.
—Jean Morgan
Roscoe, Illinois

 1/4 cup buttermilk
   2 tablespoons mayonnaise *or* salad dressing
   2 tablespoons sugar
   1 tablespoon vinegar
   6 cups torn leaf lettuce

In a small bowl, whisk the first four ingredients. Toss with lettuce or serve on the side. Refrigerate any leftover dressing. **Yield:** 4 servings.

GREEN BEAN SESAME SALAD

A friend brought this refreshing salad to a church luncheon and came prepared with copies of the recipe, saying someone always asks for it. She was right!
—Mildred Sherrer
Bay City, Texas

✓ **This tasty dish uses less sugar, salt and fat. Recipe includes *Diabetic Exchanges*.**

 1 pound fresh green beans
 2 tablespoons olive *or* vegetable oil
 1 tablespoon lemon juice
 2 tablespoons sesame seeds, toasted

SPICY BEEF SALAD

(Pictured above)

This recipe was inspired by my love of spicy flavors and light, nutritious entrees. The pretty salad has an appealing variety of textures. I make it year-round because it's fast and easy to prepare. —*Peggy Allen*
Pasadena, California

✓ **This tasty dish uses less sugar, salt and fat. Recipe includes *Diabetic Exchanges*.**

 1/2 pound boneless sirloin steak
 1/3 cup fresh lime juice
   1 tablespoon brown sugar
   1 tablespoon soy sauce
   1 tablespoon minced fresh basil *or* 1 teaspoon dried basil
   2 teaspoons minced fresh mint *or* 3/4 teaspoon dried mint
   1 jalapeno pepper, minced
   2 to 3 garlic cloves, minced
   1 teaspoon grated fresh gingerroot *or* 1/4 to 1/2 teaspoon ground ginger
   1 large sweet red pepper, julienned
 1/2 medium cucumber, chopped
   6 cups torn mixed salad greens

1 garlic clove, minced
1/2 teaspoon salt, optional
1/2 teaspoon crushed red pepper flakes
1/8 teaspoon pepper

In a saucepan, cover beans with water; cook until crisp-tender. Drain and rinse in cold water; place in a serving bowl. Sprinkle with remaining ingredients; toss to coat. Serve at room temperature. **Yield:** 6 servings. **Diabetic Exchanges:** One serving (prepared without salt) equals 1 vegetable, 1 fat; also, 82 calories, 8 mg sodium, 0 cholesterol, 6 gm carbohydrate, 2 gm protein, 6 gm fat.

WILTED LETTUCE

Here's an easy, old-fashioned salad that makes for a different-tasting side dish. You can use less bacon drippings to cut down on the fat. —*Jennie Wilburn Long Creek, Oregon*

8 cups torn leaf lettuce *or* spinach
1/2 medium onion, sliced into rings
3 bacon strips, diced
1/4 cup vinegar
2 tablespoons water
1/2 teaspoon salt
1/2 teaspoon pepper
1 hard-cooked egg, chopped

Place lettuce and onion in a large salad bowl; set aside. In a skillet, cook bacon until crisp (do not drain). Stir in vinegar, water, salt and pepper. Pour over lettuce and toss gently until well coated. Top with egg. Serve immediately. **Yield:** 6 servings.

MARINATED VIDALIA ONIONS

My husband, Raymond, and I grow a large crop of Vidalia onions with our son and daughter-in-law. So it's no wonder onions are always on my menu! Here a light dressing really complements the sweet onions. —*Ruby Jean Bland Glennville, Georgia*

3/4 cup sugar
3/4 cup vegetable oil
1/4 cup vinegar
1/2 teaspoon salt
1/8 teaspoon pepper
4 medium Vidalia *or* sweet onions, sliced
2 medium carrots, thinly sliced

In a large salad bowl, combine the first five ingre-

dients. Add onions and carrots; toss to coat. Cover and refrigerate 24 hours, stirring occasionally. **Yield:** 8 servings.

TURKEY FRUIT SALAD
(Pictured below)

This salad is a great way to use leftover turkey. The fruit makes it refreshing, and the apples and toasted nuts give it a nice crunch. Just serve it with rolls or breadsticks to make a lovely lunch. —*Mary Anne Mayberry Fairmont, Minnesota*

1/2 cup mayonnaise
2 tablespoons honey
1/8 teaspoon ground ginger
2 cups cubed cooked turkey
1 can (11 ounces) mandarin oranges, drained
1 cup chopped unpeeled apple
1 cup grape halves
1 can (8-1/4 ounces) pineapple chunks, drained
1/2 cup pecan halves, toasted

In a large bowl, combine mayonnaise, honey and ginger. Stir in turkey, oranges, apple, grapes and pineapple. Refrigerate for 1 hour. Sprinkle with pecans just before serving. **Yield:** 8 servings.

SALMON-STUFFED TOMATOES

You can serve this salmon salad in a tomato as suggested or by itself on a bed of lettuce. Either way, folks will rave about the wonderful flavor.
—Glennis Stuart Liles
Greenup, Kentucky

> 1 can (14-3/4 ounces) red salmon, drained, deboned and flaked
> 1 cup thinly sliced celery
> 2 tablespoons chopped sweet pickle
> 2 tablespoons snipped fresh chives
> 1 tablespoon chopped green pepper
> 1/2 cup mayonnaise
> 2 tablespoons lemon juice
> 1/2 teaspoon salt
> 1/4 teaspoon lemon-pepper seasoning
> 6 medium tomatoes

In a bowl, combine salmon, celery, pickle, chives and green pepper. Combine mayonnaise, lemon juice, salt and lemon pepper. Add to salmon mixture and mix gently. Cover and refrigerate for 2 hours. Core tomatoes; cut into four to six wedges, not cutting all the way through. Place tomatoes on salad plates; top with salmon salad. **Yield:** 6 servings.

MEXICAN POTATO SALAD

(Pictured above)

This fun, fresh-tasting potato salad is a colorful and zesty variation of the average potato salad. It looks great and people love it. —*Danette Hofer*
Cedar Rapids, Iowa

> ✓ **This tasty dish uses less sugar, salt and fat. Recipe includes** *Diabetic Exchanges.*

> 1/4 cup low-sodium chicken broth
> 2 tablespoons white wine vinegar

> 2 tablespoons pickled jalapeno pepper juice
> 2 tablespoons olive *or* vegetable oil
> 1-1/2 pounds red potatoes
> 1 cup sliced carrots
> 2 celery ribs, thinly sliced
> 1/2 cup chopped onion
> 1/2 cup frozen peas, thawed
> 1/3 cup sliced green onions
> 1 tablespoon minced pickled jalapeno peppers
> 1/4 teaspoon pepper

In a large bowl, combine the first four ingredients; set aside. Place potatoes in a saucepan and cover with water; bring to a boil. Cook until almost tender, about 15 minutes. Add carrots and cook until carrots and potatoes are tender; drain. When cool enough to handle, cube potatoes. Add potatoes and carrots to broth mixture. Add remaining ingredients; toss to coat. Serve at room temperature or slightly chilled. **Yield:** 12 servings. **Diabetic Exchanges:** One 1/2-cup serving equals 1/2 starch, 1/2 fat; also, 62 calories, 148 mg sodium, 0 cholesterol, 10 gm carbohydrate, 2 gm protein, 2 gm fat.

SALLY'S POTATO SALAD

Broccoli, cauliflower, green beans and red pepper give traditional potato salad a new twist. It's a fresh-tasting salad that makes a nice addition to all your meals.
—Sally Burek
Fenton, Michigan

> ✓ **This tasty dish uses less sugar, salt and fat. Recipe includes** *Diabetic Exchanges.*

> 6 medium red potatoes, cubed
> 1-1/2 cups chopped celery
> 1-1/2 cups fresh broccoli florets
> 3/4 cup cut fresh green beans, blanched
> 1/2 cup fresh cauliflowerets
> 1/2 cup julienned sweet red pepper
> 1/4 cup fat-free Italian salad dressing
> 1/2 cup low-fat mayonnaise
> 2 teaspoons fat-free dry ranch salad dressing mix
> 1/4 teaspoon pepper

Cook potatoes in boiling water until tender. In a large bowl, combine the celery, broccoli, beans, cauliflower, red pepper and Italian dressing. Drain potatoes and add to the vegetable mixture. Combine mayonnaise, salad dressing mix and pepper; pour over the vegetable mixture and toss to coat. Cover and chill for at least 2 hours. **Yield:** 16 servings. **Diabetic Exchanges:** One 1/2-cup serving equals 1 vegetable, 1/2 fat; also, 37 calories, 75 mg sodium, 2 mg cholesterol, 4 gm carbohydrate, 1 gm protein, 2 gm fat.

MINTED POTATO SALAD

Here parsley adds a pretty green color while still allowing the subtle mint flavor to come through.
—Shirley Glaab
Hattiesburg, Mississippi

✓ **This tasty dish uses less sugar, salt and fat. Recipe includes *Diabetic Exchanges*.**

  4 medium potatoes (about 1 pound)
1/2 cup chopped fresh parsley
  3 tablespoons olive *or* vegetable oil
  2 tablespoons lemon juice
  1 tablespoon chopped fresh mint
  1 garlic clove, minced
1/2 teaspoon salt, optional
Pinch pepper

In a saucepan, cook potatoes in boiling water until tender. Peel and cube; place in a medium bowl. Combine remaining ingredients in a small bowl. Add to potatoes and mix well. Chill for at least 1 hour before serving. **Yield:** 6 servings. **Diabetic Exchanges:** One 1/2-cup serving (prepared without salt) equals 1 starch, 1 fat; also, 113 calories, 5 mg sodium, 0 cholesterol, 12 gm carbohydrate, 2 gm protein, 7 gm fat.

WILD ASPARAGUS SALAD

When most fresh vegetables are yet to sprout, the first shoots of asparagus make a mouth-watering treat. This is the first vegetable dish on our table every year.
—Karen Grasley
Quadville, Ontario

3/4 pound wild asparagus, trimmed
  2 tablespoons chopped stuffed olives
  1 hard-cooked egg, chopped
1/2 cup vegetable oil
  5 tablespoons lemon juice
  3 tablespoons vinegar
  2 teaspoons sugar
1/2 teaspoon salt
1/2 teaspoon paprika
1/2 teaspoon ground mustard
Dash cayenne pepper
Cherry tomatoes, halved

Cook asparagus until crisp-tender; drain and rinse in cold water. Place in a shallow dish; top with olives and egg. In a jar with tight-fitting lid, combine oil, lemon juice, vinegar, sugar, salt, paprika, mustard and cayenne pepper; shake well. Pour over asparagus. Chill for several hours or overnight. Garnish with tomatoes. **Yield:** 4 servings.

TROPICAL TURKEY SALAD
(Pictured above)

This delicious salad is lovely with all the colors, and satisfying with a mixture of turkey, fruits and vegetables. And the dressing is irresistible.
—Rosalind Canada
White Bluff, Tennessee

  5 cups torn fresh spinach
  3 cups torn lettuce
  2 cups cooked cubed turkey
  2 slices red onion, separated into rings
1/2 cup chopped green pepper
1/2 cup mandarin oranges
1/2 cup sliced celery
1/2 cup pineapple chunks
1/3 cup vegetable oil
1/4 cup raspberry syrup
  2 tablespoons red wine vinegar
1-1/2 teaspoons honey
1/2 teaspoon celery seed
1/2 cup sliced almonds, toasted
1/4 cup flaked coconut, toasted

Line a large salad bowl with spinach and lettuce. Combine the next six ingredients; spoon into bowl. In a jar with tight-fitting lid, combine oil, raspberry syrup, vinegar, honey and celery seed; shake well. Pour over the salad. Top with almonds and coconut. Serve immediately. **Yield:** 6 servings.

STRAWBERRY GELATIN SALAD

Even though it's low-fat, this salad is always a hit when served at church dinners and family reunions. Strawberries, bananas and pineapple give this dish its delightful natural sweetness.
—Ruth Barton
Millsap, Texas

✓ **This tasty dish uses less sugar, salt and fat. Recipe includes *Diabetic Exchanges*.**

2 cups unsweetened frozen strawberries
2 medium ripe bananas
3 packets sugar substitute
1 package (.6 ounce) sugar-free strawberry gelatin
2 cups boiling water
1 can (8 ounces) crushed pineapple in natural juices, undrained
1 carton (8 ounces) plain low-fat yogurt

Mash strawberries, bananas and sugar substitute; set aside. Dissolve gelatin in boiling water. Stir in strawberry mixture and pineapple. Pour half into an 8-in. square dish coated with nonstick cooking spray. Chill until firm. Combine yogurt and the remaining gelatin mixture; spoon over the first layer. Chill until firm, about 3 hours. **Yield:** 8 servings. **Diabetic Exchanges:** One serving equals 1 fruit, 1/4 skim milk; also, 86 calories, 76 mg sodium, 2 mg cholesterol, 18 gm carbohydrate, 3 gm protein, 1 gm fat.

EGGNOG MOLDED SALAD

(Pictured above)

This gelatin salad looks pretty on a platter and tastes good with a hint of eggnog flavor.
—Alice Ceresa
Rochester, New York

1 teaspoon unflavored gelatin
1/4 cup water

1 can (16 ounces) sliced pears
1 package (6 ounces) lemon gelatin
1 cup (8 ounces) sour cream
3/4 cup eggnog
1 can (11 ounces) mandarin oranges, drained
Orange slices, maraschino cherries and mint leaves, optional

In a small bowl, combine gelatin and water; set aside. Drain pears, reserving juice; set pears aside. Add enough water to the juice to measure 2 cups. Pour into a saucepan; bring to a boil. Remove from the heat; stir in gelatin mixture and lemon gelatin until completely dissolved. Cool for about 15 minutes. Stir in sour cream and eggnog until well blended. Chill until partially set. Cut the oranges and pears into chunks; add to eggnog mixture. Pour into an oiled 6-cup mold. Chill until firm. Garnish with oranges, cherries and mint if desired. **Yield:** 10-12 servings.

BLACK BEAN AND CORN SALAD

Even folks who normally don't care for black beans will find this fresh dish delicious. With its contrasting colors and wonderful cumin dressing, this salad is a great addition to any meal.
—Margaret Allen
Abingdon, Virginia

✓ **This tasty dish uses less sugar, salt and fat. Recipe includes *Diabetic Exchanges*.**

1/3 cup olive *or* vegetable oil
1 tablespoon red wine vinegar
1 teaspoon cider vinegar
1 garlic clove, minced
1/2 teaspoon ground cumin
1/2 teaspoon dried oregano
1/2 teaspoon salt, optional
1/4 teaspoon sugar
1/8 teaspoon ground red *or* cayenne pepper
2 cans (15 ounces *each*) black beans, rinsed and drained
1 can (8 ounces) whole kernel corn, drained
3/4 cup chopped red onion
1/2 cup chopped sweet red pepper

In a bowl, whisk the first nine ingredients until well blended. Add the beans, corn, onion and red pepper; toss well. Cover and chill 8 hours or overnight. **Yield:** 12 servings. **Diabetic Exchanges:** One 1/2-cup serving (prepared without salt) equals 1 starch, 1 fat; also, 111 calories, 146 mg sodium, 0 cholesterol, 12 gm carbohydrate, 3 gm protein, 6 gm fat.

PEACHY APPLESAUCE SALAD

I've been revising many recipes and creating new ones since my husband developed diabetes a couple of years ago. Folks will enjoy this dish whether it's served as a salad or dessert.
—*Marcille Meyer*
Battle Creek, Nebraska

✓ **This tasty dish uses less sugar, salt and fat. Recipe includes *Diabetic Exchanges*.**

- 1 cup diet lemon-lime soda
- 1 package (.3 ounce) peach *or* mixed fruit sugar-free gelatin
- 1 cup unsweetened applesauce
- 2 cups reduced-calorie whipped topping
- 1/8 teaspoon ground nutmeg
- 1/8 teaspoon vanilla extract
- 1 fresh peach, peeled and chopped

In a saucepan, bring soda to a boil. Remove from the heat; stir in gelatin until dissolved. Add applesauce; chill until partially set. Fold in whipped topping, nutmeg and vanilla. Fold in peach. Chill until firm. **Yield:** 6 servings. **Diabetic Exchanges:** One 1/2-cup serving equals 1 fruit, 1 fat; also, 99 calories, 6 mg sodium, 0 cholesterol, 15 gm carbohydrate, trace protein, 3 gm fat.

SEAFOOD-STUFFED TOMATOES

A tempting combination of tiny shrimp, crabmeat, hard-cooked eggs and rice makes a cool, hearty salad perfect for warm days. Our teenage daughter likes to prepare this salad for company. It's so easy to fix.
—*Gwen Landry*
Jennings, Louisiana

- 2 cups cooked rice
- 1 cup cooked salad shrimp
- 2 cans (6 ounces *each*) crabmeat, rinsed, drained and cartilage removed
- 4 hard-cooked eggs, chopped
- 1/2 cup chopped celery
- 1/2 cup chopped green pepper
- 1/4 cup chopped onion
- 1/4 cup chopped dill pickle
- 1 jar (2 ounces) chopped pimientos, drained
- 3/4 cup mayonnaise
- 2 tablespoons lemon juice
- 1 teaspoon salt
- 1/2 teaspoon dill weed
- 1/4 teaspoon pepper
- 6 to 8 large tomatoes

Combine the first nine ingredients in a bowl; set aside. In a small bowl, combine mayonnaise, lemon juice, salt, dill and pepper; mix well. Pour over rice mixture; toss gently. Cover and chill for at least 1 hour. Just before serving, cut a thin slice from the top of each tomato, or scallop the top with a sharp knife. Scoop out pulp and discard, leaving a 1/2-in.-thick shell. Fill each tomato with about 1/2 cup of salad. Serve immediately. **Yield:** 6-8 servings.

GUACAMOLE SALAD BOWL

This salad's dressing features avocado—an important crop in our state. The bowl is usually "licked clean" when I make this hearty salad for our Grange group. I sometimes substitute tuna for the shrimp.
—*Ann Eastman*
Greenville, California

- 5 cups torn leaf lettuce
- 2 medium tomatoes, cut into wedges
- 1 cup (4 ounces) shredded cheddar cheese
- 1 cup cooked salad shrimp
- 1 cup corn chips
- 1/2 cup sliced ripe olives
- 1/4 cup sliced green onions

AVOCADO DRESSING:
- 1/2 cup mashed ripe avocado
- 1 tablespoon lemon juice
- 1/2 cup sour cream
- 1/3 cup vegetable oil
- 1 garlic clove, minced
- 1/2 teaspoon sugar
- 1/2 teaspoon chili powder
- 1/4 teaspoon salt
- 1/4 teaspoon hot pepper sauce

In a large salad bowl, combine the first seven ingredients; set aside. In a mixing bowl or blender, combine dressing ingredients; beat or process until smooth. Pour over salad and toss. Serve immediately. **Yield:** 6-8 servings.

Lettuce Know-How

Look for heads or bunches with unblemished leaves. The lettuce should have good green color and appear crisp and moist.

To keep salads crisp longer, chill the serving bowl or salad plates.

One pound of lettuce will yield about 6 cups when torn.

As a general rule, the greener the leaf, the higher its food value.

LEMON RICE SALAD
(Pictured above)

This refreshing salad is wonderful served year-round. I have taken it to potluck suppers and made it for family barbecues, picnics and dinner parties. People seem to enjoy the combination of flavors in this dish. I like that it can be prepared ahead.
— Margery Richmond
Lacombe, Alberta

  1 cup vegetable *or* olive oil
1/3 cup white wine vinegar
  1 garlic clove, minced
  1 to 2 teaspoons grated lemon peel
  2 teaspoons sugar
  1 teaspoon Dijon mustard
1/2 teaspoon salt
  6 cups cooked long grain rice
  2 cups cooked wild rice
  2 cups diced seeded cucumbers
2/3 cup thinly sliced green onions
1/4 cup minced fresh parsley
1/4 cup minced fresh basil *or* 1 tablespoon
    dried basil
1/2 teaspoon pepper
1/2 cup chopped pecans, toasted

In a jar with a tight-fitting lid, combine the first seven ingredients; shake well. In a large bowl, combine long grain and wild rice; add dressing and toss. Cover and refrigerate overnight. Add the cucumbers, green onions, parsley, basil and pepper;

mix well. Chill for 2 hours. Fold in pecans just before serving. **Yield:** 16-18 servings.

MARINATED GARDEN PLATTER

Sharing this mouth-watering vegetable medley with others is a treat. The delicate flavor of the fresh green beans really comes through.
— Patty Kile
Greentown, Pennsylvania

1-1/2 pounds fresh green beans
  3/4 cup vegetable oil
  1/3 cup cider vinegar
    1 tablespoon sugar
    2 teaspoons Dijon mustard
  1/2 teaspoon salt
  1/2 teaspoon pepper
    1 pint cherry tomatoes, halved
    2 tablespoons finely chopped
      red onion
  1/2 cup sliced fresh mushrooms

In a saucepan, cover beans with water; cook until crisp-tender. Meanwhile, in a small jar with tight-fitting lid, combine the next six ingredients and shake well. In a bowl, combine tomatoes, onion and 1/4 cup dressing. Combine mushrooms and 2 tablespoons dressing in another bowl. Drain the beans; place in a bowl. Add remaining dressing. Chill the vegetables in their separate bowls for at least 1 hour. To serve, arrange vegetables on a platter. **Yield:** 8-10 servings.

BEET MACARONI SALAD

Just mention the word "beet" and most kids turn up their noses. Our two children never rushed to the table for beets...but now, when I mention that I'm serving this salad, the response is just the opposite. My mother would prepare this dish for me when I was a little girl. It was the only way I'd eat this ruby vegetable.
— Sue Gronholz
Columbus, Wisconsin

  1 package (7 ounces) shell macaroni, cooked
    and drained
  1 package (10 ounces) frozen peas, cooked
    and drained
1/4 cup diced celery
1/4 cup chopped onion
  2 cans (16 ounces *each*) diced beets, drained
  1 cup mayonnaise
Salt and pepper to taste

In a large bowl, combine all ingredients. Cover and refrigerate for several hours or overnight. **Yield:** 16 servings.

TOSSED SALAD WITH CREAMY GARLIC DRESSING

I often mix some escarole and spinach with leaf lettuce for this salad. But no matter what greens I use, folks always compliment me on the pleasant dressing.
—*Phyllis Hickey*
Bedford, New Hampshire

    1/4 cup red wine vinegar
    1/4 cup water
      2 tablespoons finely chopped onion
      1 to 2 garlic cloves, minced
    1/3 cup sugar
    1/2 cup mayonnaise *or* salad dressing
  1-1/2 cups (12 ounces) sour cream
    1/4 teaspoon salt
    1/4 teaspoon pepper
      8 cups torn lettuce
      1 large carrot, shredded
      3 tablespoons bacon bits
Croutons, optional

In a small saucepan, combine vinegar, water, onion and garlic; simmer until the onion is tender, about 5 minutes. Add sugar; simmer until dissolved. Cool to room temperature. Stir in mayonnaise, sour cream, salt and pepper. In a large salad bowl, toss the lettuce, carrots and bacon bits; add dressing and toss to coat. Top with croutons if desired. **Yield:** 6-8 servings.

THREE-BEAN SALAD

This old-time favorite is updated with a touch of garlic and a not-so-sweet dressing. Since I freeze some of my homegrown green and wax beans each summer, we can enjoy this salad year-round. —*Katie Koziolek*
Hartland, Minnesota

    1 pound fresh green beans
    1 pound fresh wax beans
    1 can (16 ounces) kidney beans, rinsed
       and drained
    1 cup Italian salad dressing
  1/4 cup finely chopped onion
    2 garlic cloves, minced
    1 tablespoon dried parsley flakes

Cut green and wax beans into 1-1/4-in. pieces; place in a saucepan. Cover with water and cook until

crisp-tender. Drain; place in a large bowl. Add remaining ingredients; mix gently. Cover and chill for several hours before serving. **Yield:** 12-16 servings.

SUMMER RICE SALAD

(Pictured above)

Tangy dressing and flavorful ingredients make for a very tasty side dish that's a refreshing alternative to potato salad. People can't seem to stop eating this unique salad. It's great with chicken or hamburgers.
—*Laura Panfil*
Niles, Michigan

    2 cups cooked brown rice
    1 cup quartered cherry tomatoes
  1/3 cup chopped red onion
    1 can (2-1/4 ounces) sliced ripe olives,
       drained
    3 tablespoons cider vinegar
    2 tablespoons vegetable oil
    2 tablespoons minced fresh parsley
  1/2 teaspoon sugar
  1/2 teaspoon salt
Leaf lettuce, optional

In a large bowl, combine rice, tomatoes, onion and olives. In a small bowl, combine vinegar, oil, parsley, sugar and salt; mix well. Pour over rice mixture and toss to coat. Cover and chill for at least 2 hours. Serve in a lettuce-lined bowl if desired. **Yield:** 4-6 servings.

Beet Basics

Small and medium beets are usually the most tender. Plus, they should be firm and smooth with good round shape.

Fresh uncooked beets will keep in the refrigerator for about 1 month.

ANTIPASTO SALAD
(Pictured below)

I take this fresh-tasting, colorful salad to potluck dinners throughout the year, since everyone who tries it loves it. The pasta, garbanzo beans and pepperoni make it a nice hearty dish. —Agnes Bulkley
Hicksville, New York

- 1 package (16 ounces) rotini pasta
- 1 can (15 ounces) garbanzo beans, rinsed and drained
- 1 package (3-1/2 ounces) sliced pepperoni, halved
- 1 can (2-1/4 ounces) sliced ripe olives, drained
- 1/2 cup diced sweet red pepper
- 1/2 cup diced green pepper
- 4 medium fresh mushrooms, sliced
- 2 garlic cloves, minced
- 2 tablespoons minced fresh basil *or* 2 teaspoons dried basil
- 2 teaspoons salt
- 1-1/2 teaspoons minced fresh oregano *or* 1/2 teaspoon dried oregano
- 1/2 teaspoon pepper
- 1/4 teaspoon cayenne pepper
- 1 cup olive *or* vegetable oil
- 2/3 cup lemon juice

Cook the pasta according to package directions; drain and rinse with cold water. Place in a large salad bowl. Add the next 12 ingredients; mix well. In a jar with tight-fitting lid, shake oil and lemon juice. Pour over salad and toss. Cover and refrigerate 6 hours or overnight. Stir before serving. **Yield:** 12-16 servings.

APPLE BEET SALAD

When I'm looking for a unique side dish to serve, this salad is the first thing that comes to mind. The tasty combination of tart apples and pickled beets add zest and color to this one-of-a-kind salad.

—Shirley Glaab
Hattiesburg, Mississippi

- 1/3 cup sweet pickle relish
- 1/4 cup sliced green onions
- 1/4 cup mayonnaise
- 2 tablespoons cider vinegar
- 1 tablespoon sugar
- 1/4 teaspoon salt
- 1/8 teaspoon pepper
- 2 cups diced peeled apples
- 2 cups diced pickled beets
- Lettuce leaves, optional
- 1 hard-cooked egg, chopped, optional

In a bowl, combine the first seven ingredients. Gently fold in apples and beets. If desired, serve on a lettuce-lined plate and top with chopped egg. **Yield:** 6-8 servings.

MODERN CAESAR SALAD

I've had several versions of Caesar salad but like this one the best. I think it's the robust flavor that distinguishes it from all others. I hope your family likes it as mush as mine does. —Dorothy Pritchett
Wills Point, Texas

- 3 slices bread
- 1/2 cup vegetable oil
- 1/4 cup red wine vinegar
- 2 teaspoons Worcestershire sauce
- 1 garlic clove, minced
- 1/4 teaspoon salt
- Dash pepper
- 8 cups torn romaine and leaf lettuce
- 1/2 cup grated *or* shredded Parmesan cheese
- 1/4 cup crumbled blue cheese

Cut bread into 1-in. cubes and place on a baking sheet. Toast at 225° for 1-2 hours or until crisp, turning occasionally. Meanwhile, combine the oil, vinegar, Worcestershire sauce, garlic, salt and pepper in a jar with tight-fitting lid; shake well. Refrigerate for several hours. In a large salad bowl, toss lettuce, cheeses and croutons. Shake the dressing; pour over the salad and toss to coat. Serve immediately. **Yield:** 6-8 servings.

BETTER THAN POTATO SALAD

(Pictured above)

As soon as our family tried this delicious salad, it became a favorite, especially during the warmer months. It's a flavorful change of pace from traditional potato salad that's easy to prepare. Even our two kids enjoy it.
—Susan McCurdy
Elmhurst, Illinois

    4 cups cooked long grain rice
    8 radishes, sliced
    4 hard-cooked eggs, chopped
    1 medium cucumber, seeded and chopped
    2 cups thinly sliced celery
  1/2 cup chopped onion
1-1/2 cups mayonnaise
    3 tablespoons prepared mustard
  3/4 teaspoon salt

In a large bowl, combine rice, radishes, eggs, cucumber, celery and onion. Combine mayonnaise, mustard and salt; mix well. Pour over rice mixture and toss. Cover and refrigerate at least 1 hour. **Yield:** 12-14 servings.

MARSHMALLOW LIME SALAD

Cool, fluffy and green, this salad has lots of kid appeal despite the cottage cheese and mayonnaise mixed in it. My daughter enjoyed this salad as a child, and now her two children love it, too.
—Fleda Collins
Talbott, Tennessee

    1 package (3 ounces) lime gelatin
    1 package (3 ounces) lemon gelatin

    2 cups boiling water
    2 cups miniature marshmallows
    1 can (20 ounces) crushed pineapple, undrained
    1 carton (8 ounces) small curd cottage cheese
    1 cup mayonnaise

In a bowl, dissolve both packages of gelatin in boiling water. Add marshmallows and stir until dissolved. Chill until partially set. Combine pineapple, cottage cheese and mayonnaise; stir into gelatin. Pour into a 9-in. square dish. Chill until firm. **Yield:** 9-12 servings.

HORSERADISH BEET SALAD

The horseradish marinade sparks the flavor of this simple salad and the beets look particularly pretty on a bed of your favorite lettuce.
—Doris Heath
Bryson City, North Carolina

    2 tablespoons sugar
    2 tablespoons cider vinegar
    1 tablespoon prepared horseradish
1-1/2 pounds beets, cooked and julienned
Lettuce leaves

In a bowl, combine sugar, vinegar and horseradish. Add the beets and toss to coat. Cover and chill for 6 hours or overnight. Serve on lettuce. **Yield:** 6 servings.

DOUBLE APPLE SALAD

Two kinds of apples in this recipe add great flavor as well as color. This scrumptious salad is delicious with chicken or turkey dishes.
—Nila Tower
Baird, Texas

    1 large Golden Delicious apple, diced
    1 large Red Delicious apple, diced
    1 teaspoon lemon juice
    1 can (20 ounces) pineapple chunks, drained
    1 cup miniature marshmallows
  2/3 cup flaked coconut
  1/2 cup chopped walnuts
  1/4 cup raisins
  1/4 cup mayonnaise
    2 tablespoons thinly sliced celery

In a bowl, toss apples with lemon juice. Add remaining ingredients and mix well. Cover and chill for at least 1 hour. **Yield:** 10-12 servings.

Soups & Sandwiches

A bowl brimming with hearty soup and a plate stacked high with an assortment of sandwiches is a classic combination that everyone will find hard to resist.

DILLY TURKEY MELT

(Pictured above)

This is a hearty grilled sandwich. The pickle slices add a bit of fun, and the barbecue sauce provides a hint of sweetness that's irresistible. —Henry Mujica
North Riverside, Illinois

   2 **medium onions, sliced**
   4 **tablespoons butter *or* margarine, *divided***
   4 **tablespoons barbecue sauce**
   8 **slices sourdough bread**
   8 **slices Monterey Jack cheese**
   8 **slices Canadian bacon**
   8 **slices cooked turkey**
Dill pickle slices

In a large skillet, saute onions in 1 tablespoon of butter until tender; remove and set aside. Spread barbecue sauce on four slices of bread. Layer each with one slice of cheese, bacon, turkey, pickles, onions and another slice of cheese. Cover with remaining slices of bread. In the same skillet over medium-low heat, melt remaining butter. Cook sandwiches on both sides until golden brown and cheese is melted (skillet may be covered the last few minutes to help melt cheese if necessary). **Yield:** 4 servings.

WILD DUCK GUMBO

Our family and friends just love this delightful, rich gumbo—it's such a unique way to serve this wild bird. We like that the meat is tender but not greasy. —Doris Heath
Bryson City, North Carolina

   2 **wild ducks, cut up**
   1/2 **cup cooking oil**

   2/3 **cup all-purpose flour**
   1 **pound smoked sausage, sliced**
   2 **cups chopped onion**
   1-1/2 **cups chopped green pepper**
   1-1/2 **cups sliced celery**
   2 **tablespoons minced fresh parsley**
   1 **tablespoon minced garlic**
   1 **can (14-1/2 ounces) stewed tomatoes**
   2 **bay leaves**
   2 **tablespoons Worcestershire sauce**
   1-1/2 **teaspoons pepper**
   1 **teaspoon salt**
   1 **teaspoon dried thyme**
   1/4 **teaspoon cayenne pepper**
   2 **quarts water**
Hot cooked rice

In a Dutch oven over medium heat, brown duck in batches in oil. Remove and set aside. Discard all but 2/3 cup drippings. Add flour to drippings; cook and stir over medium heat until brown, 12-14 minutes. Add sausage, onion, green pepper, celery, parsley and garlic. Cook for 10 minutes, stirring occasionally. Add next eight ingredients; mix well. Add duck; bring to a boil. Reduce heat; cover and simmer 60-75 minutes or until duck is tender. Remove duck. Cool. Debone and cut into chunks; return to pan. Simmer 5-10 minutes or until heated through. Remove bay leaves. Serve with rice. **Yield:** 16 servings (4 quarts).

BEET BORSCHT

My mother used to make this hearty soup from her garden's bountiful crop of beets and other vegetables. —Ruth Andrewson
Leavenworth, Washington

   2 **cups shredded fresh beets**
   1 **cup shredded carrots**
   1 **cup chopped onion**
   2 **cups water**
   1/2 **teaspoon salt**
   2 **cans (14-1/2 ounces *each*) beef broth**
   1 **cup shredded cabbage**
   1 **tablespoon butter *or* margarine**
   1 **tablespoon lemon juice**
Sour cream, optional

In a saucepan, bring the beets, carrots, onion, water and salt to a boil. Reduce heat; cover and simmer for 20 minutes. Add broth, cabbage and butter; simmer, uncovered, for 15 minutes. Just before serving, stir in lemon juice. Top each serving with a dollop of sour cream if desired. **Yield:** 8 servings (2 quarts).

EGG SALAD SUPREME

This dressed-up egg salad is a tasty change of pace. It's easily made the night before so the flavors have time to blend. I'm constantly getting requests to serve this yummy egg salad. —Sherry Krenz
Woodworth, North Dakota

    1 package (3 ounces) cream cheese, softened
1/4 cup mayonnaise *or* salad dressing
1/2 teaspoon prepared mustard
1/2 teaspoon salt
1/2 teaspoon dill weed
Pinch pepper
    6 hard-cooked eggs, chopped
1/2 cup chopped celery
    1 can (2-1/4 ounces) sliced ripe olives, drained
    2 tablespoons chopped onion
    1 tablespoon chopped pimientos
Bread *or* pita bread

In a bowl, combine the first six ingredients; mix well. Add eggs, celery, olives, onion and pimientos; mix well. Cover and chill for at least 1 hour. Serve on bread or pita bread, using about 1/2 cup for each sandwich. **Yield:** 6 servings.

BACHELOR CHILI

As a single male, I prepare my own meals night after night. This prize-winning chili I concocted years ago appeared in a local cookbook. —Dan Ellison
Herman, Minnesota

    1 boneless venison, elk, moose *or* beef chuck roast (3 to 3-1/2 pounds)
    1 tablespoon cooking oil
    2 medium onions, chopped
    1 medium green pepper, chopped
    2 garlic cloves, minced
1/4 to 1/2 teaspoon crushed red pepper flakes
    4 cans (14-1/2 ounces *each*) diced tomatoes, undrained
    1 cup water
    1 can (12 ounces) tomato paste
    1 tablespoon sugar
1/2 teaspoon ground cumin
1/2 teaspoon dried oregano
1/4 teaspoon pepper

Cut meat into 1/4-in. pieces. In a 4-qt. Dutch oven, brown meat in oil; remove with a slotted spoon and set aside. In the same pan, saute onions, green pepper, garlic and red pepper flakes until vegetables are tender. Return meat to pan. Add remaining in-

gredients; bring to a boil. Reduce heat; cover and simmer for 3 hours or until the meat is tender. **Yield:** 10-12 servings (3 quarts).

MEXICAN CHICKEN CORN CHOWDER

(Pictured below)

When company comes to visit, I like to make this smooth creamy soup. Its zippy flavor gives it Southwestern flair that appeals to all. —Susan Garoutte
Georgetown, Texas

1-1/2 pounds boneless skinless chicken breasts
    1/2 cup chopped onion
    1 to 2 garlic cloves, minced
    3 tablespoons butter *or* margarine
    2 chicken bouillon cubes
    1 cup hot water
  1/2 to 1 teaspoon ground cumin
    2 cups half-and-half cream
    2 cups (8 ounces) shredded Monterey Jack cheese
    1 can (16 ounces) cream-style corn
    1 can (4 ounces) chopped green chilies, undrained
  1/4 to 1 teaspoon hot pepper sauce
    1 medium tomato, chopped
Fresh cilantro *or* parsley, optional

Cut chicken into bite-size pieces. In a Dutch oven, brown chicken, onion and garlic in butter until chicken is no longer pink. Dissolve bouillon in hot water. Add to pan along with cumin; bring to a boil. Reduce heat; cover and simmer for 5 minutes. Add cream, cheese, corn, chilies and hot pepper sauce. Cook and stir over low heat until cheese is melted. Stir in tomato. Serve immediately; garnish with cilantro if desired. **Yield:** 6-8 servings (2 quarts).

HOT TUNA SANDWICHES

If you're looking for a deliciously different kind of sandwich, why not try this recipe? These tasty tuna sandwiches are great either warmed up or cold.
—Lucile Proctor
Panguitch, Utah

  1 can (6 ounces) tuna, drained and flaked
  1 cup (4 ounces) shredded cheddar cheese
  3 hard-cooked eggs, chopped
  3 tablespoons *each* chopped green pepper,
    sweet pickle, ripe olives and onion
  1/2 cup mayonnaise *or* salad dressing
  6 sandwich buns, split

Combine tuna, cheese, eggs, green pepper, pickle, olives, onion and mayonnaise; spread about 1/3 cup onto each bun. Wrap each sandwich in waxed paper; microwave on high for 30-45 seconds (per sandwich) or until cheese melts. **Yield:** 6 servings.

BAKED SOUTHWEST SANDWICHES

(Pictured above)

I like to prepare these tasty sandwiches whenever I have a few friends over for an informal lunch. The combination of toppings is out of this world. I'm often asked for the recipe.
—Holly Sorensen
Reedley, California

  1 can (4-1/4 ounces) chopped ripe olives,
    drained
  1/2 teaspoon chili powder
  1/2 teaspoon ground cumin
  1/4 teaspoon salt

  1/2 cup mayonnaise
  1/3 cup sour cream
  1/3 cup chopped green onions
  8 slices Italian bread
  3/4 to 1 pound thinly sliced cooked turkey
  2 medium tomatoes, thinly sliced
  2 ripe avocados, sliced
  3/4 cup shredded cheddar cheese
  3/4 cup shredded Monterey Jack cheese

In a bowl, combine olives, chili powder, cumin and salt; set aside 2 tablespoons. Add the mayonnaise, sour cream and onions to the remaining olive mixture. Place bread on an ungreased baking sheet; spread 1 tablespoon of mayonnaise mixture on each slice. Top with turkey and tomatoes. Spread with another tablespoon of mayonnaise mixture; top with avocados and cheeses. Sprinkle with reserved olive mixture. Bake at 350° for 15 minutes or until heated through. **Yield:** 8 servings.

SLOW-COOKED CHILI

This hearty chili can cook up to 10 hours on low in the slow cooker. It's so good to come home to its wonderful aroma after a long day away.
—Sue Call
Beech Grove, Indiana

  ✓ **This tasty dish uses less sugar, salt and fat.
    Recipe includes *Diabetic Exchanges*.**

  2 pounds ground beef
  2 cans (16 ounces *each*) kidney beans, rinsed
    and drained
  2 cans (14-1/2 ounces *each*) diced tomatoes,
    undrained
  1 can (8 ounces) tomato sauce
  2 medium onions, chopped
  1 green pepper, chopped
  2 garlic cloves, minced
  2 tablespoons chili powder
  2 teaspoons salt, optional
  1 teaspoon pepper
Shredded cheddar cheese, optional

In a skillet, brown beef; drain. Transfer to a slow cooker. Add the next nine ingredients. Cover and cook on low for 8-10 hours or on high for 4 hours. Garnish individual servings with cheese if desired. **Yield:** 10 servings. **Diabetic Exchanges:** One 1-cup serving (prepared with extra-lean ground beef and without salt or cheese) equals 3 meat, 1-1/2 starch, 1 vegetable; also, 330 calories, 337 mg sodium, 60 mg cholesterol, 29 gm carbohydrate, 26 gm protein, 13 gm fat.

SAUCY PIZZA BURGERS

These burgers are simple and taste like a little bit of Italy. The mushrooms in the sauce are a nice surprise. These are a favorite of the men in the family.
—Diane Hixon
Niceville, Florida

1 pound ground beef
1/2 teaspoon garlic salt
1 cup (4 ounces) shredded mozzarella cheese
1 can (8 ounces) pizza sauce
1 can (4 ounces) mushroom stems and pieces, drained
1/2 teaspoon dried oregano
1 medium onion, sliced
1 tablespoon butter *or* margarine
4 hamburger buns, split

In a bowl, combine beef and garlic salt. Shape into eight patties; top four of the patties with cheese. Cover with remaining patties; press edges to seal. Refrigerate. In a saucepan, combine the pizza sauce, mushrooms and oregano; cover and simmer for 10 minutes, stirring occasionally. In a skillet, saute onion in butter until tender; set aside. Pan-fry, grill or broil burgers until no longer pink. Spread bottoms of buns with a little of the sauce; top with burgers, onion and remaining sauce. Replace tops. **Yield:** 4 servings.

ZESTY HAMBURGERS

These lean patties get a little zip from horseradish and stay moist while cooking.   *—Sue Travnik Schiller*
Western Springs, Illinois

✓ **This tasty dish uses less sugar, salt and fat. Recipe includes *Diabetic Exchanges*.**

1 pound ground beef *or* turkey
4 teaspoons prepared horseradish
2 teaspoons Dijon mustard
1 teaspoon paprika
1/4 teaspoon pepper
1/8 teaspoon salt, optional
4 hamburger buns, split

In a bowl, combine the first six ingredients; mix well. Shape into four patties. Pan-fry, grill or broil until no longer pink. Serve on buns. **Yield:** 4 servings. **Diabetic Exchanges:** One serving (prepared with ground turkey breast and without added salt) equals 3 very lean meat, 2 starch; also, 240 calories, 355 mg sodium, 35 mg cholesterol, 24 gm carbohydrate, 31 gm protein, 4 gm fat.

ASPARAGUS CHICKEN CHOWDER

(Pictured above)

It makes me feel great to prepare this delicious soup and set it on the table in my favorite soup tureen.
—Jona Fell
Appleton, Wisconsin

1 broiler/fryer chicken (3 to 3-1/2 pounds)
3-1/2 quarts water
2 teaspoons chicken bouillon granules
5 bacon strips, diced
2 medium carrots, chopped
1 medium onion, chopped
1/2 pound fresh asparagus, cut into 1/2-inch pieces*
2 cups cubed peeled potatoes
1 tablespoon salt
1-1/2 teaspoons dried thyme
1/2 teaspoon pepper
1/2 cup all-purpose flour
1-1/2 cups whipping cream
2 tablespoons chopped fresh parsley

Place chicken, water and bouillon in a Dutch oven or soup kettle. Cover and bring to a boil; skim fat. Reduce heat; cover and simmer for 1 to 1-1/2 hours or until chicken is tender. Remove chicken; cool. Remove 1 cup of broth and set aside. In a skillet over medium heat, cook bacon until crisp. Remove bacon; drain and discard all but 2 tablespoons drippings. Saute carrots, onion and asparagus in drippings over medium heat until crisp-tender. Add to kettle along with potatoes, salt, thyme and pepper; return to a boil. Reduce heat; cover and simmer for 20 minutes or until potatoes are tender. Combine flour and reserved broth; stir into soup. Bring to a boil; cook and stir for 2 minutes. Debone chicken and cut into thin strips; add to soup along with cream and parsley. Heat through (do not boil). Sprinkle with bacon just before serving. **Yield:** 16-18 servings (4-1/2 quarts). ***Editor's Note:** If fresh asparagus is unavailable, a 10-ounce box of frozen cut asparagus (thawed) may be used. Add it to the soup with the chicken, cream and parsley.

SAUSAGE-STUFFED LOAF
(Pictured above)

I love to serve this hearty sandwich of sausage and ground beef in a zesty spaghetti sauce stuffed inside a loaf of French bread. Topped with melted cheese, it's a real crowd-pleaser every time. —Mary Koehler
Portland, Oregon

  2 Italian sausages
1/2 pound ground beef
1/2 cup chopped onion
1/4 cup chopped green pepper
  1 medium tomato, chopped
  1 can (15 ounces) chunky Italian-style tomato sauce
1/2 teaspoon dried basil
1/2 teaspoon dried oregano
1/2 teaspoon sugar
1/4 teaspoon aniseed
1/4 teaspoon salt
1/8 teaspoon garlic powder
  1 loaf (1 pound) French bread
1/4 to 1/2 cup shredded Parmesan cheese
Coarsely ground pepper

In a skillet, cook sausages until no longer pink. Remove and set aside. In the same skillet, cook beef, onion and green pepper until beef is no longer pink; drain. Stir in tomato, tomato sauce and seasonings. Cut sausages in half lengthwise and slice; add to meat sauce. Cut a wedge out of top of the bread, about 2 in. wide and three-fourths of the way through the loaf. Fill loaf with meat sauce. Sprinkle with Parmesan cheese and pepper. Wrap in heavy-duty foil. Bake at 400° for 15-20 minutes or until heated through. **Yield:** 6 servings.

HEARTY CHICKEN CLUB

I discovered the recipe for this sizable sandwich a while back and modified it to suit my family's tastes.

We love it...the only problem is trying to open wide enough to take a bite! —Debbie Johanesen
Missoula, Montana

1/4 cup mayonnaise
  2 tablespoons salsa
  4 slices seven-grain sandwich bread
  2 lettuce leaves
  4 slices tomato
  8 ounces sliced cooked chicken *or* turkey
  4 bacon strips, cooked
  4 slices cheddar cheese
  1 ripe avocado, sliced

Combine mayonnaise and salsa; spread on two slices of bread. Layer with lettuce, tomato, chicken or turkey, bacon, cheese and avocado. Top with remaining bread. **Yield:** 2 servings.

PAUL'S BURGERS ON THE GRILL

My wife, Julie, sometimes jokes she married me for better, for worse and for my cooking! I spent a lot of time in the kitchen while I was growing up and still enjoy doing so today. —Paul Miller
Green Bay, Wisconsin

  1 pound ground beef
1/4 cup ketchup
1/4 cup finely chopped onion
  2 teaspoons Italian seasoning
  1 teaspoon garlic powder
1/2 teaspoon salt
  4 hamburger buns, split
Lettuce leaves and tomato slices, optional

Combine the first six ingredients in a medium bowl; mix well. Shape into four patties. Grill over medium coals for 4-5 minutes per side or until no longer pink. Serve on buns; top with lettuce and tomato if desired. **Yield:** 4 servings.

CHILLED SORREL SOUP

This is a tart, refreshing cold soup with lovely spring green color. I especially like serving sorrel this way.
—Sara Seltzer
Sacramento, California

1/2 pound fresh sorrel
  4 cups water
  1 tablespoon lemon juice
  2 egg yolks

1 teaspoon salt
1/4 teaspoon pepper
Sour cream
Additional chopped fresh sorrel, optional

Remove center ribs and stems from sorrel; tie ribs and stems in a bundle and wrap in cheesecloth. Chop leaves into thin strips. In a 2-qt. saucepan, combine water, lemon juice, sorrel leaves and bundle of stems. Simmer for 20 minutes; discard stem bundle. In a small bowl, beat egg yolks; add a small amount of sorrel mixture, stirring constantly. Return all to the pan. Cook and stir until soup thickens (do not boil). Cool; chill for several hours. Add salt and pepper. Garnish with a dollop of sour cream and additional sorrel if desired. **Yield:** 4 servings (1 quart).

HARVEST TURKEY SOUP

The recipe for this super soup evolved over the years. I've learned to use herbs and spices to make dishes like this taste terrific. Along with a hearty broth, this soup has a colorful blend of vegetables.

—Linda Sand
Winsted, Connecticut

1 turkey carcass (from a 12- to 14-pound turkey)
5 quarts water
2 large carrots, shredded
1 cup chopped celery
1 large onion, chopped
4 chicken bouillon cubes
1 can (28 ounces) stewed tomatoes
3/4 cup fresh *or* frozen peas
3/4 cup long grain rice
1 package (10 ounces) frozen chopped spinach
1 tablespoon salt
3/4 teaspoon pepper
1/2 teaspoon dried marjoram
1/2 teaspoon dried thyme

Place the turkey carcass and water in a Dutch oven or soup kettle; bring to a boil. Reduce heat; cover and simmer for 1-1/2 hours. Remove carcass; allow to cool. Remove turkey from bones and cut into bite-size pieces; set aside. Strain broth. Add carrots, celery, onion and bouillon; bring to a boil. Reduce heat; cover and simmer for 30 minutes. Add tomatoes, peas, rice, spinach, salt, pepper, marjoram, thyme and reserved turkey. Return to a boil; cook, uncovered, for 20 minutes or until rice is tender. **Yield:** 22 servings (5-1/2 quarts).

CHEESEBURGER SOUP

(Pictured below)

After a local restaurant wouldn't share their recipe for a similar soup with me, I developed my own, starting from a recipe for potato soup. I was really pleased at how good this "all American" soup turned out.

—Joanie Shawhan
Madison, Wisconsin

1/2 pound ground beef
3/4 cup chopped onion
3/4 cup shredded carrots
3/4 cup diced celery
1 teaspoon dried basil
1 teaspoon dried parsley flakes
4 tablespoons butter *or* margarine, *divided*
3 cups chicken broth
4 cups diced peeled potatoes (1-3/4 pounds)
1/4 cup all-purpose flour
8 ounces process American cheese, cubed (2 cups)
1-1/2 cups milk
3/4 teaspoon salt
1/4 to 1/2 teaspoon pepper
1/4 cup sour cream

In a 3-qt. saucepan, brown beef; drain and set aside. In the same saucepan, saute onion, carrots, celery, basil and parsley in 1 tablespoon butter until vegetables are tender, about 10 minutes. Add broth, potatoes and beef; bring to a boil. Reduce heat; cover and simmer 10-12 minutes or until potatoes are tender. Meanwhile, in small skillet, melt remaining butter. Add flour; cook and stir 3-5 minutes or until bubbly. Add to soup; bring to a boil. Cook and stir 2 minutes. Reduce heat to low. Add cheese, milk, salt and pepper; cook and stir until cheese melts. Remove from the heat; blend in sour cream. **Yield:** 8 servings (2-1/4 quarts).

NUTTY CHICKEN PITA SANDWICHES

(Pictured above)

When company is coming for lunch, this is my favorite sandwich to make, since it looks and tastes a bit fancy. Even kids like it. —Glenda Schwarz
Morden, Manitoba

- 1 package (8 ounces) cream cheese, softened
- 3 tablespoons milk
- 1 tablespoon lemon juice
- 2 cups cubed cooked chicken
- 1/2 cup chopped green pepper
- 2 tablespoons chopped green onions
- 1 teaspoon ground mustard
- 1/2 teaspoon dried thyme
- 1/2 teaspoon salt
- 1/8 teaspoon pepper
- 1/4 cup chopped walnuts
- 3 large pita breads, halved

Alfalfa sprouts, optional

In a mixing bowl, beat cream cheese, milk and lemon juice until smooth. Stir in the chicken, green pepper, onions, mustard, thyme, salt and pepper; refrigerate. Just before serving, stir in the walnuts. Spoon about 1/2 cup filling into each pita half. Top with alfalfa sprouts if desired. **Yield:** 3-6 servings.

BIG SANDWICH

One look at this impressive sandwich and your family and friends will know their taste buds are in for a treat.

I have served it many times for casual lunches and suppers. The tall layers prompt people to ask how they're supposed to eat it. I encourage them to simply dig in and enjoy every bite! —Margaret Yost
Tipp City, Ohio

- 1 unsliced round loaf of bread (8 inches)
- 2 tablespoons horseradish
- 1/2 pound thinly sliced cooked roast beef
- 2 tablespoons prepared mustard
- 1/2 pound thinly sliced fully cooked ham *or* turkey
- 4 slices Swiss cheese
- 2 tablespoons mayonnaise
- 1 small tomato, thinly sliced
- 6 bacon strips, cooked
- 4 slices American cheese
- 1 small onion, thinly sliced
- 1/4 cup butter *or* margarine, melted
- 1 tablespoon sesame seeds
- 1/2 teaspoon onion salt

Slice bread horizontally into five equal layers. Spread bottom layer with horseradish; top with roast beef. Place the next slice of bread over beef; spread with mustard and top with ham or turkey and Swiss cheese. Add the next slice of bread; spread with mayonnaise and top with tomato and bacon. Add the next slice of bread; top with American cheese and onion. Cover with remaining bread. Combine butter, sesame seeds and onion salt; brush over top and sides of loaf. Place on a baking sheet; loosely tent with heavy-duty foil. Bake at 400° for 15-20 minutes or until heated through. Carefully slice into eight wedges. **Yield:** 8 servings.

HEARTY SPLIT PEA SOUP

This recipe puts a different spin on traditional split pea soup. The flavor is peppery rather than smoky, and the corned beef is a pleasant change of pace.
—Barbara Link
Alta Loma, California

- 1 bag (1 pound) dry split peas
- 8 cups water
- 2 medium potatoes, peeled and cubed
- 2 large onions, chopped
- 2 medium carrots, chopped
- 2 cups cubed cooked corned beef *or* ham
- 1/2 cup chopped celery
- 5 teaspoons chicken bouillon granules
- 1 teaspoon dried marjoram
- 1 teaspoon poultry seasoning

1 teaspoon rubbed sage
1/2 to 1 teaspoon pepper
1/2 teaspoon dried basil
1/2 teaspoon salt

In a Dutch oven or soup kettle, combine all ingredients; bring to a boil. Reduce heat; cover and simmer for 1-1/4 to 1-1/2 hours or until peas and vegetables are tender. **Yield:** 12 servings (3 quarts).

CREAM OF MUSHROOM SOUP

I love to experiment with recipes. I developed this recipe after years of trying many different combinations of ingredients. —*Jim Cosgrove Burlington, Ontario*

    2 garlic cloves, minced
    1 cup butter *or* margarine, *divided*
    2 medium onions, diced
    3 celery ribs, diced
    1 small green pepper, diced
2-1/2 pounds fresh mushrooms, sliced
    6 cups chicken broth
    1 cup all-purpose flour
    9 cups milk
    2 teaspoons salt
1/2 teaspoon pepper
1/4 teaspoon ground nutmeg

In a large kettle, saute garlic in 2 tablespoons butter. Add onions, celery and green pepper; saute until tender. Add mushrooms; saute for 5 minutes. Stir in broth and simmer for 20 minutes. In a saucepan, melt remaining butter; stir in flour until smooth. Gradually stir in milk. Cook and stir over low heat until mixture comes to a boil; boil for 2 minutes. Add to mushroom mixture; stir in seasonings. **Yield:** 16-18 servings (4-3/4 quarts).

DILLY ROAST BEEF SANDWICH

The seasoned cream cheese spread is a nice change of pace from ordinary mayonnaise and makes this sandwich something extra special. —*Betsey Bishop Jeffersonton, Virginia*

    3 tablespoons cream cheese, softened
Pinch *each* dill weed, garlic powder and pepper
    2 slices bread
    2 slices cooked roast beef
    3 tomato slices
Alfalfa sprouts

Combine cream cheese, dill, garlic powder and pepper; spread on one slice of bread. Top with beef, tomato, sprouts and remaining bread. **Yield:** 1 serving.

RASPBERRY-CRANBERRY SOUP

(Pictured below)

Served hot, this beautiful tangy soup helps beat the winter "blahs". On a sunny summer day, it's refreshing cold. I have fun serving it because people are so intrigued with the idea of a fruit soup. —*Susan Stull Chillicothe, Missouri*

    2 cups fresh *or* frozen cranberries
    2 cups apple juice
    1 cup fresh *or* frozen unsweetened
      raspberries, thawed
1/2 to 1 cup sugar
    1 tablespoon lemon juice
1/4 teaspoon ground cinnamon
    2 cups half-and-half cream, *divided*
    1 tablespoon cornstarch
Whipped cream, additional raspberries and
    mint, optional

In a 3-qt. saucepan, bring cranberries and apple juice to a boil. Reduce heat; simmer, uncovered, for 10 minutes. Press through a sieve; return to pan. Also press raspberries through the sieve; discard skin and seeds. Add to cranberry mixture; bring to a boil. Add sugar, lemon juice and cinnamon; remove from the heat. Cool 4 minutes. Stir 1 cup into 1-1/2 cups cream. Return all to pan; bring to a gentle boil. Mix cornstarch with remaining cream; stir into soup. Cook and stir for 2 minutes. Serve hot or chilled. Garnish with whipped cream, raspberries and mint if desired. **Yield:** 4 servings.

TURKEY BURGERS

(Pictured above)

I created this recipe on a whim for company. It was a hit. Now my family asks me quite often to prepare these healthy, hearty burgers. —*Brenda Jones*
Homestead, Florida

✓ **This tasty dish uses less sugar, salt and fat. Recipe includes *Diabetic Exchanges*.**

1 pound ground turkey breast
Egg substitute equal to 1 egg
  1/4 cup dry bread crumbs
    1 teaspoon steak sauce
    1 teaspoon spicy brown mustard
  1/4 teaspoon dried thyme
  1/4 teaspoon pepper
    4 hamburger buns, split
Lettuce leaves and tomato slices

In a bowl, combine the first seven ingredients. Shape into four burgers (for easier shaping, use cold wet hands). Pan-fry, grill or broil until no longer pink. Serve on buns with lettuce and tomato. **Yield: 4 servings. Diabetic Exchanges:** One serving equals 4 very lean meat, 2 starch; also, 285 calories, 411 mg sodium, 35 mg cholesterol, 26 gm carbohydrate, 33 gm protein, 6 gm fat.

ITALIAN CHICKEN SOUP

Nothing chases the winter chills away like a steaming bowl of this chicken soup. It's a comforting dish that brings back memories of Mom. —*John Croce*
Yarmouthport, Massachusetts

  4 chicken breast halves (bone in)
  1 large onion, halved
  1 large carrot, quartered
  3 celery ribs with leaves, chopped
  2 cans (14-1/2 ounces *each*) chicken broth
  2 cups water
  2 chicken bouillon cubes

  2 bay leaves
  1 can (14-1/2 ounces) diced tomatoes, undrained
  6 to 8 green onions, thinly sliced
1/2 cup chopped fresh parsley
1/4 cup ketchup
  1 teaspoon salt
  1 teaspoon dried rosemary, crushed
1/2 teaspoon dried basil
  2 garlic cloves, minced
1/2 teaspoon pepper
  2 cans (15-1/2 ounces *each*) kidney beans, rinsed and drained
1/4 cup grated Romano cheese

In a 5-qt. Dutch oven, combine the first eight ingredients; bring to a boil. Reduce heat; leaving cover ajar, simmer for 1-1/2 hours. Remove chicken; strain and reserve broth. Discard vegetables and bay leaves. When the chicken is cool enough to handle, remove skin and bones; discard. Cut chicken into bite-size pieces; set aside. Return broth to kettle; add tomatoes, onions, parsley, ketchup, salt, rosemary, basil, garlic and pepper; bring to a boil. Reduce heat; leaving cover ajar, simmer for 45 minutes. Add beans, cheese and chicken; heat through. **Yield:** 12-14 servings (3-1/2 quarts).

FOUR-ONION SOUP

This mellow, rich-tasting onion soup is a mainstay for our family meals throughout the year. I'm happy to share the recipe. —*Margaret Adams*
Pacific Grove, California

  1 medium yellow onion
  1 medium red onion
  1 medium leek (white portion only)
  5 green onions with tops
  1 garlic clove, minced
  2 tablespoons butter *or* margarine
  2 cans (14-1/2 ounces *each*) beef broth
  1 can (10-1/2 ounces) beef consomme
  1 teaspoon Worcestershire sauce
1/2 teaspoon ground nutmeg
  1 cup (4 ounces) shredded Swiss cheese
  6 slices French bread (3/4 inch thick), toasted
  6 tablespoons grated Parmesan cheese, optional

Slice all onions 1/4 in. thick. In a 3-qt. saucepan over medium-low heat, saute onions and garlic in butter for 15 minutes or until tender and golden, stirring occasionally. Add broth, consomme, Worcestershire sauce and nutmeg; bring to a boil. Reduce heat; cover and simmer for 30 minutes. Sprinkle 1 tablespoon of Swiss cheese in the bottom of six ovenproof 8-oz. bowls. Ladle hot soup into bowls. Top each with a slice of bread. Sprinkle with remaining Swiss cheese and Parmesan cheese if desired. Broil until cheese melts. Serve immediately. **Yield:** 6 servings.

MUSHROOM BARLEY SOUP
(Pictured above)

With beef, barley and vegetables, this soup is hearty enough to be a meal. A big steaming bowl and a slice of crusty bread tastes great on a cold day.
—Lynn Thomas
London, Ontario

1-1/2 pounds boneless beef chuck, cut into
      3/4-inch cubes
  1 tablespoon cooking oil
  2 cups finely chopped onion
  1 cup diced carrots
1/2 cup sliced celery
  1 pound fresh mushrooms, sliced
  2 garlic cloves, minced
1/2 teaspoon dried thyme
  1 can (14-1/2 ounces) beef broth
  1 can (14-1/2 ounces) chicken broth
  2 cups water
1/2 cup medium pearl barley
  1 teaspoon salt
1/2 teaspoon pepper
  3 tablespoons chopped fresh parsley

In a Dutch oven or soup kettle, brown meat in oil. Remove meat with a slotted spoon and set aside. Saute onion, carrots and celery in drippings over medium heat until tender, about 5 minutes. Add mushrooms, garlic and thyme; cook and stir for 3 minutes. Add broth, water, barley, salt and pep-

per. Return meat to pan; bring to a boil. Reduce heat; cover and simmer for 1-1/2 to 2 hours or until barley and meat are tender. Stir in parsley. **Yield:** about 10 servings (2-3/4 quarts).

STUFFED PEPPER SOUP

Some of us cooks at the restaurant where I work were talking about stuffed peppers and decided to stir up similar ingredients for a soup. Customer response was overwhelming to our creation! —Krista Muddiman
Meadville, Pennsylvania

  2 pounds ground beef
  2 quarts water (8 c.)
  1 can (28 ounces) diced tomatoes, undrained
  1 can (28 ounces) tomato sauce
  2 cups cooked long grain white rice
  2 cups chopped green pepper
  2 beef bouillon cubes
1/4 cup packed brown sugar
  2 teaspoons salt
  1 teaspoon pepper , 2-3 tsp. chili powder

In a large saucepan or Dutch oven, brown beef; drain. Add remaining ingredients; bring to a boil. Reduce heat; cover and simmer for 30-40 minutes or until peppers are tender. **Yield:** 10 servings.

SALMON-SALAD SANDWICHES

These are perfect to pack in your kids' lunch boxes when they can't face another boring sandwich. The carrots and celery add a nice crunch. —Yvonne Shust
Shoal Lake, Manitoba

  1 package (3 ounces) cream cheese, softened
  1 tablespoon mayonnaise
  1 tablespoon lemon juice
  1 teaspoon dill weed
1/4 to 1/2 teaspoon salt
1/8 teaspoon pepper
  1 can (6 ounces) pink salmon, drained, skin
    and bones removed
1/2 cup shredded carrot
1/2 cup chopped celery
Lettuce leaves
  2 whole wheat buns, split

In a mixing bowl, beat cream cheese, mayonnaise, lemon juice, dill, salt and pepper until smooth. Add the salmon, carrot and celery; mix well. Place a lettuce leaf and about 1/2 cup salmon salad on each bun. **Yield:** 2 servings.

SIZZLING RICE SOUP

(Pictured below)

My family enjoys food with flair like this unique Oriental soup. Whenever I serve it, it's such a hit that no one has much room for the main course.
— *Mary Woodke*
Gardiner, New York

    1 **cup uncooked long grain rice**
    8 **cups chicken broth**
    2 **cups cubed cooked chicken**
    2 **cups sliced fresh mushrooms**
1/4 **cup chopped green onions**
    1 **can (8 ounces) bamboo shoots, drained**
    1 **can (8 ounces) sliced water chestnuts, drained**
    4 **chicken bouillon cubes**
1/2 **teaspoon garlic powder**
    1 **package (10 ounces) frozen peas**
1/4 **cup cooking oil**

Cook rice according to package directions. Spread on a greased 15-in. x 10-in. x 1-in. baking pan. Bake at 325° for 2 hours or until dried and browned, stirring occasionally; set aside. In a large soup kettle or Dutch oven, combine the broth, chicken, mushrooms, onions, bamboo shoots, water chestnuts, bouillon and garlic powder. Cover and simmer for 1 hour. Add peas; cook for 15 minutes. Just before serving, heat oil in a skillet. Fry rice in hot oil until it is slightly puffed. Ladle soup into serving bowls. Immediately spoon some hot rice into each bowl and it will sizzle. **Yield:** 10-12 servings (3 quarts).

POOR BOY SANDWICH

The original poor boy sandwiches called for oysters, but I made this meal more economical by substituting tuna instead. The horseradish in this recipe really wakes up an ordinary tuna sandwich. —*Violet Beard*
Marshall, Illinois

    1 **French *or* submarine roll**
    1 **tablespoon butter *or* margarine, softened**
1/4 **teaspoon celery seed**
    1 **can (6 ounces) tuna, drained and flaked**
1/4 **cup chopped celery**
1/4 **cup chopped fresh parsley**
    3 **tablespoons mayonnaise**
    1 **tablespoon horseradish**
1/2 **teaspoon grated lemon peel**
1/8 **teaspoon pepper**

Cut a thin slice off top of roll; set aside. Hollow out center, reserving 1/2 cup of bread and leaving a 1/4-in. shell. Combine butter and celery seed; spread over inside of roll and on cut surface of top. Combine remaining ingredients and reserved bread; spoon into roll. Replace top. **Yield:** 1 serving.

COUNTRY MUSHROOM SOUP

The big fresh-mushroom flavor of this dish sets it apart from other mushroom soup recipes I've tried.
— *Elsie Cathrea*
Elmira, Ontario

1/4 **cup butter *or* margarine**
1/4 **cup all-purpose flour**
    2 **cups chicken broth**
1/2 **teaspoon salt**
1/4 **teaspoon pepper**
    1 **to 2 bay leaves**
2/3 **cup finely chopped celery**
1/4 **cup finely chopped onion**
    3 **tablespoons cooking oil**
    4 **to 5 cups sliced fresh mushrooms (about 1 pound)**
2/3 **cup half-and-half cream *or* milk**

In a 2-qt. saucepan, melt butter; stir in flour until smooth. Gradually stir in broth until smooth. Add salt, pepper and bay leaves. Simmer, uncovered, for 15 minutes, stirring occasionally. Meanwhile, in another saucepan, saute celery and onion in oil until tender. Add mushrooms; cook and stir until tender. Add to broth mixture; bring to a boil. Reduce heat; simmer, uncovered, for 15 minutes, stirring occasionally. Add cream; heat through. Discard bay leaves. **Yield:** 4 servings.

HAM AND BEAN SOUP

A mix of colorful beans and two types of meat make this a hearty meal. —Margaret Shauers
Great Bend, Kansas

- 1 package (20 ounces) 15-bean blend
- 5 quarts water, *divided*
- 1 pound fully cooked ham, cubed
- 2 smoked *or* precooked bratwurst links, sliced
- 1 cup chopped green pepper
- 1/2 cup chopped onion
- 1/2 cup chopped celery
- 1/2 cup sliced carrots
- 2 garlic cloves, minced *1/4 tsp. garlic powder*
- 2 tablespoons Worcestershire sauce
- 1 teaspoon dried basil
- 3/4 teaspoon salt
- 3/4 teaspoon pepper
- 1/2 teaspoon dried marjoram
- 1/2 teaspoon hot pepper sauce
- 2 cans (14-1/2 ounces *each*) diced tomatoes, undrained
- 1 can (4 ounces) chopped green chilies

Rinse dry beans and place in a Dutch oven with 3 qts. of water. Bring to a boil; boil for 3-5 minutes. Remove from the heat; cover and let stand for 1 hour. Drain and rinse beans. Return to pan; add remaining water and the next 13 ingredients. Bring to a boil. Reduce heat; cover and simmer for 2-1/2 to 3 hours or until beans are almost tender. Add tomatoes and chilies; bring to a boil. Reduce heat; cover and simmer for 30 minutes. **Yield:** 18 servings (4-1/2 quarts).

MEXICAN BEEF BURGERS

(Pictured above right)

One night for dinner, half the family requested hamburgers and the others wanted tacos. My daughter-in-law and I came up with this compromise to satisfy everyone's tastes. —Stanny Barta
Pisek, North Dakota

- 2 eggs, beaten
- 2 cans (4 ounces *each*) chopped green chilies
- 1/4 cup finely minced onion
- 1/3 cup salsa
- 1 teaspoon salt
- 1/2 teaspoon pepper
- 1 garlic clove, minced
- 3/4 cup finely crushed corn chips
- 2 pounds ground beef

- 8 flour tortillas (10 inches), warmed
- **TOPPINGS:**
- **Chopped tomatoes**
- **Chopped ripe olives**
- **Shredded cheddar cheese**
- **Shredded lettuce**
- **Salsa**
- **Sour cream**

In a bowl, combine the first seven ingredients. Add chips and beef; mix well. Shape into eight patties. Pan-fry, grill or broil until no longer pink. Wrap burgers and desired toppings in tortillas. **Yield:** 8 servings.

FRENCH DIP

Seasonings give the broth a wonderful flavor, and the meat cooks up tender and juicy. —Margaret McNeil
Memphis, Tennessee

- 1 beef chuck roast (3 pounds), trimmed
- 2 cups water
- 1/2 cup soy sauce
- 1 teaspoon dried rosemary
- 1 teaspoon dried thyme
- 1 teaspoon garlic powder
- 1 bay leaf
- 3 to 4 whole peppercorns
- 8 French rolls, split

Place roast in a slow cooker. Add water, soy sauce and seasonings. Cover and cook on high for 5-6 hours or until beef is tender. Remove meat from broth; shred with forks and keep warm. Strain broth; skim off fat. Pour broth into small cups for dipping. Serve beef on rolls. **Yield:** 8 servings.

VEGETABLE BARLEY SOUP

People always comment on the wonderful flavor and are often surprised to hear that a touch of mint is added to the broth. —Mary Kay Dixson
Catlin, Illinois

1-1/2 quarts beef broth
    1 can (46 ounces) V-8 juice
    2 cups water
    1 cup diced celery
    1 cup diced peeled potato
    1 cup sliced carrots
    1 cup chopped onion
    3/4 cup uncooked barley
    4 garlic cloves, minced
    2 tablespoons Italian seasoning
    1 to 2 teaspoons lemon-pepper seasoning
    2 teaspoons dried rosemary, crushed
    1 teaspoon fennel seed
    1 teaspoon dried mint
Parmesan cheese, optional

In a large kettle or Dutch oven, combine all ingredients except the cheese; bring to a boil. Reduce heat; cover and simmer for 3 hours. Top each serving with cheese if desired. **Yield:** 12-14 servings (3-1/4 quarts).

MUSHROOM CHEESE STROMBOLI

(Pictured above right)

I got the recipe for this hearty crowd-pleaser from a friend. We find it especially delicious since our state is well known for its wonderful fresh mushrooms.
—Patty Kile
Greentown, Pennsylvania

1/4 pound fresh mushrooms, sliced
    1 tablespoon butter *or* margarine
    1 loaf (1 pound) frozen bread dough, thawed
    3 ounces thinly sliced pepperoni
    6 ounces thinly sliced mozzarella cheese
1/4 pound thinly sliced Provolone cheese
    1 cup grated Parmesan cheese
1/3 cup spaghetti sauce
    1 tablespoon dried parsley flakes
1/2 teaspoon dried oregano
    1 egg yolk
1/2 teaspoon water
Additional Parmesan cheese, optional

In a skillet, saute mushrooms in butter until tender; set aside. On a lightly floured board, roll dough into a 30-in. x 8-in. rectangle; cut into two 15-in. x 8-in. pieces. On the long side of each piece, layer pepperoni, cheeses, mushrooms, spaghetti sauce, parsley and oregano. Fold over dough and pinch to seal. Combine egg and water; brush over edges and ends of dough. With a sharp knife, cut five small steam vents in the top of each roll. Place on greased baking sheets. Sprinkle with Parmesan if desired. Bake at 350° for 27-30 minutes or until golden brown. Slice and serve warm. **Yield:** 36 slices. **Editor's Note:** Baked stromboli may be frozen for up to 1 month.

ITALIAN SLOPPY JOES

My mother used to make these for us when we were kids. When I left home, I was sure to take the recipe with me, and now it's one of my husband's favorites.
—Kimberly Speakman
McKinney, Texas

    1 pound bulk Italian sausage
    1 pound bulk hot Italian sausage
    4 garlic cloves, minced
    1 cup chopped green pepper
1/2 cup chopped onion
    1 can (15 ounces) tomato sauce
    2 tablespoons minced fresh parsley
    1 teaspoon dried oregano
1/2 teaspoon chili powder
1/4 teaspoon fennel seed
    8 to 10 French *or* submarine rolls, split
3/4 cup shredded mozzarella cheese

In a large saucepan or Dutch oven over medium heat, cook sausage, garlic, green pepper and onion until the sausage is no longer pink; drain. Add the tomato sauce and seasonings; bring to a boil. Reduce heat; cover and simmer for 30 minutes. Spoon about 1/2 cup onto each roll; sprinkle with cheese. **Yield:** 8-10 servings.

CHICKEN SALAD SANDWICHES

These sandwiches give kids two of their favorite foods—sunflower seeds and grapes. —*Diane Hixon*
Niceville, Florida

2 cups cubed cooked chicken
1 cup diced Monterey Jack cheese
1/2 cup seedless green grapes, halved
1/2 cup mayonnaise
1/4 cup thinly sliced celery
1/4 cup sunflower seeds
1/4 teaspoon salt
1/4 teaspoon pepper
Lettuce leaves
4 pita breads, halved *or* 8 slices bread

In a bowl, combine the first eight ingredients. Line pita or bread with lettuce; add 1/2 cup chicken salad. **Yield:** 4 servings.

SPLIT PEA SOUP

This hearty classic is a great dish for all cooks, whether a beginner or more experienced. Not only is it nourishing and inexpensive, it's simple to make.
—*John Croce*
Yarmouthport, Massachusetts

1 pound green split peas
2 smoked ham hocks (about 1-1/2 pounds)
2 celery ribs, finely chopped
1 medium onion, finely chopped
1 medium carrot, finely chopped
2 chicken bouillon cubes
1 teaspoon garlic powder
1 teaspoon salt
1/2 teaspoon dried oregano
1/4 teaspoon pepper
8 to 10 cups water
1 bay leaf

In a large saucepan, combine all of the ingredients; bring to a boil. Reduce heat; leaving cover ajar, simmer for 3 hours, stirring occasionally. Remove and discard bay leaf. Remove the ham hocks; when cool enough to handle, cut meat into bite-size pieces. Return meat to the soup and heat through. **Yield:** 6-8 servings (2 quarts).

CREAMY TURKEY SOUP

(Pictured below)

My mother always prepared a holiday turkey much larger than our family could ever eat in one meal so there'd be plenty of leftovers to use in dishes like this.
—*Kathleen Harris*
Galesburg, Illinois

1 large onion, chopped
3 celery ribs with leaves, cut into 1/4-inch pieces
6 tablespoons butter *or* margarine
6 tablespoons all-purpose flour
1 teaspoon salt
1/4 teaspoon pepper
1/4 teaspoon garlic powder
1/2 teaspoon *each* dried thyme, savory and parsley flakes
1-1/2 cups milk
4 cups cubed cooked turkey
5 medium carrots, cut into 1/4-inch pieces
1 to 2 cups turkey *or* chicken broth
1 package (10 ounces) frozen peas

In a large kettle, saute onion and celery in butter until tender, about 10 minutes. Stir in the flour and seasonings; gradually add milk, stirring constantly until thickened. Add turkey and carrots. Add enough broth until soup is desired consistency. Cover and simmer for 15 minutes. Add peas; cover and simmer for 15 minutes or until vegetables are tender. **Yield:** 6-8 servings (2 quarts).

DOUBLE-DECKER BURGERS
(Pictured above)

These man-sized sandwiches look as delectable as they taste. We especially like the variety of flavors in the special cheese spread.
—*Marcy Schewe*
Danube, Minnesota

2 pounds ground beef
1/4 cup finely chopped onion
2 eggs, beaten
2 teaspoons Worcestershire sauce
1 teaspoon salt
1/4 teaspoon pepper
1-1/2 cups (6 ounces) shredded cheddar cheese
3 tablespoons mayonnaise
4 teaspoons prepared mustard
4 teaspoons dill pickle relish
Shredded lettuce
6 onion slices
6 hamburger buns, split
6 tomato slices

In a large bowl, combine the first six ingredients; mix well. Shape into 12 thin patties. Broil 4 in. from the heat for 7-8 minutes on each side or until no longer pink. In a small bowl, combine the cheese, mayonnaise, mustard and relish; mix well. Spoon 2 tablespoons on each burger. Return to the broiler just until cheese softens. Place lettuce and onion on bottom of buns; top each with two burgers, tomato and top of bun. **Yield:** 6 servings.

LUCKY BEAN SOUP

One lucky day, I received a bag of mixed beans at a church bazaar, so I developed a bean soup gift pack

that has become a popular church fund-raiser. We provide the recipe, the beans and a packet containing the spices. The recipient just adds water and a can of tomatoes for a delicious pot of savory soup.
—*Doris Cox*
South Orange, New Jersey

1/4 cup *each* dry yellow split peas, lentils, black beans, great northern beans, pinto beans, baby lima beans and kidney beans
1/2 cup *each* dry green split peas, black-eyed peas and navy beans
2 quarts water
1/3 cup dried minced onion
1 tablespoon salt
1 teaspoon dried thyme
1 teaspoon dried rosemary, crushed
1 teaspoon garlic powder
1/2 teaspoon celery seed
1/2 teaspoon dried basil
1/4 to 1/2 teaspoon crushed red pepper flakes
2 bay leaves
1 can (28 ounces) crushed tomatoes

Place peas, lentils and beans in a Dutch oven or soup kettle; add enough water to cover. Bring to a boil; boil for 2 minutes. Remove from the heat; let stand for 1 hour. Drain and discard liquid. Add 2 qts. water and seasonings; bring to a boil. Reduce heat; cover and simmer for 1-1/2 to 2 hours or until beans are just tender. Stir in tomatoes; increase heat to medium. Cook, uncovered, for 15-30 minutes. Discard bay leaves before serving. **Yield:** 14 servings (3-1/2 quarts).

GRILLED HAM AND EGG SALAD SANDWICHES

An aunt shared this wonderful recipe with me years ago when I was looking for some low-budget family meals. The hearty ham and toasted bread make it a deliciously different kind of egg salad sandwich.
—*Beverly Stiger*
Wolf Creek, Montana

6 hard-cooked eggs, chopped
1 cup diced fully cooked ham
1/2 cup finely chopped celery
1 tablespoon minced onion
1/2 cup mayonnaise
2 teaspoons prepared mustard
1/2 teaspoon salt
1/4 teaspoon pepper
12 slices whole wheat *or* white bread
Cooking oil

BATTER:
   1/2 cup cornmeal
   1/2 cup all-purpose flour
   1 teaspoon baking powder
   1 teaspoon salt
   2 cups milk
   2 eggs, lightly beaten

Combine eggs, ham, celery, onion, mayonnaise, mustard, salt and pepper; spread on six slices of bread. Top with remaining bread and set aside. In a bowl, whisk batter ingredients until well blended. Heat about 1/2 in. of oil in a large deep skillet. Dip sandwiches into batter. Fry in hot oil for 3 minutes on each side or until golden brown. Drain on paper towels. **Yield:** 6 servings.

BEEF BARLEY SOUP

When most folks think of barley, they picture it served up in a delicious soup. I'm no exception! This is a hearty soup that's a meal in itself. —Jan Spencer
McLean, Saskatchewan

✓ **This tasty dish uses less sugar, salt and fat. Recipe includes** *Diabetic Exchanges*.

   2 pounds beef short ribs with bones
   5 cups water
   1 can (14-1/2 ounces) diced tomatoes, undrained
   1 medium onion, chopped
   1 to 1-1/2 teaspoons salt, optional
   1/8 teaspoon pepper
   2 cups sliced carrots
   1 cup sliced celery
   1 cup chopped cabbage
   2/3 cup quick-cooking barley
   1/4 cup minced fresh parsley

In a large saucepan or Dutch oven, combine ribs, water, tomatoes, onion, salt if desired and pepper; bring to a boil over medium heat. Reduce heat; cover and simmer for 1-1/2 to 2 hours or until meat is tender. Remove ribs; allow to cool. Skim fat. Remove meat from bones and cut into bite-size pieces; return to broth. Add carrots, celery and cabbage; bring to a boil. Reduce heat; cover and simmer for 15 minutes. Add barley; return to a boil. Reduce heat; cover and cook for 10-15 minutes or until barley and vegetables are tender. Stir in parsley. **Yield:** 8 servings (2 quarts). **Diabetic Exchanges:** One 1-cup serving (prepared without salt) equals 3 meat, 1 vegetable, 1 starch; also, 314 calories, 156 mg sodium, 72 mg cholesterol, 19 gm carbohydrate, 27 gm protein, 15 gm fat.

GOLDEN SQUASH SOUP
(Pictured below)

This recipe, from my mother-in-law, is one I enjoy making. It's a special rich soup that dresses up the table.
—Maryann Klein
Washington Township, New Jersey

   3 leeks (white portion only), sliced
   4 medium carrots, chopped
   5 tablespoons butter *or* margarine
   3 pounds butternut squash, peeled and cubed
   6 cups chicken broth
   3 medium zucchini, peeled and sliced
   2 teaspoons salt
   1/2 teaspoon dried thyme
   1/4 teaspoon white pepper
   1 cup half-and-half cream
   1/2 cup milk
Grated Parmesan cheese and chives, optional

In a Dutch oven or soup kettle over medium heat, saute leeks and carrots in butter for 5 minutes, stirring occasionally. Add squash, broth, zucchini, salt, thyme and pepper; bring to a boil. Reduce heat; cover and simmer until vegetables are tender, about 30 minutes. Cool until lukewarm. In a blender or food processor, puree soup in small batches until smooth; return to kettle. Add cream and milk; mix well and heat through (do not boil). Garnish with Parmesan cheese and chives if desired. **Yield:** 12-14 servings (3-1/2 quarts).

TUNA BURGERS

(Pictured above)

I gave Mom's original recipe a boost by adding onion and green pepper to these delightfully different tuna sandwiches. The filling is very fresh. —Nancy Selig
Lunenburg, Nova Scotia

- 6 hard-cooked eggs, chopped
- 2 cans (6 ounces *each*) tuna, drained and flaked
- 1 cup (4 ounces) shredded sharp cheddar cheese
- 1/2 cup chopped green pepper
- 1/2 cup chopped onion
- 3/4 teaspoon garlic salt
- 3/4 teaspoon pepper
- 1 cup mayonnaise *or* salad dressing
- 8 Kaiser rolls, split

In a bowl, combine eggs and tuna. Add the cheese, green pepper, onion, garlic salt and pepper; mix well. Stir in the mayonnaise. Spoon about 1/2 cup onto each roll; wrap individually in heavy-duty foil. Bake at 400° for 15 minutes or until heated through. **Yield:** 8 servings.

VIDALIA ONION SOUP

There's no question of the star in this traditional favorite soup. Rich Swiss cheese delightfully tops off a heaping bowlful of sweet, succulent Vidalia onions. —Ruby Jean Bland
Glennville, Georgia

- 4 to 5 large Vidalia *or* sweet onions, chopped
- 3 tablespoons butter *or* margarine
- 1/4 teaspoon pepper
- 1 tablespoon all-purpose flour
- 4 cups beef broth
- 1-1/2 cups water

- 1 bay leaf
- 8 slices French bread, toasted
- 1/2 cup shredded Swiss cheese

In a Dutch oven or soup kettle, saute the onions in butter until lightly browned. Sprinkle with pepper and flour. Cook and stir for 1 minute. Add the broth, water and bay leaf; simmer for 30-40 minutes, stirring occasionally. Discard bay leaf. Ladle into ovenproof soup bowls; top with bread and cheese. Bake at 400° for 10 minutes or until cheese is golden brown. **Yield:** 8 servings (2 quarts).

ITALIAN BEEF SANDWICHES

Before leaving for work, I put these ingredients in the slow cooker. Then supper is ready when I get home. —Carol Allen
McLeansboro, Illinois

- 1 boneless beef chuck roast (3 to 4 pounds), trimmed
- 3 tablespoons dried basil
- 3 tablespoons dried oregano
- 1 cup water
- 1 envelope dry onion soup mix
- 10 to 12 Italian rolls *or* sandwich buns

Place the roast in a slow cooker. Combine basil, oregano and water; pour over roast. Sprinkle with soup mix. Cover and cook on low for 7-8 hours or until meat is tender. Remove meat from broth; shred with a fork and keep warm. Strain broth; skim off fat. Serve meat on rolls; use broth for dipping if desired. **Yield:** 10-12 servings.

BEAN SOUP WITH DUMPLINGS

I let my slow cooker simmer this nicely spiced, bean-filled broth while I'm busy or running errands. —Jane Mullins
Livonia, Missouri

- 3 cups water
- 1 can (16 ounces) kidney beans, rinsed and drained
- 1 can (15 ounces) black beans, rinsed and drained
- 1 can (14-1/2 ounces) Mexican-style stewed tomatoes
- 1 can (4 ounces) chopped green chilies
- 1 package (10 ounces) frozen corn, thawed
- 1 cup chopped onion
- 1 cup chopped carrots

        3 beef bouillon cubes
        3 garlic cloves, minced
        1 teaspoon chili powder
    1/2 teaspoon salt
    1/4 teaspoon pepper
DUMPLINGS:
    1/2 cup all-purpose flour
    1/4 cup yellow cornmeal
        1 teaspoon baking powder
Dash salt and pepper
        1 egg white, beaten
        3 tablespoons milk
        1 tablespoon vegetable oil

In a large saucepan over medium heat, combine the first 13 ingredients; bring to a boil. Reduce heat; cover and simmer for 1 hour or until vegetables are tender. For dumplings, combine flour, cornmeal, baking powder, salt and pepper. Combine egg white, milk and oil; stir into dry ingredients. Drop into eight mounds onto boiling soup. Reduce heat; cover and simmer for 15-20 minutes (do not lift the cover). **Yield:** 8 servings (2-1/4 quarts).

SAUSAGE KALE SOUP

Several years ago, I had a dish in a local restaurant that was so good I was determined to duplicate it at home. I played with the recipe until I finally got it right. That gratifying experience sparked my interest in creating tasty dishes like this. —John Croce
Yarmouthport, Massachusetts

        1 pound bulk pork sausage
        2 medium onions, chopped
        2 tablespoons olive *or* vegetable oil
        2 garlic cloves, minced
        3 cans (14-1/2 ounces *each*) chicken broth
        2 cups water
        3 chicken bouillon cubes
    1/2 pound fresh kale, chopped
        3 medium potatoes, peeled and cubed
        2 cans (16 ounces *each*) kidney beans,
            rinsed and drained

In a 5-qt. Dutch oven over medium heat, cook sausage and onions in oil for 5 minutes or until sausage is browned; drain. Add garlic; cook for 1-2 minutes. Add broth, water, bouillon and kale; bring to a boil. Reduce heat; leaving the cover ajar, simmer for 1 hour. Add the potatoes and cook for 15 minutes. Add the beans; cook until potatoes are tender and beans are heated through. **Yield:** 10-12 servings (3-1/4 quarts). **Editor's Note:** Fresh spinach may be used in place of kale. Add it along with the beans.

ZESTY VEGETABLE BEEF SOUP
(Pictured below)

My family loves to come to the table for hot homemade biscuits and a bowl of this flavorful filling soup.
—Brenda Wood
Portage la Prairie, Manitoba

BROTH:
        2 quarts water
        3 pounds beef short ribs with bones
        1 large onion, quartered
        2 medium carrots, quartered
        2 celery ribs, quartered
        8 whole allspice
        2 bay leaves
        1 tablespoon salt
    1/2 teaspoon pepper
SOUP:
        1 quart V-8 juice
        3 celery ribs, sliced
        2 medium potatoes, peeled and cubed
        2 medium carrots, sliced
        1 medium onion, diced
        2 teaspoons Worcestershire sauce
    1/2 teaspoon hot pepper sauce
    1/2 teaspoon dried oregano
    1/2 teaspoon dried basil
    1/4 teaspoon chili powder
        1 cup uncooked noodles

In a Dutch oven or soup kettle, bring broth ingredients to a boil. Reduce heat; cover and simmer for 2 hours or until meat is tender. Remove ribs; allow to cool. Skim fat and strain broth; discard vegetables and seasonings. Remove meat from bones and cut into bite-size pieces; return to broth. Add the first 10 soup ingredients; bring to a boil. Reduce heat; cover and simmer for 1 hour or until vegetables are tender. Stir in noodles. Return to a boil; cook, uncovered, for 15 minutes or until noodles are tender. **Yield:** 12-14 servings (3-3/4 quarts).

GAZPACHO

(Pictured above)

This dish comes in handy for luncheons in summer since it's so colorful and refreshing. —Pat Waymire
Yellow Springs, Ohio

✓ **This tasty dish uses less sugar, salt and fat. Recipe includes *Diabetic Exchanges*.**

4 cups tomato juice
2 cups chopped seeded peeled tomatoes
1 cup diced green pepper
1 cup diced celery
1 cup diced seeded cucumber
2 garlic cloves, minced
1/2 cup diced onion
1/3 cup tarragon vinegar
2 tablespoons minced fresh parsley
1 tablespoon minced chives
1 teaspoon Worcestershire sauce
1 teaspoon salt, optional
1/2 teaspoon pepper
2 tablespoons vegetable oil

In a large bowl, combine the first 13 ingredients. Cover and chill for at least 4 hours. Stir in oil before serving. Serve cold. **Yield:** 8 servings. **Diabetic Exchanges:** One 1-cup serving (prepared with low-sodium tomato juice and without salt) equals 2 vegetable, 1 fat; also, 96 calories, 56 mg sodium, 0 cholesterol, 13 gm carbohydrate, 2 gm protein, 4 gm fat.

GREEK BURGERS

A friend served these lamb patties at a barbecue party. After tasting them, I wouldn't leave without the recipe! The rosemary and lamb make a taste sensation. —Michelle Curtis
Baker City, Oregon

1 pound ground lamb
1 tablespoon Dijon mustard
1 tablespoon lemon juice
1 tablespoon minced onion
1 garlic clove, minced
1/2 teaspoon dried rosemary, crushed
1/2 teaspoon salt
1/4 teaspoon pepper
4 hamburger buns *or* hard rolls, split
Sliced cucumbers and tomatoes, optional
Ranch salad dressing, optional

In a medium bowl, combine the first eight ingredients; mix well. Shape into four patties. Pan-fry, grill or broil until no longer pink. Serve on buns with cucumbers, tomatoes and ranch dressing if desired. **Yield:** 4 servings.

Growing Garlic

Break up bulbs of garlic and plant cloves with pointed end up about 1 inch deep and 4 inches apart. Keep the soil moist for bigger bulbs.

HEARTY HAM SANDWICHES

When our granddaughter needed sandwiches for a gathering after a high-school dance, I created this recipe. Now these sandwiches and some soup make a nice meal for me and my husband, Claude.
—Rena Charmasson
Woodward, Oklahoma

2 tablespoons mayonnaise
1 tablespoon prepared horseradish
1 tablespoon prepared mustard
1 tablespoon chopped onion
8 slices rye *or* sourdough bread
8 slices fully cooked ham
4 slices Swiss cheese

In a small bowl, combine mayonnaise, horseradish, mustard and onion; mix well. Spread on four slices of bread. Layer with ham and cheese; top with remaining bread. **Yield:** 4 servings.

BARBECUED HOT DOGS

I grew up in a family of eight kids, and we never complained if Mom made these terrific hot dogs often for birthday parties and other family gatherings. Even

with all those hungry brothers and sisters, we never had leftovers with these. —Joyce Koehler
Watertown, Wisconsin

- 3/4 **cup chopped onion**
- 3 **tablespoons butter *or* margarine**
- 1-1/2 **cups chopped celery**
- 1-1/2 **cups ketchup**
- 3/4 **cup water**
- 1/3 **cup lemon juice**
- 3 **tablespoons brown sugar**
- 3 **tablespoons vinegar**
- 1 **tablespoon Worcestershire sauce**
- 1 **tablespoon yellow mustard**
- 2 **packages (1 pound *each*) hot dogs**
- 20 **hot dog buns, split**

In a saucepan over medium heat, saute onion in butter until tender. Add celery, ketchup, water, lemon juice, sugar, vinegar, Worcestershire sauce and mustard; bring to a boil. Reduce heat; cover and simmer 30 minutes. Cut three 1/4-in.-deep slits on each side of hot dogs; place in a 2-1/2-qt. baking dish. Pour sauce over hot dogs. Cover and bake at 350° for 40-45 minutes or until heated through. Serve on buns. **Yield:** 20 servings.

HAM AND CHEESE SOUP

While I was growing up, my family had a big garden. Mom would turn that produce into some wonderful meals...that's where I get my love of cooking. I share one of my favorite recipes with you here.
—Paul Miller
Green Bay, Wisconsin

- 1 **cup chopped onion**
- 1/2 **cup chopped celery**
- 1/2 **cup chopped carrot**
- 1/4 **cup minced fresh parsley**
- 2 **garlic cloves, minced**
- 1/4 **cup butter *or* margarine**
- 1/4 **cup all-purpose flour**
- 1 **tablespoon ground mustard**
- 1/8 **teaspoon pepper**
- 1 **cup chopped fully cooked ham**
- 2-1/2 **cups chicken broth**
- 2 **cups milk**
- 3/4 **pound process American cheese, cubed**

Popped popcorn, optional

In a large saucepan over medium heat, saute onion, celery, carrot, parsley and garlic in butter for 5 minutes or until the vegetables are crisp-tender. Stir in flour, mustard and pepper. Add ham; cook for 1 minute, stirring constantly. Gradually add broth and milk; bring to a boil over medium heat. Cook and stir for 2 minutes or until slightly thickened. Stir in cheese; reduce heat. Cook and stir until cheese is melted (do not boil). Garnish servings with popcorn if desired. **Yield:** 6 servings.

ALOHA BURGERS

(Pictured below)

I love hamburgers and pineapple, so it just seemed natural for me to combine them. My family frequently requsts these unique burgers. It's a nice change of pace from the same old boring hamburger.
—Joi McKim-Jones
Waikoloa, Hawaii

- 1 **can (8 ounces) pineapple slices**
- 3/4 **cup teriyaki sauce**
- 1 **pound ground beef**
- 1 **large sweet onion, sliced**
- 1 **tablespoon butter *or* margarine**
- 4 **lettuce leaves**
- 4 **onion *or* sesame seed buns, split and toasted**
- 4 **slices Swiss cheese**
- 4 **bacon strips, cooked**

Drain pineapple juice into a small bowl; add teriyaki sauce. Place 3 tablespoons in a resealable plastic bag. Add pineapple and rotate to coat; set aside. Shape beef into four patties; place in an 8-in. square baking dish. Pour the remaining teriyaki sauce mixture over patties; marinate for 5-10 minutes, turning once. In a skillet, saute onion in butter until tender, about 5 minutes. Grill or broil burgers until no longer pink. Place pineapple on grill or under broiler to heat through. Layer lettuce and onion on bottom of buns. Top with burgers, cheese, pineapple and bacon. Replace tops; serve immediately. **Yield:** 4 servings.

Side Dishes

Rice, vegetables, potatoes and pasta take top billing in these splendid dishes. They're perfect complements to all of your everyday dinners and special-occasion meals.

and parsley; bring to a boil. Reduce heat; cover and simmer for 20 minutes. Cool for 30 minutes. Stir in egg, cheese, basil and pepper. Moisten hands with water and shape 1/4 cupfuls into logs. Roll in crumbs. In an electric skillet, heat 1/4 in. of oil to 365°. Fry croquettes, a few at time, for 3-4 minutes or until crisp and golden, turning often. Drain on paper towels. Garnish with parsley if desired. **Yield:** 16 croquettes.

CREAMY ASPARAGUS AND CARROTS

Here in Missouri, asparagus season is short, so we savor every delicious bite of this delicacy. Of course, this vegetable freezes so well I'm able to prepare tasty dishes like this year-round. —Darlene Schafer
Corder, Missouri

2 medium carrots, cut into 1/4-inch slices
2/3 cup water
1 pound fresh asparagus, cut into 1-inch pieces
1 package (3 ounces) cream cheese, softened
1 teaspoon all-purpose flour
1/4 teaspoon salt
1/8 teaspoon ground nutmeg
Pinch pepper
1 tablespoon sliced almonds, toasted

In a saucepan, bring carrots and water to a boil; cover and cook for 4 minutes. Add asparagus; cover and cook for 3 minutes or until just tender. Drain, reserving liquid; add enough water to liquid to equal 1/3 cup. Set vegetables aside; return liquid to skillet. Combine cream cheese, flour, salt, nutmeg and pepper; add to liquid. Cook over low heat, stirring constantly, until cheese melts and sauce is bubbly, about 3 minutes. Stir in vegetables and heat through. Garnish with almonds. **Yield:** 4 servings.

THREE-RICE PILAF
(Pictured at right)

My family's favorite rice dish is this tempting medley of white, brown and wild rice. I prepare it as a side dish or a stuffing. In fall I add chopped dried apricots, and for the holidays I mix in dried cranberries. My guests always ask for seconds. —Ricki Bingham
Ogden, Utah

1/2 cup uncooked brown rice
1/2 cup finely chopped carrots

RICE CROQUETTES
(Pictured above)

As a newlywed, I used to agonize over meal preparation. Through the years, I've come to enjoy trying new recipes. This tasty side dish turned out to be very popular with my family. These croquettes are crisp and golden and add some fun to a simple dinner like roast chicken and salad. —Lucia Edwards
Cotati, California

1/2 cup chopped onion
2 tablespoons butter *or* margarine
1 cup uncooked long grain rice
2-1/4 cups chicken broth
2 tablespoons chopped fresh parsley
1 egg, lightly beaten
1/2 cup grated Parmesan cheese
1 teaspoon dried basil
1/4 teaspoon pepper
1/2 cup dry bread crumbs
Cooking oil
Additional fresh parsley, optional

In a large saucepan, saute onion in butter until tender. Add rice; saute for 3 minutes. Stir in broth

1/2 cup chopped onion
1/2 cup sliced fresh mushrooms
  2 tablespoons cooking oil
1/2 cup uncooked wild rice
  3 cups chicken broth
1/4 teaspoon dried thyme
1/4 teaspoon dried rosemary, crushed
1/2 cup uncooked long grain rice
1/3 cup chopped dried apricots
  2 tablespoons minced green onions
1/4 teaspoon salt
1/8 teaspoon pepper
1/2 cup chopped pecans, toasted

In a large saucepan, saute brown rice, carrots, onion and mushrooms in oil for 10 minutes or until rice is golden. Add wild rice, broth, thyme and rosemary; bring to a boil. Reduce heat; cover and simmer for 25 minutes. Stir in long grain rice; cover and simmer for 25 minutes or until liquid is absorbed and wild rice is tender. Remove from the heat; stir in apricots, green onions, salt and pepper. Cover and let stand for 5 minutes. Sprinkle with pecans just before serving. **Yield:** 8-10 servings.

SLICE 'N' FRY POTATO PANCAKES

When you want a break from ordinary potato pancakes, reach for this recipe. It makes quite a few servings, so you can feed a hungry crowd. But with such fantastic flavor, don't be surprised if they disappear quickly!
—Carl Wanasek
Rogers, Arkansas

  2 pounds potatoes, peeled, cooked and shredded
  1 egg, beaten
  1 tablespoon minced onion
  1 teaspoon salt
1/4 teaspoon pepper
3/4 to 1 cup all-purpose flour
Cooking oil
Applesauce, optional

In a bowl, combine potatoes, egg, onion, salt and pepper; stir in 3/4 cup flour. Add enough remaining flour to form a firm dough. Turn onto a lightly floured board; knead for 1 minute. Shape into a 9-in. x 2-in. roll. Cut into 1/3-in. slices; roll into 4-in. circles. Fry pancakes in a small amount of oil until browned, about 4 minutes per side. Serve with applesauce if desired. **Yield:** 27 pancakes.

BAKED MUSHROOM RICE

With fresh mushrooms and a nice blend of seasonings, this rice recipe complements any meat you serve as a main course. Best of all, it cooks in one pot for a no-hassle dish. I hope you like it!
—Alcy Thorne
Los Molinos, California

✓ **This tasty dish uses less sugar, salt and fat. Recipe includes** *Diabetic Exchanges.*

1/2 cup uncooked long grain rice
1-1/3 cups reduced-sodium fat-free chicken broth
  1 cup sliced fresh mushrooms
  1 medium onion, chopped
1/4 teaspoon dried basil
1/4 teaspoon dried oregano
1/8 teaspoon lemon-pepper seasoning

Combine all ingredients in a 1-1/2-qt. casserole coated with nonstick cooking spray. Cover and bake at 350° for 45 minutes or until rice is tender. **Yield:** 4 servings. **Diabetic Exchanges:** One 3/4-cup serving equals 1 starch, 1/2 vegetable; also, 96 calories, 63 mg sodium, 0 cholesterol, 20 gm carbohydrate, 3 gm protein, trace fat.

SWEET POTATO PUFF

(Pictured above)

I prepare this sweet potato dish mostly around the holidays, but it's good anytime. For added convenience, you can prepare it the night before and just pop it in the oven the next day. It's a joy to serve this delicious fluffy casserole to my five children and their families.

—Fay Miller
Denham Springs, Louisiana

   3 **cups cold mashed sweet potatoes**
     (without added milk or butter)
1/2 **cup sugar**
1/2 **cup butter *or* margarine, melted**
   2 **eggs, beaten**
1/3 **cup milk**
   1 **teaspoon vanilla extract**
1/2 **cup flaked coconut**
TOPPING:
1/2 **cup packed brown sugar**
1/2 **cup chopped pecans**
   2 **tablespoons butter *or* margarine, melted**
1/4 **cup all-purpose flour**

In a mixing bowl, beat sweet potatoes, sugar, butter, eggs, milk and vanilla until fluffy. Stir in coconut. Spoon into a greased 2-1/2-qt. baking dish. Combine topping ingredients until well blended; sprinkle over sweet potatoes. Bake, uncovered, at 350° for 35-40 minutes or until golden brown. **Yield:** 8 servings.

POTATO-SPINACH CASSEROLE

As much as my family loves mashed potatoes, once in a while I'll want to dress them up by preparing this recipe. Spinach and chives give this potato dish wonderful flavor, not to mention terrific color.

—Mary Allen
Orange, California

   2 **pounds potatoes, peeled and cubed**
2/3 **cup milk**
   6 **tablespoons butter *or* margarine, softened**
   1 **teaspoon salt**
1/4 **teaspoon pepper**
   2 **packages (10 ounces *each*) frozen chopped spinach, thawed and well drained**
1/4 **cup snipped fresh chives**
   1 **teaspoon dill weed**

In a saucepan over medium heat, cook potatoes in boiling salted water until tender; drain. In a mixing bowl, mash potatoes until no lumps remain. Add the milk, butter, salt and pepper; beat until light and fluffy. Stir in spinach, chives and dill. Spread in a greased 2-1/2-qt. casserole. Cover and bake at 350° for 30-40 minutes or until heated through. **Yield:** 10-12 servings.

GARLICKY GREEN BEANS

Crisp-tender green beans are delicious tossed with a garlic butter sauce. With its pretty green color, this fresh dish is an attractive addition to your table.
—Ruth Marie Lyons
Boulder, Colorado

  1 **pound fresh green beans**
1/2 **cup water**
  2 **to 3 garlic cloves, minced**
  3 **tablespoons butter *or* margarine**
1/8 **teaspoon salt**
Pinch pepper

In a saucepan, bring beans and water to a boil; reduce heat to medium. Cover and cook for 10-15 minutes or until beans are crisp-tender; drain and set aside. In a large skillet, saute garlic in butter until lightly browned, about 1 minute. Add beans, salt and pepper; heat through. **Yield:** 4-6 servings.

BASIL SPAETZLE

My interest in cooking started when I was 10 years old. I like to experiment with recipes and give the old standbys a new twist. In this traditional dish, I added fresh basil with delicious results.   *—Bob Foust*
Indianapolis, Indiana

  3 **cups all-purpose flour**
1/3 **cup finely chopped fresh basil leaves**
  3 **teaspoons salt, *divided***
  4 **eggs, beaten**
1/2 **cup cold water**
  4 **quarts water**
  2 **tablespoons butter *or* margarine**

In a bowl, combine flour, basil and 1 teaspoon salt. Stir in eggs and cold water; mix until dough is smooth. In a large kettle, bring water and remaining salt to a boil; reduce heat. With a rubber spatula, press dough through a colander into simmering water. Simmer for 2-3 minutes, stirring gently so spaetzle do not stick together. Drain; toss with butter. **Yield:** 6-8 servings.

Storing Sweet Potatoes
Keep sweet potatoes in a cool, dry place, but not in the refrigerator. Also, don't stack them since that promotes spoilage.

GARLIC AU GRATIN TOMATOES

You'll likely reach for this recipe when you have a bumper crop of tomatoes. The distinctive taste of garlic nicely enhances sweet juicy tomatoes.
—Dorothy Pritchett
Wills Point, Texas

    8 **medium tomatoes**
1-1/2 **cups soft bread crumbs**
    2 **to 4 garlic cloves, minced**
  1/2 **cup grated Parmesan cheese**
  1/3 **cup chopped fresh parsley**
  1/2 **teaspoon salt**
  1/4 **teaspoon pepper**
  1/3 **cup olive *or* vegetable oil**

Cut a thin slice from the top of each tomato. Scoop out the pulp, leaving a 1/2-in.-thick shell. Invert tomatoes onto paper towels to drain. Meanwhile, in a bowl, combine crumbs, garlic, cheese, parsley, salt and pepper. Stuff tomatoes; place in a greased shallow baking dish. Drizzle with oil. Bake, uncovered, at 400° for 15-20 minutes or until stuffing is lightly browned. **Yield:** 4-6 servings. **Editor's Note:** To make appetizers, stuff 48 cherry tomatoes with crumb mixture; bake for 8-10 minutes.

PEAS AND CARROTS WITH MINT

If you're looking for an easy way to dress up ordinary peas and carrots, reach for this simple recipe. Fresh mint adds a refreshing subtle flavor that'll keep folks coming back for more.   *—Margie Snodgrass*
Gig Harbor, Washington

  4 **large carrots, julienned**
  3 **tablespoons butter *or* margarine**
1/2 **pound sugar snap peas**
  1 **to 2 tablespoons finely chopped fresh mint**
1/4 **teaspoon salt**
1/8 **teaspoon pepper**

Place carrots in a saucepan with enough water to cover; bring to a boil. Reduce heat; cook, uncovered, for 4 minutes or until crisp-tender. Drain. Add remaining ingredients. Cook and stir for 3-4 minutes or until the peas are crisp-tender. **Yield:** 6-8 servings.

MOM'S EASY BEAN BAKE

My mom's baked beans are the best I've ever tasted. Family and friends expect me to bring a pot of these beans to gatherings...they've become my trademark.
—Sue Gronholz
Columbus, Wisconsin

2-1/2 cups dry great northern beans (about 1 pound)
1 teaspoon salt
1 pound sliced bacon, cooked and crumbled
1 cup packed brown sugar
3 tablespoons molasses
3 small onions, chopped

Place beans and salt in a saucepan; cover with water. Bring to a boil; boil for 2 minutes. Remove from the heat; cover and let stand for 1 hour. Drain, discarding liquid, and return beans to pan. Cover with fresh water; bring to a boil. Reduce heat; cover and simmer for 1 hour or until beans are tender. Drain, reserving liquid. Combine beans, 1 cup liquid and the remaining ingredients in a greased 2-1/2-qt. baking dish. Cover and bake at 350° for 1-1/4 hours or until beans are tender, stirring occasionally (add additional reserved liquid if needed). **Yield:** 8-10 servings.

AU GRATIN CARROTS

Our children would never eat carrots, and I could never find a recipe to please their taste buds. Then a friend shared this recipe, and sure enough...they loved it! Now they request this dish.　—Sherry Johnson
Glenfield, North Dakota

2 pounds carrots, sliced
1/2 cup chopped onion
1/4 cup butter *or* margarine, *divided*
3 tablespoons all-purpose flour
1/2 teaspoon salt
1/8 teaspoon pepper
1-1/2 cups milk
4 ounces process American cheese, cubed
2 tablespoons chopped fresh parsley
2 cups cornflakes, crushed

Cook the carrots until crisp-tender; drain and set aside. In a saucepan over medium heat, saute onion in 3 tablespoons butter until tender. Stir in flour, salt and pepper. Gradually add milk; bring to a boil, stirring constantly. Cook for 1 minute or until thickened. Stir in the cheese just until melt-ed. Add carrots and parsley. Pour into a greased 8-in. square baking dish. Melt remaining butter; add cornflakes. Sprinkle over carrots. Bake, uncovered, at 350° for 20-25 minutes or until bubbly. **Yield:** 8-10 servings.

GARLIC PASTA

This is one of many recipes I obtained while living in France. It makes an excellent side dish.
—Sandi Pichon
Slidell, Louisiana

1 whole garlic bulb
1/2 cup olive *or* vegetable oil
1/2 cup chopped fresh parsley
1/4 cup chopped fresh oregano *or* 4 teaspoons dried oregano
1 teaspoon salt
1/4 teaspoon pepper
1 pound pasta, cooked and drained

Separate garlic into cloves; remove papery skins. In a large skillet over low heat, saute garlic in oil for 20 minutes or until golden brown. Remove from the heat; add parsley, oregano, salt and pepper. Toss with pasta; serve immediately. **Yield:** 4 servings.

CALICO RICE

This dish goes together quickly. So I use it frequently when I need to put dinner on the table in a hurry. It's a good way to use up bits of frozen peppers.
—Dorothy Collins
Winnsboro, Texas

1 medium green pepper, chopped
1 medium sweet red pepper, chopped
2 tablespoons butter *or* margarine
1/4 teaspoon salt
3 cups hot cooked rice

In a skillet over medium heat, saute peppers in butter for 8-10 minutes or until tender. Sprinkle with salt; toss with rice. **Yield:** 6-8 servings.

HERBED GREEN BEANS

The herb butter makes this bean dish so pleasant. If you want to cut down on the fat and sodium, simply use margarine and eliminate the salt. I always serve this with a ham dinner...don't forget the hot rolls!

—Bernice Morris
Marshfield, Missouri

✓ **This tasty dish uses less sugar, salt and fat. Recipe includes *Diabetic Exchanges.***

1-1/2 pounds fresh green beans
1/2 cup finely chopped onion
2 tablespoons butter *or* margarine
3 tablespoons lemon juice
1 tablespoon chopped fresh parsley
1 teaspoon salt, optional
1-1/2 teaspoons chopped fresh thyme *or*
1/2 teaspoon dried thyme
1/4 teaspoon paprika

In a saucepan, cover beans with water; cook until crisp-tender. Meanwhile, in a skillet, saute the onion in butter until tender. Add the lemon juice, parsley, salt if desired, thyme and paprika. Drain beans; add herb butter and stir to coat. Serve immediately. **Yield:** 6 servings. **Diabetic Exchanges:** One serving (prepared with margarine and without salt) equals 1 vegetable, 1 fat; also, 76 calories, 42 mg sodium, 0 cholesterol, 10 gm carbohydrate, 2 gm protein, 4 gm fat.

SWEET-AND-SOUR BEETS

With their jewel tones and tangy glaze, these beets will take center stage at all of your meals. Whenever I present them, they win me rave reviews.

—Emily Chaney
Penobscot, Maine

✓ **This tasty dish uses less sugar, salt and fat. Recipe includes *Diabetic Exchanges.***

1/2 cup water
1/4 cup vinegar
2 teaspoons cornstarch
4 teaspoons sugar
2 cups sliced cooked beets

In a saucepan, combine water, vinegar and cornstarch; bring to a boil. Cook and stir for 1-2 minutes; remove from the heat. Add sugar and beets; let stand for 1 hour. Heat through just before serving. **Yield:** 4 servings. **Diabetic Exchanges:** One serving equals 2 vegetable; also, 49 calories, 37 mg sodium, 0 cholesterol, 12 gm carbohydrate, 1 gm protein, trace fat.

CRANBERRY WILD RICE PILAF
(Pictured above)

This wonderful, moist side dish is perfect anytime a meal requires a special touch. Dried cranberries, currants and almonds add color and texture.

—Pat Gardetta
Osage Beach, Missouri

3/4 cup uncooked wild rice
3 cups chicken broth
1/2 cup pearl barley
1/4 cup dried cranberries
1/4 cup dried currants
1 tablespoon butter *or* margarine
1/3 cup sliced almonds, toasted

Rinse and drain rice; place in a saucepan. Add broth and bring to a boil. Reduce heat; cover and simmer for 10 minutes. Remove from the heat; stir in barley, cranberries, currants and butter. Spoon into a greased 1-1/2-qt. baking dish. Cover and bake at 325° for 55 minutes or until liquid is absorbed and rice is tender. Add almonds and fluff with a fork. **Yield:** 6-8 servings.

15 minutes more or until barley is tender and corn is heated through. **Yield:** 12 servings. **Diabetic Exchanges:** One 1/2-cup serving (prepared with low-sodium reduced-fat chicken broth and without salt) equals 1 starch, 1 vegetable; also, 108 calories, 36 mg sodium, 1 mg cholesterol, 21 gm carbohydrate, 4 gm protein, 2 gm fat.

SLOW-COOKED SAGE DRESSING

Preparing this dressing in a slow cooker makes it moist and delicious. My family enjoys it so much that I serve it alongside a variety of main meals.
—Ellen Benninger
Stoneboro, Pennsylvania

  14 to 15 cups day-old bread cubes
   3 cups chopped celery
1-1/2 cups chopped onion
1-1/2 teaspoons rubbed sage
   1 teaspoon salt
 1/2 teaspoon pepper
1-1/4 cups butter *or* margarine, melted

In a large bowl, combine bread, celery, onion, sage, salt and pepper; mix well. Add butter and toss. Spoon into a 5-qt. slow cooker. Cover and cook on low for 4-5 hours, stirring once. **Yield:** about 12 servings.

HERBED ZUCCHINI

This simple side dish is made extra-special with the addition of bacon, two kinds of cheese and seasonings. My bumper crop of zucchini disappears quickly when this is the featured fare.
—Diana Nutter
Mount Dora, Florida

   5 bacon strips, diced
   1 cup chopped onion
   1 cup chopped celery
   1 garlic clove, minced
   1 can (14-1/2 ounces) diced tomatoes, undrained
   4 to 5 cups sliced zucchini
   1 tablespoon chopped fresh parsley
1-1/2 teaspoons snipped fresh sage *or* 1/2 teaspoon rubbed sage
 1/2 teaspoon dried basil
 1/2 teaspoon dried oregano
 1/4 teaspoon pepper

BARLEY AND CORN CASSEROLE

(Pictured above)

This hearty colorful casserole goes well with pork, chicken or fish. For convenience, it can be made ahead and refrigerated before serving. —Diane Molberg
Emerald Park, Saskatchewan

✓ **This tasty dish uses less sugar, salt and fat. Recipe includes *Diabetic Exchanges*.**

   3 garlic cloves, minced
   1 cup chopped onion
 2/3 cup chopped carrots
   1 tablespoon cooking oil
   3 cups chicken broth
   1 cup pearl barley
 1/4 teaspoon salt, optional
 1/8 teaspoon pepper
   2 cups frozen corn, thawed
 1/2 cup chopped fresh parsley

In a skillet over medium heat, saute garlic, onion and carrots in oil until tender. Transfer to a greased 2-qt. baking dish; add broth, barley, salt if desired and pepper. Mix well. Cover and bake at 350° for 1 hour. Stir in corn and parsley. Cover and bake 10-

2 tablespoons grated Parmesan cheese
1/3 cup shredded mozzarella cheese

In a skillet over medium heat, cook bacon until crisp. Remove bacon and discard all but 1 tablespoon drippings. Saute onion, celery and garlic in drippings until tender. Add tomatoes, zucchini, parsley and seasonings; bring to a boil. Reduce heat; cover and simmer for 6-8 minutes or until zucchini is tender. Sprinkle with cheeses and bacon. Serve with a slotted spoon. **Yield:** 4-6 servings.

TANGY GREEN BEAN CASSEROLE

Here's a bean dish my family requests often. It's easy to prepare and makes a wonderful addition to a buffet supper or potluck dinner. —Judy Rush
Newport, Rhode Island

    2 **pounds fresh green beans, cut into**
      1-1/2-inch pieces
    2 **tablespoons finely chopped onion**
    2 **tablespoons olive *or* vegetable oil**
    1 **tablespoon vinegar**
    1 **garlic clove, minced**
1/2 **teaspoon salt**
1/4 **teaspoon pepper**
    2 **tablespoons dry bread crumbs**
    2 **tablespoons grated Parmesan cheese**
    1 **tablespoon butter *or* margarine, melted**

In a saucepan, cover beans with water. Cook until crisp-tender; drain. Add the onion, oil, vinegar, garlic, salt and pepper; toss to coat. Transfer to an ungreased 2-qt. baking dish. Toss crumbs, cheese and butter; sprinkle over bean mixture. Bake, uncovered, at 350° for 20-25 minutes or until golden brown. **Yield:** 6-8 servings.

LEMON RICE PILAF

My husband and I produce jasmine rice, which is a long grain variety that has a wonderful aroma as it cooks (many people say it reminds them of popcorn) and a nutty flavor. This is one of my favorite recipes I share with customers. —Linda Raun
El Campo, Texas

    1 **cup uncooked jasmine rice *or* long grain**
      white rice
    1 **cup sliced celery**

    1 **cup thinly sliced green onions**
    2 **tablespoons butter *or* margarine**
    1 **tablespoon grated lemon peel**
    1 **teaspoon salt**
1/4 **teaspoon pepper**

Cook rice according to package directions. Meanwhile, in a skillet over medium heat, saute celery and onions in butter until tender. Add rice, lemon peel, salt and pepper; toss lightly. Cook and stir until heated through. **Yield:** 4-6 servings.

OVEN-BAKED ASPARAGUS

I like to use recipes that call for fresh produce I've grown in my garden. Here's a simple way to prepare tender spears that brings out their flavor and maintains their bright green color. —Bob Foust
Indianapolis, Indiana

    1 **pound fresh asparagus, trimmed**
    2 **tablespoons butter *or* margarine**
Salt and pepper to taste

Place the asparagus on a large piece of heavy-duty aluminum foil. Dot with butter. Bring edges of foil together and seal tightly; place foil packet on a baking sheet. Bake at 350° for 25-30 minutes or until asparagus is crisp-tender. Carefully open foil to allow steam to escape. Season with salt and pepper. **Yield:** 4 servings.

GARLIC MASHED POTATOES

I love both mashed potatoes and garlic, so this seemed like the perfect recipe for me. People say these potatoes rival varieties some restaurants are now serving. —Myra Innes
Auburn, Kansas

    6 **medium potatoes, peeled and quartered**
    4 **to 5 garlic cloves**
    5 **cups water**
    2 **tablespoons olive *or* vegetable oil**
1/2 **to 1 teaspoon salt**
Pinch pepper

In a medium saucepan, bring potatoes, garlic and water to a boil. Reduce heat; cover and cook for 20 minutes or until potatoes are tender. Drain, reserving 2/3 cup cooking liquid. Mash the potatoes. Add oil, salt, pepper and reserved liquid; stir until smooth. **Yield:** 4-6 servings.

Main Dishes

These palate-pleasing casseroles, oven entrees, skillet suppers and grilled favorites feature beef, poultry, pork, game and more. Build your meals around these recipes, then get ready to hear some compliments!

4 eggs, lightly beaten
1 turkey (16 to 18 pounds)
1 cup chicken broth

In a pan, bring broth, butter and salt to a boil. Add herbs; set aside. Toast bread; cut into 1/2-in. cubes. Place in a bowl. In a skillet, brown sausage; remove with slotted spoon and add to bread. Add butter to drippings; saute celery, carrots, mushrooms, ham and onions for 15 minutes. Add to bread mixture; stir in next eight ingredients. Add eggs and 3/4 cup basting sauce; mix lightly. Stuff turkey with about 8 cups dressing. Skewer openings; tie drumsticks together. Place on a rack in a roasting pan. Baste with some of remaining basting sauce. Bake, uncovered, at 325° for 5 to 5-1/2 hours or until thermometer reads 185°, basting every 30 minutes. When turkey begins to brown, cover lightly with foil. Add broth to remaining dressing and mix lightly. Place in a greased 2-1/2-qt. baking dish; chill. Cover and bake at 325° for 1 hour; uncover and bake 10 minutes. **Yield:** 14-16 servings (18 cups dressing).

HERBED TURKEY AND DRESSING
(Pictured above)

Whenever I serve this succulent golden turkey and delectable dressing, guests fill their plates and I'm buried in compliments. This recipe always makes a special dinner one to remember. —Marilyn Clay
Palatine, Illinois

BASTING SAUCE:
2-1/4 cups chicken broth
1/2 cup butter *or* margarine
1/2 teaspoon salt
1 teaspoon dried thyme
1/4 teaspoon *each* dried marjoram, rosemary
and rubbed sage
1/4 cup chopped fresh parsley
2 tablespoons dried chives
DRESSING:
1 loaf (1 pound) sliced bread
1 pound bulk pork sausage
1/2 cup butter *or* margarine
4 cups thinly sliced celery
3 cups thinly sliced carrots
1/2 pound fresh mushrooms, chopped
1/2 pound cubed fully cooked ham
2 cups sliced green onions
2 cups chopped pecans
1 large tart apple, chopped
1 cup chopped dried apricots
1 tablespoon rubbed sage
2 teaspoons dried marjoram
1 teaspoon dried rosemary
1 teaspoon salt
1/8 teaspoon ground nutmeg

CHICKEN VEGETABLE MEDLEY

Garden-fresh vegetables and tender, juicy chicken combine in this dish to provide a mouth-watering meal that's sure to receive raves from your family. The pleasant blend of herbs makes it particularly tasty.
—Kim Marie Van Rheenen
Mendota, Illinois

✓ This tasty dish uses less sugar, salt and fat. Recipe includes *Diabetic Exchanges.*

6 boneless skinless chicken breast halves
(1-1/2 pounds)
4 tablespoons olive *or* vegetable oil, *divided*
8 ounces fresh mushrooms, sliced
4 garlic cloves, minced
3 tomatoes, peeled, seeded and chopped
2 medium eggplant, peeled and diced
2 large green peppers, diced
2 medium zucchini, diced
1 large onion, diced
1 can (8 ounces) tomato sauce
1 bay leaf
1 teaspoon dried basil
1 teaspoon dried oregano
1/2 teaspoon dried marjoram
1/2 teaspoon dried thyme
1/2 teaspoon salt, optional
1/4 teaspoon pepper

In a large skillet or Dutch oven over medium heat, brown chicken in 1 tablespoon of oil; set chicken aside. Add remaining oil to skillet; saute mushrooms, garlic, tomatoes, eggplant, green pepper, zucchini and onion for 10-15 minutes or until vegetables are tender. Add remaining ingredients; bring to a boil. Return chicken to skillet. Reduce heat; cover and simmer for 30-40 minutes or until chicken juices run clear. Remove bay leaf before serving. **Yield:** 6 servings. **Diabetic Exchanges:** One serving (prepared with no-salt-added tomato sauce and without salt) equals 4 very lean meat, 1-1/2 fat, 1 starch; also, 298 calories, 88 mg sodium, 73 mg cholesterol, 16 gm carbohydrate, 32 gm protein, 13 gm fat.

PARTY BEEF CASSEROLE
(Pictured above)

Round steak is economical and delicious. That's why I was thrilled to find the recipe for this comforting meal-in-one casserole. With a salad and rolls, it's an inexpensive, hearty dinner. —Kelly Hardgrave
Hartman, Arkansas

  3 tablespoons all-purpose flour
  1 teaspoon salt
1/2 teaspoon pepper
  2 pounds boneless round steak, cut into 1/2-inch cubes
  2 tablespoons cooking oil
  1 cup water
1/2 cup beef broth
  1 garlic clove, minced
  1 tablespoon dried minced onion
1/2 teaspoon dried thyme

1/4 teaspoon dried rosemary, crushed
  2 cups sliced fresh mushrooms
  2 cups frozen peas, thawed
  3 cups mashed potatoes (mashed with milk and butter)
  1 tablespoon butter *or* margarine, melted
Paprika

In a large resealable plastic bag, combine flour, salt and pepper; add beef cubes and shake to coat. In a skillet over medium heat, brown beef in oil. Place beef and drippings in a greased shallow 2-1/2-qt. baking dish. To skillet, add water, broth, garlic, onion, thyme and rosemary; bring to a boil. Simmer, uncovered, for 5 minutes; stir in mushrooms. Pour over meat; mix well. Cover and bake at 350° for 1-1/2 to 1-3/4 hours or until beef is tender. Sprinkle peas over meat. Spread potatoes evenly over top. Brush with butter; sprinkle with paprika. Bake 15-20 minutes more. **Yield:** 6-8 servings.

BOHEMIAN BEEF DINNER

One of my favorite things to do when I was growing up was to help my mother in the kitchen while she prepared traditional Czech dishes like this. It's a savory stick-to-your-ribs meal with beef and sauerkraut covered in a creamy sauce. —Carl Wanasek
Rogers, Arkansas

3/4 cup all-purpose flour
  1 teaspoon salt
1/4 teaspoon pepper
  2 pounds beef stew meat, cut into 1-inch cubes
  2 tablespoons cooking oil
  2 medium onions, chopped
  1 garlic clove, minced
  1 teaspoon dill weed
  1 teaspoon caraway seed
  1 teaspoon paprika
1/2 cup water
  1 cup (8 ounces) sour cream
  1 can (27 ounces) sauerkraut
Additional paprika

In a bowl or plastic bag, combine flour, salt and pepper. Add beef; dredge or shake to coat. In a Dutch oven, brown the beef, half at a time, in oil; drain. Add onions, garlic, dill, caraway, paprika and water. Cover and simmer for 2 hours or until meat is tender, stirring occasionally. Stir in sour cream; heat through but do not boil. Heat sauerkraut; drain and spoon onto a serving platter. Top with the beef mixture. Sprinkle with paprika. **Yield:** 6 servings.

AMY'S GREEN EGGS AND HAM
(Pictured above)

This whimsically named dish is a great way to use hard-cooked eggs. It's a favorite at our house at Easter and all year-round.
—*Amy Church*
Camby, Indiana

 1 **package (10 ounces) frozen**
  chopped broccoli, cooked and drained
 6 **hard-cooked eggs, halved**
1/4 **cup mayonnaise**
 2 **tablespoons Dijon mustard**
1/4 **cup chopped fully cooked ham**
 1 **tablespoon sliced green onions**
CHEESE SAUCE:
 2 **tablespoons butter** *or* **margarine**
 2 **tablespoons all-purpose flour**
1-1/4 **cups milk**
Dash salt and paprika
 1 **cup (4 ounces) shredded cheddar cheese**
 2 **tablespoons grated Parmesan cheese**

In a greased 11-in. x 7-in. x 2-in. baking dish, layer broccoli and eggs. Combine the mayonnaise, mustard, ham and onions; spread over eggs. In a saucepan, melt butter; add flour. Cook and stir until bubbly. Gradually add milk, salt and paprika; cook and stir until boiling. Cook and stir 2 minutes more. Remove from the heat; stir in cheddar cheese until melted. Pour over casserole. Sprinkle with Parmesan cheese. Bake, uncovered, at 400° for 10-12 minutes or until heated through. **Yield:** 6 servings.

OVEN SWISS STEAK

I was really glad to find this recipe since it's a great way to use round steak and it picks up fabulous flavor from one of my favorite herbs—tarragon. I am a homemaker with three children and enjoy cooking tasty dinners like this one for my family. —*Lorna Dickau*
Vanderhoof, British Columbia

 8 **bacon strips**
 2 **pounds round steak (3/4 inch thick)**
 2 **cups sliced fresh mushrooms**
 1 **can (14-1/2 ounces) diced tomatoes,**
  undrained
1/2 **cup chopped onion**
 1 **to 2 teaspoons dried tarragon**
 2 **tablespoons cornstarch**
 2 **tablespoons water**
 1 **cup whipping cream**

In a large ovenproof skillet, cook bacon until crisp. Remove, crumble and set aside. Discard all but 1/4 cup of drippings. Trim beef; cut into serving-size pieces. Brown on both sides in drippings. Top meat with mushrooms, tomatoes and onion. Sprinkle with tarragon and bacon. Cover and bake at 325° for 1-1/4 to 1-3/4 hours or until meat is tender, basting twice. Remove meat to a serving platter; keep warm. Combine cornstarch and water; add to the skillet and bring to a boil. Cook and stir for 2 minutes. Reduce heat; stir in cream. Simmer, uncovered, for 3-4 minutes or until sauce thickens. Serve over meat. **Yield:** 6-8 servings.

MARINATED SIRLOIN STEAK

I once knew a nun who cooked the best marinated steaks. I found this recipe in my quest to fix steaks as good as hers. This delicious versatile meat makes a special main dish. —*Karen Mattern*
Spokane, Washington

 2 **to 2-1/2 pounds sirloin steak (about 1 inch**
  thick)
1-1/2 **cups water**
 3/4 **cup soy sauce**
 1/4 **cup Worcestershire sauce**
 1 **medium onion, chopped**
 2 **tablespoons white wine vinegar**
 2 **tablespoons lemon juice**
 2 **tablespoons Dijon mustard**
 2 **garlic cloves, minced**
 2 **teaspoons dried parsley flakes**
 1 **teaspoon dried thyme**
 1 **teaspoon Italian seasoning**
 1 **teaspoon pepper**

Place steak in a shallow dish or large heavy-duty resealable plastic bag. Combine remaining ingredients; pour over the meat. Cover or seal and refrigerate overnight. Remove meat; discard marinade. Grill, uncovered, over medium coals until meat is cooked as desired, about 6-7 minutes per side for rare, 8-10 minutes per side for medium or 11-13 minutes for well-done. **Yield:** 6 servings.

HUEVOS RANCHEROS

(Pictured above)

I like to spice up my meals with these tempting whole eggs poached in a zesty tomato sauce. You can enjoy the Southwestern flair of this egg dish anytime—for breakfast, lunch or supper. —Olga Koetting
Terre Haute, Indiana

1 small onion, finely chopped
1 medium green pepper, finely chopped
2 garlic cloves, minced
1 tablespoon cooking oil
2 cans (14-1/2 ounces *each*) stewed
   tomatoes, undrained
2 to 4 teaspoons seeded minced jalapeno
   pepper
2 teaspoons dried oregano
1 teaspoon chili powder
1/2 teaspoon ground cumin
1/2 teaspoon pepper
6 eggs
1 cup (4 ounces) shredded cheddar cheese
Flour tortillas, warmed, optional

In a large skillet, saute onion, green pepper and garlic in oil until tender. Stir in tomatoes and seasonings; simmer, uncovered, for 15 minutes. Make six indentations in the tomato mixture with a spoon. Break eggs into indentations. Cover and cook on low heat for 5 minutes or until eggs are set. Sprinkle with cheese; cover and cook until melted, about 1 minute. Serve with tortillas if desired. **Yield:** 6 servings.

CHICKEN RICE BURRITOS

(Pictured below)

For a nice alternative to beef and bean burritos, I use this recipe I discovered a while back. If I fix the chicken mixture the night before, the next day's dinner is a snap. My 14-year-old loves them. —Suzanne Adams
Laguna Niguel, California

1/3 cup sliced green onions
1 garlic clove, minced
2 tablespoons butter *or* margarine
7 cups shredded cooked chicken
1 tablespoon chili powder
2-1/2 cups chicken broth, *divided*
1 jar (16 ounces) picante sauce, *divided*
1 cup uncooked long grain rice
1/2 cup sliced ripe olives
3 cups (12 ounces) shredded cheddar
   cheese, *divided*
12 flour tortillas (10 inches), warmed
Additional picante sauce and cheddar cheese

In a skillet, saute onions and garlic in butter until tender. Stir in the chicken, chili powder, 1/4 cup of broth and 3/4 cup of picante sauce. Heat through; set aside. In a medium saucepan, bring rice and remaining broth to a boil. Reduce heat; cover and simmer for 20 minutes. Stir in remaining picante sauce; cover and simmer 5-10 minutes or until rice is tender. Stir into chicken mixture. Add olives and 2 cups cheese. Spoon 1 cup filling, off center, on each tortilla. Fold sides and ends over filling, then roll up. Arrange burritos in two ungreased 13-in. x 9-in. x 2-in. baking dishes. Sprinkle with the remaining cheese. Cover and bake at 375° for 10-15 minutes or until heated through. Garnish with picante sauce and cheese. **Yield:** 6 servings.

TURKEY POTPIE

(Pictured above)

Family and guests rave about this hearty potpie and its light flaky crust. The "secret" crust ingredients are Parmesan cheese and instant mashed potato flakes. On busy days, I prepare this entree in the morning and just bake it in the evening. —Cheryl Arnold
Lake Zurich, Illinois

    1 can (10-3/4 ounces) condensed cream of
      mushroom soup, undiluted
    1 can (5 ounces) evaporated milk
 1/4 cup minced fresh parsley *or* 1 tablespoon
      dried parsley flakes
 1/2 teaspoon dried thyme
    3 cups cubed cooked turkey
    1 package (10 ounces) frozen mixed
      vegetables, thawed
 1/4 teaspoon salt
 1/4 teaspoon pepper
CRUST:
 3/4 cup instant mashed potato flakes
 3/4 cup all-purpose flour
 1/4 cup grated Parmesan cheese
 1/3 cup butter *or* margarine
 1/4 cup ice water
Half-and-half cream

In a bowl, combine the first four ingredients. Stir in turkey, vegetables, salt and pepper. Spoon into a greased 11-in. x 7-in. x 2-in. baking dish. For crust, combine potato flakes, flour and Parmesan in a bowl; cut in butter until crumbly. Add water, 1 tablespoon at a time, tossing lightly with a fork until the dough forms a ball. On a lightly floured surface, roll the dough to fit baking dish. Cut vents in crust, using a small tree or star cutter if desired.

Place over filling; flute edges. Brush pastry with cream. Bake at 400° for 25-30 minutes or until golden brown. If necessary, cover edges of crust with foil to prevent overbrowning. **Yield:** 6 servings.

MUSHROOM SPAGHETTI SAUCE

Our three boys don't seem to mind the flavor of mushrooms, green peppers and onions in my spaghetti sauce as much as the chunks. Through the years, I've learned to chop the vegetables very fine so there's nothing for them to search for and pick out. —LaVonne Hegland
St. Michael, Minnesota

    2 pounds ground beef
    2 large onions, finely chopped
    1 large green pepper, finely chopped
    1 can (28 ounces) diced tomatoes,
      undrained
    2 cans (15 ounces *each*) tomato sauce
    2 cans (one 12 ounces, one 18 ounces)
      tomato paste
 1/2 pound fresh mushrooms, finely chopped
    4 cups water
    2 bay leaves
    2 teaspoons *each* dried parsley flakes, basil
      and oregano
    2 teaspoons *each* garlic powder, sugar and
      salt
    1 teaspoon chili powder
    1 teaspoon pepper

In a Dutch oven, brown beef, onions and green pepper until the beef is no longer pink; drain. Add remaining ingredients; bring to a boil. Reduce heat; simmer, uncovered, for 2-3 hours. Remove the bay leaves before serving. **Yield:** 16 cups.

PEPPER STEAK

I attended a cooking class a while back, and this was one of the recipes we learned to prepare. Everyone in the class just loved it. So I tried it out on my family, and they all raved about the delicious flavor. It's become an often-requested dish. —Jeanne Bunders
Wauzeka, Wisconsin

 ✓ **This tasty dish uses less sugar, salt and fat.**
   Recipe includes *Diabetic Exchanges*.

    1 pound boneless sirloin steak
    2 tablespoons cooking oil
    1 garlic clove, minced

1 teaspoon ground ginger
1 teaspoon salt, optional
1/2 teaspoon pepper
3 large green peppers, thinly sliced
2 large onions, thinly sliced
3/4 teaspoon beef bouillon granules
3/4 cup hot water
1 can (8 ounces) sliced water chestnuts, drained
1 tablespoon cornstarch
1/4 cup soy sauce
1/4 cup cold water
1/2 teaspoon sugar

Cut steak into 2-in. x 1/8-in. strips. In a large skillet or wok, brown steak in oil. Add garlic, ginger, salt if desired and pepper; cook for 1 minute. Remove meat and keep warm. Add green peppers and onions to skillet; cook and stir for 5 minutes or until crisp-tender. Dissolve bouillon in hot water; add to skillet with water chestnuts. Combine cornstarch, soy sauce, cold water and sugar; stir into skillet. Add meat. Cook and stir until mixture boils; cook and stir 2 minutes more. **Yield:** 6 servings. **Diabetic Exchanges:** One serving (prepared with low-sodium bouillon and light soy sauce and without added salt) equals 3 vegetable, 2 lean meat; also, 188 calories, 453 mg sodium, 29 mg cholesterol, 16 gm carbohydrate, 15 gm protein, 8 gm fat.

KIELBASA AND BEANS

When I was a bachelor, I really began experimenting with cooking. This casserole is a recipe I created back then because it's tasty, simple and hearty.
—Wade Harmon
Orange, Massachusetts

1/2 pound sliced bacon
1 pound smoked kielbasa, sliced and halved
1 large onion, chopped
1 medium sweet red pepper, chopped
2 cans (16 ounces *each*) kidney beans, rinsed and drained
1/2 cup chicken broth
Pepper to taste

In a large skillet, cook bacon until crisp; remove to paper towel to drain. Discard all but 1 tablespoon drippings; cook kielbasa in drippings until lightly browned. Drain. Add onion, red pepper, beans, broth and pepper. Cover and simmer for 1 hour, stirring occasionally. Crumble the bacon on top. **Yield:** 6 servings.

PEPPERED BEEF TENDERLOIN

(Pictured below)

This peppery, tempting tenderloin is perfect for folks who really savor meat. It's important to let it rest for a few minutes before carving to allow the juices to work through the meat.
—Margaret Ninneman
La Crosse, Wisconsin

✓ This tasty dish uses less sugar, salt and fat. Recipe includes *Diabetic Exchanges.*

1 teaspoon dried oregano
1 teaspoon paprika
1 teaspoon dried thyme
1 teaspoon salt, optional
1/2 teaspoon garlic powder
1/2 teaspoon onion powder
1/2 teaspoon pepper
1/2 teaspoon white pepper
1/8 to 1/4 teaspoon cayenne pepper
1 beef tenderloin (3 pounds)

Combine seasonings and rub over entire tenderloin. Place on a rack in a roasting pan. Bake, uncovered, at 425° until meat is cooked as desired. Allow approximately 45-50 minutes for rare or until a meat thermometer reads 140°, 55-60 minutes for medium-rare (150°), 62-65 minutes for medium (160°) and 67-70 minutes for well-done (170°). Let stand 10 minutes before carving. **Yield:** 8-10 servings. **Editor's Note:** After seasoning, the uncooked tenderloin may be wrapped tightly and refrigerated overnight for a more intense flavor. **Diabetic Exchanges:** One 3-oz. serving (prepared without salt) equals 4 lean meat; also, 179 calories, 67 mg sodium, 61 mg cholesterol, 1 gm carbohydrate, 28 gm protein, 7 gm fat.

1 cup dry bread crumbs
1-1/2 teaspoons salt
1/8 teaspoon pepper
1-1/2 pounds ground venison
2 tablespoons brown sugar
2 tablespoons spicy brown mustard
2 tablespoons vinegar

In a large bowl, lightly beat eggs; add the tomato sauce, onion, crumbs, salt and pepper. Add venison and mix well. Press into an ungreased 9-in. x 5-in. x 3-in. loaf pan. Combine the brown sugar, mustard and vinegar; pour over meat loaf. Bake, uncovered, at 350° for 70 minutes. **Yield:** 6-8 servings.

SPICED PORK CHOPS

Being a widow who likes to cook big meals, I frequently invite family and friends for dinner. On busy days, I rely on this easy recipe, which I got from a dear friend. It's hearty and satisfying. —Joan MacKinnon
Brooklyn, Nova Scotia

1/2 cup all-purpose flour
1-1/2 teaspoons garlic powder
1-1/2 teaspoons ground mustard
1-1/2 teaspoons paprika
1/2 teaspoon celery salt
1/4 teaspoon ground ginger
1/8 teaspoon dried oregano
1/8 teaspoon dried basil
1/8 teaspoon salt
Pinch pepper
4 pork loin chops (about 3/4 inch thick)
1 to 2 tablespoons cooking oil
1 cup ketchup
1 cup water
1/4 cup packed brown sugar

In a shallow dish, combine the first 10 ingredients; dredge pork chops on both sides. In a skillet, brown the chops in oil on both sides. Place in a greased 13-in. x 9-in. x 2-in. baking dish. Combine ketchup, water and brown sugar; pour over chops. Bake, uncovered, at 350° for 1 hour or until tender. **Yield:** 4 servings.

GRILLED CHICKEN KABOBS

I have fun trying new recipes and creating dishes of my own. I especially enjoy main entrees like this that are

RED FLANNEL HASH

(Pictured above)

This is an old-fashioned meal that satisfies big appetites with its hearty mix of ingredients. It gets its name from the rosy color the dish picks up from the beets.
—Jesse and Anne Foust
Bluefield, West Virginia

3 tablespoons cooking oil
1 can (15 ounces) sliced beets, drained and chopped
2 cups chopped cooked corned beef
2-1/2 cups diced cooked potatoes
1 medium onion, chopped
1/4 cup half-and-half cream
2 tablespoons butter *or* margarine, melted
2 teaspoons dried parsley flakes
1 teaspoon Worcestershire sauce
1/4 teaspoon salt
1/8 teaspoon pepper

Heat oil in a 12-in. skillet. Add all remaining ingredients. Cook and stir over low heat for 20 minutes or until lightly browned and heated through. **Yield:** 4 servings.

VENISON MEAT LOAF

My mother, who claims she can detect venison in any recipe, didn't have a clue it was in this tender meat loaf until we told her after dinner. She raved about this flavorful main dish the entire time she was eating it!
—Liz Gilchrist
Bolton, Ontario

2 eggs
1 can (8 ounces) tomato sauce
1 medium onion, finely chopped

a little lighter and that let the food's natural flavors come through. They grill in no time. —Paul Miller
Green Bay, Wisconsin

2 teaspoons ground mustard
1 tablespoon Worcestershire sauce
1/2 cup water
1/2 cup soy sauce
1 tablespoon vegetable oil
4 boneless skinless chicken breast halves
2 medium zucchini, cut into 1-1/2-inch slices
1 medium onion, cut into wedges
1 medium green pepper, cut into chunks
8 to 12 medium fresh mushrooms

In a resealable plastic bag, combine the mustard and Worcestershire sauce. Add water, soy sauce and oil; remove 1/3 cup and set aside for basting. Cut chicken into 1-1/2-in. pieces; add to bag. Seal and refrigerate for 1-1/2 to 2 hours. Drain, discarding marinade. Thread chicken and vegetables alternately on skewers. Baste with reserved marinade. Grill over hot coals for 10 minutes. Turn and baste. Cook 10 minutes more or until chicken juices run clear. **Yield:** 4-6 servings.

TANGY BEEF STROGANOFF

This is one of my favorite recipes. It features sirloin strips covered in a rich sour cream sauce with hints of caraway, mustard and tomato. It's a mouth-watering main dish for two people. —Bob Foust
Indianapolis, Indiana

1/2 cup sour cream
1 tablespoon all-purpose flour
1 tablespoon tomato paste
1 tablespoon Dijon mustard
2 teaspoons Worcestershire sauce
1 teaspoon beef bouillon granules
1/2 teaspoon caraway seed
8 ounces boneless beef sirloin, thinly sliced
1 cup sliced fresh mushrooms
1 small onion, sliced into rings
1 garlic clove, minced
1 tablespoon butter *or* margarine
Basil Spaetzle (recipe on page 57) *or* hot cooked noodles

In a small bowl, combine sour cream and flour until smooth. Add tomato paste, mustard, Worcestershire sauce, bouillon and caraway; mix well. Set aside. In a skillet over medium heat, cook beef, mushrooms, onion and garlic in butter until beef is browned and vegetables are tender. Add the sour

cream mixture; heat through but do not boil. Serve over spaetzle or noodles. **Yield:** 2 servings.

HERBED POT ROAST
(Pictured below)

I prepare this delicious main dish several times a month. The herbs and vegetables give the beef an excellent taste. My husband, Jack, a real meat-and-potatoes man, enjoys the leftovers. —Christel McKinley
East Liverpool, Ohio

1 boneless beef rump *or* chuck roast (3 to 3-1/2 pounds)
1 tablespoon cooking oil
1 teaspoon salt
1 teaspoon dried marjoram
1 teaspoon dried thyme
1/2 teaspoon dried oregano
1/2 teaspoon garlic powder
1/2 teaspoon pepper
1 can (10-1/2 ounces) condensed beef broth
8 carrots, cut into thirds
8 medium potatoes, peeled and quartered
1 large onion, quartered
1 cup water

In a Dutch oven, brown roast in oil. Combine the seasonings; sprinkle over meat. Add broth and bring to a boil. Cover and bake at 325° for 2 hours, basting occasionally. Add carrots, potatoes, onion and water. Cover and bake for 1 hour or until vegetables are tender. Thicken pan juices for gravy if desired. **Yield:** 8 servings.

EGG PIZZAS

I taught high school home economics classes for 33 years. I always included a session on eggs, and this is a recipe my students enjoyed. It's a fun way to dress up scrambled eggs.
—Olive Ranck
Williamsburg, Indiana

4 eggs
3 tablespoons finely chopped green pepper
3 tablespoons milk
Dash salt and pepper
1/2 teaspoon dried oregano
1 tablespoon butter *or* margarine
4 English muffins
4 to 6 tablespoons pizza sauce
1/2 cup bulk pork sausage, cooked and drained
2 tablespoons sliced ripe olives
2 tablespoons grated Parmesan cheese

In a bowl, beat eggs; add green pepper, milk, salt, pepper and oregano. Melt butter in a skillet; add the egg mixture. Cook and stir over medium heat until eggs are set. Remove from the heat. Split and toast English muffins; spread with pizza sauce. Spoon the egg mixture onto muffins. Sprinkle with sausage, olives and cheese. Place under broiler for a few minutes to heat through. **Yield:** 4 servings.

PHEASANT IN MUSTARD SAUCE
(Pictured above)

Until I met my husband, an avid hunter, I'd never cooked or eaten pheasant. I tried several different recipes before creating this one. —*Joan Mihalko*
Elkton, South Dakota

2 boneless skinless pheasant breast halves
1/4 teaspoon salt
1/8 teaspoon pepper
1 tablespoon cooking oil
1 tablespoon butter *or* margarine
1/4 cup chopped onion
1 garlic clove, minced
1/2 cup chicken broth
2 tablespoons lemon juice
3 tablespoons Dijon mustard
3/4 teaspoon dried marjoram
Hot cooked rice

Sprinkle pheasant with salt and pepper. In a skillet over medium heat, brown pheasant in oil and butter on both sides, about 6-8 minutes. Combine onion, garlic, broth, lemon juice, mustard and marjoram; add to skillet. Bring to a boil. Reduce heat; cover and simmer for 15-20 minutes or until pheasant juices run clear. Serve over rice. **Yield:** 2 servings.

OLD-FASHIONED LAMB STEW

This hearty stew is chock-full of tender lamb chunks and lots of vegetables. Sometimes I prepare this recipe in my slow cooker for added convenience.
—*Michelle Wise*
Spring Mills, Pennsylvania

1/4 cup all-purpose flour
1 teaspoon salt
1/2 teaspoon pepper
3 pounds boneless lamb, cut into 3-inch pieces
2 tablespoons cooking oil
1 can (28 ounces) diced tomatoes, undrained
1 medium onion, cut into eighths
1 tablespoon dried parsley flakes
2 teaspoons dried rosemary, crushed
1/4 teaspoon garlic powder
4 large carrots, cut into 1/2-inch pieces
4 medium potatoes, peeled and cut into 1-inch pieces
1 package (10 ounces) frozen peas
1 can (4 ounces) mushroom stems and pieces, drained

In a large resealable plastic bag, combine the flour, salt and pepper; add lamb and toss to coat. In a Dutch oven, brown the lamb in oil; drain. Add the tomatoes, onion, parsley, rosemary and garlic powder. Cover and simmer for 2 hours. Add the carrots and potatoes; cover and cook 1 hour longer or until the meat is tender. Add peas and mushrooms; heat through. Thicken if desired. **Yield:** 10-12 servings.

SHORT RIBS WITH DUMPLINGS

(Pictured above)

I've heard that these tender ribs and cornmeal dumplings were typical chuck-wagon fare for cowboys on the trail. I like making them for me and my husband, Bud, on cold rainy days. —Evelyn Hynd
Gravette, Arkansas

3 pounds boneless beef short ribs
2 tablespoons cooking oil
1 medium onion, cut into wedges
1 garlic clove, minced
1 can (28 ounces) diced tomatoes, undrained
1 cup beef broth, *divided*
2 tablespoons soy sauce
1 tablespoon sugar
1/2 teaspoon salt
1/4 teaspoon pepper
1/4 teaspoon crushed red pepper flakes
1/8 teaspoon ground nutmeg
2 to 3 tablespoons cornstarch
CORNMEAL DUMPLINGS:
3/4 cup water
1/2 cup cornmeal
1/2 teaspoon salt
1 egg, beaten
1/2 cup all-purpose flour
1 teaspoon baking powder
Dash pepper
1 can (7 ounces) whole kernel corn, drained

Cut ribs into 1-in. pieces. In a Dutch oven, brown ribs on all sides in oil. Add onion and garlic; cook until onion is tender, stirring occasionally. Stir in tomatoes, 1/2 cup broth, soy sauce and seasonings; bring to a boil. Reduce heat; cover and simmer for 1-1/2 to 2 hours or until meat is tender. Combine cornstarch and remaining broth; stir into the beef mixture. Bring to a boil, stirring constantly. For dumplings, combine water, cornmeal and salt in a saucepan; bring to a boil. Cook and stir for 1-2 minutes or until thickened; remove from the heat. Stir a small amount into egg; return all to pan. Combine flour, baking powder and pepper; stir into cornmeal mixture. Add corn. Drop by rounded tablespoonfuls into simmering stew. Cover and simmer for 10-12 minutes (do not lift lid) or until dumplings test done. **Yield:** 6-8 servings.

MUSHROOM LAMB CHOPS

(Pictured below)

Fresh lamb chops are a real treat for us, and this is how I always fix them. As far as I'm concerned, there's no better way to serve lamb. —Ruth Andrewson
Leavenworth, Washington

6 blade lamb chops (about 3 pounds)
1 tablespoon olive *or* vegetable oil
1/2 teaspoon dried thyme
1/2 teaspoon salt
1/4 teaspoon pepper
1/2 cup chopped celery
1/2 cup chopped green onions
1 can (10-1/2 ounces) beef consomme, undiluted
3 tablespoons all-purpose flour
1/4 cup water
1 can (4 ounces) button mushrooms, drained
1 tablespoon minced fresh parsley
Hot cooked noodles

In a large skillet, brown the chops in oil; drain. Sprinkle with thyme, salt and pepper. Add celery, onions and consomme; cover and simmer for 40-45 minutes or until meat is tender. Remove chops and keep warm. Combine flour and water until smooth; gradually stir into skillet and bring to a boil. Cook and stir for 2 minutes. Add mushrooms and parsley; heat through. Serve over chops and noodles. **Yield:** 6 servings.

4 cups cooked wild rice
1 pound uncooked lean ground beef
2 cups (8 ounces) shredded cheddar cheese
1 cup dry bread crumbs
1 cup finely chopped onion
1/2 cup all-purpose flour
2 eggs, beaten
1-1/4 teaspoons salt
1 teaspoon rubbed sage
3/4 teaspoon pepper

Combine all ingredients in a large bowl; mix well. Firmly press into a greased 9-in. x 5-in. x 3-in. loaf pan. Bake, uncovered, at 350° for 70 minutes. Cover with foil during the last 15 minutes if the top is browning too quickly. **Yield:** 4-6 servings.

TURKEY PASTA SUPREME

Since this dish combines turkey and pasta, even our children love it. It's fun to make turkey a different way, and you can't beat the creamy, cheesy sauce.
—Cassie Dion
South Burlington, Vermont

3/4 pound uncooked turkey breast
2 garlic cloves, minced
2 tablespoons butter *or* margarine
1-1/4 cups whipping cream
2 tablespoons minced fresh basil *or* 2 teaspoons dried basil
1/4 cup grated Parmesan cheese
Dash pepper
3 to 4 cups hot cooked pasta

Cut turkey into 2-in. x 1/4-in. pieces. In a skillet, saute turkey and garlic in butter until turkey is browned and no longer pink, about 6 minutes. Add cream, basil, Parmesan and pepper; bring to a boil. Reduce heat; simmer for 3 minutes, stirring frequently. Stir in pasta and toss to coat. Serve immediately. **Yield:** 4 servings.

CHICKEN IN PLUM SAUCE
(Pictured above)

The secret is in the sauce in this delicious main dish. Honey, plums and garlic combine to make a sauce that adds mouth-watering flavor to tender, juicy chicken.
—Patricia Collins
Imbler, Oregon

1 broiler/fryer chicken (3-1/2 to 4 pounds), cut up
3/4 cup all-purpose flour
3 tablespoons cooking oil
2 cans (16-1/2 ounces *each*) whole plums, pitted
1/2 cup honey
1 tablespoon vinegar
1 to 2 garlic cloves, minced

Coat chicken pieces with flour; brown in oil in a large skillet over medium heat. Transfer to a greased 13-in. x 9-in. x 2-in. baking pan. Drain plums, reserving syrup; remove pits and coarsely chop plums in a food processor. Pour into a measuring cup; add enough syrup to equal 2 cups. Place in a saucepan. Add honey, vinegar and garlic; bring to a boil. Cook and stir for 2 minutes. Pour over chicken. Bake, uncovered, at 350° for 45 minutes or until chicken juices run clear. **Yield:** 4-6 servings.

WILD RICE MEAT LOAF

I've shared this recipe with many friends. The unique, hearty meat loaf is full of surprises—tangy wild rice and pockets of cheddar cheese make it extra special. Even so, it's not that tricky to prepare...try it and see!
—Genie Lang
Jamestown, North Dakota

Mighty Good Meat Loaf

To please picky eaters in your family who don't like chunks of onion or green pepper in their meat loaf, put those ingredients in the blender and blend before adding to the ground beef.

If your family won't eat liver, add ground cooked liver to your meat loaf. They'll never know it's in there, but they'll think it's delicious.

PARMESAN CHICKEN

This chicken is moist and saucy with great Parmesan flavor. Whenever I take it to a potluck, it disappears quickly and people often request the recipe.

—Cara Flora
Kokomo, Indiana

✓ **This tasty dish uses less sugar, salt and fat. Recipe includes *Diabetic Exchanges*.**

  8 boneless skinless chicken breast halves (2 pounds)
  1 cup fat-free mayonnaise
1/2 cup grated fat-free Parmesan cheese
  2 teaspoons dried oregano
1/8 teaspoon pepper
Paprika, optional

Place chicken in a shallow 3-qt. baking dish that has been coated with nonstick cooking spray. Bake, uncovered, at 400° for 20 minutes. Combine the mayonnaise, cheese, oregano and pepper; spread over chicken. Sprinkle with paprika if desired. Bake 20 minutes more or until chicken juices run clear. **Yield:** 8 servings. **Diabetic Exchanges:** One serving equals 4 very lean meat, 1/2 starch; also, 183 calories, 371 mg sodium, 73 mg cholesterol, 7 gm carbohydrate, 30 gm protein, 3 gm fat.

MULTIGRAIN PANCAKES

My husband and I love the goodness of foods prepared with whole grains. But our children are different—their idea of good bread is store-bought soft white sandwich bread. So I developed this to appeal to their love of sweet toppings while giving them a taste of whole-grain cooking.

—Ann Harris
Lancaster, California

✓ **This tasty dish uses less sugar, salt and fat. Recipe includes *Diabetic Exchanges*.**

1/2 cup all-purpose flour
1/4 cup whole wheat flour
1/4 cup cornmeal
  2 tablespoons sugar
1/2 teaspoon baking soda
1/2 teaspoon salt
  1 egg
  1 cup buttermilk
  2 tablespoons butter *or* margarine, melted
Maple syrup

In a large bowl, combine dry ingredients. In a small bowl, beat egg; add buttermilk and butter. Stir into dry ingredients just until moistened. Pour batter by 1/4 cupfuls onto a lightly greased hot griddle; turn when bubbles form on top of pancakes. Cook until second side is golden brown. Serve with syrup. **Yield:** 4 servings. **Diabetic Exchanges:** Two pancakes (prepared with margarine) served with 2 tablespoons sugar-free maple-flavored syrup equals 2-1/2 starch, 1-1/2 fat; also, 250 calories, 621 mg sodium, 55 mg cholesterol, 38 gm carbohydrate, 7 gm protein, 8 gm fat.

BARLEY-STUFFED PEPPERS

(Pictured below)

My mother cooked with barley a lot, so when I found this recipe for stuffed peppers, I knew it would be great. I just made a few changes to suit our tastes, and now it's a weekday dinner standby.

—Rosella Peters
Gull Lake, Saskatchewan

  4 large green peppers
1/2 pound bulk Italian sausage
  1 cup chopped onion
  1 to 2 garlic cloves, minced
  1 can (8 ounces) tomato sauce
  3 cups cooked barley
1/4 teaspoon dried thyme
1/2 teaspoon salt
1/8 teaspoon pepper

Cut tops off peppers; remove seeds. In a large kettle, blanch peppers in boiling water for 3 minutes. Drain and rinse in cold water; set aside. In a skillet over medium heat, cook sausage, onion and garlic until onion is tender and sausage is no longer pink; drain. Stir in tomato sauce, barley, thyme, salt and pepper; heat through. Spoon into peppers; place in an ungreased 8-in. square baking dish. Cover and bake at 350° for 25-30 minutes or until peppers are tender and filling is hot. **Yield:** 4 servings.

ORANGE ONION CHICKEN

(Pictured above)

Folks really enjoy this tasty chicken. It's a light, refreshing dinner that appeals to all palates.
—*Alcy Thorne*
Los Molinos, California

✓ **This tasty dish uses less sugar, salt and fat.
Recipe includes *Diabetic Exchanges*.**

    4 boneless skinless chicken breast halves
        (1-1/4 pounds)
    2 tablespoons cooking oil
1-1/4 cups water, *divided*
  1/2 cup orange juice
  1/4 cup chopped onion
  1/4 cup reduced-sodium fat-free chicken
        broth
  1/4 to 1/2 teaspoon ground ginger
    2 tablespoons cornstarch
    2 oranges, peeled and sectioned

In a skillet, brown the chicken in oil; drain. Add 1 cup water, orange juice, onion, broth and ginger. Cover and simmer until chicken juices run clear, 20-25 minutes. Remove chicken; keep warm. Mix cornstarch with remaining water; stir into skillet. Cook and stir until thickened and bubbly; cook and stir for 2 minutes more. Add the orange sections and heat through. Serve over the chicken. **Yield:** 4 servings. **Diabetic Exchanges:** One serving equals 4 very lean meat, 1 fruit, 1 fat; also, 239 calories, 68 mg sodium, 73 mg cholesterol, 16 gm carbohydrate, 28 gm protein, 7 gm fat.

SAGE BREAKFAST SAUSAGE

I added some more seasonings to a recipe my mother-in-law gave me, and now my family prefers these patties to any frozen variety.   —*Karla Krenik Mayer*
Le Sueur, Minnesota

    1 pound ground pork
1-1/2 teaspoons rubbed sage
    1 teaspoon salt
  1/2 teaspoon poultry seasoning

  1/2 teaspoon pepper
Pinch ground allspice

In a bowl, combine all ingredients; mix well. Shape into six patties. Chill at least 1 hour. In a skillet over medium heat, fry patties for 3-4 minutes per side or until browned and no longer pink in the center. **Yield:** 6 servings.

SPRING BREAKFAST STRATA

Eggs are the star of this hearty breakfast fare. Filled with tasty ingredients like ham, mushrooms, cheddar cheese and asparagus, this dish is super. You can prepare it the night before for a no-fuss breakfast, brunch or dish to pass.   —*Maryellen Hays*
Fort Wayne, Indiana

    8 eggs
    3 cups milk
    1 tablespoon Dijon mustard
    2 teaspoons dried basil
    1 teaspoon salt
    2 tablespoons butter *or* margarine, melted
    2 tablespoons all-purpose flour
    2 cups (8 ounces) shredded cheddar cheese
    1 pound fully cooked ham, cubed
    1 package (10 ounces) frozen cut asparagus,
        thawed *or* 2 cups cut fresh asparagus,
        cooked
    2 cups sliced fresh mushrooms
   10 cups cubed bread

In a large bowl, beat eggs; add milk, mustard, basil and salt. Gently stir in remaining ingredients until well mixed. Pour into a greased 13-in. x 9-in. x 2-in. baking dish. Cover and refrigerate 8 hours or overnight. Remove from the refrigerator 30 minutes before baking. Bake, uncovered, at 350° for 1 hour or until a knife inserted near the center comes out clean. Let stand 5 minutes before cutting. **Yield:** 12 servings.

GARLIC ROSEMARY TURKEY

The house smells so good while this turkey is cooking that my family can hardly wait 'til it's done! This is a beautiful, succulent main dish.   —*Cathy Dobbins*
Rio Rancho, New Mexico

✓ **This tasty dish uses less sugar, salt and fat.
Recipe includes *Diabetic Exchanges*.**

    1 whole turkey (10 to 12 pounds)
    6 to 8 garlic cloves

2 large lemons, halved
2 tablespoons chopped fresh rosemary *or*
  2 teaspoons dried rosemary, crushed
1 tablespoon chopped fresh sage *or* 1
  teaspoon rubbed sage

Cut six to eight small slits in turkey skin; insert garlic between skin and meat. Squeeze two lemon halves inside the turkey and leave them inside. Squeeze remaining lemon over outside of turkey. Spray turkey with nonstick cooking spray; sprinkle with rosemary and sage. Place on a rack in a roasting pan. Bake, uncovered, at 325° for 1 hour. Cover and bake 2-1/2 to 3-1/2 hours longer or until a meat thermometer reads 185°. **Yield:** 8-10 servings. **Diabetic Exchanges:** One serving (4 ounces of white meat without skin) equals 4 very lean meat; also, 144 calories, 57 mg sodium, 88 mg cholesterol, trace carbohydrate, 31 gm protein, 1 gm fat.

BAKED ITALIAN CHICKEN

This recipe is a variation on one calling for pork chops. I like this delicious main dish because it doesn't dirty a pile of pots and pans.
—*Jim Cosgrove*
Burlington, Ontario

6 boneless skinless chicken breast halves
1/2 cup all-purpose flour
2 eggs, beaten
3/4 cup dry bread crumbs
1/2 cup grated Parmesan cheese, *divided*
1 tablespoon cooking oil
SAUCE:
2 tablespoons butter *or* margarine
2 tablespoons all-purpose flour
1-1/4 cups milk
1 teaspoon salt
1/2 teaspoon dried basil
1/2 teaspoon dried oregano
1/4 teaspoon pepper
1 can (8 ounces) tomato sauce
1 cup (4 ounces) shredded mozzarella cheese

Pound chicken breasts. Coat with flour; dip into eggs. Combine bread crumbs and 1/4 cup Parmesan cheese; pat onto both sides of chicken. Brush oil onto a foil-lined 13-in. x 9-in. x 2-in. baking pan; place chicken in pan. Bake, uncovered, at 400° for 20 minutes. Meanwhile, for sauce, melt butter in a saucepan; stir in the flour until smooth. Whisk in milk; bring to a boil. Cook and stir for 2 minutes. Add seasonings. Pour over chicken. Drizzle with tomato sauce; sprinkle with mozzarella and remaining Parmesan. Bake 15 minutes longer or until the cheese is lightly browned. **Yield:** 6 servings.

TACO PIZZA
(Pictured below)

This slightly spicy pizza is a colorful, delicious change of pace from the ordinary kind. You'll have a hard time eating just one slice!
—*Gladys Shaffer*
Elma, Washington

1-1/4 cups cornmeal
1-1/4 cups all-purpose flour
2 teaspoons baking powder
1-1/2 teaspoons salt
2/3 cup milk
1/3 cup butter *or* margarine, melted
1/2 pound ground beef
1/2 pound bulk pork sausage
1 can (6 ounces) tomato paste
1 can (14-1/2 ounces) diced tomatoes,
  undrained
1 envelope taco seasoning mix
3/4 cup water
1-1/2 cups (6 ounces) shredded cheddar cheese
1 cup (4 ounces) shredded Monterey Jack
  cheese
2 cups chopped lettuce
1 cup diced fresh tomato
1/2 cup sliced ripe olives
1/2 cup sliced green onions

In a medium bowl, combine the cornmeal, flour, baking powder and salt. Add milk and butter; mix well. Press onto the bottom and sides of a 12- to 14-in. pizza pan. Bake at 400° for 10 minutes or until edges are lightly browned. Cool. In a large skillet, brown beef and sausage; drain. Stir in the tomato paste, canned tomatoes, taco seasoning and water; bring to a boil. Simmer, uncovered, for 5 minutes. Spread over crust. Combine cheeses; sprinkle 2 cups over the meat layer. Bake at 400° for 15 minutes or until cheese melts. Top with lettuce, fresh tomato, olives, onions and remaining cheese. **Yield:** 4-6 servings.

SCOTT'S BEEF BRISKET

(Pictured below and on front cover)

My brother and I made special grills to cook and smoke 20 briskets at a time for parties. I created this recipe to achieve a similar fork-tender, sweet and spicy brisket using the oven. —Scott Post
Clayton, North Carolina

1/2 teaspoon *each* ground allspice, chili powder, garlic powder, onion powder, paprika, seasoned salt and sugar
1/4 teaspoon pepper
1 fresh beef brisket* (3 to 4 pounds)
1/2 cup cola
1/3 cup Worcestershire sauce
1/2 cup cider vinegar
1/2 cup butter *or* margarine, melted
1/3 cup soy sauce
3/4 cup barbecue sauce
Additional barbecue sauce, optional

Combine the dry seasonings; cover and set aside. Place brisket in a shallow dish or large heavy-duty resealable plastic bag. Combine the cola and Worcestershire sauce; pour over meat. Cover or seal and refrigerate overnight. Drain meat; discard marinade. Rub seasoning mix over brisket; place in a large shallow roasting pan. Combine vinegar, butter and soy sauce; pour over meat. Cover and bake at 325° for 2 hours, basting occasionally. Drain drippings. Pour barbecue sauce over meat. Cover and bake for 1 hour or until the meat is tender. Remove meat from pan; let stand 15 minutes before slicing. Serve with additional barbecue sauce if desired. **Yield:** 6-8 servings. ***Editor's Note:** This is a fresh brisket, not corned beef.

GRILLED FAJITAS

A special marinade gives the meat in these fajitas outstanding flavor that's always a hit with my family. It's a fun summer main dish. —Cheryl Smith
The Dalles, Oregon

1 beef flank steak (about 1 pound)
1 envelope onion soup mix
1/4 cup vegetable oil
1/4 cup lime juice
1/4 cup water
2 garlic cloves, minced
1 teaspoon grated lime peel
1 teaspoon ground cumin
1/2 teaspoon dried oregano
1/4 teaspoon pepper
1 medium onion, thinly sliced
Green, sweet red *and/or* yellow peppers, julienned
1 tablespoon cooking oil
8 flour tortillas (7 inches), warmed

Place the flank steak in a glass dish. Combine the next nine ingredients; pour over meat. Cover and refrigerate 4 hours or overnight. Drain and discard marinade. Grill meat over hot coals until it is cooked as desired, about 4 minutes per side for medium, 5 minutes per side for medium-well. Meanwhile, in a skillet, saute onion and peppers in oil for 3-4 minutes or until crisp-tender. Slice meat into thin strips across the grain; place on tortillas. Top with vegetables; roll up and serve immediately. **Yield:** 4 servings.

CHICKEN MUSHROOM STEW

The flavors blend beautifully in this pot of chicken, vegetables and herbs as it simmers slowly. You'll find it's a convenient recipe to have on hand for busy weekdays and hectic weekends. —Kim Marie Van Rheenen
Mendota, Illinois

✓ **This tasty dish uses less sugar, salt and fat. Recipe includes** *Diabetic Exchanges.*

6 boneless skinless chicken breast halves (1-1/2 pounds)
2 tablespoons cooking oil, *divided*
8 ounces fresh mushrooms, sliced
1 medium onion, diced
3 cups diced zucchini
1 cup diced green pepper
4 garlic cloves, minced
3 medium tomatoes, diced
1 can (6 ounces) tomato paste

   3/4 cup water
   2 teaspoons salt, optional
   1 teaspoon *each* dried thyme, oregano, marjoram and basil

Cut chicken into 1-in. cubes; brown in 1 tablespoon of oil in a large skillet. Transfer to a slow cooker. In the same skillet, saute the mushrooms, onion, zucchini, green pepper and garlic in remaining oil until crisp-tender. Place in slow cooker. Add tomatoes, tomato paste, water and seasonings. Cover and cook on low for 4 hours or until vegetables are tender. **Yield:** 6 servings. **Diabetic Exchanges:** One 1-1/3-cup serving (prepared with no-salt-added tomato paste and without salt) equals 4 very lean meat, 1 vegetable, 1 fat, 1/2 starch; also, 274 calories, 102 mg sodium, 84 mg cholesterol, 16 gm carbohydrate, 34 gm protein, 9 gm fat.

SOUTHWESTERN STEW

Romping in the national forest amid tall ponderosa pines around our home gives my husband and our two little boys big appetites. They like this savory stew. Because I'm a busy firefighter, I often make it ahead and serve it when I need a meal in a hurry.
— Linda Russell
Forest Lakes, Arizona

✓ **This tasty dish uses less sugar, salt and fat. Recipe includes *Diabetic Exchanges*.**

   2 pounds beef stew meat, cut into 1-inch cubes
   2 tablespoons cooking oil
   2 cups water
1-1/4 cups chopped onion
   1 cup salsa
   2 garlic cloves, minced
   1 tablespoon dried parsley flakes
   2 teaspoons beef bouillon granules
   1 teaspoon ground cumin
1/2 teaspoon salt, optional
   3 medium carrots, cut into 1-inch pieces
   1 can (14-1/2 ounces) diced tomatoes, undrained
1-1/2 cups frozen cut green beans
1-1/2 cups frozen corn
   1 can (4 ounces) chopped green chilies
Hot pepper sauce, optional

In a 4-qt. Dutch oven over medium heat, brown meat in oil; drain. Add the next eight ingredients; bring to a boil. Reduce heat; cover and simmer for 1 hour. Add carrots; return to a boil. Reduce heat and simmer for 20 minutes. Add tomatoes, beans, corn and chilies; return to a boil. Reduce heat; cover and simmer for 15-20 minutes or until beef and vegetables are tender. Season with hot pepper sauce if desired. This stew is good served over rice. **Yield:** 8 servings. **Diabetic Exchanges:** One serving (prepared with lean meat and low-sodium tomatoes and without salt and hot pepper sauce) equals 3 lean meat, 1 starch, 1 vegetable, 1/2 fat; also, 293 calories, 525 mg sodium, 82 mg cholesterol, 17 gm carbohydrate, 31 gm protein, 11 gm fat.

TURKEY IN A HURRY

(Pictured above)

This dish is easy to prepare and really brings some variety to mealtime. It's a delicious non-traditional way to fix turkey, which cooks up moist and tasty.
— Denise Goedeken
Platte Center, Nebraska

   2 turkey tenderloins (1-1/2 pounds)
1/4 cup butter *or* margarine
3/4 teaspoon dried thyme
1/2 teaspoon dried rosemary, crushed
1/4 teaspoon paprika
1/8 teaspoon garlic powder

Cut tenderloins in half lengthwise, then into serving-size pieces. Place on rack of broiler pan. In a small saucepan, heat remaining ingredients until butter is melted. Broil turkey until lightly browned on one side. Brush with the herb butter; turn and brown the other side. Brush with butter. Continue cooking 6-8 minutes or until no longer pink, brushing often with butter. **Yield:** 6 servings.

EASY TACO CASSEROLE
(Pictured above)

Your family will enjoy this mildly spicy, quick-and-easy meal with Southwestern flair. —Flo Burtnett
Gage, Oklahoma

- 1 pound ground beef
- 1 cup salsa
- 1/2 cup mayonnaise *or* salad dressing
- 2 teaspoons chili powder
- 2 cups crushed tortilla chips
- 1 cup (4 ounces) shredded Colby cheese
- 1 cup (4 ounces) shredded Monterey Jack cheese
- 1 medium tomato, chopped
- 2 cups shredded lettuce

In a saucepan, brown ground beef; drain. Add salsa, mayonnaise and chili powder; mix well. In an ungreased 2-qt. baking dish, layer half of the meat mixture, chips and cheeses. Repeat layers. Bake, uncovered, at 350° for 20-25 minutes or until heated through. Just before serving, top with tomato and lettuce. **Yield:** 6 servings.

DELUXE HAM OMELET

Ham, vegetables and two cheeses are what make this omelet deluxe. It's a hearty meal for one or two.
—Iola Egle
McCook, Nebraska

- 3 eggs
- 2 tablespoons half-and-half cream
- 2 tablespoons snipped fresh chives
- 1/2 teaspoon garlic salt
- 1/4 teaspoon pepper
- 1 tablespoon olive *or* vegetable oil
- 1/2 cup finely chopped fully cooked ham

- 2 tablespoons chopped green pepper
- 2 tablespoons chopped tomato
- 2 fresh mushrooms, sliced
- 2 tablespoons shredded cheddar cheese
- 2 tablespoons shredded mozzarella cheese

In a small bowl, beat the eggs, cream, chives, garlic salt and pepper. Heat oil in a 10-1/2-in. nonstick skillet; add the egg mixture and cook over medium heat. As the eggs set, lift edges, letting uncooked portion flow underneath. Sprinkle with ham, green pepper, tomato and mushrooms. When eggs are set, remove from the heat and fold omelet in half. Sprinkle with cheese; cover for 1-2 minutes or until cheese melts. **Yield:** 1-2 servings.

BRAISED LAMB SHANKS

These lamb shanks turn out tender and savory. It's a perfect one-pot meal for hectic days. —Billie Moss
El Sobrante, California

- 2 lamb shanks (about 2 pounds)
- 2 tablespoons cooking oil
- 1 medium onion, diced
- 2 garlic cloves, minced
- 1 tablespoon all-purpose flour
- 2 beef bouillon cubes
- 1/4 cup boiling water
- 1 can (14-1/2 ounces) diced tomatoes, undrained
- 1/2 cup chopped celery
- 1/2 cup chopped carrot
- 1/2 teaspoon dried marjoram
- 1/4 teaspoon salt

In a large skillet, brown lamb in oil; remove and set aside. Add the onion and garlic; saute until tender. Stir in flour; cook and stir for 1 minute. Add bouillon and water; stir to dissolve. Return lamb to pan. Add remaining ingredients; bring to a boil. Reduce heat; cover and simmer for 1-1/2 hours or until meat is tender. **Yield:** 2 servings.

ROAST LAMB WITH PLUM SAUCE

Cloves of garlic inserted into slits cut into the meat are the secret to this recipe's success. Plus, you'll find the plum sauce delightfully different. —Dorothy Pritchett
Wills Point, Texas

- 1 leg of lamb (5 to 6 pounds)
- 3 garlic cloves, peeled

1/2 cup thinly sliced green onions
1/4 cup butter *or* margarine
1 jar (12 ounces) plum jam
1/2 cup chili sauce
1/4 cup white grape juice
1 tablespoon lemon juice
1/2 teaspoon ground allspice
1 tablespoon dried parsley flakes

Remove the thin fat covering from the roast. Make three deep cuts in meat; insert a garlic clove in each. Place roast on a rack in a large roasting pan. Bake, uncovered, at 325° for 1-1/2 hours. Meanwhile, make the plum sauce. In a medium saucepan, saute onions in butter until tender but not brown. Add jam, chili sauce, grape juice, lemon juice and allspice; bring to a boil, stirring occasionally. Simmer, uncovered, for 10 minutes. Baste roast with sauce. Roast 1 hour longer, basting occasionally, or until a meat thermometer reads 160°. Bring the remaining sauce to a boil; stir in parsley. Serve with the roast. **Yield:** 10-12 servings.

RED BEANS AND SAUSAGE

Turkey sausage, beans and a zesty blend of spices make this a deliciously unique meal.—Cathy Webster
Morris, Illinois

✓ **This tasty dish uses less sugar, salt and fat. Recipe includes *Diabetic Exchanges*.**

2 garlic cloves, minced
1 medium green pepper, diced
1 medium onion, chopped
1 tablespoon vegetable oil
2 cans (16 ounces *each*) kidney beans, rinsed and drained
1/2 pound smoked turkey sausage, sliced
3/4 cup water
1 teaspoon Cajun seasoning
1/8 teaspoon hot pepper sauce
Hot cooked rice, optional

In a saucepan, saute the garlic, green pepper and onion in oil until tender, about 5 minutes. Add the next five ingredients; bring to a boil. Reduce heat; cook for 5-7 minutes or until the sausage is heated through. Serve over rice if desired. **Yield:** 6 servings. **Diabetic Exchanges:** One 2/3-cup serving (calculated without rice) equals 1-1/2 starch, 1 meat, 1 vegetable; also, 221 calories, 627 mg sodium, 20 mg cholesterol, 29 gm carbohydrate, 14 gm protein, 6 gm fat.

CHICKEN STIR-FRY
(Pictured below)

This is a tasty, healthy meal that everyone in my family enjoys! The broccoli and carrots in this dish give it an attractive color. —Lori Schlecht
Wimbledon, North Dakota

✓ **This tasty dish uses less sugar, salt and fat. Recipe includes *Diabetic Exchanges*.**

4 boneless skinless chicken breast halves (1 pound)
3 tablespoons cornstarch
2 tablespoons soy sauce
1/2 teaspoon ground ginger
1/4 teaspoon garlic powder
3 tablespoons cooking oil, *divided*
2 cups broccoli florets
1 cup sliced celery (1/2-inch pieces)
1 cup thinly sliced carrots
1 small onion, cut into wedges
1 cup water
1 teaspoon chicken bouillon granules

Cut chicken into 1/2-in. strips; place in a resealable plastic bag. Add cornstarch and toss to coat. Combine soy sauce, ginger and garlic powder; add to bag and shake well. Refrigerate for 30 minutes. In a large skillet or wok, heat 2 tablespoons of oil; stir-fry chicken until no longer pink, about 3-5 minutes. Remove and keep warm. Add remaining oil; stir-fry broccoli, celery, carrots and onion for 4-5 minutes or until crisp-tender. Add water and bouillon. Return chicken to pan. Cook and stir until thickened and bubbly. **Yield:** 4 servings. **Diabetic Exchanges:** One serving (prepared with light soy sauce and low-sodium bouillon) equals 3 lean meat, 2 vegetable, 1 fat, 1/2 starch; also, 306 calories, 239 mg sodium, 73 mg cholesterol, 18 gm carbohydrate, 30 gm protein, 14 gm fat.

MUSHROOM BEEF PATTIES

(Pictured above)

Even though I'm a "city boy", my co-workers have said I'm the most country city boy they have ever run across. Maybe that's because of the hearty recipes I share, like this ground beef dish. —Dale Thelen
Bedford, Texas

    1 pound ground beef
1/4 cup dry bread crumbs
    2 tablespoons milk
    1 tablespoon Worcestershire sauce
    1 teaspoon salt, *divided*
1/2 teaspoon pepper
1/2 teaspoon garlic powder
1/2 pound fresh mushrooms, sliced
    1 teaspoon dried basil
    5 tablespoons butter *or* margarine, *divided*
    2 tablespoons all-purpose flour
1/2 cup half-and-half cream
1/2 to 3/4 cup water
1/4 teaspoon hot pepper sauce
1/4 cup shredded cheddar cheese
    2 tablespoons chopped green onions

Combine beef, crumbs, milk, Worcestershire sauce, 1/2 teaspoon of salt, pepper and garlic powder; mix well. Shape into three or four oval patties; cook on both sides until no longer pink. In another skillet, cook the mushrooms and basil in 2 tablespoons butter over medium-high heat until tender; remove mushrooms and set aside. Melt the remaining butter; stir in flour. Increase heat to high; cook and stir until most of the liquid evaporates. Gradually blend in cream. Add 1/2 cup water, hot pepper sauce and remaining salt; cook and stir on low until thickened and bubbly. Cook and stir for 2 minutes more. Add enough remaining water to make a medium-thin sauce. Return mushrooms to sauce and heat through. Serve over beef patties; top with cheese and onions. **Yield:** 3-4 servings.

ZESTY STUFFED PEPPERS

Since I discovered this recipe, I've never made stuffed peppers any other way. People are pleasantly surprised to find corn in the stuffing of these peppers.
—Margery Bryan
Royal City, Washington

    6 medium green peppers, tops and seeds removed
    1 pound ground beef
1/4 cup chopped onion
    1 can (11 ounces) whole kernel corn, drained
    1 can (8 ounces) tomato sauce
    1 cup cooked rice
1/4 cup steak sauce
1/4 teaspoon salt
1/4 teaspoon pepper

In a large kettle over medium-high heat, blanch peppers in boiling salted water for 3-5 minutes. Drain and rinse in cold water; set aside. In a skillet over medium heat, brown beef and onion; drain. Add remaining ingredients and mix well. Loosely stuff into peppers. Place in a 9-in. square baking pan. Bake, uncovered, at 350° for 30-35 minutes or until peppers are done and filling is hot. **Yield:** 6 servings.

AUTUMN PORK ROAST

Although this main meal captures the fabulous flavor of fall, don't hesitate to serve it throughout the year. Your family will flock to the table when they smell this delicious roast. It's a hearty dish that makes everyday dinners more special. —Kathy Barbarek
Joliet, Illinois

    1 bone-in pork loin roast (5 pounds)
    8 medium potatoes, peeled and quartered
    8 carrots, halved lengthwise
    2 medium onions, quartered
    1 small pumpkin *or* butternut squash, peeled and cut into 1-1/2-inch chunks
    1 cup water
    3 tablespoons snipped fresh sage *or* 1 tablespoon rubbed sage
1/4 teaspoon pepper
    2 tablespoons butter *or* margarine
    4 baking apples, quartered

Place roast in a large baking pan. Arrange potatoes, carrots, onions and pumpkin around roast. Add water to pan. Sprinkle meat and vegetables with sage and pepper; dot vegetables with butter. Bake, uncovered, at 400° for 15 minutes. Reduce heat to 350°; bake, uncovered, for 1 hour. Place apples around roast; cover and bake for 1-1/4 hours, basting every 30 minutes, or until a meat thermometer reads 160°-170°. If desired, thicken pan juices for gravy. **Yield:** 6-8 servings.

SPINACH PASTA SAUCE

People are always surprised to hear that the "secret" ingredient in this special sauce is to add a touch of anise. The herb nicely complements the zippy Italian sausage and chunky tomatoes. —Margaret Allen
Abingdon, Virginia

1-1/2 pounds bulk mild Italian sausage
   3 cups sliced fresh mushrooms
  1/2 cup *each* chopped carrot, green pepper
     and onion
   1 can (28 ounces) crushed tomatoes
   1 can (15 ounces) tomato sauce
   1 can (6 ounces) tomato paste
  1/2 cup grated Parmesan cheese
  1/2 cup beef broth *or* red wine
  3/4 teaspoon *each* aniseed, seasoned salt,
     pepper, garlic powder, brown sugar, dried
     basil and oregano
   4 cups coarsely chopped fresh spinach
Hot cooked pasta
   2 cups (8 ounces) shredded mozzarella
     cheese
  1/4 cup cooked crumbled bacon

In a Dutch oven, cook and crumble sausage until browned; drain. Add mushrooms, carrot, green pepper and onion; saute for 5 minutes. Add tomatoes, sauce, paste, Parmesan, broth and seasonings; cover and simmer for 1 hour. Add spinach; heat through. Serve over pasta; top with mozzarella and bacon. **Yield:** 8-10 servings.

ONE-SKILLET SPAGHETTI
(Pictured at right)

I call this medley my "homemade hamburger helper". Everything—including the spaghetti—cooks right in the same skillet. I serve this meal often to my family. It's so convenient and they all really love it.
—Joanne Shew Chuk
St. Benedict, Saskatchewan

   1 pound ground beef
   2 medium onions, chopped
   1 package (7 ounces) ready-cut spaghetti

   1 can (28 ounces) diced tomatoes, undrained
  3/4 cup chopped green pepper
  1/2 cup water
   1 can (8 ounces) sliced mushrooms, drained
   1 teaspoon chili powder
   1 teaspoon dried oregano
   1 teaspoon sugar
   1 teaspoon salt
   1 cup (4 ounces) shredded cheddar cheese

In a large skillet, brown beef and onions; drain. Stir in uncooked spaghetti and the next eight ingredients; bring to a boil. Reduce heat; cover and simmer for 30 minutes or until the spaghetti is tender. Sprinkle with cheese; cover and heat until melted. **Yield:** 4-6 servings.

PORK CHOP SUPPER

This is a great way to serve pork chops. It's so easy to prepare. You can just let it simmer while you do your other chores. This was one of my mother's favorite meals to make on washday. —Ruth Andrewson
Leavenworth, Washington

   6 pork loin chops (3/4 inch thick)
  1/2 cup all-purpose flour
   2 tablespoons olive *or* vegetable oil
   2 teaspoons dried thyme
   2 teaspoons salt
  1/4 teaspoon pepper
   4 large potatoes (about 2-1/4 pounds)
   5 medium carrots, sliced 1/4 inch thick
   1 medium onion, cut into wedges
   3 cups beef broth

Dredge pork in flour. Heat oil in a large skillet; brown the chops on both sides. Sprinkle with thyme, salt and pepper. Peel potatoes and cut into 3/4-in. cubes; add to skillet along with the carrots and onion. Pour broth over all; bring to a boil. Reduce heat; cover and simmer for 40-50 minutes or until pork and vegetables are tender. **Yield:** 6 servings.

SWEET-AND-SOUR POT ROAST
(Pictured above)

I grew up on a farm and we ate beef often. I was so pleased to find this recipe since it gives pot roast a new mouth-watering flavor. I'm always looking for no-fuss delicious meals, and this slow-cooked supper is definitely one of them. —Erica Warkentin
Dundas, Ontario

  12 small white potatoes, peeled
   1 boneless beef chuck roast (about 3 pounds)
   1 tablespoon cooking oil
   1 cup chopped onion
   1 can (15 ounces) tomato sauce
 1/4 cup packed brown sugar
   2 to 3 tablespoons Worcestershire sauce
   2 tablespoons cider vinegar
   1 teaspoon salt

Place potatoes in a slow cooker. Trim fat from roast; brown in hot oil on all sides in a skillet. Place meat in the slow cooker. Discard all but 1 tablespoon drippings from skillet; saute onion until tender. Stir in tomato sauce, brown sugar, Worcestershire sauce, vinegar and salt. Pour over meat and potatoes. Cover and cook on high for 4-5 hours or until meat is tender. Before serving, pour sauce into a skillet. Cook and stir over medium-high heat until thickened; serve with potatoes and meat. **Yield:** 6-8 servings.

RABBIT WITH TARRAGON SAUCE

Golden rabbit pieces covered in a savory herbed gravy make this a satisfying, stick-to-your-ribs main dish. One of my favorite herbs, tarragon, provides subtle flavor that goes so well with rabbit. —Yvonne Kessler
Pangman, Saskatchewan

 1/2 cup all-purpose flour
   2 teaspoons dried tarragon

1-1/2 teaspoons salt
   1 teaspoon pepper
   2 rabbits (2 to 2-1/2 pounds *each*), cut up
 1/4 cup butter *or* margarine
 1/4 cup cooking oil
   2 cups chicken broth

In a resealable plastic bag, combine flour, tarragon, salt and pepper. Add the rabbit pieces, one at a time, and shake well. In a large skillet, melt butter; add oil. Saute the rabbit pieces, a few at a time, until browned. Add broth; cover and simmer for 50-60 minutes or until tender. Thicken the pan juices if desired. **Yield:** 8 servings.

MEXICAN-STYLE SPAGHETTI

A good friend of mine shared this delicous recipe with me. When my family gets tired of the same old spaghetti, I like to serve this dish for a change! It provides a flavorful alternative to the Italian version. It's also a great dish when you don't have a lot of time to spend in the kitchen. —Mary Detweiler
West Farmington, Ohio

✓ **This tasty dish uses less sugar, salt and fat. Recipe includes *Diabetic Exchanges*.**

   2 pounds ground beef
   2 medium onions, chopped
   1 medium green pepper, chopped
   3 garlic cloves, minced
   1 can (29 ounces) tomato puree
   1 can (15-1/2 ounces) kidney beans, rinsed and drained
   1 cup water
 1/4 cup chopped fresh parsley
   2 tablespoons chili powder
   1 teaspoon ground cumin
   1 teaspoon dried marjoram
   1 teaspoon dried oregano
   1 teaspoon salt, optional
 1/4 to 1/2 teaspoon cayenne pepper
   1 package (12 ounces) spaghetti, cooked and drained

In a Dutch oven, brown beef, onions, green pepper and garlic; drain. Add the next 10 ingredients and mix well. Cover and simmer for 2 hours, stirring occasionally. Serve over spaghetti. **Yield:** 8 servings. **Diabetic Exchanges:** One serving (1 cup sauce prepared without salt, served with 1-1/2 ounces spaghetti) equals 3 starch, 2 lean meat, 2 vegetable; also, 379 calories, 699 mg sodium, 61 mg cholesterol, 59 gm carbohydrate, 35 gm protein, 4 gm fat.

STEAK 'N' GRAVY

Slow cooking in a zesty tomato sauce for hours helps the round steak become nice and tender. This nicely spiced steak and gravy makes a satisfying meal served over rice or mashed potatoes. —Betty Janway
Ruston, Louisiana

    1 **pound round steak, trimmed**
    1 **tablespoon cooking oil**
1-1/2 **cups water**
    1 **can (8 ounces) tomato sauce**
    1 **teaspoon ground cumin**
    1 **teaspoon garlic powder**
1/2 **teaspoon salt**
1/4 **teaspoon pepper**
    2 **tablespoons all-purpose flour**
1/4 **cup cold water**
Hot cooked rice *or* mashed potatoes

Cut beef into bite-size pieces; brown in oil in a skillet. Transfer to a slow cooker. Cover with water; add tomato sauce and seasonings. Cover and cook on low for 8 hours, or on high for 4 hours, or until meat is tender. In a small bowl, combine flour and cold water to make a paste; stir into liquid in slow cooker. Cover and cook on high 30 minutes longer or until gravy is thickened. Serve over rice or potatoes. **Yield:** 4 servings.

TURKEY POTATO PANCAKES

My husband and our four children like pancakes, and I appreciate quick suppers...so I gave this recipe a try when I saw it. Adding turkey turns golden side-dish potato pancakes into a simple main dish we all savor. —Kathi Duerr
Fulda, Minnesota

    3 **eggs**
    3 **cups shredded peeled potatoes**
1-1/2 **cups finely chopped cooked turkey**
1/4 **cup sliced green onions with tops**
    2 **tablespoons all-purpose flour**
1-1/2 **teaspoons salt**
Cooking oil
Cranberry sauce, optional

In a bowl, beat the eggs. Add potatoes, turkey, onions, flour and salt; mix well. Heat about 1/4 in. of oil in a large skillet. Pour batter by 1/3 cupfuls into hot oil. Fry 5-6 minutes on each side or until potatoes are tender and pancakes are golden brown. Serve with cranberry sauce if desired. **Yield:** 12 pancakes.

BLUEBERRY SOUR CREAM PANCAKES

(Pictured below)

When our family of 10 goes blueberry picking, we have a bounty of blueberries in no time. They taste great in these melt-in-your-mouth pancakes. —Paula Hadley
Forest Hill, Louisiana

1/2 **cup sugar**
    2 **tablespoons cornstarch**
    1 **cup water**
    4 **cups fresh *or* frozen blueberries**
PANCAKES:
    2 **cups all-purpose flour**
1/4 **cup sugar**
    4 **teaspoons baking powder**
1/2 **teaspoon salt**
    2 **eggs**
1-1/2 **cups milk**
    1 **cup (8 ounces) sour cream**
1/3 **cup butter *or* margarine, melted**
    1 **cup fresh *or* frozen blueberries**

In a medium saucepan, combine sugar and cornstarch. Gradually stir in water. Add blueberries; bring to a boil over medium heat. Boil for 2 minutes, stirring constantly. Remove from the heat; cover and keep warm. For pancakes, combine dry ingredients in a bowl. In another bowl, beat the eggs. Add milk, sour cream and butter; mix well. Stir into dry ingredients just until blended. Fold in the blueberries. Pour batter by 1/4 cupfuls onto a greased hot griddle; turn when bubbles form on top of pancakes. Cook until the second side is golden brown. Serve with blueberry topping. **Yield:** about 20 pancakes (3-1/2 cups topping).

CHICKEN WITH CUCUMBERS

(Pictured above)

Although most often eaten raw, cucumber can also be enjoyed cooked in recipes like this. This interesting chicken dish has an irresistible fresh flavor.
—Angela Avedon
Moorseville, North Carolina

    1 broiler/fryer chicken (3-1/2 to 4 pounds),
       cut up
    2 tablespoons cooking oil
  1/4 pound fresh mushrooms, sliced
    1 garlic clove, minced
    3 tablespoons all-purpose flour
1-3/4 cups water
    1 tablespoon chicken bouillon granules
    2 large cucumbers
    1 cup (8 ounces) sour cream

In a large skillet over medium heat, brown chicken in oil. Remove chicken and set aside. To drippings, add mushrooms and garlic; saute 2 minutes. Stir in flour until mushrooms are coated. Gradually add water and bouillon; cook and stir over medium heat until bubbly. Return chicken to skillet; bring to a boil. Reduce heat; cover and simmer for 30 minutes, stirring occasionally. Meanwhile, slice one cucumber into thin slices; set aside. Peel remaining cucumber; slice in half lengthwise and remove seeds. Cut into 1-in. chunks. Add to skillet and simmer for 20 minutes or until chicken juices run clear. Stir sour cream into sauce; heat through but do not boil. Garnish with reserved cucumber slices. **Yield:** 4-6 servings.

NAVY BEAN STEW

Whenever my husband and I get a taste for a nice hearty stew, this recipe immediately comes to mind. My husband's on a low-salt diet, so this dish is perfect for him. We both enjoy this flavorful stew.
—Margaret Bourgoujian
Oswego, New York

    1 pound dry navy beans
    4 quarts water, *divided*
1-1/2 pounds Italian sausage, cut into 1/4-inch
       slices
    2 cans (14-1/2 ounces *each*) chicken broth
    2 cups chopped onion
1-1/2 cups thinly sliced carrots
    1 can (15 to 16 ounces) whole kernel corn
    1 tablespoon minced fresh parsley
1-1/2 teaspoons Italian seasoning

Soak beans in 2 qts. of water overnight; drain. Place in a large saucepan and add remaining water. Bring to a boil; boil for 2 minutes. Reduce heat; cover and simmer for 60-70 minutes or until beans are tender. Drain. In a Dutch oven, brown sausage. Add broth, onion, carrots, corn, parsley, Italian seasoning and beans. Cover and bake at 350° for 30 minutes. Uncover and bake 30 minutes longer or until bubbly. **Yield:** 8-10 servings.

RICE-STUFFED PEPPERS

Mother used to fix this wonderful, easy dish when we had company. She was from a family of fantastic Cajun cooks, so our food was always well-seasoned. The cheese sauce in this recipe sets these stuffed peppers apart from any others I've tried. —Lisa Easley
Longview, Texas

    2 pounds ground beef
    1 medium onion, chopped
    1 small green pepper, chopped
    2 garlic cloves, minced
1-1/2 teaspoons salt
  1/2 teaspoon pepper
    1 can (10 ounces) diced tomatoes with
       chilies, undrained
    1 can (14-1/2 ounces) diced tomatoes,
       undrained
    1 can (15 ounces) tomato sauce
3-3/4 cups water
    1 tablespoon ground cumin
    3 cups uncooked instant rice
    4 medium green peppers
CHEESE SAUCE:
1-1/2 pounds process American cheese, cubed
    1 can (10 ounces) diced tomatoes with
       chilies, undrained

1/2 cup chili sauce
1/4 cup packed brown sugar
1 teaspoon soy sauce
1/8 teaspoon cayenne pepper

Cook cabbage in boiling water just until the leaves fall off head. Reserve 10 large leaves (save remaining cabbage for another use). Combine pork, barley, garlic, onion, soy sauce, ketchup, brown sugar, ginger, salt and pepper; mix well. Spoon about 1/2 cup onto each cabbage leaf. Fold in sides, starting at an unfolded edge; roll up completely to enclose filling. Place rolls, seam side down, in a greased 13-in. x 9-in. x 2-in. baking dish. In a saucepan over medium heat, combine sauce ingredients; heat until sugar is melted and sauce is hot. Pour over rolls. Cover and bake at 350° for 80-90 minutes. **Yield:** 8-10 servings.

COUNTRY-FRIED STEAKS

(Pictured above)

This down-home recipe calls for cube steak instead of round steak, so there's no need to pound the meat. I just dip and coat the beef, then cook it in my cast-iron skillet. They always turn out scrumptious.
—Bonnie Malloy
Norwood, Pennsylvania

5 tablespoons all-purpose flour, *divided*
1/4 cup cornmeal
1/2 teaspoon salt
1/4 teaspoon pepper
4 beef cube steaks (about 1 pound)
1 egg white
1 teaspoon water
2 tablespoons cooking oil, *divided*

GRAVY:
1 tablespoon butter *or* margarine
2 tablespoons all-purpose flour
1-1/2 cups milk
1 teaspoon beef bouillon granules
1/2 teaspoon dried marjoram
1/4 teaspoon dried thyme
1/8 teaspoon pepper

Combine 3 tablespoons flour, cornmeal, salt and pepper; set aside. Coat steaks with remaining flour. Beat egg white and water; dip steaks, then dredge in cornmeal mixture. In a skillet over medium-high heat, cook two steaks in 1 tablespoon oil for 5-7 minutes on each side or until crisp, lightly browned and cooked as desired. Remove steaks and keep warm. Repeat with the remaining oil and steaks. Meanwhile, for gravy, melt butter in a saucepan; stir in flour until well blended. Gradually add milk; bring to a boil over medium heat. Boil for 2 minutes, stirring constantly; reduce heat to medium-low. Add bouillon, marjoram, thyme and pepper; simmer, uncovered, for 4-5 minutes, stirring occasionally. Serve over steaks. **Yield:** 4 servings.

COOL CUCUMBER CHICKEN

My husband really likes chicken and he's especially fond of this recipe. It's so versatile because it can be served hot or cold. —Andria Barosi-Stampone
Randolph, New Jersey

✓ **This tasty dish uses less sugar, salt and fat. Recipe includes *Diabetic Exchanges*.**

4 boneless skinless chicken breast halves (1 pound)
2 tablespoons olive *or* vegetable oil
1 medium cucumber, seeded and chopped
1/2 cup plain low-fat yogurt
2 tablespoons reduced-fat mayonnaise
1 tablespoon minced fresh dill
1/8 teaspoon pepper

Brush both sides of chicken with oil. Broil 5 in. from the heat or grill over medium coals, turning occasionally, for 10-14 minutes or until juices run clear. Meanwhile, combine remaining ingredients in a small bowl. Spoon over warm chicken; serve immediately. Or, to serve cold, spoon sauce over chicken and refrigerate several hours or overnight. **Yield:** 4 servings. **Diabetic Exchanges:** One serving equals 4 very lean meat, 1-1/2 fat, 1 vegetable; also, 256 calories, 134 mg sodium, 75 mg cholesterol, 7 gm carbohydrate, 29 gm protein, 12 gm fat.

GOLDEN CATFISH FILLETS

(Pictured above)

These delicious fillets cook up moist with an irresistible crisp, golden coating. Whether your fish comes from a nearby lake or the grocery store, it makes a terrific summer meal. —Tammy Moore-Worthington
Artesia, New Mexico

    1 egg white
    1 cup milk
    1 cup cornmeal
  3/4 teaspoon salt
  1/4 teaspoon garlic powder
  1/4 to 1/2 teaspoon cayenne pepper
  1/8 teaspoon pepper
    4 catfish fillets (8 ounces *each*)
Cooking oil
Lemon *or* lime wedges, optional

In a shallow bowl, beat the egg white until foamy; add milk and mix well. In another shallow bowl, combine the cornmeal, salt, garlic powder, cayenne and pepper. Dip the fillets in milk mixture, then coat with cornmeal mixture. Heat 1/4 in. of oil in a large skillet; fry fish over medium-high for 3-4 minutes per side or until it flakes easily with a fork. Garnish with lemon or lime if desired. **Yield:** 4 servings.

BLUEBERRY FRENCH TOAST

This is the most flavorful unique breakfast dish I've ever tasted. But it's hard to tell whether it's a breakfast dish or a dessert. With luscious berries inside and in a sauce that drizzles over each slice, it looks and tastes more like a dessert. The recipe was shared with me by a local blueberry grower when I asked for suggestions on how to use this juicy fruit. —Patricia Walls
Aurora, Minnesota

   12 slices day-old white bread, crusts removed
    2 packages (8 ounces *each*) cream cheese
    1 cup fresh *or* frozen blueberries
   12 eggs
    2 cups milk
  1/3 cup maple syrup *or* honey
SAUCE:
    1 cup sugar
    2 tablespoons cornstarch
    1 cup water
    1 cup fresh *or* frozen blueberries
    1 tablespoon butter *or* margarine

Cut bread into 1-in. cubes; place half in a greased 13-in. x 9-in. x 2-in. baking dish. Cut cream cheese into 1-in. cubes; place over bread. Top with blueberries and remaining bread. In a large bowl, beat eggs. Add milk and syrup; mix well. Pour over bread mixture. Cover and chill 8 hours or overnight. Remove from the refrigerator 30 minutes before baking. Cover and bake at 350° for 30 minutes. Uncover; bake 25-30 minutes more or until golden brown and the center is set. In a saucepan, combine sugar and cornstarch; add water. Bring to a boil over medium heat; boil for 3 minutes, stirring constantly. Stir in blueberries; reduce heat. Simmer for 8-10 minutes or until berries have burst. Stir in butter until melted. Serve over French toast. **Yield:** 6-8 servings (1-3/4 cups sauce).

TURKEY PRIMAVERA

We grow herbs and vegetables in our garden, so I incorporate them into recipes whenever possible. This dish has tender turkey and mushrooms, onions and green pepper covered in a zippy tomato sauce. It's a favorite among our family and friends. —Zita Wilensky
North Miami Beach, Florida

  1/4 cup all-purpose flour
    2 teaspoons minced fresh parsley
1-1/2 pounds turkey tenderloins, cubed
    2 tablespoons olive *or* vegetable oil
  1/2 cup chicken broth
    1 cup sliced fresh mushrooms
    1 medium onion, chopped
    4 garlic cloves, minced
  1/2 medium green pepper, chopped
    1 can (14-1/2 ounces) beef broth
  3/4 cup tomato puree

1/2 teaspoon dried thyme
1/2 teaspoon dried rosemary, crushed
1/2 teaspoon dried basil
1 bay leaf
1/4 teaspoon salt
1/8 teaspoon pepper
Hot cooked fettuccine *or* spaghetti
Parmesan cheese, optional

Combine flour and parsley; add turkey and toss to coat. In a skillet, brown turkey in oil; remove with a slotted spoon and set aside. In the same skillet, combine chicken broth, mushrooms, onion, garlic and green pepper. Cook and stir for 3-4 minutes. Add beef broth, tomato puree and seasonings. Cook and stir for 20-25 minutes or until sauce is desired consistency. Add turkey; heat through. Remove the bay leaf. Serve over pasta; sprinkle with Parmesan if desired. **Yield:** 4-6 servings.

HEARTY RIBS AND BEANS

This is one of my favorite ways to prepare pork spareribs. The celery and red pepper really add a lot of color to this meaty main meal, and it always gets rave reviews from family and friends.
—Marlene Muckenhirn
Delano, Minnesota

    3 to 3-1/2 pounds country-style pork
      spareribs
1/4 cup water
    1 can (14-1/2 ounces) tomato sauce
    1 envelope dry onion soup mix
1/3 cup packed brown sugar
    2 tablespoons prepared mustard
1/8 teaspoon hot pepper sauce
    2 cans (15-1/2 ounces *each*) great northern
      beans, rinsed and drained
    2 cans (16 ounces *each*) kidney beans,
      rinsed and drained
1-1/2 cups thinly sliced celery
    1 sweet red pepper, thinly sliced

Place ribs in an ungreased 13-in. x 9-in. x 2-in. baking dish; add water. Cover and bake at 350° for 1-1/2 hours. Drain, reserving liquid; skim fat. Set ribs aside. Add enough water to liquid to equal 1 cup; place in a saucepan. Add the tomato sauce, soup mix, sugar, mustard and hot pepper sauce. Simmer for 10 minutes; remove 1/2 cup. To the remaining sauce, add beans, celery and red pepper. Pour into the baking dish; add ribs. Pour reserved sauce over ribs. Cover and bake for 45 minutes. **Yield:** 6-8 servings.

CREOLE SKILLET DINNER
(Pictured below)

While living in Canada, I sampled this colorful dish at a neighbor's. The next Christmas, I served it instead of turkey, and everyone loved it. —Bonnie Brann
Pasco, Washington

    4 cups chicken broth
2-1/2 cups uncooked long grain rice
    1 cup chopped red onion
    3 garlic cloves, minced, *divided*
1-1/4 teaspoons chili powder
    1 teaspoon salt
1/2 teaspoon ground turmeric
1/4 teaspoon pepper
    1 bay leaf
    1 sweet red pepper, julienned
    1 green pepper, julienned
    2 green onions, sliced
    1 teaspoon chopped fresh parsley
1/2 teaspoon dried basil
1/2 teaspoon dried thyme
1/4 teaspoon hot pepper sauce
    2 tablespoons butter *or* margarine
    1 cup sliced fresh mushrooms
    1 medium tomato, chopped
    1 cup frozen peas
    1 pound boneless skinless chicken breasts,
      thinly sliced
    2 tablespoons lemon juice
1/3 cup sliced almonds, toasted

In a saucepan, bring broth, rice, onion, 1 teaspoon garlic, chili powder, salt, turmeric, pepper and bay leaf to a boil. Reduce heat; cover and simmer 20 minutes or until rice is tender. Discard bay leaf. In a skillet over medium-high heat, saute the next seven ingredients and remaining garlic in butter for 2 minutes. Add mushrooms; cook until peppers are crisp-tender. Add tomato and peas; heat through. Remove from the heat. Add rice; keep warm. Over medium-high heat, cook and stir chicken in lemon juice until chicken juices run clear. Add to rice mixture; toss. Top with almonds. **Yield:** 6-8 servings.

CURRIED RICE HAM ROLLS

(Pictured above)

My mother gave me this recipe, which had been hand-ed down to her. She prepared these hearty ham rolls for church luncheons, and they were a huge success every time. I find that even people who have never tried curry rave about the flavor. —Pamela Witte
Hastings, Nebraska

> 1/2 cup chopped onion
> 2 tablespoons butter *or* margarine
> 4 cups cooked brown *or* long grain rice
> 1 tablespoon dried parsley flakes
> 1 teaspoon salt
> 1/2 teaspoon curry powder
> 12 slices deli ham (1/8 inch thick)
> 4 hard-cooked eggs, sliced

CURRY SAUCE:

> 1/4 cup butter *or* margarine
> 2 tablespoons cornstarch
> 1/4 teaspoon curry powder
> 1/4 teaspoon salt
> 2 cups milk, *divided*

In a skillet, saute onion in butter until tender, about 3 minutes. In a large bowl, combine rice, parsley, salt, curry powder and onion; mix well. Spoon about 1/3 cup down the center of each ham slice; roll up. Secure with toothpicks if desired. Place seam side down in a greased 13-in. x 9-in. x 2-in. baking pan. Arrange eggs on top. For sauce, melt butter in a saucepan. Combine cornstarch, curry powder, salt and 1/3 cup milk; mix well. Gradual-ly stir into butter. Add remaining milk; bring to a boil, stirring constantly. Cook and stir for 2 minutes. Pour over the ham rolls. Cover and bake at 375° for 25 minutes. Uncover and bake for 10 minutes. **Yield:** 6 servings.

TROPICAL CHICKEN

This hearty, colorful dish makes a convenient all-in-one meal. I serve it often, and my family never seems
to get tired of it. They like the way the sweetness of the pineapple in this recipe balances the garlic and hot pepper. —Leah Johnson
Pearl City, Hawaii

> 1 broiler/fryer chicken (3-1/2 to 4 pounds), cut up
> 3 tablespoons cooking oil, *divided*
> 3/4 cup chopped onion
> 2 garlic cloves, minced
> 3 medium tomatoes, peeled and chopped
> 3 cups fresh *or* canned pineapple chunks
> 1/4 cup pineapple juice
> 1 hot red pepper (4-1/2 to 5 inches), seeded and chopped
> 3/4 teaspoon salt
> 1/4 teaspoon pepper
> 1 can (8 ounces) sliced water chestnuts, drained
> 1/2 pound fresh snow peas
> 1 tablespoon chopped fresh chives

Hot cooked rice

In a skillet over medium heat, brown the chicken in 2 tablespoons of oil; remove and set aside. In the same skillet, saute the onion and garlic in remain-ing oil until tender. Add tomatoes, pineapple, pine-apple juice, red pepper, salt, pepper and water chestnuts. Return chicken to the pan; bring to a boil. Reduce heat; cover and simmer for 45 min-utes. Add peas and chives; cover and simmer for 10-15 minutes or until peas are tender and chick-en juices run clear. Thicken pan juices if desired. Serve over rice. **Yield:** 6 servings.

ELK PARMESAN

Wyoming is a paradise for people like us who enjoy hunting. My husband was thrilled when our jobs brought us here over 20 years ago. I've been cooking game since I was a girl, so I use recipes like this en-ticing elk dish often. With its delicious Italian flavor, this is a scrumptious meal. —Dolores Crock
Cheyenne, Wyoming

> 1-1/2 pounds boneless elk steak
> 1/4 to 1/2 teaspoon garlic salt
> 1/8 teaspoon pepper
> 1/2 cup dry Italian bread crumbs
> 1/2 cup grated Parmesan cheese
> 2 eggs
> 1/4 cup water
> 1/2 cup all-purpose flour
> 1/4 cup olive *or* vegetable oil
> 1-1/2 cups spaghetti sauce
> 6 slices mozzarella cheese

Hot cooked noodles
Snipped fresh parsley

Cut meat into six pieces; pound with a meat mallet to tenderize. Sprinkle with garlic salt and pepper. Combine bread crumbs and Parmesan cheese in a bowl. In another bowl, beat eggs with water. Dip both sides of meat into flour, then into egg mixture. Press each side of meat into crumb mixture; refrigerate for 20 minutes. Heat oil in a large skillet; brown meat on both sides. Place in a greased 13-in. x 9-in. x 2-in. baking pan. Spoon 2 tablespoons spaghetti sauce over each piece. Cover with mozzarella cheese; top with remaining spaghetti sauce. Bake, uncovered, at 350° for 30 minutes or until meat is tender. Serve over noodles; garnish with parsley if desired. **Yield:** 6 servings.

TURKEY DRUMSTICK DINNER
(Pictured above)

I love this recipe because it uses economical turkey drumsticks. Our family and friends enjoy this savory meat-and-potatoes meal. The flavorful sauce turns plain drumsticks into a feast. —Alice Balliet
Kane, Pennsylvania

  4 **uncooked turkey drumsticks (about 3 pounds)**
  2 **tablespoons cooking oil**
  1 **tablespoon butter *or* margarine**
  1 **medium onion, sliced**
  1 **can (14-1/2 ounces) stewed tomatoes**
  3 **chicken bouillon cubes**
  1 **teaspoon garlic salt**
1/2 **teaspoon dried oregano**
1/2 **teaspoon dried basil**
  4 **large potatoes, peeled, cooked and quartered**
  2 **medium zucchini, cut into 3/4-inch slices**
  2 **tablespoons cornstarch**
  2 **tablespoons water**
Snipped fresh parsley

In a large skillet, brown drumsticks in oil and butter. Place in a 3-qt. Dutch oven. Top with onion slices. In the same skillet, heat tomatoes, bouillon and seasonings until bouillon is dissolved. Pour over the drumsticks. Cover and bake at 325° for 2 hours, basting once or twice. Add the potatoes and zucchini. Cover and bake for 20 minutes. Remove drumsticks and vegetables to a serving dish and keep warm. Combine the cornstarch and water until smooth; stir into tomato mixture. Return to the oven, uncovered, for 10-15 minutes or until slightly thickened. Pour over drumsticks and vegetables. Sprinkle with parsley. **Yield:** 4 servings.

BEEF AND ASPARAGUS STIR-FRY

With tasty tender slices of beef and fresh colorful vegetables, this mouth-watering stir-fry was designated "a keeper" by my husband the first time I made it. He loves the beef and asparagus, and I appreciate how quick it is to make. —JoLynn Hill
Roosevelt, Utah

  2 **tablespoons cornstarch**
1/2 **cup plus 2 tablespoons water, *divided***
1/2 **teaspoon salt**
1/4 **teaspoon pepper**
1/8 **teaspoon hot pepper sauce**
  1 **pound boneless round steak (3/4 inch thick)**
  3 **tablespoons cooking oil, *divided***
  2 **cups fresh asparagus pieces *or* broccoli florets**
  1 **cup sliced cauliflower**
  1 **small sweet red *or* green pepper, julienned**
  1 **small onion, cut into 1/4-inch wedges**
  2 **teaspoons beef bouillon granules**
  1 **tablespoon soy sauce**
  1 **tablespoon ketchup**
  1 **teaspoon red wine vinegar**
Hot cooked rice

Combine cornstarch, 2 tablespoons water, salt, pepper and hot pepper sauce. Slice beef into thin 3-in. strips; toss with the cornstarch mixture. In a large skillet or wok over medium-high heat, stir-fry half of the beef in 1 tablespoon oil until cooked as desired; remove from the skillet. Repeat with remaining beef and 1 tablespoon oil. Stir-fry the asparagus and cauliflower in remaining oil for 4 minutes. Add red pepper and onion; stir-fry for 2 minutes. Return beef to skillet. Combine the bouillon, soy sauce, ketchup, vinegar and remaining water; add to the skillet. Cook and stir for 2 minutes. Serve over rice. **Yield:** 6 servings.

Breads, Rolls & Muffins

Oven-fresh quick breads, coffee cakes, muffins, buns and rolls are an enticing way to invite family and friends to the table... morning, noon and night!

BANANA CRUMB MUFFINS

I've tried many banana muffin and quick bread recipes. But this is definitely one of my favorites. These are the only kind of muffin our 4-year-old will eat.
—*Wendy Masters*
Grand Valley, Ontario

      1-1/2 cups all-purpose flour
          1 teaspoon baking soda
          1 teaspoon baking powder
      1/2 teaspoon salt
          3 large ripe bananas, mashed
      3/4 cup sugar
          1 egg, lightly beaten
      1/3 cup butter *or* margarine, melted
TOPPING:
      1/3 cup packed brown sugar
          1 tablespoon all-purpose flour
      1/8 teaspoon ground cinnamon
          1 tablespoon cold butter *or* margarine

In a large bowl, combine dry ingredients. Combine bananas, sugar, egg and butter; mix well. Stir into dry ingredients just until moistened. Fill greased or paper-lined muffin cups three-fourths full. Combine the first three topping ingredients; cut in butter until crumbly. Sprinkle over muffins. Bake at 375° for 18-20 minutes or until muffins test done. Cool in pan 10 minutes before removing to a wire rack. **Yield:** about 1 dozen.

POPPY SEED KOLACHES

Preparing and sharing recipes I made as a boy are what keep me young at heart. And since I'm retired, I have plenty of time to bake treats like this for our children, grandchildren and great-grandchildren.
—*Carl Wanasek*
Rogers, Arkansas

          1 package (1/4 ounce) active dry yeast
      1/4 cup warm water (110° to 115°)
      1/2 cup butter *or* margarine, melted
          1 cup milk
          1 egg plus 2 egg yolks
      1/4 cup sugar
      3/4 teaspoon salt
      1/4 teaspoon ground mace
      1/4 teaspoon grated lemon peel
          3 to 3-1/2 cups all-purpose flour
Additional melted butter *or* margarine
POPPY SEED FILLING:
      3/4 cup poppy seeds
      1/2 cup water
      1/2 cup milk

DROP DOUGHNUTS

(Pictured above)

For 30 years, I've been using leftover mashed potatoes to make these light, fluffy doughnuts. The recipe was originally created by my neighbor's mother-in-law. They're great for breakfast or as a snack.
—*Marilyn Kleinfall*
Elk Grove Village, Illinois

      1/2 cup mashed potatoes (mashed with milk
          and butter)
      1/4 cup sugar
          1 egg, beaten
      1/2 cup sour cream
      1/2 teaspoon vanilla extract
      1-1/2 cups all-purpose flour
      1/2 teaspoon baking soda
      1/4 teaspoon baking powder
Cooking oil for deep-fat frying
Additional sugar *or* confectioners' sugar,
      optional

In a bowl, combine potatoes, sugar, egg, sour cream and vanilla. Combine dry ingredients; stir into potato mixture. Heat oil in an electric skillet or deep-fat fryer to 375°. Drop dough by teaspoonfuls, 5 to 6 at a time, into hot oil. Fry for 1 minute per side or until golden brown. Drain on paper towels. Roll in sugar if desired. Serve immediately. **Yield:** 3 to 3-1/2 dozen.

1/4 cup raisins
1/2 cup sugar
  2 teaspoons butter *or* margarine
1/2 teaspoon vanilla extract
1/4 teaspoon ground cinnamon
1/4 cup graham cracker crumbs
Confectioners' sugar glaze, optional

In a mixing bowl, dissolve yeast in water. Add the next seven ingredients and 2 cups of flour; beat until smooth. Add enough remaining flour to form a soft dough. Turn onto a floured board; knead until smooth and elastic, about 6-8 minutes. Place in a greased bowl, turning once to grease top. Cover and let rise in a warm place until doubled, about 1 hour. Punch dough down. Shape into walnut-size balls; roll each into a 2-1/2-in. circle. Place 2 in. apart on greased baking sheets; brush with butter. Cover and let rise until doubled, about 30 minutes. Meanwhile, in a saucepan, bring poppy seeds and water to a boil; boil 1 minute or until thickened. Add milk and raisins; simmer for 10 minutes. Add sugar, butter, vanilla and cinnamon; simmer for 5 minutes. Remove from the heat; stir in crumbs. Make a depression, about 1-1/2 in. in diameter, in the center of each roll; fill with 2 teaspoons of filling. Bake at 400° for 7-10 minutes or until golden brown. Cool on wire racks. Drizzle with glaze if desired. **Yield:** 3 dozen.

CINNAMON BREAD ROLLS

My aunt shared this recipe with me years ago. Now my kids and I make them assembly-line style. They love to help prepare these creamy rolls, but I think they enjoy eating them even more! —Cathy Stanfield
Bernie, Missouri

24 **slices soft white sandwich bread, crust removed**
 2 **packages (8 ounces *each*) cream cheese, softened**
1-1/2 **cups sugar, *divided***
 2 **egg yolks**
 2 **teaspoons ground cinnamon**
 1 **cup butter *or* margarine, melted**

Flatten bread with a rolling pin. In a mixing bowl, beat cream cheese, 1/2 cup sugar and yolks. Spread on bread; roll up, jelly-roll style. Combine cinnamon and remaining sugar. Lightly dip rolls in butter, then in cinnamon-sugar. Place on ungreased baking sheets. Bake at 350° for 20 minutes. **Yield:** 2 dozen.

BLUEBERRY STREUSEL COFFEE CAKE
(Pictured below)

This coffee cake smells wonderful as it bakes and tastes even better. The moist cake filled with juicy berries and crunchy pecans is a family favorite. It never lasts long at our house. —Lori Snedden
Sherman, Texas

  2 **cups all-purpose flour**
3/4 **cup sugar**
  2 **teaspoons baking powder**
1/4 **teaspoon salt**
  1 **egg, beaten**
1/2 **cup milk**
1/2 **cup butter *or* margarine, softened**
  1 **cup fresh *or* frozen blueberries**
  1 **cup chopped pecans**
STREUSEL:
1/2 **cup sugar**
1/3 **cup all-purpose flour**
1/4 **cup cold butter *or* margarine**

In a mixing bowl, combine flour, sugar, baking powder and salt. Add egg, milk and butter; beat well. Fold in blueberries and pecans. Spread into a greased 9-in. square baking pan. In another bowl, combine sugar and flour; cut in the butter until crumbly. Sprinkle over the batter. Bake at 375° for 35-40 minutes or until a wooden pick inserted near the center comes out clean. **Yield:** 9 servings.

out clean. Cool in pans 10 minutes before removing to wire racks to cool completely. **Yield:** 3 loaves.

SOUR CREAM 'N' CHIVE BISCUITS
(Pictured on the front cover)

I grow chives in my front yard and like to use them in as many recipes as I can. These moist, tender biscuits are delectable as well as attractive.
—Lucille Proctor
Panguitch, Utah

   2 cups all-purpose flour
   1 tablespoon baking powder
1/2 teaspoon salt
1/4 teaspoon baking soda
1/3 cup shortening
3/4 cup sour cream
1/4 cup milk
1/4 cup snipped fresh chives

In a bowl, combine dry ingredients. Cut in shortening until mixture resembles coarse crumbs. With a fork, stir in sour cream, milk and chives until the mixture forms a ball. On a lightly floured surface, knead five to six times. Roll to 3/4-in. thickness; cut with a 2-in. biscuit cutter. Place on an ungreased baking sheet. Bake at 350° for 12-15 minutes or until golden brown. **Yield:** 12-15 biscuits.

ORANGE KNOTS
(Pictured above right)

These orange rolls are a little time-consuming to prepare, but my family tells me they're definitely worth the extra effort. They bake up feather-light with a sweet and tangy flavor. We love them on Easter morning.
—Bernice Morris
Marshfield, Missouri

   1 package (1/4 ounce) active dry yeast
1/4 cup warm water (110° to 115°)
   1 cup warm milk (110° to 115°)
1/3 cup sugar
1/2 cup butter *or* margarine, softened
   1 teaspoon salt
   2 eggs
1/4 cup orange juice
   2 tablespoons grated orange peel
5-1/4 to 5-3/4 cups all-purpose flour
ORANGE ICING:
   1 cup confectioners' sugar

APPLE ORANGE BREAD
(Pictured above)

I love to take advantage of the wonderful citrus fruits from our state. I make these lovely loaves, with refreshing orange zip, for our church's Christmas bazaar bake sale. They don't last long!
—Norma Poole
Auburndale, Florida

   2 large unpeeled baking apples, cored and quartered
   1 large unpeeled orange, quartered
1-1/2 cups raisins
2/3 cup shortening
   2 cups sugar
   4 eggs
   1 teaspoon lemon extract
   4 cups all-purpose flour
   2 teaspoons baking powder
1-1/2 teaspoons baking soda
   1 teaspoon salt
2/3 cup orange juice
   1 cup chopped walnuts

In a blender or food processor, process apples, orange and raisins until finely chopped; set aside. In a large mixing bowl, cream shortening and sugar. Add eggs, one at a time, beating well after each addition; beat until light and fluffy. Beat in extract. Combine dry ingredients; add to creamed mixture alternately with orange juice. Stir in fruit mixture and nuts. Pour into three greased 8-in. x 4-in. x 2-in. loaf pans. Bake at 350° for 50-55 minutes or until a wooden pick inserted near the center comes

each into a 5-in. rope. Twist two pieces together. Moisten ends with water and pinch to seal. Dip in butter, then in cheese mixture. Place on a greased baking sheet. Bake at 400° for 10-14 minutes or until golden brown. Serve with pizza sauce for dipping if desired. **Yield:** 16 servings.

"THE BROWN BAG, a small restaurant/bakery in Rockland, Maine, makes wonderful muffins," informs Eunice Stadler of South Thomaston.

"My favorite kind is called A.M. Delight Muffins. They're full of apples, raisins, carrots, coconut and nuts…people around here love them. I hope the owners will share the recipe with *Taste of Home!*"

Happy to oblige is Anne Maher, co-owner of The Brown Bag with her sisters, Claire Holmes, Barbara Fifield and Debra Orosz.

"We've been making A.M. Delight Muffins daily since we opened back in 1987," relates Anne. "The recipe is a combination of our favorites from home. We bake at least 30 dozen muffins for the shop every morning."

Building on their tradition of made-from-scratch, wholesome food, the sisters recently opened a second location in Brewer, Maine.

A.M. DELIGHT MUFFINS

        2 cups all-purpose flour
    3/4 cup sugar
        2 teaspoons baking soda
1-1/2 teaspoons ground cinnamon
    1/2 teaspoon salt
        3 eggs
    1/2 cup vegetable oil
    1/2 cup milk
1-1/2 teaspoons vanilla extract
        2 cups chopped peeled apples
        2 cups grated carrots
    1/2 cup flaked coconut
    1/2 cup raisins
    1/2 cup sliced almonds

In a large bowl, combine flour, sugar, baking soda, cinnamon and salt. In another bowl, beat eggs; add oil, milk and vanilla. Mix well; stir into dry ingredients just until moistened. Fold in the remaining ingredients. Fill greased or paper-lined muffin cups three-fourths full. Bake at 375° for 20-25 minutes or until muffins test done. **Yield:** 1-1/2 dozen.

---

2 tablespoons orange juice
1 teaspoon grated orange peel

In a mixing bowl, dissolve yeast in water. Add the next seven ingredients and 3 cups flour; beat until smooth. Add enough remaining flour to form a soft dough. Turn onto a floured board; knead until smooth and elastic, about 6-8 minutes. Place in a greased bowl, turning once to grease top. Cover and let rise in a warm place until doubled, about 2 hours. Punch dough down; roll into a 16-in. x 10-in. rectangle, about 1/2 in. thick. Cut into 10-in. x 3/4-in. strips; roll lightly and tie into a knot. Place on greased baking sheets; tuck the ends under. Cover and let rise until doubled, about 30 minutes. Bake at 400° for 10-12 minutes or until golden brown. Cool on wire racks. Combine icing ingredients; drizzle over rolls. **Yield:** 1-1/2 dozen.

PARMESAN BREADSTICKS

These soft breadsticks are so easy to make and have wonderful homemade flavor. We enjoy them warm from the oven dipped in pizza sauce. But they also taste great with a spaghetti dinner. —Marlene Muckenhirn Delano, Minnesota

    3/4 cup grated Parmesan cheese
1-1/2 teaspoons dried Italian seasoning
    1 loaf (1 pound) frozen white bread dough, thawed
1/4 cup butter *or* margarine, melted
Warm pizza sauce, optional

Combine cheese and Italian seasoning in a shallow bowl; set aside. Divide dough into 32 sections; roll

cardamom. Cut in butter until crumbly. Add yeast mixture and whole egg; mix well. Stir in cherries, raisins and pecans. Turn onto a floured board; knead until smooth and elastic, about 6-8 minutes. Place in a greased bowl, turning once to grease top. Cover and let rise in a warm place for 1 hour (dough will not double in size). Punch dough down; divide into four pieces. Roll three pieces into 15-in. ropes. Braid ropes; place on a greased baking sheet. Divide last portion of dough in half; roll each into a 15-in. rope. Twist ropes. Press an indentation down the center of braided loaf; place twisted dough in indentation. Cover and let rise until doubled, about 30 minutes. Beat egg yolk and water; brush over loaf. Bake at 350° for 20 minutes. Cover loosely with foil; bake 20-25 minutes more. Cool on a wire rack. Combine sugar and milk; drizzle over loaf. Decorate with cherries if desired. **Yield:** 1 loaf.

PINEAPPLE NUT BREAD

This lovely loaf has true Hawaiian taste with lots of luscious pineapple and macadamia nuts. Welcome your family and friends with a tempting slice today.
—Brittany Jewett
Ewa Beach, Hawaii

      3 tablespoons butter *or* margarine, softened
      2 eggs
  3/4 cup packed brown sugar
1-3/4 cups all-purpose flour
      2 teaspoons baking powder
  1/2 teaspoon salt
  1/4 teaspoon baking soda
  3/4 cup coarsely chopped macadamia nuts
      1 cup finely chopped fresh pineapple
      1 tablespoon sugar
  1/4 teaspoon ground cinnamon

In a mixing bowl, beat butter, eggs and brown sugar. Combine the flour, baking powder, salt, baking soda and nuts; stir half into egg mixture. Add pineapple, then remaining flour mixture. Pour into a greased 8-in. x 4-in. x 2-in. loaf pan. Combine sugar and cinnamon; sprinkle over loaf. Bake at 350° for 50-55 minutes or until bread tests done. Cool on a wire rack. **Yield:** 1 loaf.

ALMOND RHUBARB COFFEE CAKE

This moist golden cake stirs up quickly and is long on

HOLIDAY BRAID

(Pictured above)

I make this bread year-round, eliminating the candied cherries and serving it for breakfast.
—Brenda Mowrey
Taylors, South Carolina

      1 package (1/4 ounce) active dry yeast
      1 cup warm milk (110° to 115°)
      4 cups all-purpose flour
  1/2 cup sugar
      1 teaspoon salt
      1 teaspoon grated lemon peel
  1/4 teaspoon ground cardamom
  1/2 cup butter *or* margarine
      1 egg plus 1 egg yolk
  1/2 cup chopped red and green candied
          cherries
  1/4 cup raisins
  1/4 cup chopped pecans
      1 tablespoon water
GLAZE:
  1/2 cup confectioners' sugar
      1 tablespoon milk
Additional candied cherries, optional

In a small bowl, dissolve yeast in milk. In a large bowl, combine flour, sugar, salt, lemon peel and

old-fashioned flavor. The sliced almonds add to the sweet and crunchy topping. —Dawn Fagerstrom
Warren, Minnesota

1-1/2 cups packed brown sugar
  2/3 cup vegetable oil
    1 egg
    1 teaspoon vanilla extract
2-1/2 cups all-purpose flour
    1 teaspoon salt
    1 teaspoon baking soda
    1 cup milk
1-1/2 cups finely chopped fresh *or* frozen
    rhubarb
  1/2 cup sliced almonds
TOPPING:
  1/3 cup sugar
    1 tablespoon butter *or* margarine, melted
  1/4 cup sliced almonds

In a mixing bowl, beat brown sugar, oil, egg and vanilla until smooth. Combine flour, salt and baking soda; add to sugar mixture alternately with milk. Beat until smooth. Stir in rhubarb and almonds. Pour into two greased 9-in. round cake pans. For topping, combine sugar and butter; stir in almonds. Sprinkle over batter. Bake at 350° for 30-35 minutes or until a wooden pick inserted near the center comes out clean. **Yield:** 12-14 servings.

APRICOT MUFFINS

"Fruity and fantastic" is how most folks describe these pretty, moist muffins. —Ruth Bolduc
Conway, New Hampshire

    1 cup chopped dried apricots
    1 cup boiling water
    1 cup sugar
  1/2 cup butter *or* margarine, softened
    1 cup (8 ounces) sour cream
    2 cups all-purpose flour
    1 teaspoon baking soda
  1/2 teaspoon salt
    1 tablespoon grated orange peel
  1/2 cup chopped nuts

Soak apricots in water for 5 minutes. In a large mixing bowl, cream sugar and butter until fluffy. Add sour cream; mix well. Combine dry ingredients; stir into creamed mixture just until moistened. Drain apricots, discarding liquid. Fold apricots, orange peel and nuts into batter. Fill greased or paper-lined muffin cups three-fourths full. Bake at 400° for 18-20 minutes or until muffins test done. Cool 10 minutes before removing to a wire rack. **Yield:** about 1 dozen.

RHUBARB NUT MUFFINS
(Pictured below)

Muffins are my weakness! They must appeal to other people as well—whenever I make these treats to take to a gathering, I come home with an empty plate. —Mary Kay Morris
Cokato, Minnesota

1-1/2 cups all-purpose flour
  3/4 cup packed brown sugar
  1/2 teaspoon baking soda
  1/2 teaspoon salt
  1/3 cup vegetable oil
    1 egg, lightly beaten
  1/2 cup buttermilk
    1 teaspoon vanilla extract
    1 cup diced fresh *or* frozen rhubarb
  1/2 cup chopped walnuts
TOPPING:
  1/4 cup packed brown sugar
  1/4 cup chopped walnuts
  1/2 teaspoon ground cinnamon

In a large bowl, combine flour, brown sugar, baking soda and salt. Combine oil, egg, buttermilk and vanilla; stir into dry ingredients just until moistened. Fold in rhubarb and walnuts. Fill greased or paper-lined muffin cups two-thirds full. Combine topping ingredients; sprinkle over muffins. Bake at 375° for 20-25 minutes or until muffins test done. Cool 10 minutes before removing to a wire rack. **Yield:** about 10 muffins.

GOLDEN RAISIN BUNS
(Pictured below)

These delightful buns will remind you of old-fashioned cream puffs with a mild lemon flavor. They look appealing on a platter and sure get snatched up quickly.
—Kathy Scott
Hemingford, Nebraska

    2 cups hot water, *divided*
1/2 cup golden raisins
1/2 cup butter *or* margarine
    1 teaspoon sugar
1/4 teaspoon salt
    1 cup all-purpose flour
    4 eggs
ICING:
    1 tablespoon butter *or* margarine
    4 to 5 teaspoons half-and-half cream
    1 cup confectioners' sugar
1/2 teaspoon lemon juice
1/2 teaspoon vanilla extract

In a small bowl, pour 1 cup of water over raisins; let stand for 5 minutes. Drain; set raisins aside. In a large saucepan, bring butter, sugar, salt and remaining water to a boil. Add flour all at once; stir until a smooth ball forms. Remove from the heat; beat by hand for 2 minutes. Add eggs, one at a time, beating well after each addition. Beat until mixture is well blended, about 3 minutes. Stir in the raisins. Drop by tablespoonfuls 2 in. apart onto greased baking sheets. Bake at 375° for 30-35 minutes or until golden brown. Transfer to a wire rack. For icing, melt the butter in a small saucepan; stir in cream. Remove from the heat; add sugar, lemon juice and vanilla. Spread on buns while still warm. Serve warm if desired. **Yield:** 20 servings.

SPECIAL CINNAMON ROLLS

I found that adding instant pudding mix to my mom's delicious roll recipe really enhances the flavor.
—Brenda Deveau
Van Buren, Maine

    2 packages (1/4 ounce *each*) active dry yeast
1/2 cup warm water (110° to 115°)
    8 cups all-purpose flour
    1 package (3.4 ounces) instant vanilla
        pudding mix
    2 cups warm milk (110° to 115°)
    2 eggs, lightly beaten
1/2 cup sugar
1/2 cup vegetable oil
    2 teaspoons salt
1/4 cup butter *or* margarine, melted
FILLING:
    1 cup packed brown sugar
    2 teaspoons ground cinnamon
    1 cup raisins
    1 cup chopped walnuts
GLAZE:
    1 cup confectioners' sugar
    1 to 2 tablespoons milk
1/4 teaspoon vanilla extract

In a mixing bowl, dissolve yeast in water. Add next seven ingredients; mix well (do not knead). Place in a greased bowl; turn once to grease top. Cover and let rise in a warm place until doubled, about 1 hour. Punch down. Turn onto a lightly floured board; divide in half. Roll each half into a 12-in. x 8-in. rectangle; brush with butter. Combine filling ingredients; spread over dough. Roll up from long side; seal seam. Slice each roll into 12 rolls; place cut side down in two greased 13-in. x 9-in. x 2-in. baking pans. Cover and let rise until nearly doubled, 45 minutes. Bake at 350° for 25-30 minutes or until golden brown. Combine glaze ingredients; drizzle over rolls. Cool in pans on wire racks. **Yield:** 2 dozen.

SWEDISH COFFEE BREAD

One day, I discovered a recipe for these tasty loaves. My wife, Sharon, challenged me to make them. It took a bit of time, but she said they were delicious!
—Wade Harmon
Orange, Massachusetts

    2 packages (1/4 ounce *each*) active dry yeast
1/2 cup warm water (110° to 115°)
    2 cups warm milk (110° to 115°)
1/2 cup butter *or* margarine, melted
1-1/4 cups sugar

4 eggs, lightly beaten
1-1/4 teaspoons ground cardamom
1 teaspoon salt
10 to 11 cups all-purpose flour
TOPPING:
2 tablespoons all-purpose flour
2 tablespoons sugar
2 tablespoons butter *or* margarine
GLAZE:
1/4 cup water
2 tablespoons sugar
1 egg yolk

In a large mixing bowl, dissolve yeast in water. Stir in milk, butter, sugar, eggs, cardamom and salt; beat until smooth. Gradually add 8 cups flour; beat until smooth. Stir in enough remaining flour to form a soft dough. Turn onto a floured board; knead until smooth and elastic, about 6-8 minutes. Place in a greased bowl, turning once to grease top. Cover and let rise in a warm place until doubled, about 1 hour. Punch dough down. Divide into nine equal portions. On a floured board, shape each into a 14-in. rope. For each loaf, braid three ropes together on a greased baking sheet; pinch ends to seal. Cover and let rise for 30 minutes. Meanwhile, for topping, combine flour and sugar; cut in butter until mixture resembles coarse crumbs. Sprinkle over loaves. Bake at 325° for 25 minutes or until golden brown. Combine glaze ingredients until smooth; brush over loaves. Bake for 5 minutes. Brush again; bake 5-10 minutes more. Remove from pans to cool on wire racks. **Yield:** 3 loaves.

CHOCOLATE CHIP MINI-MUFFINS

I bake a lot of different muffins, but I use this recipe the most. My family and friends always comment that these little bitefuls are packed with lots of wonderful flavor.
—Joanne Shew Chuk
St. Benedict, Saskatchewan

1/2 cup sugar
1/4 cup shortening
1 egg
1/2 cup milk
1/2 teaspoon vanilla extract
1 cup all-purpose flour
1/2 teaspoon baking soda
1/2 teaspoon baking powder
1/4 teaspoon salt
2/3 cup miniature semisweet chocolate chips

In a large mixing bowl, cream sugar and shortening until fluffy. Add egg, milk and vanilla; mix well. Combine the dry ingredients. Gradually add to the creamed mixture and mix well. Fold in chocolate chips. Spoon about 1 tablespoon of batter into each greased or paper-lined mini-muffin cup. Bake at 375° for 10-13 minutes or until muffins test done. Cool in pan 10 minutes before removing to a wire rack. **Yield:** about 3 dozen.

PUMPKIN DATE BREAD

My husband is diabetic, so I appreciate recipes that fit his restricted diet. Canned pumpkin makes this sweet bread nice and moist, while seasonings add flavor.
—Ruth McKay
Hopkins, Minnesota

✓ **This tasty dish uses less sugar, salt and fat. Recipe includes *Diabetic Exchanges*.**

1/3 cup margarine, softened
3 tablespoons brown sugar
Egg substitute equivalent to 2 eggs
1 cup solid-pack pumpkin
1 cup whole wheat flour
1/2 cup all-purpose flour
1 teaspoon baking powder
1 teaspoon baking soda
1-1/2 teaspoons ground cinnamon
1/2 teaspoon ground nutmeg
1/4 teaspoon salt
1/4 teaspoon ground cloves
1/4 teaspoon ground allspice
1/2 cup buttermilk
1 cup quick-cooking oats
1/2 cup chopped dates

In a mixing bowl, cream margarine and sugar. Beat in egg substitute and pumpkin. Combine the dry ingredients; add to the creamed mixture alternately with buttermilk. Stir in oats and dates. Pour into an 8-in. x 4-in. x 2-in. loaf pan coated with non-stick cooking spray. Bake at 350° for 75 minutes or until a wooden pick inserted near the center comes out clean. Cool in pan 10 minutes; remove to a wire rack to cool. **Yield:** 1 loaf (15 slices). **Diabetic Exchanges:** One slice equals 1-1/2 starch, 1 fat; also, 148 calories, 198 mg sodium, 0 cholesterol, 21 gm carbohydrate, 4 gm protein, 6 gm fat.

No More Unraveling Rolls!

To prevent cinnamon rolls from unrolling when serving, be careful not to spread too much filling over the dough—abundant filling does not allow the roll to seal as it rises.

ITALIAN EASTER BREAD
(Pictured above)

Both the Italians and the Swiss prepare this festive Easter bread with colored eggs embedded in the dough. Not only do you get a beautifully baked bread, you get hard-cooked eggs that are ready to eat.
—Dolores Skrout
Summerhill, Pennsylvania

   3 to 3-1/2 cups all-purpose flour
1/4 cup sugar
   1 package (1/4 ounce) active dry yeast
   1 teaspoon salt
2/3 cup warm milk (120° to 130°)
   2 tablespoons butter *or* margarine, softened
   7 eggs
1/2 cup chopped mixed candied fruit
1/4 cup chopped blanched almonds
1/2 teaspoon aniseed
Vegetable oil

In a mixing bowl, combine 1 cup flour, sugar, yeast and salt. Add milk and butter; beat 2 minutes on medium. Add 2 eggs and 1/2 cup flour; beat 2 minutes on high. Stir in fruit, nuts and aniseed; mix well. Stir in enough remaining flour to form a soft dough. Turn onto a lightly floured board; knead until smooth and elastic, 6-8 minutes. Place in a greased bowl; turn once to grease top. Cover and let rise in a warm place until doubled, about 1 hour. If desired, dye remaining eggs (leave them uncooked); lightly rub with oil. Punch dough down. Divide in half; roll each piece into a 24-in.

rope. Loosely twist ropes together; place on a greased baking sheet and form into a ring. Pinch ends together. Gently split ropes and tuck eggs into openings. Cover and let rise until doubled, about 30 minutes. Bake at 350° for 30-35 minutes or until golden brown. Remove from pan; cool on a wire rack. **Yield:** 1 bread.

SWEDISH ANISE TWISTS

My family loves the subtle taste of anise, so it's no surprise these pretty twists are often requested. Because anise appears in the dough and topping, everyone gets a doubly delicious dose of their favorite herb.
—Geraldine Grisdale
Mt. Pleasant, Michigan

   2 packages (1/4 ounce *each*) active dry yeast
1/2 cup warm water (110° to 115°)
3/4 cup warm milk (110° to 115°)
1/2 cup butter *or* margarine, melted
1/2 cup sugar
   2 eggs, beaten
   1 teaspoon salt
1-1/2 teaspoons crushed aniseed
4-1/2 to 5 cups all-purpose flour
TOPPING:
   1 egg, beaten
1/2 cup sugar
1/2 teaspoon crushed aniseed

In a mixing bowl, dissolve yeast in water. Add milk, butter, sugar, eggs, salt, aniseed and 3 cups of flour; beat until smooth. Add enough remaining flour to form a soft dough. Turn onto a floured board; knead until smooth and elastic, about 6-8 minutes. Place in a greased bowl, turning once to grease top. Cover and let rise in a warm place until doubled, about 1 hour. Punch dough down; roll into a 16-in. x 9-in. rectangle. Cut into three 16-in. x 3-in. pieces. Cut each piece into sixteen 3-in. x 1-in. strips. Twist each strip; place 1-1/2 in. apart on greased baking sheets. Cover and let rise until doubled, about 30 minutes. Combine topping ingredients; brush over twists. Bake at 375° for 12-15 minutes or until browned. Cool on wire racks. **Yield:** 4 dozen.

HAM AND CHEESE MUFFINS
(Pictured above right)

These savory biscuit-like muffins are delicious at breakfast or accompanying a hearty bowl of soup. Of

course, your family will enjoy them no matter what time of day you put them out. —Doris Heath
Bryson City, North Carolina

 2 cups self-rising flour*
1/2 teaspoon baking soda
 1 cup milk
1/2 cup mayonnaise
1/2 cup finely chopped fully cooked ham
1/2 cup shredded cheddar cheese

In a large bowl, combine flour and baking soda. Combine remaining ingredients; stir into dry ingredients just until moistened. Fill greased or paper-lined muffin cups two-thirds full. Bake at 425° for 16-18 minutes or until muffins test done. **Yield:** about 1 dozen. ***Editor's Note:** As a substitute for each cup of self-rising flour, place 1-1/2 teaspoons baking powder and 1/2 teaspoon salt in a measuring cup. Add enough all-purpose flour to equal 1 cup.

HOT CROSS BUNS
(Pictured at right)
This recipe came from my niece in Ballwin, Missouri, who's one of the best cooks in the world. These buns have become an Easter morning tradition.
—Dorothy Pritchett
Wills Point, Texas

 2 packages (1/4 ounce *each*) active dry yeast
1/2 cup warm water (110° to 115°)
 1 cup warm milk (110° to 115°)
1/2 cup sugar
1/4 cup butter *or* margarine, softened
 1 teaspoon vanilla extract
 1 teaspoon salt
1/2 teaspoon ground nutmeg
6-1/2 to 7 cups all-purpose flour

 4 eggs
1/2 cup dried currants
1/2 cup raisins
GLAZE/ICING:
 2 tablespoons water
 1 egg yolk
 1 cup confectioners' sugar
 4 teaspoons milk
1/4 teaspoon vanilla extract

In a mixing bowl, dissolve yeast in water. Add milk, sugar, butter, vanilla, salt, nutmeg and 3 cups of flour; beat until smooth. Add eggs, one at a time, beating well after each. Stir in the currants, raisins and enough remaining flour to form a soft dough. Turn onto a floured board; knead until smooth and elastic, 6-8 minutes. Place in a greased bowl, turning once to grease top. Cover and let rise in a warm place until doubled, about 1 hour. Punch dough down; shape into 30 balls. Place on greased baking sheets. Cut a cross on top of each roll with a sharp knife. Cover and let rise until doubled, about 30 minutes. Beat water and egg yolk; brush over rolls. Bake at 375° for 12-15 minutes. Cool on wire racks. For the icing, combine sugar, milk and vanilla until smooth; drizzle over rolls. **Yield:** 2-1/2 dozen.

Country-Style Condiments

Tastefully top off your favorite foods with this appealing assortment of salad dressings, relishes, spreads, sauces, salsa and more. You'll relish every mouth-watering bite!

RHUBARB-STRAWBERRY SAUCE

Every spring, I search for recipes that allow me to use my abundance of tangy rhubarb. My family is always delighted to see me preparing this pretty sauce. They enjoy spooning it over hot muffins and waffles or creamy vanilla ice cream. —Earlene Ertelt
Woodburn, Oregon

> 1 pound fresh *or* frozen rhubarb, cut into 1-inch pieces
> 1 jar (12 ounces) currant jelly
> 2 cups sliced fresh *or* frozen strawberries
> 1/4 cup sugar

In a large saucepan over medium heat, bring rhubarb and jelly to a boil, stirring frequently. Reduce heat; cover and simmer for 8-10 minutes or until rhubarb is tender. Remove from the heat. Mash with a potato masher. Stir in the strawberries and sugar; bring to a boil. Cook and stir for 1 minute. Remove from the heat; cool. Pour into freezer containers; refrigerate or freeze. Serve as a side dish or over ice cream or waffles. **Yield:** 2 pints.

PINEAPPLE CHUTNEY
(Pictured above)

I love relish, so when I discovered the recipe for this tangy chutney, I knew I had to try it. I've made it many times since to serve with ham and pork or as an appetizer over cream cheese. Its sweet, spicy flavor adds zing to any dish. —Shirley Watanabe
Kula, Hawaii

> 2 cans (20 ounces *each*) pineapple tidbits, drained
> 4 cups diced onion
> 3 cups packed brown sugar
> 2 cups golden raisins
> 2 cups vinegar
> 2 teaspoons salt
> 2 teaspoons mustard seed
> 2 teaspoons ground turmeric
> 4 teaspoons grated orange peel
> 2 teaspoons grated lemon peel
> 2 medium yellow banana peppers, seeded and chopped, optional

In a saucepan over medium heat, combine all ingredients; bring to a boil. Reduce heat; simmer, uncovered, for 1 to 1-1/2 hours or until chutney reaches desired thickness. Refrigerate. Serve with meat or over cream cheese as an appetizer spread. **Yield:** about 6 cups.

EASY SALSA

Cooking is especially fun when you're making a favorite snack that tastes better than the store-bought version. Garden tomatoes and onions make this homemade salsa so much better than salsa from a jar. —Mikel Chapman
Helena, Oklahoma

> 4 medium tomatoes, chopped
> 1 medium onion, chopped
> 1/4 cup chunky salsa
> 1/2 teaspoon salt
> 1/4 teaspoon pepper
> 1/4 cup canned chopped green chilies, optional

In a large bowl, combine the tomatoes, onion, salsa, salt and pepper. Add the chilies if desired. Cover and refrigerate for several hours. **Yield:** 4-1/2 to 5 cups.

POPPY SEED PARMESAN SALAD DRESSING

We've been serving this quick and easy dressing at our restaurant for years. It's sure to tantalize your taste buds. —Steve Sparkman
Madison, Mississippi

> 1 cup sugar
> 1/2 cup white wine vinegar
> 2 cups mayonnaise

1-1/4 cups Italian salad dressing
    1 cup shredded Parmesan cheese
  1/4 cup poppy seeds
    1 teaspoon white pepper
  1/2 teaspoon salt

In a small bowl, stir sugar and vinegar until sugar is dissolved. Whisk in mayonnaise and Italian dressing. Stir in the Parmesan, poppy seeds, pepper and salt until smooth. Cover and refrigerate. **Yield:** about 5 cups.

RHUBARB RELISH

I've been making this relish for years. The whole family likes it, especially on cold roast beef. It's a new and interesting way to use up homegrown rhubarb.
—Mina Dyck
Boissevain, Manitoba

    2 cups finely chopped fresh *or* frozen rhubarb
    2 cups finely chopped onion
2-1/2 cups packed brown sugar
    1 cup vinegar
    1 teaspoon salt
  1/2 teaspoon ground cinnamon
  1/2 teaspoon ground allspice
  1/4 teaspoon ground cloves
  1/4 teaspoon pepper

In a saucepan, combine all ingredients. Cook over medium heat for 30 minutes or until thickened, stirring occasionally. Cool; store in the refrigerator. Relish is a nice condiment to poultry, pork or beef. **Yield:** 3-1/3 cups.

RANCH-STYLE DRESSING

Looking for a low-fat dressing for salads without the preservatives of already-prepared varieties? Then this recipe is for you. It's a creamy topping for any crispy greens. You'll want to keep plenty on hand...it disappears quickly!
—Sheree Feero
Golden, Colorado

✓ **This tasty dish uses less sugar, salt and fat. Recipe includes *Diabetic Exchanges*.**

2/3 cup low-fat cottage cheese
  3 tablespoons skim milk
  1 tablespoon tarragon vinegar
  1 garlic clove, minced
  1 tablespoon sliced green onion tops

In a blender or food processor, blend cottage cheese, milk, vinegar and garlic until smooth. Add onion tops; blend just until combined. Store in the refrigerator. **Yield:** 3/4 cup. **Diabetic Exchanges:** One serving (2 tablespoons) equals a free food; also, 23 calories, 107 mg sodium, 1 mg cholesterol, 1 gm carbohydrate, 3 gm protein, trace fat.

FOUR-BERRY SPREAD
(Pictured above)

For a big berry taste, you can't beat this tasty spread. With a flavorful foursome of blackberries, blueberries, raspberries and strawberries, this lovely jam brightens any breakfast.
—Marie St. Thomas
Sterling, Massachusetts

    1 cup fresh *or* frozen blackberries
    1 cup fresh *or* frozen blueberries
1-1/2 cups fresh *or* frozen strawberries
1-1/2 cups fresh *or* frozen raspberries
    1 box (1-3/4 ounces) powdered fruit pectin
    7 cups sugar

Crush berries in large kettle. Stir in pectin; bring to full rolling boil over high heat, stirring constantly. Stir in sugar; return to full rolling boil. Boil for 1 minute, stirring constantly. Remove from heat; skim off any foam. Pour hot into hot jars, leaving 1/4-in. headspace. Adjust caps. Process for 10 minutes in a boiling-water bath. **Yield:** about 7 half-pints.

1/2 teaspoon salt
1/2 teaspoon sugar
1/4 teaspoon pepper
1/4 teaspoon ground mustard
Pinch ground nutmeg
2 to 3 tablespoons prepared horseradish
1 tablespoon lemon juice

In a saucepan, melt butter; stir in flour until smooth. Gradually add milk and cream; bring to a boil. Cook and stir for 2 minutes. Remove from the heat; add the seasonings, horseradish and lemon juice. Serve over roast beef or spread on beef sandwiches. **Yield:** 1-1/4 cups.

STRAWBERRY SALSA
(Pictured above)

This deliciously different salsa is versatile, fresh-tasting and colorful. People are surprised to see a salsa made with strawberries, but it's excellent over grilled chicken and pork. —Jean Giroux
Belchertown, Massachusetts

1 pint fresh strawberries, diced
4 plum tomatoes, seeded and diced
1 small red onion, diced
1 to 2 medium jalapeno peppers, minced
Juice of 1 lime
2 garlic cloves, minced
1 tablespoon olive or vegetable oil

In a bowl, combine strawberries, tomatoes, onion and peppers. Stir in the lime juice, garlic and oil. Cover and chill for 2 hours. Serve with cooked poultry or pork or as a dip for tortilla chips. **Yield:** 4 cups.

HORSERADISH SAUCE

The combination of mustard and horseradish gives this flavorful sauce just the right amount of zip. It's perfect for spicing up all kinds of beef. —Jim Cosgrove
Burlington, Ontario

2 tablespoons butter *or* margarine
2 tablespoons all-purpose flour
1 cup milk
1/4 cup half-and-half cream

ITALIAN SALAD DRESSING
(Pictured above)

As a diabetic who likes salads, I was tired of plain vinegar and oil topping the greens. So I came up with this tongue-tingling dressing. —George Greenauer
Spencerport, New York

✓ **This tasty dish uses less sugar, salt and fat. Recipe includes *Diabetic Exchanges*.**

1/4 cup vegetable oil
1/4 cup red wine vinegar
1 garlic clove, minced
1 teaspoon finely chopped onion
1/2 teaspoon ground mustard
1/2 teaspoon celery seed

1/2 teaspoon paprika
1/4 teaspoon Italian seasoning
Artificial sweetener equivalent to 2 to 4
   teaspoons sugar

Combine all ingredients in a jar with a tight-fitting lid; shake well. Refrigerate overnight. **Yield:** 2/3 cup. **Diabetic Exchanges:** One serving (2 tablespoons) equals 2 fat; also, 96 calories, 1 mg sodium, 0 cholesterol, 1 gm carbohydrate, 0 protein, 10 gm fat.

CRANBERRY PEAR CHUTNEY
(Pictured below)

My husband, Jack, is a diabetic who likes to round out a meal with this lovely sauce. The ingredients in this sugar-free treat give it a natural sweetness.
—Carol Bricke
Tempe, Arizona

✓ **This tasty dish uses less sugar, salt and fat. Recipe includes *Diabetic Exchanges*.**

   2 cups fresh *or* frozen cranberries
3/4 cup frozen apple juice concentrate,
       thawed
   1 medium pear, peeled and cubed
1/2 cup raisins

In a saucepan over medium heat, bring cranberries and concentrate to a boil. Cook and stir for 5 minutes. Add pear and raisins; cook and stir until berries pop and pear is tender, about 5-7 minutes. Pour into a serving bowl; chill overnight. **Yield:** 2 cups. **Diabetic Exchanges:** One 1/4-cup serving equals 1-1/2 fruit; also, 99 calories, 8 mg sodium, 0 cholesterol, 25 gm carbohydrate, 1 gm protein, trace fat.

CRISP SWEET RELISH
(Pictured above)

Friends share their garden bounty, so I needed a recipe to make good use of cucumbers. I adapted this recipe from one my mother used. This mouth-watering relish even won a blue ribbon at our county fair.
—Joyce Hallisey
Mt. Gilead, North Carolina

   8 cups ground cucumbers (about 5 pounds)
   4 cups ground onions
   2 cups ground carrots
   5 tablespoons salt
   7 cups sugar
   4 cups vinegar
   2 teaspoons celery seed
   1 teaspoon ground turmeric
   1 teaspoon ground nutmeg
1/2 teaspoon pepper

Combine the cucumbers, onions and carrots in a large bowl; sprinkle with salt. Cover with ice cubes. Let stand for 6 hours; drain. Rinse and drain thoroughly. In a large kettle, combine sugar, vinegar, celery seed, turmeric, nutmeg and pepper. Add vegetables; bring to a boil over medium heat, stirring often. Reduce heat; simmer, uncovered, for 20 minutes, stirring occasionally. Pack hot into hot jars, leaving 1/2-in. headspace. Adjust caps. Process for 10 minutes in a boiling-water bath. **Yield:** 8 pints.

ALL-DAY APPLE BUTTER

I make several batches of this simple and delicious apple butter to freeze in jars. Depending on the sweetness of the apples used, you can adjust the sugar to taste.
—Betty Ruenholl
Syracuse, Nebraska

5-1/2 pounds apples, peeled and finely chopped
    4 cups sugar
    2 to 3 teaspoons ground cinnamon
    1/4 teaspoon ground cloves
    1/4 teaspoon salt

Place apples in a slow cooker. Combine sugar, cinnamon, cloves and salt; pour over apples and mix well. Cover and cook on high for 1 hour. Reduce heat to low; cover and cook for 9-11 hours or until thickened and dark brown, stirring occasionally (stir more frequently as it thickens to prevent sticking). Uncover and cook on low 1 hour longer. If desired, stir with a wire whisk until smooth. Spoon into freezer containers, leaving 1/2-in. headspace. Cover and refrigerate or freeze. **Yield:** 4 pints.

LOW-FAT GRAVY
(Pictured below)

With this special sauce, folks on restricted diets don't have to pass on the gravy. Instead, they can say, "Please pass the gravy!" Now you can smother slices of turkey without guilt.
—Mary Fry
Cedar Rapids, Iowa

✓ **This tasty dish uses less sugar, salt and fat.**
   Recipe includes *Diabetic Exchanges*.

1/2 cup finely chopped onion
1/2 cup finely chopped fresh mushrooms

BLUEBERRY JELLY
(Pictured above)

My mother brought this old family recipe with her when she moved here from Scotland. My children and husband especially love spreading this fruitful jelly on slices of homemade bread.
—Elaine Soper
Trinity Bay, Newfoundland

    2 quarts fresh *or* frozen blueberries
    4 cups water
  12 cups sugar
    2 pouches (3 ounces *each*) liquid fruit pectin

Place blueberries in a large kettle and crush slightly. Add water; bring to a boil. Reduce heat to medium; cook, uncovered, for 45 minutes. Strain through a jelly bag, reserving 6 cups juice. Pour juice into a large kettle; gradually stir in sugar until dissolved. Bring to a boil over high heat, stirring constantly. Add pectin; bring to a full rolling boil. Boil for 1 minute, stirring constantly. Remove from the heat. Skim foam. Pour hot into sterilized hot jars, leaving 1/4-in. headspace. Adjust caps. Process for 5 minutes in a boiling-water bath. **Yield:** 6 pints.

2 tablespoons chopped fresh parsley
2 cups reduced-sodium fat-free beef *or*
  chicken broth, *divided*
2 tablespoons cornstarch
Pinch pepper

In a saucepan over medium heat, saute onion, mushrooms and parsley in 1/4 cup of broth until vegetables are tender. Combine cornstarch, pepper and 1/2 cup of broth; stir until smooth. Add to saucepan along with remaining broth. Bring to a boil, stirring occasionally; boil for 2 minutes. **Yield:** 2 cups. **Diabetic Exchanges:** One 1/4-cup serving equals a free food; also, 19 calories, 28 mg sodium, 2 mg cholesterol, 3 gm carbohydrate, 1 gm protein, 1 gm fat.

SWEET PEPPER RELISH

The homemade fresh flavor really comes through in this tangy, sweet relish, and the green and red peppers provide appealing color. It makes a terrific topper for hot dogs and hamburgers. —Sue Thomas
Casa Grande, Arizona

7-1/2 cups diced sweet red pepper
6-1/2 cups diced green pepper
  6 cups diced onion
  2 quarts boiling water
  3 cups cider vinegar
2-1/2 cups sugar
  1 tablespoon canning salt
  2 teaspoons mustard seed
  1 teaspoon celery seed

In a large container, combine peppers and onion. Pour water over and let stand for 20 minutes; drain well. In a large kettle, combine the remaining ingredients; bring to a boil. Add pepper mixture; cover and simmer for 20 minutes. Pour hot into hot jars, leaving 1/4-in. headspace. Adjust lids. Process for 15 minutes in a boiling-water bath. **Yield:** 7 pints.

EASY PICKLED BEETS

Here's an easy way to spice up canned beets. It's a perfect dish for large gatherings. —Cordie Cash
Silsbee, Texas

  1 tablespoon mixed pickling spices
  2 cups vinegar
  2 cups sugar
  1 teaspoon ground cinnamon

  1 teaspoon salt
  4 cans (16 ounces *each*) sliced beets

Place pickling spices in a cheesecloth bag. In a large saucepan, combine vinegar, sugar, cinnamon, salt and the spice bag; bring to a boil. Drain the beets, reserving 3/4 cup of juice. Stir beets and reserved juice into saucepan. Pour into a 1-1/2-qt. glass container. Cover and refrigerate overnight. Remove spice bag before serving. **Yield:** 18-20 servings.

THREE-HOUR
REFRIGERATOR PICKLES
(Pictured below)

I can't wait for my husband to get our garden ready each year. Cucumber seeds are the first to be planted. My grandchildren love to help me make these pickles and proudly carry a big jar home. —Sandra Jones
Troy, North Carolina

  6 pounds cucumbers
  4 medium onions
  4 cups sugar
  4 cups vinegar
1/2 cup salt
  1 teaspoon celery salt
  1 teaspoon mustard seed
1-1/2 teaspoons ground turmeric

Slice the cucumbers 1/4 in. thick. Slice onions 1/8 in. thick. Place both in a large nonmetallic bowl. Combine remaining ingredients; pour over cucumbers and onions. Stir well for 5 minutes. Cover and refrigerate 3 hours before serving. Store in the refrigerator for up to 3 months, stirring occasionally. **Yield:** 2-1/2 quarts.

Cookies & Bars

Your family's days will be a little sweeter when you present them with an assortment of melt-in-your-mouth cookies, tempting bars and scrumptious brownies.

FUDGE BROWNIES

(Pictured above)

These brownies are rich and chocolaty, which makes them a hit with everyone. My children always looked forward to these after-school snacks. They're so fudgy they don't need icing. —Hazel Fritchie
Palestine, Illinois

      1 cup butter *or* margarine
      6 squares (1 ounce *each*) unsweetened
         chocolate
      4 eggs
      2 cups sugar
      1 teaspoon vanilla extract
  1/2 teaspoon salt
      1 cup all-purpose flour
      2 cups chopped walnuts
Confectioners' sugar, optional

In a saucepan over low heat, melt butter and chocolate; cool for 10 minutes. In a mixing bowl, beat eggs, sugar, vanilla and salt. Stir in the chocolate mixture. Add flour and nuts; mix well. Pour into a greased 9-in. square baking pan. Bake at 350° for 45 minutes or until brownies test done with a wooden pick. Cool. Dust with confectioners' sugar if desired. **Yield:** 16 servings.

SNACK BARS

If your family likes granola bars, they're sure to love these tempting treats. Full of hearty ingredients, they're a perfect snack for taking along on picnics and bike trips or for packing in brown-bag lunches.
—Carolyn Fisher
Kinzer, Pennsylvania

      9 cups Rice Chex, crushed
      6 cups quick-cooking oats
      1 cup graham cracker crumbs
      1 cup flaked coconut
  1/2 cup wheat germ
      2 bags (one 16 ounces, one 10 ounces)
         large marshmallows
      1 cup butter *or* margarine
  1/2 cup honey
1-1/2 cups chocolate chips, mini M&M's *or*
         raisins, optional

In a very large bowl, combine the first five ingredients. In a saucepan over low heat, cook and stir marshmallows and butter until the marshmallows are melted. Add honey and mix well. Pour over cereal mixture; mix well. Add chips, M&M's or raisins if desired. Pat two-thirds into a greased 15-in. x 10-in. x 1-in. pan and the remaining third into a 9-in. square pan. Cool. **Yield:** 4-5 dozen.

TOASTED COCONUT COOKIES

These cookies have coconut, walnuts and oats to make them a satisfying snack no matter what time of day. They're a hit with everyone who tries them.
—Cindy Colley
Othello, Washington

  1/2 cup butter *or* margarine
  1/2 cup shortening
  3/4 cup sugar
  3/4 cup packed brown sugar
      2 eggs
      2 teaspoons vanilla extract
      2 cups all-purpose flour
      1 teaspoon baking powder
      1 teaspoon baking soda
  3/4 teaspoon salt
1-1/2 cups quick-cooking oats
1-1/2 cups flaked coconut, toasted
  3/4 cup chopped walnuts, toasted

In a mixing bowl, cream butter, shortening and sugars until fluffy. Add eggs and vanilla; beat well. Combine flour, baking powder, baking soda and salt; gradually add to creamed mixture. Fold in oats, coconut and nuts. Drop by tablespoonfuls onto greased baking sheets. Bake at 375° for 10-11 minutes or until golden brown. Cool 2-3 minutes before removing to a wire rack. **Yield:** about 5 dozen.

JEWELED COOKIES

Candied fruits give a stained-glass look to these specialties. They're like a shortbread, but dressed up. They make an attractive addition to your buffet table.

—Ruth Ann Stelfox
Raymond, Alberta

   1 pound butter (no substitutes), softened
2-1/2 cups sugar
   3 eggs
   5 cups all-purpose flour
   1 teaspoon baking soda
1-1/2 cups raisins
   1 cup coarsely chopped walnuts
   1/2 cup *each* chopped red and green candied cherries
   1/2 cup chopped candied pineapple

In a mixing bowl, cream butter and sugar. Add eggs, one at a time, beating well after each. Combine flour and baking soda; add to creamed mixture. Stir in raisins, nuts, cherries and pineapple; mix well. Shape into 2-in. rolls; wrap in waxed paper or foil. Freeze at least 2 hours. Cut into 1/4-in. slices; place on greased baking sheets. Bake at 350° for 8-10 minutes or until lightly browned. Cool on wire racks. **Yield:** 12-14 dozen.

EGGNOG COOKIES
(Pictured above)

At Christmastime, our family loves to spend time together baking a variety of sweet treats. Our kids especially like decorating these cookies. We then wrap them in pretty paper and give them away as gifts. This cookie's flavor fits right into the holiday spirit.

—Myra Innes
Auburn, Kansas

   1 cup butter *or* margarine, softened
   2 cups sugar
   1 cup store-bought eggnog
   1 teaspoon baking soda
   1/2 teaspoon ground nutmeg
5-1/2 cups all-purpose flour
   1 egg white, lightly beaten
Colored sugar

In a mixing bowl, cream butter and sugar. Beat in eggnog, baking soda and nutmeg. Gradually add flour and mix well. Cover and chill for 1 hour. On a lightly floured surface, roll out half of the dough to 1/8-in. thickness. Cut into desired shapes; place on ungreased baking sheets. Repeat with remaining dough. Brush with egg white; sprinkle with colored sugar. Bake at 350° for 6-8 minutes or until edges are lightly browned. Cool on wire racks. **Yield:** about 16 dozen.

HAZELNUT CRUNCHERS

The flavor of these treats smacks of harvesttime. I often make ice cream sandwiches using these yummy cookies. They're a favorite with my grandchildren.

—Ruth Sayles
Pendleton, Oregon

   1/2 cup butter *or* margarine, softened
   1/2 cup packed dark brown sugar
   1/3 cup sugar
   1 egg
   1/2 teaspoon vanilla extract
   1 cup plus 2 tablespoons all-purpose flour
   1/2 teaspoon baking soda
Pinch salt
   1 cup (6 ounces) vanilla chips
   1 cup chopped hazelnuts *or* filberts, toasted

In a large mixing bowl, cream butter and sugars. Add egg and vanilla; mix well. Combine dry ingredients; add to creamed mixture and mix well. Stir in chips and nuts. Shape into 1-1/2-in. balls; place on greased baking sheets. Flatten to 1/2-in. thickness with a glass dipped in sugar. Bake at 350° for 10-12 minutes or until lightly browned. Remove to a wire rack to cool. **Yield:** about 2 dozen.

Tempting Taste Treats

Give regular Rice Krispies Treats a pleasing flavor by adding 1 tablespoon cinnamon for every 10 ounces of marshmallows. Everyone will enjoy the subtle, sweet flavor.

PEPPERMINT KISSES

(Pictured above)

These fun and refreshing cookies really melt in your mouth. Plus, they're low in fat—just perfect when you're trying to watch what you eat during the holidays!
—Lynn Bernstetter
Lake Elmo, Minnesota

    2 egg whites
1/8 teaspoon salt
1/8 teaspoon cream of tartar
1/2 cup sugar
    2 peppermint candy canes (one green, one red), crushed

In a mixing bowl, beat egg whites until foamy. Add salt and cream of tartar; beat until soft peaks form. Beat in sugar, 1 tablespoon at a time, until stiff and glossy. Spoon meringue into a pastry bag or a resealable plastic bag. If using a plastic bag, cut a 1-in. hole in a corner. Squeeze 1-1/2-in. kisses of meringue onto ungreased foil-lined baking sheets. Sprinkle half with red crushed candy canes and half with green candy canes. Bake at 225° for 1-1/2 to 2 hours or until dry but not brown. Cool; remove from foil. Store in an airtight container. **Yield:** about 3 dozen.

CRANBERRY DROP COOKIES

*I found this recipe in a children's cookbook some 20 years ago. After all those years, my grown daughter in-*sists on baking these treats each holiday season. They're a nice change from ordinary Christmas cookies.*
—Pam Baker
South Charleston, West Virginia

1/2 cup butter *or* margarine, softened
    1 cup sugar
    1 cup packed brown sugar
    1 egg
1/4 cup milk
    2 tablespoons lemon juice
    3 cups all-purpose flour
    1 teaspoon baking powder
1/2 teaspoon salt
1/4 teaspoon baking soda
    1 package (12 ounces) fresh *or* frozen cranberries, chopped
    1 cup chopped walnuts

In a mixing bowl, cream butter and sugars. Add egg, milk and lemon juice; mix well. Combine dry ingredients; add to creamed mixture and mix well. Stir in cranberries and nuts. Drop by heaping teaspoonfuls 2 in. apart onto greased baking sheets. Bake at 375° for 13-15 minutes or until golden brown. Cool on wire racks. **Yield:** about 5 dozen.

CREAM FILBERTS

These cookies remind me of "mothball candy" I used to buy with dimes Grandma gave me. Everyone raves about these crisp cookies with a rich, buttery flavor.
—Deanna Richter
Elmore, Minnesota

    1 cup shortening
3/4 cup sugar
    1 egg
    1 teaspoon vanilla extract
2-1/2 cups all-purpose flour
1/2 teaspoon baking powder
1/8 teaspoon salt
3/4 cup whole filberts *or* hazelnuts
GLAZE:
    2 cups confectioners' sugar
    3 tablespoons water
    2 teaspoons vanilla extract
Granulated sugar *or* about 60 crushed sugar cubes

In a mixing bowl, cream shortening and sugar. Add egg and vanilla; mix well. Combine the dry ingredients and add to creamed mixture. Roll heaping teaspoonfuls into balls; press a filbert into each and reshape so dough covers nut. Place on ungreased baking sheets. Bake at 375° for 12-15 minutes or until lightly browned. Cool on wire racks. Combine the first three glaze ingredients; dip entire top of cookies. Roll in sugar. **Yield:** about 5 dozen.

RICH CHOCOLATE BROWNIES
(Pictured above)

I'm one of those people who need chocolate on a regular basis. I looked high and low for a rich brownie recipe that called for cocoa instead of chocolate squares...and this is it. My family loves these brownies—they never last more than a day at our house.
—Karen Trapp
North Weymouth, Massachusetts

   1 cup sugar
   2 eggs
 1/2 teaspoon vanilla extract
 1/2 cup butter *or* margarine, melted
 1/2 cup all-purpose flour
 1/3 cup baking cocoa
 1/4 teaspoon baking powder
 1/4 teaspoon salt
FROSTING:
   3 tablespoons butter *or* margarine, melted
   3 tablespoons baking cocoa
   2 tablespoons warm water
   1 teaspoon instant coffee granules
1-1/2 cups confectioners' sugar

In a mixing bowl, beat sugar, eggs and vanilla. Add butter; mix well. Combine dry ingredients; add to batter and mix well. Pour into a greased 8-in. square baking pan. Bake at 350° for 25-30 minutes or until brownies test done with a wooden pick. Cool in pan on a wire rack. For frosting, combine butter, co-

coa, water and coffee; mix well. Gradually stir in sugar until smooth, adding additional warm water if necessary to achieve a spreading consistency. Frost the brownies. **Yield:** 12-16 servings.

"A COOKIE on the dessert table in the Garden Buffet at Harveys in Lake Tahoe, Nevada was the very best I've ever eaten!" reports Harriet Richardson of Soccoro, New Mexico.

"Similar to a coconut macaroon, it was full of finely chopped nuts and topped with a candied cherry. I'd truly love to have the recipe. These cookies would make excellent holiday gifts!"

Contacting Harveys, a resort hotel including eight different restaurants, we discovered the cookie that delighted Harriet has an international background.

Informs Executive Chef Norbert Koblitz, a native of Germany, "This recipe originated nearly 100 years ago at Gerstner & Koeble Konditory, a pastry shop in Vienna, Austria, which has delivered cakes, pastries and cookies to the Vienna Opera House since 1945."

Chef Koblitz modified the macaroon slightly and first served it in 1992 for Sunday brunch at the hotel's top-floor signature restaurant. It was met with rave reviews and has become a trademark of the restaurant.

HARVEYS COCONUT MACAROONS

   1 cup shredded coconut
3-1/2 cups almond paste
   1 cup all-purpose flour
 2/3 cup sugar
   5 eggs
 1/2 cup chopped walnuts
Red candied cherries, halved

In a food processor or blender, process coconut until finely chopped; set aside. In a mixing bowl, beat almond paste until crumbled. Gradually add flour, sugar and coconut; mix well. Add eggs, one at a time; beat until smooth. Stir in nuts. Place dough in a pastry bag with a large star tip; pipe onto baking sheets covered with parchment paper or foil. Top with cherries. Bake at 350° for 15-20 minutes or until golden brown. Cool 5 minutes before removing to wire racks. **Yield:** about 4 dozen.

CHOCOLATE SANDWICH COOKIES

(Pictured above)

Because they get a head start from packaged cake mixes, I don't mind whipping up a batch of these chewy cookies whenever I'm asked.
—Karen Bourne
Magrath, Alberta

- 2 packages (18-1/4 ounces *each*) devil's food cake mix
- 4 eggs, lightly beaten
- 2/3 cup vegetable oil
- 1 package (8 ounces) cream cheese, softened
- 1/2 cup butter *or* margarine, softened
- 3 to 4 cups confectioners' sugar
- 1/2 teaspoon vanilla extract
- Red *and/or* green food coloring, optional

In a mixing bowl, beat cake mixes, eggs and oil (batter will be very stiff). Roll into 1-in. balls; place on ungreased baking sheets and flatten slightly. Bake at 350° for 8-10 minutes or until a slight indentation remains when lightly touched. Cool. In another mixing bowl, beat cream cheese and butter. Add sugar and vanilla; mix until smooth. If desired, tint with food coloring. Spread on bottom of half of the cookies. Top with remaining cookies. **Yield:** 4 dozen.

SOFT LEMONADE COOKIES

I remember my mother making these cookies. They just go perfectly with warm days. They're so lovely and moist, you won't be able to stop eating them.
—Margo Neuhaser
Bakersfield, California

- 1 cup butter *or* margarine, softened
- 1 cup sugar

- 2 eggs
- 3 cups all-purpose flour
- 1 teaspoon baking soda
- 1 can (6 ounces) frozen lemonade concentrate, thawed, *divided*
- Additional sugar

In a mixing bowl, cream butter and sugar; add eggs. Combine flour and baking soda; add to the creamed mixture alternately with 1/3 cup of lemonade concentrate. Mix well. Drop by rounded teaspoonfuls onto ungreased baking sheets. Bake at 400° for 8 minutes. Remove to wire racks. Brush with remaining lemonade concentrate; sprinkle with sugar. Cool. **Yield:** 6 dozen.

MOCHA BROWNIES

My husband doesn't drink coffee, but he loves the taste of these brownies. Since trying this recipe from a co-worker, I'll never make any other kind of brownies.
—Suzanne Strocsher
Bothell, Washington

- 1 package (21-1/2 ounces) brownie mix
- 1/2 cup water
- 1/4 cup vegetable oil
- 1 egg
- 2 teaspoons instant coffee granules
- 1 teaspoon vanilla extract
- FILLING:
- 1/4 cup butter *or* margarine, softened
- 1/2 cup packed brown sugar
- 1 egg
- 2 teaspoons instant coffee granules
- 1 teaspoon vanilla extract
- 1 cup chopped walnuts
- 3/4 cup semisweet chocolate chips
- ICING:
- 1/2 cup semisweet chocolate chips
- 1 tablespoon butter *or* margarine
- 1/4 teaspoon instant coffee granules
- 1 to 2 teaspoons milk

In a bowl, combine the first six ingredients and mix well by hand. Spread into a greased 13-in. x 9-in. x 2-in. baking pan. Bake at 350° for 30-35 minutes or until brownies test done with a wooden pick. Meanwhile, in a small mixing bowl, cream butter and sugar until light and fluffy. Add egg, coffee and vanilla; mix well. Stir in the walnuts and chocolate chips. Spread over brownies. Bake at 350° for 17 minutes. For icing, melt the chocolate chips and butter in a saucepan over low heat, stirring constantly. Whisk in coffee and enough milk to reach a drizzling consistency. Drizzle over warm brownies. Cool before cutting. **Yield:** 3 dozen.

CHEWY GINGER COOKIES

These moist, delicious ginger cookies have an old-fashioned appeal that'll take you back to Grandma's kitchen. I'm never surprised when these treats quickly disappear from my cookie jar. —Bernice Smith
Sturgeon Lake, Minnesota

  3/4 cup shortening
1-1/4 cups sugar, *divided*
    1 egg
  1/4 cup molasses
    1 teaspoon vanilla extract
    2 cups all-purpose flour
    1 teaspoon ground cinnamon
    1 teaspoon ground ginger
    1 teaspoon baking soda
  1/2 teaspoon salt
  1/2 teaspoon ground cloves

In a mixing bowl, cream shortening and 1 cup sugar. Add the egg, molasses and vanilla; mix well. Combine dry ingredients; add to creamed mixture and mix well. Roll into 1-in. balls; roll in remaining sugar. Place 1-1/2 in. apart on ungreased baking sheets. Bake at 375° for 10 minutes or until lightly browned. Cool on wire racks. Store in an airtight container. **Yield:** about 4 dozen.

BLACK WALNUT BROWNIES

These brownies, studded with big chunks of black walnuts, are crisp on top and chewy inside. Our friends have given this treat rave reviews, especially those in areas where black walnuts are hard to come by.
—Catherine Berra Bleem
Walsh, Illinois

    1 cup sugar
  1/4 cup vegetable oil
    2 eggs
    1 teaspoon vanilla extract
  1/2 cup all-purpose flour
    2 tablespoons baking cocoa
  1/2 teaspoon salt
  1/2 cup chopped black walnuts

In a mixing bowl, combine sugar and oil. Add eggs and vanilla; mix well. Combine flour, cocoa and salt; add to sugar mixture and mix well. Stir in wal-

nuts. Pour into a greased 8-in. square baking pan. Bake at 350° for 30-35 minutes or until brownies test done with a wooden pick. Cool on a wire rack. **Yield:** 16 servings.

SUGARLESS HEART COOKIES

(Pictured below)

These melt-in-your-mouth cookies are a wonderful treat, even for those not watching their sugar intake. It's fun to try various flavors of gelatin.—Becky Jones
Akron, Ohio

✓ **This tasty dish uses less sugar, salt and fat. Recipe includes *Diabetic Exchanges*.**

  3/4 cup margarine, softened
    1 package (.3 ounce) mixed fruit sugar-free gelatin
Egg substitute equivalent to 1 egg
    1 teaspoon vanilla extract
1-3/4 cups all-purpose flour
  1/2 teaspoon baking powder

In a mixing bowl, cream margarine and gelatin. Beat in egg substitute and vanilla. Add flour and baking powder; mix well. Chill for 1 hour. Roll out on a lightly floured board to 1/4-in. thickness. Cut with a 1-1/4-in. cookie cutter. Place on ungreased baking sheets. Bake at 400° for 6-7 minutes or until bottoms are lightly browned and cookies are set. Cool on wire racks. **Yield:** 6 dozen. **Diabetic Exchanges:** One serving (2 cookies) equals 1/2 starch, 1/2 fat; also, 59 calories, 49 mg sodium, trace cholesterol, 5 gm carbohydrate, 1 gm protein, 4 gm fat.

Gingerbread House 'Goes Up' Easily

HERE'S a set of tasty "house plans"! "You don't have to be an expert baker—or architect—to build a basic house like this one using my recipe and 'building tips'!" assures Christa Currie of Milwaukie, Oregon, who has 300 edible edifices to her credit. A sample is pictured at right.

GINGERBREAD HOUSE DOUGH

2 cups shortening (no substitutes)
2 cups sugar
2 cups dark molasses
2 tablespoons ground cinnamon
2 teaspoons baking soda
1 teaspoon salt
9 to 10 cups all-purpose flour

In a 5-qt. pan, heat shortening, sugar and molasses on low, stirring constantly until sugar is dissolved. Remove from heat; add cinnamon, baking soda and salt. Stir in flour, 1 cup at a time, until dough can be formed into a ball. Using remaining flour, lightly flour a wooden board. Turn dough onto the board; knead until even in color and smooth (not crumbly or dry), adding more flour if needed. Form into a log. Cut into five equal pieces; wrap in plastic wrap.

Referring to diagrams below, cut patterns out of paper or cardboard. Line a baking sheet with foil and lightly grease the foil. Lay a damp towel on counter; place prepared pan on towel (to prevent slipping). Unwrap one portion of dough. Using a very lightly floured rolling pin, roll out dough directly on baking sheet to a 15-in. x 10-1/2-in. rectangle about 1/4 in. thick. Position patterns at least 1/2 in. apart on dough as shown. Cut around patterns with a sharp knife or pizza cutter; remove patterns. Remove dough scraps; cover and save to re-roll if needed.

Bake at 375° for 10-14 minutes or until cookie springs back when lightly touched. Remove from oven; immediately replace patterns on dough. Cut around the edges to trim off excess cookie. Cool 3-4 minutes or until cookies begin to firm up. Carefully remove to a wire rack; cool. Repeat with remaining dough and patterns.

ICING AND ASSEMBLY

8 cups confectioners' sugar
6 tablespoons meringue powder*
3/4 to 1 cup warm water
Decorating bag
Large dot (#12) decorating tip
Spice jars
Candies and cookies for decorating

In a large mixing bowl, beat the sugar, meringue powder and 3/4 cup water on low until blended. Beat on high for 8-10 minutes or until stiff peaks form, adding additional water, 1 tablespoon at a time, if needed. Place a damp paper towel over bowl and cover tightly until ready to use. *Meringue powder

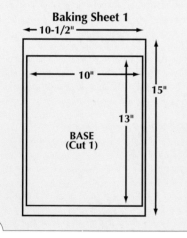

Baking Sheet 1
← 10-1/2" →
10"
15"
13"
BASE (Cut 1)

Baking Sheet 2
8"
6-3/4"
SIDE A (Cut 1)
8"
6-3/4"
SIDE B (Cut 1)

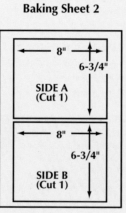

Baking Sheet 3
9"
ROOF A (Cut 1)
6"
9"
ROOF B (Cut 1)
6"

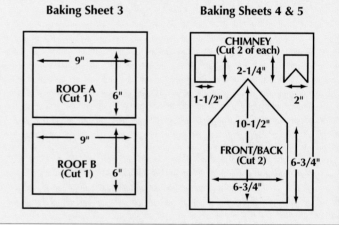

Baking Sheets 4 & 5
CHIMNEY (Cut 2 of each)
2-1/4"
1-1/2"
2"
10-1/2"
FRONT/BACK (Cut 2)
6-3/4"
6-3/4"

FRUITCAKE COOKIES

Oatmeal adds extra texture and subtle sweetness to these old-fashioned goodies. I think you'll find them fun, colorful and chewy without being sticky.
—Dorcas Wright
Guelph, Ontario

1/2 cup butter *or* margarine, softened
1/2 cup shortening
1/2 cup sugar
1/2 cup packed brown sugar
1 egg
1 teaspoon vanilla extract
1 cup all-purpose flour
1/2 teaspoon baking soda
1/2 teaspoon salt
2 cups old-fashioned oats
1 cup flaked coconut
1/2 cup chopped dates
1/2 cup *each* chopped red and green candied

is available where cake decorating supplies are sold. Or you may order it by contacting Wilton Enterprises, 2240 W. 75th St., Woodridge IL 60517; 1-708/963-7100.

To assemble frame of the house, test your cookie pieces to make sure they fit together snugly. If necessary, file carefully with a serrated knife or an emery board to make fit. Fill decorating bag two-thirds full with icing. Beginning with the front of the house, squeeze a 3/8-in.-wide strip of icing onto the bottom edge of the front piece. Position on the cookie base, 3 in. from the front edge of the base. Prop it upright with spice jars for 2-3 minutes or until icing hardens; remove jars.

To add the sides, squeeze icing on lower edge of one side piece and side edge of the front piece. Align pieces at a right angle, making sure they are as tight as possible. Repeat with the other side.

To add the back, squeeze icing on the bottom and side edges of the back piece; position with the other assembled pieces. For added stability, squeeze icing along the *inside* edge of all pieces and corners.

To assemble the roof, working with one side at a time, squeeze icing on the upper edge of the slant of the front and back pieces on one side. Also squeeze icing on the adjoining side piece. Carefully place roof piece on the slants so that the roof's peak is even with the points of the front and back. (There will be an overhang of 1/2 in.) Repeat with other side of the roof.

To decorate, add a chimney if desired (see photo for assembly). Decorate the house with remaining icing, candies and cookies of your choice.

cherries
1/2 cup chopped candied pineapple

In a mixing bowl, cream butter, shortening and sugars. Add egg and vanilla; mix well. Combine the flour, baking soda, salt and oats; add to creamed mixture and mix well. Stir in the coconut, dates, cherries and pineapple. Shape into 1-in. balls; place on greased baking sheets. Bake at 325° for 15 minutes or until lightly browned. Cool on wire racks. **Yield:** 5-6 dozen.

ROSETTES
(Pictured below)

Dipping the edges of these traditional favorites in icing beautifully defines their lacy pattern. People are always impressed to see a plate of these crisp cookies presented on the table at Christmas. —Iola Egle
McCook, Nebraska

> 2 eggs
> 2 teaspoons sugar
> 1 cup milk
> 1 tablespoon vanilla extract
> 1 cup all-purpose flour
> 1/4 teaspoon salt
> Cooking oil for deep-fat frying
> ICING:
> 2 cups confectioners' sugar
> 1 teaspoon vanilla extract
> 1 to 3 tablespoons water

In a mixing bowl, beat eggs and sugar; stir in milk and vanilla. Combine flour and salt; add to batter and beat until smooth. Heat 2-1/2 in. of oil to 365° in a deep-fat fryer or electric skillet. Place rosette iron in hot oil, then dip in batter, three-fourths up on sides of iron (do not let batter run over top of iron). Immediately place into hot oil; loosen rosette with fork and remove iron. Fry 1-2 minutes per side or until golden. Remove to a wire rack covered with paper towel. Repeat with remaining batter. For icing, combine the sugar, vanilla and enough water to make a dipping consistency. Dip edges of rosettes into icing; dry on wire racks. **Yield:** 4-5 dozen.

CHOCOLATE PINWHEELS
(Pictured above)

I prepare these eye-catching sweets every Christmas. My husband's 95-year-old grandfather was intrigued with how the swirls got in these cookies!

—Patricia Kile
Greentown, Pennsylvania

    1/2 **cup butter** *or* **margarine, softened**
      1 **cup sugar**
    1/4 **cup packed brown sugar**
      1 **egg**
1-1/2 **teaspoons vanilla extract**
      2 **cups all-purpose flour**
      1 **teaspoon baking powder**
Pinch salt
FILLING:
      2 **cups (12 ounces) semisweet chocolate**
        chips
      2 **tablespoons butter** *or* **margarine**
    1/4 **teaspoon vanilla extract**
Pinch salt

In a mixing bowl, cream butter and sugars. Add egg and vanilla; beat until light and fluffy. Combine dry ingredients; beat into creamed mixture. Divide dough in half; place each half between two sheets of waxed paper. Roll into 12-in. x 10-in. rectangles. Chill until almost firm, about 30 minutes. In a saucepan over low heat, melt chips and butter. Add vanilla and salt; mix well. Spread over dough. Carefully roll up each rectangle into a tight jelly roll; wrap in waxed paper. Chill for 2 hours or until firm. Cut into 1/8-in. slices with a sharp thin knife; place on greased or parchment-lined baking sheets. Bake at 350° for 7-10 minutes or until lightly browned. Cool on wire racks. **Yield:** about 9 dozen.

BANANA OATMEAL COOKIES

To help interest my kids in cooking, I started with this recipe from my own childhood. My mom made these cookies when I was young. Now my seven children like them as much as I did. We quadruple the recipe to serve our big family, so the kids get to practice their math skills and have fun at the same time.

—Jacqueline Wilson
Armstrong Creek, Wisconsin

1-1/2 **cups all-purpose flour**
      1 **cup sugar**
      1 **teaspoon salt**
    1/2 **teaspoon baking soda**
    1/2 **teaspoon ground cinnamon**
    1/4 **teaspoon ground nutmeg**
    3/4 **cup butter** *or* **margarine, softened**
      1 **egg**
      1 **cup mashed ripe bananas (about 2)**
1-3/4 **cups quick-cooking oats**
      1 **cup (6 ounces) semisweet chocolate chips**
    1/2 **cup chopped walnuts**

In a mixing bowl, combine dry ingredients; beat in butter until mixture resembles coarse crumbs. Add egg, bananas and oats; mix well. Stir in chips and nuts. Drop by tablespoonfuls onto greased baking sheets. Bake at 375° for 13-15 minutes or until golden brown. Cool on wire racks. **Yield:** 4 dozen.

QUICK GHOST COOKIES

When I don't have time to make cookies from scratch, I simply spruce up store-bought cookies. These are a real hit with "goblins" of all ages. —Denise Smith
Lusk, Wyoming

    1 **pound white confectionery coating*,**
      cut into small chunks
    1 **package (1 pound) Nutter Butter peanut**
      butter cookies
Mini semisweet chocolate chips

In top of double boiler over simmering water, melt confectionery coating, stirring occasionally. Dip cookies into chocolate, covering completely. Set on waxed paper to cool. Brush ends with a pastry brush dipped in chocolate where fingers touched cookies. While chocolate is still warm, immediately place two chips on each cookie for eyes. **Yield:** about 3 dozen. ***Editor's Note:** White confectionery coating is found in the baking section of most grocery stores. It is sometimes labeled "almond bark" or "candy coating" and is often sold in bulk packages of 1 to 1-1/2 pounds.

HARVEST PUMPKIN BROWNIES

(Pictured above)

These lightly spiced pumpkin brownies are a nice change from the typical chocolate variety. They're moist and delicious and make a festive treat.

—*Iola Egle*
McCook, Nebraska

1 can (16 ounces) pumpkin
4 eggs
3/4 cup vegetable oil
2 teaspoons vanilla extract
2 cups all-purpose flour
2 cups sugar
1 tablespoon pumpkin pie spice
2 teaspoons ground cinnamon
2 teaspoons baking powder
1 teaspoon baking soda
1/2 teaspoon salt
FROSTING:
6 tablespoons butter *or* margarine,
softened
1 package (3 ounces) cream cheese, softened
1 teaspoon vanilla extract
1 teaspoon milk
1/8 teaspoon salt
1-1/2 to 2 cups confectioners' sugar

In a mixing bowl, beat pumpkin, eggs, oil and vanilla until well mixed. Combine dry ingredients; stir into pumpkin mixture and mix well. Pour into a greased 15-in. x 10-in. x 1-in. baking pan. Bake at 350° for 20-25 minutes or until brownies test done with a wooden pick. Cool. In

a small mixing bowl, beat the butter, cream cheese, vanilla, milk and salt until smooth. Add confectioners' sugar; mix well. Frost brownies. Store in the refrigerator. **Yield:** 5-6 dozen.

SUGAR DIAMONDS

(Pictured below)

I admit it—I don't have a lot of patience for decorating, so I look for tasty recipes with interesting shapes and textures, like these cookies. Folks will never know you didn't fuss!

—*Gladys De Boer*
Castleford, Idaho

1 cup butter (no substitutes), softened
1 cup sugar
1 egg, *separated*
1/2 teaspoon vanilla extract
2 cups all-purpose flour
1/2 teaspoon ground cinnamon
Pinch salt
1/2 cup chopped pecans

In a mixing bowl, cream butter and sugar. Add egg yolk and vanilla; mix well. Combine flour, cinnamon and salt; gradually add to creamed mixture. Spoon into a greased 15-in. x 10-in. x 1-in. baking pan. Cover dough with plastic wrap and press evenly into pan; remove wrap. In another mixing bowl, beat egg white until foamy; brush over dough. Sprinkle with pecans. Bake at 300° for 30 minutes. Cut into 1-1/2-in. diamond shapes while warm. **Yield:** about 6 dozen.

DIABETIC ORANGE COOKIES
(Pictured above)

These good-for-you cookies have a wonderful citrus flavor and just the right amount of natural sweetness. You'll find they appeal to everyone—even to folks who aren't on restricted diets. —Ginette Martino
Deltona, Florida

✓ **This tasty dish uses less sugar, salt and fat. Recipe includes *Diabetic Exchanges*.**

1-1/2 cups all-purpose flour
   1 teaspoon baking powder
Sugar substitute equivalent to 3/4 cup sugar*
   2 teaspoons grated orange peel
  1/4 teaspoon salt
  1/8 teaspoon ground nutmeg
  1/2 cup margarine spread (70% vegetable oil)
  1/3 cup chopped raisins
  1/4 cup egg substitute
   2 tablespoons orange juice

In a medium bowl, combine the first six ingredients; mix well. Cut in margarine until mixture resembles coarse crumbs. Stir in raisins. Add egg substitute and orange juice; mix well. Drop by teaspoonfuls onto baking sheets coated with nonstick cooking spray. Flatten with a fork dipped in flour. Bake at 375° for 13-15 minutes. **Yield:** 30 cookies. **Diabetic Exchanges:** One serving (2 cookies) equals 1 starch, 1/2 fat; also, 102 calories,

137 mg sodium, 0 cholesterol, 14 gm carbohydrate, 2 gm protein, 4 gm fat. ***Editor's Note:** Use an artificial sweetener recommended for baking, such as Sweet 'N Low or Sweet One.

SLICE-AND-BAKE COOKIES

I love this cookie dough since it's so versatile. You can add any kind of chips or nuts you like. Plus, there's no rolling...they easily slice into delicious treats.
—Monica Gibbons
Dayton, Ohio

   1 cup shortening
  3/4 cup packed brown sugar
  3/4 cup sugar
   2 eggs
   1 teaspoon vanilla extract
2-1/4 cups all-purpose flour
   1 teaspoon salt
   1 teaspoon baking soda
1-1/2 cups "extras" (any one or combination of the following: chocolate, butterscotch, toffee or peanut butter chips, chopped candied cherries or nuts)

In a mixing bowl, cream shortening and sugars. Add eggs and vanilla. Combine flour, salt and baking soda; add to the creamed mixture and mix well. Fold in 1-1/2 cups "extras". Shape into a 15-in. x 2-in. roll; wrap tightly with plastic wrap. Chill 2 hours or up to 1 week. To bake, cut into 1/2-in. slices. Place 3 in. apart on ungreased baking sheets. Bake at 350° for 10 minutes. Cool 5 minutes; remove to wire racks. **Yield:** 2-1/2 dozen.

PEANUT COOKIES

I use my grandmother's recipe to make these crisp peanutty cookies, which are a hearty between-meal snack...especially when you're traveling. They are my husband's all-time favorites. —Wendy Masters
Grand Valley, Ontario

  2/3 cup shortening
1-1/3 cups packed brown sugar
   2 eggs, lightly beaten
1-1/2 teaspoons vanilla extract
1-2/3 cups all-purpose flour
  1/2 teaspoon baking soda
  1/2 teaspoon salt
   2 cups salted peanuts

In a mixing bowl, cream shortening and sugar. Beat in eggs and vanilla until light and fluffy. Combine flour, baking soda and salt; gradually add to the creamed mixture. Fold in peanuts. Drop by teaspoonfuls 2 in. apart onto greased baking sheets. Bake at 350° for 10-12 minutes or until browned and almost set (centers will be soft). Remove to a wire rack to cool. **Yield:** 4 dozen.

S'MORES BARS

You don't have to be camping to enjoy the great taste of s'mores. And since these are made in your kitchen, you don't have to put up with mosquitoes!
—Darlene Markel
Sublimity, Oregon

 3 **cups graham cracker crumbs**
3/4 **cup butter *or* margarine, melted**
1/3 **cup sugar**
 3 **cups miniature marshmallows**
 2 **cups (12 ounces) semisweet chocolate chips**

Combine crumbs, butter and sugar; press half into a greased 13-in. x 9-in. x 2-in. baking pan. Sprinkle with marshmallows and chocolate chips. Top with remaining crumb mixture; press firmly. Bake at 375° for 10 minutes. Remove from the oven and immediately press top firmly with spatula. Cool completely. Cut into bars. **Yield:** 3 dozen.

HONEY PECAN SNAPS

This recipe was originally a gingersnap cookie recipe, but I substituted honey for molasses and added pecans. Everyone just loves these cookies. They keep well, staying nice and moist. —Cheryl Christiansen
McPherson, Kansas

1/2 **cup butter *or* margarine, softened**
1/2 **cup shortening**
1-1/2 **cups sugar**
1/2 **cup honey**
 2 **eggs**
 2 **tablespoons lemon juice**
 4 **cups all-purpose flour**
2-1/2 **teaspoons baking soda**
 1 **teaspoon ground cloves**
 1 **teaspoon ground cinnamon**
1/2 **teaspoon ground ginger**
1/2 **teaspoon salt**

 1 **cup chopped pecans**
Additional sugar

In a mixing bowl, cream butter, shortening and sugar until fluffy. Add honey, eggs and lemon juice; beat well. Combine dry ingredients; gradually add to creamed mixture. Fold in pecans. Shape into 1-in. balls; roll in sugar. Place on ungreased baking sheets. Bake at 350° for 12-13 minutes or until golden brown. Cool 2 minutes; remove to wire racks. **Yield:** about 4 dozen.

CUPCAKE BROWNIES
(Pictured above)

These no-mess brownies travel well to potlucks and picnics. Pecans make them extra special.
—Nina Towler
Baird, Texas

 1 **cup butter *or* margarine**
 4 **squares (1 ounce *each*) semisweet chocolate**
 4 **eggs**
1-3/4 **cups sugar**
 1 **teaspoon vanilla extract**
 1 **cup all-purpose flour**
1-1/2 **cups chopped pecans**

In a small saucepan over low heat, melt butter and chocolate; cool for 10 minutes. In a mixing bowl, beat eggs and sugar. Add vanilla and chocolate mixture; stir in flour and nuts. Fill greased or paper-lined muffin cups two-thirds full. Bake at 350° for 18-20 minutes or until brownies test done with a wooden pick. Cool. **Yield:** about 1-1/2 dozen.

CHOCOLATE PEANUT BUTTER COOKIES

(Pictured above)

It's a snap to make a batch of tasty cookies using this recipe, which calls for a convenient boxed cake mix. My husband and son gobble them up. —Mary Pulyer Port St. Lucie, Florida

> 1 package (18-1/4 ounces) devil's food cake mix
> 2 eggs
> 1/3 cup vegetable oil
> 1 package (10 ounces) peanut butter chips

In a mixing bowl, beat cake mix, eggs and oil (batter will be very stiff). Stir in chips. Roll into 1-in. balls. Place on lightly greased baking sheets; flatten slightly. Bake at 350° for 10 minutes or until a slight indentation remains when lightly touched. Cool for 2 minutes before removing to a wire rack. **Yield:** 4 dozen.

SPIDERWEB BROWNIES

To decorate these moist brownies for Halloween, I drizzle a chocolate spiderweb on their white icing. They're so delicious and chocolaty...you'll find yourself making them for gatherings throughout the year. —Sandy Pichon Slidell, Louisiana

> 4 squares (1 ounce *each*) unsweetened chocolate
> 3/4 cup butter *or* margarine
> 2 cups sugar
> 3 eggs, beaten
> 1 teaspoon vanilla extract
> 1 cup all-purpose flour
> 1 cup chopped pecans *or* walnuts
> 1 jar (7 ounces) marshmallow creme
> 1 square (1 ounce) semisweet chocolate

In a saucepan over low heat, stir unsweetened chocolate and butter until chocolate is melted. Remove from the heat; stir in sugar. Cool for 10 minutes. Blend in eggs and vanilla. Stir in flour and nuts. Pour into a greased foil-lined 13-in. x 9-in. x 2-in. baking pan. Bake at 350° for 30 minutes or until a toothpick inserted in the center comes out clean (do not overbake). Immediately drop marshmallow creme by spoonfuls over hot brownies; spread evenly. Cool on a wire rack. Lift out of the pan; remove foil. Place on serving tray. For web decoration, melt semisweet chocolate and pour into a small resealable plastic bag. Cut a small hole in one corner of the bag; drizzle chocolate over creme in a spiderweb design. **Yield:** 2 dozen.

PISTACHIO CHIP COOKIES

Coming from a family of pistachio producers, I've collected hundreds of recipes featuring these crisp, delicious green nuts. This is one of our favorites. —Malinda Moore Davis Fresno, California

> 1-1/4 cups butter *or* margarine, softened
> 2 cups packed brown sugar
> 2 eggs
> 2 teaspoons vanilla extract
> 2-1/2 cups all-purpose flour
> 1 teaspoon baking powder
> 1 teaspoon baking soda
> 1/2 cup old-fashioned oats
> 1 package (12 ounces) vanilla chips
> 1-1/3 cups chopped pistachios, *divided*

In a mixing bowl, cream butter and sugar. Add eggs and vanilla; mix well. Combine flour, baking powder, baking soda and oats; gradually add to creamed mixture and mix well. Stir in chips and 1 cup pistachios. Shape into 1-in. balls; place 2 in. apart on ungreased baking sheets. Lightly press remaining pistachios into cookies. Bake at 350° for 10-12 minutes or until lightly browned. Cool 2 minutes before removing to wire racks. **Yield:** about 9 dozen.

SOUR CREAM ANISE COOKIES

I first made these drop cookies when I had my arm in a cast and was anxious to return to the kitchen. That should tell you just how easy these are to prepare! You'll love the subtle licorice flavor from the anise.
—Mina Dyck
Boissevain, Manitoba

1 cup shortening
1 cup packed brown sugar
1 cup honey
1 cup (8 ounces) sour cream
3 eggs
3-1/2 cups all-purpose flour
2 teaspoons baking soda
3/4 teaspoon aniseed
1/4 teaspoon salt

In a mixing bowl, cream shortening and sugar. Add the honey, sour cream and eggs; beat well. Combine flour, baking soda, aniseed and salt; add to creamed mixture and mix well. Drop by teaspoonfuls 2 in. apart onto greased baking sheets. Bake at 350° for 12-15 minutes or until lightly browned. Cool on a wire rack. **Yield:** about 8 dozen.

In the Mood for Mint?

Give your favorite brownie recipe a holiday taste by stirring in crushed candy canes or peppermint candies. To crush them, put the candy between two large plastic lids (like those from coffee cans) and tap with a hammer.

FINNISH BUTTER COOKIES

These crispy Finnish cookies have a delicate texture and wonderful almond flavor. I've been making them for the holidays for over 40 years...now my daughters are carrying on the tradition.
—Audrey Thibodeau
Mesa, Arizona

3/4 cup butter (no substitutes), softened
1/4 cup sugar
1 teaspoon almond extract
2 cups all-purpose flour
1 egg white
2 tablespoons sugar
1/3 cup ground almonds

In a mixing bowl, cream butter and sugar. Stir in extract. Add 1-1/4 cups flour; mix well. Knead in

---

remaining flour. Cover and chill at least 2 hours. Roll out on a lightly floured surface to 1/4-in. thickness. Cut with a small cookie cutter (1-1/2 to 2 in.); place on ungreased baking sheets. Beat egg white until foamy; brush over cookies. Sprinkle with sugar and almonds. Bake at 350° for 7-8 minutes or until lightly browned. Cool on wire racks. **Yield:** 4 dozen.

FOR over 60 years, Girl Scout Cookies have been America's most familiar (and flavorful) fund-raiser. Did you know that originally every one of those treats was homemade?

Individual troops began selling homemade cookies door-to-door in the 1920's. In 1935, the Girl Scouts held their first nationally coordinated cookie sale. Today, nearly a million Scouts participate in the sale annually.

To commemorate the 60th anniversary of that first nationwide sale, the Girl Scouts are pleased to share the original sugar cookie recipe used when the troops made their own.

Cut these old-fashioned cookies using any cutter, or you can purchase a cutter in the shape of the Girl Scout trefoil for under $3 by contacting your local Girl Scout Council.

Make a batch today to taste a bit of great cookie history!

GIRL SCOUT COOKIES

1 cup butter *or* margarine, softened
1 cup sugar
2 eggs
2 tablespoons milk
1 teaspoon vanilla extract
2-1/2 cups all-purpose flour
2 teaspoons baking powder
Decorator's sugar, optional

In a mixing bowl, cream butter and sugar. Add eggs, one at a time, beating well after each addition. Add milk and vanilla; beat until light and fluffy. Combine flour and baking powder; gradually add to creamed mixture and mix well. Chill at least 2 hours or overnight. On a lightly floured surface, roll the dough to 1/4-in. thickness. Cut with trefoil cookie cutter or cutter of your choice. Place cookies on ungreased baking sheets. Sprinkle with sugar if desired. Bake at 350° for 8-10 minutes or until lightly browned. Cool on wire racks. **Yield:** 4 dozen (2-1/2-inch cookies).

Cakes, Pies & Desserts

Enticing pies, sweet candies, tempting tarts and a host of delectable desserts are sure to bring your everyday dinners and special-occasion suppers to a tantalizing conclusion.

PLUM PIE

(Pictured above and on front cover)

I get lots of plums from neighbors who are glad to share. My husband loves this special dessert. Of course, he claims to only like two kinds of pies— warm ones and cold ones!
—Shirley Smith
Noti, Oregon

1/4 cup packed brown sugar
1/4 cup saltine crumbs
Pastry for double-crust pie (9 inches)
1-1/2 pounds fresh plums, pitted and quartered
1 cup sugar
1/4 cup all-purpose flour
1 teaspoon ground cinnamon
3 tablespoons cold butter *or* margarine
1 teaspoon cinnamon-sugar

In a small bowl, combine brown sugar and crumbs. Line a 9-in. pie pan with bottom crust; sprinkle with brown sugar mixture and pack gently. Cover with plums. Combine the sugar, flour and cinnamon; cut in butter until crumbly. Sprinkle over plums. Roll out remaining pastry to fit top of pie. Make small cuts or slits in top crust; place over plums. Seal and flute edges. Sprinkle with cinnamon-sugar. Bake at 400° for 30 minutes. Reduce heat to 350°; bake 25 minutes more or until golden brown. **Yield:** 6-8 servings.

CHOCOLATE PIZZA

Chocolate lovers will enjoy this delightfully sweet confection. It has a unique texture and flavor that people can't seem to resist. Whenever I make this for special occasions, I am always asked for the recipe.
—Janet Smith
Sunnyvale, California

3 cups vanilla chips, *divided*
2 cups (12 ounces) semisweet chocolate chips
2 cups miniature marshmallows
1 cup Rice Krispies
1 cup chopped walnuts
1/2 cup halved maraschino cherries, patted dry
1/4 cup flaked coconut
1 teaspoon vegetable oil

In a microwave-safe bowl, combine 2-1/2 cups vanilla chips and the chocolate chips. Microwave on high for 2 minutes; stir. Microwave for 1-2 minutes; stir until smooth. Immediately add marshmallows, cereal and walnuts; mix well. Spread evenly on a 13-in. pizza pan that has been coated with nonstick cooking spray. Arrange cherries on top; sprinkle with coconut. Microwave the remaining vanilla chips on high for 1 minute. Add oil and stir until smooth. Drizzle over pizza. Chill until firm. Serve at room temperature. **Yield:** 16-20 servings. **Editor's Note:** This recipe was tested in a 700-watt microwave.

RHUBARB RAISIN CRISP

In spring, this crisp is the first thing I make with our garden rhubarb. It's a treat my family patiently waits for all winter long.
—Martha Dayton
Alexander, New York

5 cups sliced fresh *or* frozen rhubarb
1/2 cup plus 2 tablespoons all-purpose flour, *divided*
1/2 cup raisins
3/4 cup sugar
3/4 cup packed brown sugar
1 teaspoon ground cinnamon
1/4 teaspoon salt
1/3 cup quick-cooking oats
1/3 cup cold butter *or* margarine
Vanilla ice cream, optional

Combine rhubarb and 2 tablespoons of flour; place in a greased 8-in. square baking dish. Sprinkle with raisins. Combine the sugar, brown sugar, cinnamon and salt; sprinkle over the raisins. Combine oats and remaining flour; cut in butter until crumbly. Sprinkle evenly over top. Bake at 375° for 40-45 minutes or until topping is golden brown. Serve warm with ice cream if desired. **Yield:** 6-8 servings.

ICE CREAM CAKE ROLL
(Pictured below)

Dinner guests will think you fussed all day preparing this dessert. But the cake roll can be made and filled with any ice cream flavor ahead of time, then thawed once company comes. —*Kathy Scott*
Hemingford, Nebraska

    4 eggs, *separated*
  3/4 cup sugar
    1 teaspoon vanilla extract
  3/4 cup cake flour
  1/4 cup baking cocoa
  3/4 teaspoon baking powder
  1/4 teaspoon salt
    3 cups ice cream, softened
CHOCOLATE SAUCE:
    2 squares (1 ounce *each*) unsweetened
      baking chocolate
  1/4 cup butter *or* margarine
  2/3 cup evaporated milk, heated to 160° to
      170°
    1 cup sugar

In a large mixing bowl, beat egg yolks on high for 3 minutes or until light and fluffy. Gradually add sugar and vanilla, beating until thick and lemon-colored. Combine flour, cocoa and baking powder; gradually add to egg yolk mixture. Beat on low until well mixed (mixture will be thick). Beat egg whites and salt until soft peaks form. Fold a small amount into batter until no streaks of white remain; add the remaining egg whites. Grease a 15-in. x 10-in. x 1-in. pan; line with waxed paper and grease and flour paper. Spread batter evenly in pan. Bake at 350° for 15 minutes or until cake springs back when lightly touched. Turn out onto a linen towel dusted with confectioners' sugar. Peel off pa-

per and roll up in towel. Cool for 30 minutes. Unroll cake; spread with ice cream to within 1 in. of edges. Roll up again. Cover with plastic wrap and freeze until serving. In the top of a double boiler over hot water, melt chocolate and butter. Gradually add warm milk and sugar; stir constantly for 5 minutes or until completely dissolved. Spoon over slices of cake. **Yield:** 10 servings (1-1/2 cups sauce).

"AT THE Patchwork Quilt Country Inn near Middlebury, Indiana, we ordered Buttermilk Pie to top off a wonderful home-style meal," relates Sharon Lloyd of West Terre Haute, Indiana.

"I'd love to have the recipe for that creamy delicious pie if *Taste of Home* could get it!"

Complimented by the request, Patchwork Quilt owner Maxine Zook happily shared the recipe. "Buttermilk Pie is often made by the Amish and Mennonite cooks in our area," she notes. "Our baker, Mary Hath, gave us this recipe. We've served it for years."

Maxine and husband Daryl, along with Mark and Susan Thomas, bought the bed-and-breakfast inn and restaurant in 1988. "We're located on a working farm and serve real country-style food," informs Maxine. "Buttermilk Pecan Chicken is our most popular entree, and we feature a fresh salad buffet. But we encourage guests to save room for one of our memorable desserts."

BUTTERMILK PIE

      3 cups sugar
      6 tablespoons all-purpose flour
  1-1/2 cups buttermilk, *divided*
      5 eggs
    1/2 cup butter *or* margarine, melted
      2 teaspoons vanilla extract
      2 unbaked pastry shells (9 inches *each*)
      1 cup chopped pecans, optional

In a bowl, combine sugar, flour and 3/4 cup buttermilk. Add eggs and remaining buttermilk; mix well. Stir in the butter and vanilla. Divide evenly among pie shells. Top with pecans if desired. Bake at 425° for 10 minutes. Reduce heat to 350°; bake 25-30 minutes longer or until a knife inserted near the center comes out clean. Cool completely. Store in the refrigerator. **Yield:** 12-16 servings.

COOKIES-AND-CREAM CAKE
(Pictured below)

This moist, fun-to-eat cake will remind you of Oreo cookies. I won first prize in a baking contest when I prepared this tantalizing dessert. —Pat Habiger
Spearville, Kansas

1 package (18-1/4 ounces) white cake mix
1-1/4 cups water
1/3 cup vegetable oil
3 egg whites
1 cup coarsely crushed cream-filled chocolate sandwich cookies (about 8)
FROSTING:
4 to 4-1/2 cups confectioners' sugar
1/2 cup shortening
1/4 cup milk
1 teaspoon vanilla extract
Additional cream-filled chocolate sandwich cookies, halved *and/or* crushed, optional

In a large mixing bowl, combine cake mix, water, oil and egg whites. Beat on low speed until moistened; beat on high for 2 minutes. Gently fold in the crushed cookies. Pour into two greased and floured 8-in. round cake pans. Bake at 350° for 30 minutes or until a wooden pick inserted in the center comes out clean. Cool for 10 minutes; remove from pans to wire rack to cool completely. In a mixing bowl, beat sugar, shortening, milk and vanilla until smooth. Frost cake. If desired, decorate the top with cookie halves and the sides with crushed cookies. **Yield:** 12 servings.

EASY APPLE CRISP

This is a delicious dessert perfect for young cooks to prepare. It's easy to make since there's no crust—just a crumbly topping. Plus, with apples and oats, it's a wholesome treat. —Sheri Hatten
Devil's Lake, North Dakota

10 to 11 cups sliced peeled baking apples
1/2 cup sugar
1 teaspoon ground cinnamon, *divided*
1 cup all-purpose flour
1 cup packed brown sugar
1/2 cup quick-cooking oats
1 teaspoon baking powder
1/4 teaspoon ground nutmeg
1/2 cup butter *or* margarine

Place apples in a greased 13-in. x 9-in. x 2-in. baking dish. Combine sugar and 1/2 teaspoon cinnamon; sprinkle over apples. Combine flour, brown sugar, oats, baking powder, nutmeg and remaining cinnamon; cut in butter until mixture resembles coarse crumbs. Sprinkle over the apples. Bake at 375° for 50-60 minutes or until apples are tender. **Yield:** 12-16 servings.

RASPBERRY CUSTARD KUCHEN

We love this for breakfast or as a special dessert. It's no fuss to fix and impressive to serve.
—Virginia Arndt
Sequim, Washington

1-1/2 cups all-purpose flour, *divided*
1/2 teaspoon salt
1/2 cup cold butter *or* margarine
2 tablespoons whipping cream
1/2 cup sugar
3 cups fresh raspberries
TOPPING:
1 cup sugar
1 tablespoon all-purpose flour
2 eggs, beaten
1 cup whipping cream
1 teaspoon vanilla extract

In a bowl, combine 1 cup flour and salt; cut in butter until the mixture resembles coarse crumbs. Stir in cream; pat into a greased 13-in. x 9-in. x 2-in. baking pan. Combine the sugar and remaining flour; sprinkle over crust. Arrange raspberries over crust. For topping, combine sugar and flour. Stir in eggs, cream and vanilla; pour over berries. Bake at 375° for 40-45 minutes or until lightly browned. Serve warm or chilled. Store in the refrigerator. **Yield:** 10-12 servings.

CHOCOLATE ANGEL FOOD DESSERT

"Yum!" and "Wonderful!" are typical reactions to this make-ahead dessert. And it's the perfect thing to prepare when you don't want to heat up the kitchen.
—Norma Erne
Albuquerque, New Mexico

   2 cups (12 ounces) semisweet chocolate chips
1/4 cup milk
   3 egg yolks, beaten
   2 teaspoons sugar
   2 cups whipping cream, whipped
   1 angel food cake (10 ounces)

In the top of a double boiler over boiling water, melt chocolate chips. Combine milk, egg yolks and sugar; gradually add to chocolate, stirring constantly. Cook for 2-3 minutes. Remove from the heat; cool to room temperature. Fold in cream. Tear cake into bite-size pieces; place half in a greased 13-in. x 9-in. x 2-in. baking pan. Top with half of the chocolate mixture. Repeat layers. Cover and refrigerate overnight. Serve chilled. **Yield:** 16-20 servings.

VANILLA CREAM FRUIT TART

(Pictured above right)

It's well worth the effort to prepare this spectacular tart, which is best made and served the same day.
—Susan Terzakis
Andover, Massachusetts

3/4 cup butter *or* margarine, softened
1/2 cup confectioners' sugar
1-1/2 cups all-purpose flour
   1 package (10 ounces) vanilla chips, melted and cooled
1/4 cup whipping cream
   1 package (8 ounces) cream cheese, softened
   1 pint fresh strawberries, sliced
   1 cup fresh blueberries
   1 cup fresh raspberries
1/2 cup pineapple juice
1/4 cup sugar
   1 tablespoon cornstarch
1/2 teaspoon lemon juice

In a mixing bowl, cream butter and confectioners' sugar. Beat in flour (mixture will be crumbly). Pat into the bottom of a greased 12-in. pizza pan. Bake at 300° for 25-28 minutes or until lightly browned. Cool. In another mixing bowl, beat

melted chips and cream. Add cream cheese and beat until smooth. Spread over crust. Chill for 30 minutes. Arrange berries over filling. In a saucepan, combine pineapple juice, sugar, cornstarch and lemon juice; bring to a boil over medium heat. Boil for 2 minutes or until thickened, stirring constantly. Cool; brush over fruit. Chill 1 hour before serving. Store in the refrigerator. **Yield:** 12-16 servings.

CHOCOLATE MOUSSE WITH STRAWBERRIES

You'll savor this simple tempting dessert. It's like chocolate-covered strawberries without the hassles.
—Kim Marie Van Rheenen
Mendota, Illinois

✓ This tasty dish uses less sugar, salt and fat. Recipe includes *Diabetic Exchanges.*

   1 package (1.4 ounces) instant sugar-free chocolate fudge pudding mix
   1 cup cold skim milk
1-3/4 cups light whipped topping
Whole fresh strawberries

In a mixing bowl, beat pudding and milk until blended, about 2 minutes. Fold in whipped topping. Serve with strawberries for dipping. Can also be served over slices of angel food cake. **Yield:** 2-1/2 cups. **Diabetic Exchanges:** One 2-tablespoon serving equals a free food; also, 24 calories, 70 mg sodium, trace cholesterol, 4 gm carbohydrate, 1 gm protein, trace fat.

sides of pan. Garnish with oranges and cherries.
Yield: 10-12 servings.

BROWNIE PIE

This one-of-a-kind dessert combines my family's two favorite treats—brownies and pie. "Chocoholics" will love this extra-rich treat.
—*June Formanek*
Belle Plain, Iowa

> 2 squares (1 ounce *each*) unsweetened chocolate
> 2 tablespoons butter *or* margarine
> 3 eggs
> 3/4 cup corn syrup
> 1/2 cup sugar
> 1 teaspoon vanilla extract
> 1 unbaked pastry shell (9 inches)
> 1/2 cup chopped pecans
> Vanilla ice cream *or* whipped cream, optional

In a saucepan over low heat, melt the chocolate and butter; cool slightly. In a bowl, beat eggs, corn syrup and sugar; stir in vanilla and the chocolate mixture. Pour into pastry shell. Sprinkle with nuts. Bake at 350° for 45-50 minutes or until top begins to crack and crust is golden brown. Cool. Serve with ice cream or whipped cream if desired. Store in the refrigerator. **Yield:** 8 servings.
Editor's Note: This recipe does not contain flour.

LEMON RICE PUDDING

The addition of grated lemon peel adds a flavorful twist to traditional rice puddings. Everyone will savor this refreshingly creamy dessert.
—*Barbara Parker*
Newport, New Hampshire

> ✓ This tasty dish uses less sugar, salt and fat. Recipe includes *Diabetic Exchanges.*

> 1-1/2 cups water
> 1/2 cup uncooked long grain rice
> 1/3 cup raisins
> 1/4 teaspoon ground nutmeg
> 1 package (1 ounce) instant sugar-free vanilla pudding mix
> 2 teaspoons grated lemon peel

In a saucepan, bring water, rice, raisins and nutmeg to a boil. Reduce heat; cover and simmer for 15-20 minutes or until all liquid is absorbed. Cool. Prepare pudding mix according to package directions.

ORANGE CHARLOTTE

(Pictured above)

Mom prepared this light and fluffy citrus dessert whenever Dad grilled outdoors. It gave our meals on sunny summer days a fresh-tasting finish.
—*Sue Gronholz*
Columbus, Wisconsin

> 3 envelopes unflavored gelatin
> 3/4 cup cold water
> 3/4 cup boiling water
> 1-1/2 cups orange juice
> 2 tablespoons lemon juice
> 1-1/2 teaspoons grated orange peel
> 1-1/2 cups sugar, *divided*
> 2-1/2 cups whipping cream
> 1/2 cup mandarin oranges
> 3 maraschino cherries

In a large bowl, combine gelatin and cold water; let stand for 10 minutes. Add boiling water; stir until gelatin dissolves. Add juices, orange peel and 3/4 cup sugar. Set bowl in ice water until mixture is syrupy, stirring occasionally. Meanwhile, whip cream until soft peaks form. Gradually add remaining sugar and beat until stiff peaks form. When gelatin mixture begins to thicken, fold in whipped cream. Lightly coat a 9-in. springform pan with nonstick cooking spray. Pour mixture into pan; chill overnight. Just before serving, run a knife around the edge of pan to loosen. Remove

Stir in rice mixture and lemon peel. Serve immediately or refrigerate. **Yield:** 7 servings. **Diabetic Exchanges:** One 1/2-cup serving equals 1 starch; also, 93 calories, 184 mg sodium, 0 cholesterol, 21 gm carbohydrate, 2 gm protein, 1 gm fat.

CRANBERRY ICE

This recipe dates back to 1931, but I think you'll agree the refreshing flavor is timeless. Since I was a child, I've enjoyed this dessert for many occasions, but especially around the holidays. —Eleanor Dunbar
Peoria, Illinois

   4 cups fresh *or* frozen cranberries
   4 cups cold water, *divided*
   1 package (3 ounces) lemon gelatin
   2 cups boiling water
   3 cups sugar
   1/2 cup lemon juice
   1/2 cup orange juice

In a saucepan, bring cranberries and 2 cups cold water to a boil. Reduce heat; simmer for 5 minutes. Press through a strainer to remove skins; set juice aside and discard skins. In a bowl, stir the gelatin, boiling water and sugar until dissolved. Add cranberry juice, lemon and orange juices and remaining cold water. Pour into a 13-in. x 9-in. x 2-in. pan. Cover and freeze until ice begins to form around the edges of the pan, about 1-1/2 hours; stir. Freeze until mushy, about 30 minutes. Spoon into a freezer container; cover and freeze. **Yield:** 20 servings.

APPLE PIE FILLING

My family is always delighted to see an oven-fresh apple pie cooling on the counter. What a convenience to have on hand jars of this canned homemade pie filling so I can treat them to pies year-round.
—Laurie Mace
Los Osos, California

  18 cups sliced peeled baking apples (about 6 pounds)
   3 tablespoons lemon juice
4-1/2 cups sugar
   1 cup cornstarch
   2 teaspoons ground cinnamon
   1 teaspoon salt
   1/4 teaspoon ground nutmeg
  10 cups water

In a large bowl, toss apples with lemon juice; set aside. In a Dutch oven over medium heat, combine sugar, cornstarch, cinnamon, salt and nutmeg. Add water; bring to a boil. Boil for 2 minutes, stirring constantly. Add apples; return to a boil. Reduce heat; cover and simmer until apples are tender, about 6-8 minutes. Cool for 30 minutes. Ladle into freezer containers, leaving 1/2-in. headspace. Cool at room temperature no longer than 1-1/2 hours. Seal and freeze; store for up to 12 months. **Yield:** 5-1/2 quarts (enough for about five 9-inch pies).

CRANBERRY NUT DESSERT

(Pictured below)

When time's short, I reach for this recipe—it's a pie that doesn't need a crust. It's unbelievably easy. Whole tart berries make this dessert moist and delicious.
—Peggy Van Arsdale
Trenton, New Jersey

   1 cup all-purpose flour
   1 cup sugar
   1/4 teaspoon salt
   2 cups fresh *or* frozen cranberries
   1/2 cup chopped walnuts
   1/2 cup butter *or* margarine, melted
   2 eggs, beaten
   1/2 teaspoon almond extract
Whipped cream *or* ice cream, optional

In a bowl, combine the flour, sugar and salt. Add cranberries and nuts; toss to coat. Stir in the butter, eggs and extract (mixture will be very thick if using frozen berries). Spread into a greased 9-in. pie plate. Bake at 350° for 40 minutes or until a wooden pick inserted near the center comes out clean. Serve warm with whipped cream or ice cream if desired. **Yield:** 8 servings.

SUPER STRAWBERRY SHORTCAKE

(Pictured above)

"Wow!" is what people say when I set this dessert on the table. It's fun to serve since it's attractive, not overly sweet and bursting with wondrous flavor.
—Renee Bisch
Wellesley, Ontario

    1 quart fresh strawberries, sliced
    1 to 2 tablespoons sugar
SHORTCAKE:
1-3/4 cups all-purpose flour
    2 tablespoons sugar
    1 tablespoon baking powder
1/2 teaspoon baking soda
1/2 teaspoon salt
1/4 cup cold butter *or* margarine
    1 egg
3/4 cup sour cream
TOPPING:
    1 cup whipping cream
    1 to 2 tablespoons sugar
    1 teaspoon vanilla extract

Combine the strawberries and sugar; set aside. For shortcake, combine dry ingredients in a large bowl; cut in butter until crumbly. In a small bowl, beat egg; add sour cream. Stir into the crumb mixture just until moistened. Turn onto a floured board; knead 25 times or until smooth. Roll out into a 7-1/2-in. circle. Cut a 2-in. hole in center to form a ring. Place on a lightly greased baking sheet. Bake at 425° for 12-14 minutes or until golden. Remove from baking sheet; cool on a wire rack. For topping, beat cream and sugar until stiff peaks form; stir in vanilla. Just before serving, split cake horizontally. Spoon juice from berries over bottom layer. Spoon half of berries over juice. Spread half of topping over berries. Add the top cake layer, remaining topping and berries. Cut into wedges. **Yield:** 8 servings.

GO ANYWHERE RHUBARB SQUARES

Everyone loves these squares, which travel well to picnics and potlucks. The recipe delightfuly combines rhubarb filling with a cookie crust. —Pat Habiger
Spearville, Kansas

    1 cup all-purpose flour
1/3 cup confectioners' sugar
1/3 cup butter *or* margarine
FILLING:
    1 cup sugar
1/4 cup all-purpose flour
    2 eggs, lightly beaten
    1 teaspoon vanilla extract
    3 cups finely chopped fresh *or* frozen rhubarb

In a bowl, combine the flour and confectioners' sugar; cut in butter until mixture resembles coarse crumbs. Press into the bottom of a greased 11-in. x 7-in. x 2-in. baking pan. Bake at 350° for 12 minutes. For filling, combine the first four ingredients in a bowl. Stir in the rhubarb; pour over warm crust. Bake at 350° for 35-40 minutes or until a wooden pick inserted near the center comes out clean. Cool on a wire rack. Serve warm if desired. Store in the refrigerator. **Yield:** 16 servings.

CONCORD GRAPE PIE

Instead of featuring typical fruits like cherries, blueberries, apples or peaches, this pie spotlights Concord grapes. Why not surprise your family with this delightfully different dessert tonight? —Linda Erickson
Harborcreek, Pennsylvania

4-1/2 cups Concord grapes (2 pounds)
    1 cup sugar

    1/4 cup all-purpose flour
      2 teaspoons lemon juice
    1/8 teaspoon salt
      1 unbaked pastry shell (9 inches)
STREUSEL:
    1/2 cup quick-cooking oats
    1/2 cup packed brown sugar
    1/4 cup all-purpose flour
    1/4 cup butter *or* margarine

Squeeze the end of each grape opposite the stem to separate skins from pulp. Set skins aside. Place pulp in a medium saucepan; bring to a boil. Boil and stir for 1 minute. Press through a strainer or food mill to remove seeds. Combine pulp, skins, sugar, flour, lemon juice and salt; pour into pastry shell. Combine oats, brown sugar and flour; cut in butter until crumbly. Sprinkle over filling. Cover edges of pastry with foil. Bake at 425° for 15 minutes. Remove foil; bake 20 minutes more or until golden brown. Cool on a wire rack. **Yield:** 8 servings.

CHERRY-PEACH DUMPLINGS

This fruity finale can be made on the stovetop or in an electric skillet right at the dinner table. There's no more convenient way to enjoy a delicious dessert.
—Patricia Frerk
Syracuse, New York

      1 can (21 ounces) cherry pie filling
    1/2 cup water
      2 tablespoons lemon juice
    1/2 teaspoon ground cinnamon
    1/4 teaspoon ground cloves
      1 can (16 ounces) peach slices *or* halves, drained
      1 egg
Milk
1-1/2 cups biscuit/baking mix
Additional cinnamon and whipped cream, optional

In a 10-in. skillet, combine the first five ingredients. Add peaches; bring to a boil. Place egg in a 1-cup measuring cup; add enough milk to equal 1/2 cup. Place biscuit mix in a bowl; stir in milk mixture with a fork just until moistened. Drop by six spoonfuls over top of boiling fruit. Simmer, uncovered, for 10 minutes; cover and simmer 10 minutes longer or until dumplings test done. Sprinkle with cinnamon if desired. Serve warm with whipped cream if desired. **Yield:** 6 servings.

SPICED PINEAPPLE UPSIDE-DOWN CAKE
(Pictured below)

I often bake this beautiful cake in my large iron skillet. I guarantee your family and friends will thoroughly enjoy this old-fashioned dessert.
—Jennifer Sergesketter
Newburgh, Indiana

  1-1/3 cups butter *or* margarine, softened, *divided*
      1 cup packed brown sugar
      1 can (20 ounces) pineapple slices, drained
    10 to 12 maraschino cherries
    1/2 cup chopped pecans
  1-1/2 cups sugar
      2 eggs
      1 teaspoon vanilla extract
      2 cups all-purpose flour
      2 teaspoons baking powder
    1/2 teaspoon baking soda
    1/2 teaspoon salt
    1/2 teaspoon ground cinnamon
    1/2 teaspoon ground nutmeg
      1 cup buttermilk

In a small saucepan, melt 2/3 cup of butter; stir in brown sugar. Spread in the bottom of an ungreased heavy 12-in. skillet or a 13-in. x 9-in. x 2-in. baking pan. Arrange pineapple in a single layer over sugar mixture; place a cherry in the center of each slice. Sprinkle with pecans and set aside. In a mixing bowl, cream sugar and remaining butter. Beat in eggs and vanilla. Combine the dry ingredients; add alternately to batter with buttermilk, mixing well after each addition. Carefully pour over the pineapple. Bake at 350° for 40 minutes for skillet (50-60 minutes for baking pan) or until a wooden pick inserted near the center comes out clean. Immediately invert onto a serving platter. **Yield:** 12 servings.

pie. Serve warm or at room temperature. **Yield:** 6-8 servings. **Editor's Note:** To decorate top of pie with cutouts as shown in photo, use a small pineapple-shaped cookie cutter to cut shapes from top pastry before placing pastry over filling. Place dough shapes on an ungreased baking sheet and bake at 350° for 8-10 minutes or until golden (watch closely). Cool slightly; arrange on top of baked pie after glazing.

CREAM PUFF MONSTERS

Kids of all ages will savor these delectable chocolate cream puffs that are a nice takeoff from the traditional. For extra fun, have family and friends "create" their own little monsters. —Susan Seymour
Valatie, New York

  3/4 cup plus 2 tablespoons all-purpose flour
    2 tablespoons sugar
    2 tablespoons baking cocoa
    1 cup water
  1/2 cup butter *or* margarine
    4 eggs
    1 package (3.9 ounces) instant chocolate
      pudding mix
    2 cups cold milk
  Yellow, red, blue and green food coloring
    1 can (16 ounces) vanilla frosting
  Sprinkles, small candies and slivered almonds

Combine flour, sugar and cocoa; set aside. In a saucepan over medium heat, bring water and butter to a boil; reduce heat to low. Add flour mixture all at once; stir until a smooth ball forms. Remove from heat; let stand 5 minutes. Add eggs, one at a time, beating well after each. Beat until smooth. Cover baking sheets with foil; grease foil. Drop batter by tablespoonfuls at least 2 in. apart onto baking sheets. Bake at 400° for 25-30 minutes or until lightly browned. Lift foil and transfer to a wire rack. Immediately cut a slit in each puff to allow steam to escape; cool. In a mixing bowl, beat pudding mix and milk according to package directions; set aside. When puffs are cool; split and remove soft dough from inside. Spoon pudding into puffs; replace tops. Following food coloring package directions, combine red and yellow to make orange, and red and blue to make purple. Divide frosting among three microwave-safe bowls; tint with orange, purple and green food coloring. Microwave frosting until thin (not runny). Spoon one or more colors of frosting onto puffs. Add sprinkles and candy for eyes; use almonds for teeth or whiskers. Chill. **Yield:** 2 dozen.

GLAZED PINEAPPLE PIE

(Pictured above)

With its unique glaze, this pie is a tropical treat I like to serve on cold winter days. It cuts nicely, so it makes a pretty presentation on your table. —Kathy Crow
Cordova, Alaska

    1 can (20 ounces) crushed pineapple
    1 cup sugar
  1/4 cup all-purpose flour
    1 tablespoon lemon juice
    1 tablespoon butter *or* margarine, melted
  1/4 teaspoon salt
  Pastry for double-crust pie (9 inches)
    3/4 cup flaked coconut
  1/2 cup confectioners' sugar
  1/4 teaspoon vanilla extract

Drain pineapple, reserving 1 tablespoon juice for glaze. In a medium bowl, combine pineapple, sugar, flour, lemon juice, butter and salt; mix well and set aside. Line a 9-in. pie pan with the bottom pastry. Sprinkle with coconut. Spread pineapple mixture over coconut. Top with remaining pastry; flute edges and cut slits in top. Bake at 400° for 35-40 minutes or until golden brown. Cool 20 minutes on a wire rack. Meanwhile, for glaze, combine confectioners' sugar, vanilla and reserved pineapple juice until smooth. Spread over the top of warm

SWEET POTATO CAKE

Sweet potatoes are not only tasty and versatile, they're good for you as well. Family and friends never mind eating a nutritious vegetable when it's part of this easy-to-prepare dessert. I like to serve this as a snack cake or breakfast coffee cake.
—Kathy Theriot
St. Martinville, Louisiana

- 1 cup cold mashed sweet potatoes (without added milk or butter)
- 1/3 cup shortening
- 1/3 cup water
- 1 egg
- 1-2/3 cups all-purpose flour
- 1-1/3 cups sugar
- 1 teaspoon salt
- 1 teaspoon ground cinnamon
- 1 teaspoon baking soda
- 1/4 teaspoon baking powder
- 1/4 teaspoon ground ginger
- 2/3 cup raisins
- 1/3 cup chopped pecans
- Confectioners' sugar

In a mixing bowl, beat potatoes, shortening, water and egg. Combine dry ingredients; add to potato mixture and mix well. Stir in raisins and pecans. Pour into a greased 8-cup fluted tube pan. Bake at 350° for 45-50 minutes or until a wooden pick inserted near the center comes out clean. Cool in pan 10 minutes before removing to a wire rack to cool completely. Dust with confectioners' sugar. **Yield:** 8-10 servings. **Editor's Note:** An 11-in. x 7-in. x 2-in. baking pan can be used instead of the tube pan; bake for 30-35 minutes.

CHOCOLATE ECLAIRS

(Pictured at right)

With creamy filling and fudgy frosting, these eclairs are extra special. People are thrilled when these finger-licking-good treats appear on the dessert table.
—Jessica Campbell
Viola, Wisconsin

- 1 cup water
- 1/2 cup butter *or* margarine
- 1 cup all-purpose flour
- 1/4 teaspoon salt
- 4 eggs
- FILLING:
- 1 package (5.1 ounces) instant vanilla pudding mix
- 2-1/2 cups cold milk
- 1 cup whipping cream
- 1/4 cup confectioners' sugar
- 1 teaspoon vanilla extract
- FROSTING:
- 2 squares (1 ounce *each*) semisweet chocolate
- 2 tablespoons butter *or* margarine
- 1-1/4 cups confectioners' sugar
- 2 to 3 tablespoons hot water

In a saucepan, bring water and butter to a boil, stirring constantly until butter melts. Reduce heat to low; add the flour and salt. Stir vigorously with a wooden spoon until mixture leaves sides of pan and forms a smooth ball. Remove from the heat; add eggs, one at a time, beating well after each addition until batter becomes smooth. Using a tablespoon or a pastry tube with a No. 10 or larger tip, form dough into 4-in. x 1-1/2-in. strips on a greased baking sheet. Bake at 400° for 35-40 minutes or until puffed and golden. Immediately cut a slit in each to allow steam to escape. Cool on a wire rack. In a mixing bowl, beat pudding mix and milk according to package directions. In another mixing bowl, whip the cream until soft peaks form. Beat in sugar and vanilla; fold into pudding. Split eclairs; remove soft dough from inside. Fill eclairs (chill any remaining filling for another use). For frosting, melt chocolate and butter in a saucepan over low heat. Stir in sugar and enough hot water to achieve a smooth consistency. Cool slightly. Frost eclairs. Store in the refrigerator. **Yield:** 9 servings.

CHOCOLATE BAVARIAN TORTE

(Pictured above)

Whenever I take this torte to a potluck, I get many requests for the recipe. People especially enjoy the light, creamy filling. The recipe calls for a convenient cake mix, so it's easy to make. —Edith Holmstrom
Madison, Wisconsin

  1 package (18-1/4 ounces) devil's food cake mix without pudding
  1 package (8 ounces) cream cheese, softened
2/3 cup packed brown sugar
  1 teaspoon vanilla extract
1/8 teaspoon salt
  2 cups whipping cream, whipped
  2 tablespoons grated semisweet chocolate

Mix and bake cake according to package directions, using two 9-in. cake pans. Cool in pans for 15 minutes; remove from pans and cool completely on a wire rack. In a mixing bowl, beat cream cheese, sugar, vanilla and salt until fluffy. Fold in cream. Split each cake into two horizontal layers; place one on a serving plate. Spread with a fourth of the cream mixture. Sprinkle with a fourth of the chocolate. Repeat layers. Cover and refrigerate 8 hours or overnight. **Yield:** 12 servings.

CANDY BAR FUDGE

My manager at work, who knows I like to try new treat recipes, shared this one with me. I've made this chewy

and chocolaty fudge many times since. Packed with nuts and caramel, it's like a candy bar.
—Lois Zigarac
Rochester Hills, Michigan

1/2 cup butter *or* margarine
1/3 cup baking cocoa
1/4 cup packed brown sugar
1/4 cup milk
3-1/2 cups confectioners' sugar
  1 teaspoon vanilla extract
 30 caramels
  1 tablespoon water
  2 cups salted peanuts
1/2 cup semisweet chocolate chips
1/2 cup milk chocolate chips

In a microwave-safe bowl, combine the butter, cocoa, brown sugar and milk. Microwave on high until mixture boils, about 3 minutes. Stir in confectioners' sugar and vanilla. Pour into a greased 8-in. square baking pan. In another microwave-safe bowl, heat caramels and water on high for 2 minutes or until melted. Stir in peanuts; spread over chocolate layer. Microwave chocolate chips on high for 1 minute or until melted; spread over caramel layer. Chill until firm. **Yield:** 2-3/4 pounds. **Editor's Note:** This recipe was tested using a 700-watt microwave.

SOUTHERN AMBROSIA APPLE PIE

Georgia apples and pecans make this a pie that can't be beat. In fact, it won a statewide recipe contest.
—Carolyn Griffin
Macon, Georgia

  1 pastry shell (9 inches)
1/2 cup packed brown sugar
1/2 cup apple juice
  2 tablespoons butter *or* margarine
  2 tablespoons cornstarch
1/4 teaspoon salt
  4 cups thinly sliced peeled baking apples
  2 teaspoons lemon juice
  1 egg
2/3 cup evaporated milk
1/2 cup sugar
1/2 cup flaked coconut
  2 teaspoons vanilla extract
  1 teaspoon ground cinnamon
PECAN CREAM TOPPING:
  1 package (8 ounces) cream cheese, softened
1/2 cup sugar
3/4 cup chopped pecans, toasted

1 teaspoon vanilla extract
1 carton (8 ounces) frozen whipped topping, thawed
Whole pecans, toasted, optional

Line pastry shell with foil. Bake at 450° for 5 minutes. Remove from oven; remove foil. Cool. In a saucepan over medium heat, bring brown sugar, apple juice, butter, cornstarch and salt to a boil. Stir in apples and lemon juice; cook and stir over low heat until apples are crisp-tender, 5-8 minutes. Pour into pastry shell. In a small bowl, beat egg, milk, sugar, coconut, vanilla and cinnamon; mix well. Pour over apple mixture. Bake at 350° for 40-45 minutes or until set. Cool on a wire rack. For topping, beat cream cheese and sugar in a mixing bowl. Stir in pecans and vanilla. Fold in whipped topping. Spread over pie. Garnish with pecans if desired. Chill for 4-6 hours. **Yield:** 8 servings.

COCONUT LAYER CAKE

This dessert is great for wedding or baby showers. It's a beautiful cake that's easy to bake and decorate.
—Marilyn Dick
Centralia, Missouri

1/2 cup butter *or* margarine, softened
1/2 cup shortening
2 cups sugar
5 eggs, *separated*
2 cups all-purpose flour
1 teaspoon baking soda
1 cup buttermilk
1 teaspoon vanilla extract
2 cups flaked coconut
1/2 cup chopped pecans
FROSTING:
1 package (8 ounces) cream cheese, softened
4 cups (1 pound) confectioners' sugar
1/4 cup butter *or* margarine, softened
1 teaspoon vanilla extract
1/4 cup flaked coconut, toasted
Pecan halves

In a large mixing bowl, cream the butter, shortening and sugar until light and fluffy. Add egg yolks and beat well. Combine flour and baking soda; add to creamed mixture alternately with buttermilk. Stir in vanilla. Add coconut and pecans. In a small mixing bowl, beat egg whites until stiff; gently fold into batter. Pour into two greased and floured 9-in. round cake pans. Bake at 350° for 40 minutes or until a wooden pick inserted near the center comes out clean. Cool 10 minutes in pans before remov-

ing to wire racks; cool completely. For frosting, beat cream cheese, sugar, butter and vanilla until smooth and creamy. Spread between layers and over top and sides of cake. Sprinkle with coconut; garnish with pecans. **Yield:** 12-16 servings.

PLUM UPSIDE-DOWN CAKE
(Pictured below)

Since my husband liked pineapple upside-down cake, I decided to give this recipe a try one night when we were expecting guests for dinner. Everyone pronounced this cake "Delicious!" and asked for seconds.
—Bobbie Talbott
Veneta, Oregon

1/3 cup butter *or* margarine
1/2 cup packed brown sugar
2 pounds fresh plums, pitted and halved
2 eggs
2/3 cup sugar
1 cup all-purpose flour
1 teaspoon baking powder
1/4 teaspoon salt
1/3 cup hot water
1/2 teaspoon lemon extract
Whipped cream, optional

Melt butter in a 10-in. cast-iron or ovenproof skillet. Sprinkle brown sugar over butter. Arrange plum halves, cut side down, in a single layer over sugar; set aside. In a mixing bowl, beat eggs until thick and lemon-colored; gradually beat in sugar. Combine flour, baking powder and salt; add to egg mixture and mix well. Blend water and lemon extract; beat into batter. Pour over plums. Bake at 350° for 40-45 minutes or until cake tests done. Immediately invert onto a serving plate. Serve warm with whipped cream if desired. **Yield:** 8-10 servings.

RASPBERRY RIBBON CHEESECAKE
(Pictured above)

Not only does this dessert taste wonderful with its chocolate crust, rich creamy cheesecake and tangy raspberry center and topping...it also looks lovely.
—Peggy Frasier
Indianapolis, Indiana

    2 **cups chocolate wafer crumbs**
 1/3 **cup butter *or* margarine, melted**
    3 **tablespoons sugar**
RASPBERRY SAUCE:
2-1/2 **cups fresh *or* frozen unsweetened**
      raspberries, thawed
 2/3 **cup sugar**
    2 **tablespoons cornstarch**
    2 **teaspoons lemon juice**
FILLING/TOPPING:
    3 **packages (8 ounces *each*) cream cheese,**
      softened
 1/2 **cup sugar**
    2 **tablespoons all-purpose flour**
    1 **teaspoon vanilla extract**
    2 **egg whites**
    1 **cup whipping cream**
    2 **to 3 tablespoons orange juice**
1-1/2 **cups fresh *or* frozen**
      unsweetened raspberries, thawed

Combine the first three ingredients; press into bottom and 1-1/2 in. up sides of a greased 9-in. spring-form pan. Chill 1 hour or until firm. Puree raspberries in a blender or food processor. Press through a sieve; discard seeds. Add water if necessary to measure 1 cup. In a saucepan, combine sugar and cornstarch. Stir in raspberry juice; bring to a boil. Boil 2 minutes, stirring constantly. Remove from heat; stir in lemon juice and set aside. In a mixing bowl, beat cream cheese, sugar, flour and vanilla until fluffy. Add egg whites; beat on low just until blended. Stir in cream. Pour half into crust. Top with 3/4 cup raspberry sauce (cover and refrigerate remaining sauce). Carefully spoon remaining filling over sauce. Bake at 375° for 35-40 minutes or until center is nearly set. Remove from oven; immediately run a knife around pan to loosen crust. Cool on wire rack 1 hour. Refrigerate overnight. Add orange juice to chilled raspberry sauce; gently fold in raspberries. Spoon over cheesecake. **Yield:** 12-16 servings.

PLUM IN A CLOUD

When our family first moved here, I was thrilled to find fresh plums grown everywhere. Soon I began collecting recipes calling for this tangy fruit. Chunks of plums look like jewels in this fluffy, light dessert, which is perfect after a heavy or spicy meal.
—Darlene Markel
Sublimity, Oregon

1-1/2 **cups vanilla wafer crumbs**
 1/4 **cup butter *or* margarine, melted**
  44 **large marshmallows**
    2 **tablespoons lemon juice**
    2 **tablespoons orange juice**
    1 **cup whipping cream, whipped**
    2 **cups chopped fresh plums**

In a small bowl, combine crumbs and butter. Sprinkle half into eight individual dessert dishes; set the rest aside. In a saucepan over medium heat, cook and stir the marshmallows and juices until smooth. Transfer to a bowl; cool to room temperature, about 20 minutes. Fold in cream and plums. Spoon into dishes; sprinkle with reserved crumbs. Chill until firm, about 1 hour. **Yield:** 8 servings.

HALLOWEEN LAYER CAKE

There's nothing "scary" about this cake that I always make at Halloween for husband Mike and our three children. They look forward to this dessert every year. It tastes sooo good!
—Karen Wirth
Tavistock, Ontario

    1 **cup butter *or* margarine, softened**
    2 **cups sugar**
    4 **eggs**
    3 **cups all-purpose flour**
    1 **tablespoon baking powder**
 1/2 **teaspoon salt**
    1 **cup milk**
 1/4 **cup baking cocoa**
 1/4 **cup water**

1/2 teaspoon vanilla extract
1/2 teaspoon orange extract
  1 tablespoon grated orange peel
 10 drops yellow food coloring
  6 drops red food coloring
FROSTING:
  3 packages (3 ounces *each*) cream cheese, softened
5-3/4 cups confectioners' sugar
  2 tablespoons milk
  8 drops yellow food coloring
  6 drops red food coloring
GLAZE:
  3 squares (1 ounce *each*) semisweet chocolate
1/3 cup whipping cream
Candy corn for garnish

In a mixing bowl, cream butter and sugar until light and fluffy. Add eggs, one at a time, beating well after each. Combine flour, baking powder and salt; add alternately with milk to the creamed mixture. Mix well. In a medium bowl, combine the cocoa, water and vanilla. Stir in 2 cups cake batter. Pour into a greased and floured 9-in. round baking pan. Add orange extract, orange peel and food coloring to remaining batter. Pour into two greased and floured 9-in. cake pans. Bake at 350° for 30 minutes or until a wooden pick inserted near the center comes out clean. Combine frosting ingredients in a mixing bowl; beat until smooth. Place one orange cake layer on a cake plate; spread with 1/2 cup frosting. Top with chocolate layer; spread with 1/2 cup frosting. Top with second orange layer. Frost sides and top of cake. Microwave chocolate and cream on high for 1-1/2 minutes or until melted, stirring once. Stir until smooth; let cool for 2 minutes. Slowly pour over top of cake, allowing glaze to drizzle down sides. Garnish with candy corn. **Yield:** 12-16 servings.

CREAM PUFF HEART
(Pictured at right)

This scrumptious treat looks great on a buffet table or makes a tasty finale for a special-occasion meal. It almost looks too good to eat. The strawberries provide color and a refreshing flavor.
                                     —Edna Hoffman
                                      Hebron, Indiana

  1 cup water
1/2 cup butter *or* margarine
  1 cup all-purpose flour
1/4 teaspoon salt
  4 eggs

  1 package (3 ounces) cook-and-serve vanilla pudding mix
1-1/2 cups milk
  1 cup whipping cream, whipped
  1 teaspoon vanilla extract
  2 packages (10 ounces *each*) frozen strawberries, thawed and drained *or* 2 cups sliced fresh strawberries
Confectioners' sugar

In a saucepan over medium heat, bring water and butter to a boil. Add flour and salt all at once; stir until a smooth ball forms. Remove from the heat; let stand 5 minutes. Add eggs, one at a time, beating well after each addition. Beat until smooth. Cover a baking sheet with foil; grease foil. Trace a 12-in. heart onto foil. Drop batter by rounded tablespoonfuls along the outside of the heart (mounds should be almost touching). Bake at 400° for 40-45 minutes or until golden. Lift foil and transfer to a wire rack. Immediately cut a slit in each puff to allow steam to escape; cool. In a saucepan, cook pudding mix and milk according to package directions. Cool. Fold in cream and vanilla. Place cream puffs on a serving plate; split puffs and remove soft dough from inside. Spoon filling into puffs; add strawberries. Replace tops; dust with confectioners' sugar. Chill until serving. **Yield:** 14-16 servings.

CRUSTLESS PUMPKIN PIE

Traditional pastry crusts are loaded with fat, which makes pumpkin pie a rare treat for people watching their diet. This is a satisfying treat for everyone.
—Thelia Busse
Cresco, Pennsylvania

✓ **This tasty dish uses less sugar, salt and fat. Recipe includes *Diabetic Exchanges*.**

   1 can (15 ounces) pumpkin
   1 can (12 ounces) evaporated skim milk
Egg substitute equivalent to 2 eggs
   2 egg whites
Artificial sweetener equivalent to 3/4 cup sugar*
   1 teaspoon ground cinnamon
   1/4 teaspoon ground allspice
   1/4 teaspoon ground ginger
   1/8 teaspoon salt
   1/2 cup reduced-fat graham cracker crumbs
Light whipped topping and additional cinnamon, optional

In a mixing bowl, combine pumpkin, milk, egg substitute, egg whites and sweetener; beat until smooth. Add spices and salt; beat until well mixed. Stir in graham cracker crumbs. Pour into a 9-in. pie plate that has been coated with nonstick cooking spray. Bake at 325° for 50-55 minutes or until a knife inserted near the center comes out clean. Cool. If desired, garnish with a dollop of whipped topping and sprinkling of cinnamon. Store in the refrigerator. **Yield:** 8 servings. **Diabetic Exchanges:** One serving (without garnish) equals 1 starch, 1/2 skim milk; also, 116 calories, 166 mg sodium, 2 mg cholesterol, 16 gm carbohydrate, 7 gm protein, 3 gm fat. ***Editor's Note:** Sweet 'N Low or Sweet One are recommended for baking.

SOUTHERN SHORTCAKE

(Pictured above)

Your family will rave about this dessert. Biscuits are a fun change from the usual shortcake. And fresh strawberries—lightly sweetened with sugar—make a delicious topping.
—Tommy Conley
Vero Beach, Florida

   2 quarts fresh strawberries, sliced
   1/4 to 1/2 cup sugar
   1/2 cup shortening
2-1/2 cups self-rising flour*
   1 egg
   1 cup buttermilk
Whipped cream

Combine the strawberries and sugar; set aside. In a large bowl, cut shortening into flour until crumbly. In a small bowl, beat egg; add buttermilk. Stir into flour mixture just until moistened. Turn onto a lightly floured board; knead three to four times. Roll out to 1/2-in. thickness; cut with a 3-in. round biscuit cutter. Place on a lightly greased baking sheet. Bake at 400° for 15-18 minutes or until lightly browned; cool slightly. Split biscuits lengthwise; place the bottom halves on serving plates. Top with about 1/3 cup strawberries and whipped cream. Replace biscuit tops; spoon about 1/3 cup strawberries and more whipped cream on top. Serve immediately. **Yield:** 10-12 servings. ***Editor's Note:** As a substitute for each cup of self-rising flour, place 1-1/2 teaspoons baking powder and 1/2 teaspoon salt in a measuring cup. Add enough all-purpose flour to equal 1 cup.

BERRY TARTS

These delicate tarts are lovely. A tender crust and hint of lemon make them irresistible.
—Stephanie Mullen
Whitehorse, Yukon Territory

   2 cups all-purpose flour
3/4 cup sugar
   1 teaspoon grated lemon peel
   1/4 teaspoon salt
2/3 cup cold butter *or* margarine
   2 eggs
   1 tablespoon ice water
   1 teaspoon lemon juice

FILLING:
- 2 cups wild blueberries *or* mossberries
- 3/4 cup sugar
- 1/4 cup all-purpose flour
- 1 teaspoon grated lemon peel
- 1-1/2 cups (12 ounces) sour cream
- 1 egg yolk

In a bowl, combine flour, sugar, lemon peel and salt; cut in butter until crumbly. Combine eggs, water and lemon juice until smooth; drizzle over flour mixture. Toss with a fork until mixture is moist enough to shape into a ball (dough will be sticky). Divide in half; shape into balls and wrap in plastic wrap. Refrigerate for at least 30 minutes. Remove from the refrigerator; let stand 15 minutes before rolling. On a floured surface, roll the dough to 1/8-in. thickness. Cut into 3-in. circles. Ease into 2-in. tart pans, pressing pastry onto the bottom and sides of pan. Bake at 400° for 10 minutes. Cool. Place three to four berries in each shell. In a bowl, combine sugar, flour and lemon peel. Stir in sour cream and egg yolk. Spoon 1 tablespoon of filling over berries. Place pans on a baking sheet. Bake at 350° for 15-20 minutes or until pastry is golden and filling is set. Cool in pans for 1 minute before removing to wire racks. **Yield:** 32 tarts.

BERRY BEST FRIED PIES

We would eat these wonderful fried pies faster than my mom could make them when I was growing up.
—*Sharon Garrison*
Bella Vista, Arkansas

- 1/2 cup sugar
- 1 tablespoon cornstarch
- 1/2 cup water
- 2 cups fresh *or* frozen blueberries

DOUGH:
- 2 cups all-purpose flour
- 1/4 teaspoon baking soda
- 1/4 teaspoon salt
- 1/2 cup vegetable oil
- 1/3 cup buttermilk

Cooking oil for frying

In a saucepan, combine sugar, cornstarch and water; add berries. Cook and stir over medium heat until mixture comes to a boil. Cook and stir for 2 minutes; set aside to cool. Combine flour, baking soda and salt. Combine oil and buttermilk; stir into dry ingredients until mixture forms a ball. Roll on a floured board to 1/8-in. thickness; cut into 4-1/2-in. circles. Place 1 tablespoon blueberry filling on each circle. Fold over; seal edges with a fork. In a skillet over medium heat, fry pies in 1/4 to 1/2 in. hot oil until golden brown, about 1-1/2 minutes per side. Drain on paper towels. **Yield:** 10 servings.

ALMOND CRANBERRY TART

(Pictured below)

Cranberries and currant jelly make a jewel-toned filling for the cookie-type crust in this dessert.
—*Billie Moss*
El Sobrante, California

- 1-1/4 cups sugar, *divided*
- 1 cup finely chopped toasted slivered almonds
- 1 cup all-purpose flour
- 1/2 cup butter *or* margarine
- 1 egg
- 1 teaspoon vanilla extract
- 1 envelope unflavored gelatin
- 1/4 cup water
- 1 package (12 ounces) fresh *or* frozen cranberries
- 1/2 cup red currant jelly

Whipped cream and additional chopped almonds, optional

In a bowl, combine 1/4 cup sugar, almonds and flour. Cut in the butter until crumbly. Beat egg and vanilla; add to flour mixture and stir until moistened. Cover and chill for 30 minutes. Coat fingers with flour and press mixture into the bottom and 1-1/2 in. up the sides of a greased 9-in. springform pan. Bake at 350° for 25-30 minutes or until golden brown. Cool. Meanwhile, soften gelatin in water; set aside. In a saucepan, cook cranberries, jelly and remaining sugar over medium-low heat until berries pop. Remove from the heat; stir in gelatin until dissolved. Cool; pour into crust. Chill at least 4 hours. Garnish with whipped cream and almonds if desired. **Yield:** 8-10 servings.

"VACATIONING in the Canadian Rockies, my husband and I tasted the most delicious dessert," writes Carol Sue Binder of Greenwood, Indiana. "I thought I was in pie heaven!

"We stayed at the Buffalo Mountain Lodge in Banff, Alberta and enjoyed a pie with raspberries, blueberries, strawberries, rhubarb and apples. It was as spectacular as the view! I'd love to make it myself."

The *Taste of Home* staff took Carol Sue's request to the lodge's chef, David Forestell, who says, "Bumbleberry Pie has long been a hit here. It is so popular it would be impossible to take it off the menu."

Now you can add this pleasing pie to your own menus when planning get-togethers with family and friends.

BUMBLEBERRY PIE

5-1/2 cups all-purpose flour
  1/4 teaspoon salt
    2 cups shortening
    1 egg
    1 tablespoon vinegar
  3/4 cup cold water
FILLING:
    2 cups *each* fresh *or* frozen blueberries,
      raspberries and sliced strawberries
    2 cups fresh *or* frozen chopped rhubarb
    4 cups chopped peeled baking apples
    2 cups sugar
  2/3 cup all-purpose flour
    2 tablespoons lemon juice
EGG WASH:
    1 egg yolk
    1 to 2 tablespoons water

In a bowl, combine flour and salt; cut in shortening until crumbly. Whisk egg, vinegar and water; sprinkle over dry ingredients and toss. If needed, add more water, 1 tablespoon at a time, until dough can be formed into a ball. Divide into four balls. Cover and chill for 30 minutes. On a lightly floured surface, roll out two balls to fit two 9-in. pie pans. Combine filling ingredients (partially thaw fruit if necessary); spoon into crust. Roll remaining pastry to fit pies; place over filling. Seal and flute edges. Beat yolk and water; brush over pies. Cut slits in top crust. Bake at 350° for 50-60 minutes or until golden brown. **Yield:** 16 servings (2 pies).

HEIRLOOM FRUITCAKE

I like this cake because it's not as sweet as many traditional varieties yet is loaded with fruits and nuts.
—Sharon McClatchey
Muskogee, Oklahoma

  1/3 cup butter (no substitutes), softened
    3 tablespoons brown sugar
    2 eggs, lightly beaten
    3 tablespoons honey
  1/2 cup all-purpose flour
  1/2 teaspoon salt
  1/2 teaspoon baking powder
  1/8 teaspoon ground allspice
  1/8 teaspoon ground nutmeg
    2 tablespoons half-and-half cream
    1 cup raisins
    1 cup chopped dates
    1 package (6 ounces) dried apricots, finely
      chopped
    3 cups pecan halves

In a mixing bowl, cream the butter, sugar, eggs and honey. Combine dry ingredients; add to creamed mixture alternately with cream. Beat in the raisins, dates, apricots and pecans. Pack into two greased and floured 7-3/4-in. x 3-5/8-in. x 2-1/4-in. loaf pans. Place pans on middle rack of oven; place a shallow pan of hot water on lowest rack. Bake at 300° for 60-65 minutes or until a wooden pick inserted near the center comes out clean. Cool completely in pan. Loosen edges with a knife and remove from pan. Store in an airtight container in the refrigerator. **Yield:** 2 loaves.

PUMPKIN BUNDT CAKE

When I tell people how easy it is to make this deliciously moist cake, they can't believe it. The secret ingredient is butterscotch pudding. —*Lucille Noyd*
Shrewsbury, Massachusetts

    1 package (18-1/4 ounces) yellow cake mix
    1 package (3.4 ounces) instant butterscotch
      pudding mix
    4 eggs
  1/4 cup water
  1/4 cup vegetable oil
    1 cup canned pumpkin
    2 teaspoons pumpkin pie spice
Whipped cream, optional

In a large mixing bowl, combine the first seven ingredients. Beat on low speed for 30 seconds; beat on medium for 4 minutes. Pour into a greased and floured 10-in. fluted tube pan. Bake at 350° for 50-55 minutes or until a wooden pick inserted near the center comes out clean. Cool in pan for 15 minutes before removing to a wire rack to cool completely. Serve with whipped cream if desired. **Yield:** 16 servings.

BLUE-RIBBON APPLE CAKE

A friend from New Hampshire gave me this recipe for her cake, which took a blue ribbon at the county fair. Sweet juicy apples in the batter make this dessert a hit for all who try it.
—Jennie Wilburn
Long Creek, Oregon

     3 cups all-purpose flour
2-1/4 cups sugar, *divided*
     1 tablespoon baking powder
 1/2 teaspoon salt
     4 eggs
     1 cup vegetable oil
 1/3 cup orange juice
2-1/2 teaspoons vanilla extract
     4 medium baking apples, peeled and thinly sliced
     2 teaspoons ground cinnamon
Confectioners' sugar

In a mixing bowl, combine flour, 2 cups sugar, baking powder and salt. Combine eggs, oil, orange juice and vanilla; add to the flour mixture and mix well. In a bowl, toss apples with cinnamon and remaining sugar. Spread a third of the batter into a greased 10-in. tube pan. Top with half the apples. Repeat layers. Carefully spread remaining batter over apples. Bake at 350° for 55-65 minutes or until a wooden pick inserted near the center comes out clean. Cool in pan 15 minutes before removing to a wire rack; cool. Dust with confectioners' sugar. **Yield:** 16 servings.

LEMON WHIRLIGIGS
WITH RASPBERRIES
(Pictured at right)

Golden whirligigs with a tart lemon flavor float on a raspberry sauce in this dessert. I love serving it for guests. My children also like it made with blackberries.
—Vicki Ayres
Wappingers Falls, New York

 2/3 cup sugar
     2 tablespoons cornstarch

 1/4 teaspoon ground cinnamon
 1/8 teaspoon ground nutmeg
 1/8 teaspoon salt
     1 cup water
     3 cups fresh raspberries
WHIRLIGIGS:
     1 cup all-purpose flour
     2 teaspoons baking powder
 1/2 teaspoon salt
     3 tablespoons shortening
     1 egg, lightly beaten
     2 tablespoons half-and-half cream
 1/4 cup sugar
     2 tablespoons butter *or* margarine, melted
     1 teaspoon grated lemon peel
Whipping cream and additional raspberries, optional

In a saucepan, combine sugar, cornstarch, cinnamon, nutmeg and salt. Gradually add water; bring to a boil. Reduce heat to medium; cook and stir until the sauce thickens, about 5 minutes. Place raspberries in an ungreased 1-1/2-qt. shallow baking dish; pour hot sauce over top. Bake at 400° for 10 minutes; remove from the oven and set aside. For whirligigs, combine dry ingredients in a bowl; cut in shortening until crumbly. Combine egg and cream; stir into dry ingredients to form a stiff dough. Shape into a ball; place on a lightly floured surface. Roll into a 12-in. x 6-in. rectangle. Combine sugar, butter and lemon peel; spread over dough. Roll up, jelly roll style, starting at a long side. Cut into 10 slices; pat each slice slightly to flatten. Place on top of berry mixture. Bake at 400° for 15 minutes or until whirligigs are golden. Garnish servings with cream and raspberries if desired. **Yield:** 10 servings.

BLUEBERRY CREAM PIE
(Pictured below)

Whenever I ask my family which pie they'd like me to make, everyone gives the same answer—Blueberry Cream Pie! This refreshing dessert has an enticing cream layer topped with lots of plump blueberries.
—Kim Erickson
Sturgis, Michigan

1-1/3 cups vanilla wafer crumbs
  2 tablespoons sugar
  5 tablespoons butter *or* margarine, melted
1/2 teaspoon vanilla extract
FILLING:
  1/4 cup sugar
  3 tablespoons all-purpose flour
Pinch salt
  1 cup half-and-half cream
  3 egg yolks, beaten
  3 tablespoons butter *or* margarine
  1 teaspoon vanilla extract
  1 tablespoon confectioners' sugar
TOPPING:
  5 cups fresh blueberries, *divided*
  2/3 cup sugar
  1 tablespoon cornstarch

Combine the first four ingredients; press into the bottom and sides of an ungreased 9-in. pie pan. Bake at 350° for 8-10 minutes or until crust just begins to brown. Cool. In a saucepan, combine sugar, flour and salt. Gradually whisk in cream; cook and stir over medium heat until thickened and bubbly. Cook and stir 2 minutes more. Gradually whisk half into egg yolks; return all to pan. Bring to a gentle boil; cook and stir 2 minutes. Remove from heat; stir in butter and vanilla until butter is melted. Cool 5 minutes, stirring occasionally. Pour into crust; sprinkle with confectioners' sugar. Chill 30 minutes or until set. Meanwhile, crush 2 cups of blueberries in a medium saucepan; bring to a boil. Boil 2 minutes, stirring constantly. Press berries through sieve; set aside 1 cup juice (add

water if necessary). Discard pulp. In a saucepan, combine sugar and cornstarch. Gradually stir in blueberry juice; bring to a boil. Boil 2 minutes, stirring constantly. Remove from heat; cool 15 minutes. Gently stir in remaining berries; carefully spoon over filling. Chill 3 hours or until set. Store in the refrigerator. **Yield:** 6-8 servings.

CHOCOLATE CRUNCHIES

My mother made these candies when I was young, using my grandmother's recipe. Now my daughters enjoy making them...with delicious results.
—Vanessa Pieper
Bradford, Vermont

  2 cups (12 ounces) semisweet chocolate chips
  2 cups (12 ounces) butterscotch chips
1/2 teaspoon vanilla extract
  3 cups chow mein noodles

In the top of a double boiler over simmering water, melt chips and vanilla; stir until smooth. Fold in noodles. Drop by teaspoonfuls onto waxed paper. Chill. **Yield:** 2-1/2 dozen.

BAKED APPLES IN CARAMEL CREAM

What's better on a cool fall day than baked apples? Family and friends agree this delicious dessert with yummy sauce proves the point. *—Karen Ann Bland*
Gove, Kansas

  3 tablespoons brown sugar
1/4 cup hot water
  4 large Rome Beauty apples, cored
  1 tablespoon lemon juice
  12 caramels
1/2 cup whipping cream

Combine brown sugar and water in an 8-in. square baking dish. Peel top half of each apple; brush with lemon juice. Place in the baking dish. Fill each with three caramels. Bake at 350° for 60-65 minutes or until apples are tender, basting every 20 minutes. Carefully lift apples, allowing any caramel in centers to drip into pan, and place in individual dessert dishes. Pour sauce into a small saucepan; add cream. Cook and stir over medium-low heat until sauce is smooth and thick. Spoon over apples; serve immediately. **Yield:** 4 servings.

RAISIN BUTTERSCOTCH PIE

County fair judges awarded first place to this quick dessert. Many of the recipes I've entered through the years have included our state's famous raisins.
—Arleen Owen
Fresno, California

- 1 package (3.4 ounces) instant vanilla pudding mix
- 1 package (3.4 ounces) instant butterscotch pudding mix
- 2 cups cold milk
- 2 cups (16 ounces) sour cream
- 1 cup raisins
- 1 medium firm banana, sliced into 1/4-inch pieces
- 1 pastry shell (9 inches), baked
Frozen whipped topping, thawed

In a mixing bowl, combine pudding mixes and milk; beat until thick, about 3 minutes. Fold in sour cream; stir in raisins. Place banana slices in pastry shell; top with pudding mixture. Chill until ready to serve. Garnish with whipped topping. **Yield: 6-8 servings.**

APRICOT RICE CUSTARD
(Pictured above right)

Creamy rice custard drizzled with apricot sauce makes a comforting dessert or a refreshingly different breakfast. As a young mother, housewife and substitute teacher, I haven't been cooking all that long, but it's easy to impress people with this recipe since it's simple and delicious.
—Elizabeth Montgomery
Taylorville, Illinois

- 1 cup uncooked long grain rice
- 3 cups milk
- 1/2 cup sugar
- 1/2 teaspoon salt
- 2 eggs, lightly beaten
- 1/2 teaspoon vanilla extract
- 1/4 teaspoon almond extract
Dash ground cinnamon
SAUCE:
- 1 can (8-1/2 ounces) apricot halves
- 1 can (8 ounces) crushed pineapple, undrained
- 1/3 cup packed brown sugar
- 2 tablespoons lemon juice
- 1 tablespoon cornstarch

In a large saucepan, cook rice according to package directions. Stir in milk, sugar and salt; bring to a boil. Reduce heat to low. Stir 1/2 cup into eggs; return all to the pan. Cook and stir for 15 minutes or until mixture coats a spoon (do not boil). Remove from the heat; stir in extracts and cinnamon. For sauce, drain apricot syrup into a saucepan. Chop apricots; add to syrup. Stir in remaining sauce ingredients; bring to a boil. Boil for 2 minutes, stirring occasionally. Serve sauce and custard warm or chilled. **Yield: 8-10 servings.**

WIGGLY PUMPKINS

Pumpkin-shaped cookie cutters form these festive finger snacks. They're such a nice change of pace from a regular gelatin salad.
—Frances Poste
Wall, South Dakota

- 2 packages (6 ounces *each*) orange gelatin
- 2-1/2 cups boiling water
- 1 cup cold milk
- 1 package (3.4 ounces) instant vanilla pudding mix
Candy corn
Black licorice *and/or* gumdrops

In a bowl, dissolve gelatin in water; set aside for 30 minutes. In another bowl, whisk milk and pudding mix until smooth, about 1 minute. Quickly pour into gelatin; whisk until well blended. Pour into an oiled 13-in. x 9-in. x 2-in. dish. Chill until set. Cut into circles or use a pumpkin-shaped cookie cutter. Just before serving, add candy eyes and mouths. **Yield: 14-16 servings.**

SWEETHEART MOUSSE

(Pictured above)

This refreshing mousse makes a flavorful finale for a special meal. You can use different types of molds to create various shapes depending on the occasion. It looks pretty and people love its creamy taste.

—Adeline Piscitelli
Sayreville, New Jersey

- 2 packages (3 ounces *each*) cook-and-serve vanilla pudding mix
- 5 cups milk, *divided*
- 1 package (6 ounces) cherry gelatin
- 2 packages (8 ounces *each*) cream cheese, softened

Whipped cream and maraschino cherries, optional

In a saucepan, cook pudding mix and 4 cups milk according to package directions. Remove from the heat. Sprinkle with gelatin and stir until completely dissolved. Cool for 10 minutes. In a mixing bowl, beat cream cheese and remaining milk until smooth. Gradually add gelatin mixture; mix well. Pour into oiled individual molds. Refrigerate overnight. Unmold; garnish with whipped cream and cherries if desired. **Yield:** 10-12 servings. **Editor's Note:** Recipe may also be prepared in an 8-cup heart-shaped mold.

PERFECT APPLE PIE

This recipe truly lives up to its name...it is one of the best apple pies I've ever tasted. Egg yolk glazes the top crust to a golden shine.

—Judy Oudekerk
St. Michael, Minnesota

- 2 cups all-purpose flour
- 1 teaspoon salt
- 3/4 cup shortening
- 4 to 5 tablespoons cold water

FILLING:
- 7 to 8 cups thinly sliced peeled baking apples
- 2 tablespoons lemon juice
- 1 cup sugar
- 1/4 cup all-purpose flour
- 1 teaspoon ground cinnamon
- 1/4 teaspoon salt
- 1/8 teaspoon ground nutmeg
- 2 tablespoons butter *or* margarine
- 1 egg yolk
- 1 tablespoon water

In a bowl, combine flour and salt; cut in shortening. Gradually add cold water, 1 tablespoon at a time, tossing lightly with a fork until dough forms a ball. Chill for 30 minutes. On a floured surface, roll half of dough into a 10-in. circle. Place into a 9-in. pie pan. In a bowl, toss apples with lemon juice. Combine sugar, flour, cinnamon, salt and nutmeg; add to apples and toss. Pour into crust; dot with butter. Roll out remaining pastry to fit top of pie; cut slits in top. Place over filling; seal and flute edges. Beat egg yolk and water; brush over pastry. Bake at 425° for 15 minutes. Reduce heat to 350°; bake 40-45 minutes more or until crust is golden and filling is bubbly. **Yield:** 8 servings.

HICKORY NUT CAKE

Grandma made this cake often when I was a little girl, using nuts I collected.   —Sue Gronholz
Columbus, Wisconsin

- 3/4 cup shortening
- 1-1/2 cups sugar
- 2-1/2 cups cake flour
- 2 teaspoons baking powder
- 1/4 teaspoon salt
- 1 cup water
- 1/2 teaspoon almond extract
- 1/2 teaspoon vanilla extract
- 1 ounce unsweetened chocolate, grated
- 1/2 cup chopped hickory nuts
- 1/4 cup chopped maraschino cherries
- 4 egg whites

FROSTING:
- 1/2 cup shortening
- 1/2 cup butter *or* margarine, softened
- 1/2 teaspoon vanilla extract
- 1/2 teaspoon almond extract
- 1/8 teaspoon salt
- 3 cups confectioners' sugar
- 1 to 2 tablespoons milk

In a mixing bowl, cream shortening and sugar. Combine the flour, baking powder and salt; add to the creamed mixture alternately with water. Add extracts, chocolate, nuts and cherries; mix well. In a small mixing bowl, beat egg whites until soft peaks form; fold into batter. Pour into a greased 13-in. x 9-in. x 2-in. baking pan. Bake at 350° for 30-35 minutes or until a wooden pick inserted near the center comes out clean. Cool. For frosting, cream shortening and butter in a mixing bowl. Add extracts and salt. Beat in sugar and milk. Frost cake. **Yield:** 12-16 servings.

GRAPE BAVARIAN

Our family grows Concord grapes on 235 acres near Lake Erie. Each year, we're rewarded by a crop with distinctive, robust flavor. This gelatin dessert is made with grape juice from that pretty purple fruit.
—Linda Erickson
Harborcreek, Pennsylvania

      1 package (3 ounces) lemon gelatin
  3/4 cup boiling water
      1 cup Concord grape juice
  1-3/4 cups whipped topping

In a bowl, dissolve gelatin in boiling water; stir in grape juice. Chill until slightly thickened. Gently fold in whipped topping. Pour into an oiled 4-cup mold or dessert glasses. Chill until set. **Yield:** 4 servings.

SWEET POTATO
DESSERT SQUARES

I prepare sweet potatoes every week for my family, mostly as a side dish. But I've found this vegetable also makes desserts even more delightful. These moist, rich squares have a great pecan crunch.
—Shannon Simar
Jennings, Louisiana

      1 package (18-1/4 ounces) yellow cake mix, *divided*
  1/2 cup butter *or* margarine, melted
      1 egg, beaten
FILLING:
      3 cups cold mashed sweet potatoes (without added milk or butter)
  2/3 cup milk
  1/2 cup packed brown sugar
      2 eggs, beaten
      1 tablespoon pumpkin pie spice
TOPPING:
      6 tablespoons butter *or* margarine
      1 cup chopped pecans

  1/4 cup sugar
      1 teaspoon ground cinnamon
Whipped cream and pecan halves, optional

Set aside 1 cup of the cake mix. Combine remaining mix with butter and egg; spread into a greased 13-in. x 9-in. x 2-in. baking pan. Whisk filling ingredients until smooth; pour over crust. For topping, cut butter into the reserved cake mix until crumbly. Stir in pecans, sugar and cinnamon; sprinkle over the filling. Bake at 350° for 60-65 minutes or until a knife inserted near the center comes out clean. Cool. Garnish with whipped cream and pecan halves if desired. **Yield:** 16 servings.

FRESH RASPBERRY PIE

(Pictured below)

Mouth-watering fresh raspberries star in this luscious pie. There's nothing to distract from the tangy berry flavor and gorgeous ruby color. A big slice is an excellent way to enjoy the taste of summer.
—Patricia Staudt
Marble Rock, Iowa

  1/4 cup sugar
      1 tablespoon cornstarch
      1 cup water
      1 package (3 ounces) raspberry gelatin
      4 cups fresh raspberries
      1 graham cracker crust (9 inches)
Whipped cream, optional

In a saucepan, combine sugar and cornstarch. Add the water and bring to a boil, stirring constantly. Cook and stir for 2 minutes. Remove from the heat; stir in gelatin until dissolved. Cool for 15 minutes. Place raspberries in the crust; slowly pour gelatin mixture over berries. Chill until set, about 3 hours. Garnish with whipped cream if desired. **Yield:** 6-8 servings.

'My Mom's Best Meal'

Six cooks relive memorable moments when they prepare the same meals for which their moms are fondly remembered.

Memorable birthday meal Mom prepared has become a much-requested supper throughout the year in daughter's family.

"WHEN I think of my mom's cooking, one certain menu pops into my mind," conveys Karen Wingate of Coldwater, Kansas. "It's the meal I requested for my birthday in my teen years...and the spread I missed most when graduate school took me 2,000 miles from home.

"The meal, still a standby, starts with moist Crispy Baked Chicken, which Mom, Arlene Wise (above), serves with baked potatoes.

"Her Zucchini Santa Fe, a zippy side dish made with garden vegetables, is so good with the chicken. This recipe and others Mom makes reflect her background as a third-generation Arizonian. Her cooking style revolves around the hot climate and influences from pioneer and Mexican cultures.

"A frugal cook, Mom has a knack for making plain foods taste wonderful using fresh ingredients and whole grains, like her flavorful Wholesome Wheat Bread and Mom's Strawberry Shortcake.

"Now I make this memorable meal, too, for husband Jack, a minister, and our two daughters, Katherine, 7, and Christine, 5.

"I hope you enjoy this meal as much as we do. It's truly a taste of home."

PICTURED AT LEFT: Crispy Baked Chicken, Wholesome Wheat Bread, Zucchini Santa Fe and Mom's Strawberry Shortcake (recipes are on the next page).

CRISPY BAKED CHICKEN

My siblings and I couldn't wait to sit down to supper when Mom was making this delicious chicken. The cornmeal in the coating gives each juicy golden piece a wonderful crunch.

- 1/2 cup cornmeal
- 1/2 cup all-purpose flour
- 1-1/2 teaspoons salt
- 1-1/2 teaspoons chili powder
- 1/2 teaspoon dried oregano
- 1/4 teaspoon pepper
- 1 broiler/fryer chicken (3 to 3-1/2 pounds), cut up
- 1/2 cup milk
- 1/3 cup butter *or* margarine, melted

Combine the first six ingredients. Dip chicken in milk, then roll in the cornmeal mixture. Place in a greased 13-in. x 9-in. x 2-in. baking pan. Drizzle with butter. Bake, uncovered, at 375° for 50-55 minutes or until juices run clear. **Yield:** 4-6 servings.

WHOLESOME WHEAT BREAD

My sister and I were in 4-H, and Mom was our breads project leader for years. Because of that early training, fresh homemade bread like this is a staple in my own kitchen.

✓ **This tasty dish uses less sugar, salt and fat. Recipe includes *Diabetic Exchanges*.**

- 2 packages (1/4 ounce *each*) active dry yeast
- 2-1/4 cups warm water (110° to 115°)
- 3 tablespoons sugar
- 1/3 cup butter *or* margarine, softened
- 1/3 cup honey
- 1/2 cup instant nonfat dry milk powder
- 1 tablespoon salt
- 4-1/2 cups whole wheat flour
- 2-3/4 to 3-1/2 cups all-purpose flour

In a large mixing bowl, dissolve yeast in water. Add sugar, butter, honey, milk powder, salt and whole wheat flour; beat until smooth. Add enough all-purpose flour to form a soft dough. Turn onto a floured board; knead until smooth and elastic, about 10 minutes. Place in a greased bowl, turning once to grease top. Cover and let rise in a warm place until doubled, about 1 hour. Punch down. Shape dough into traditional loaves or divide into fourths and roll each portion into a 15-in. rope. Twist two ropes together. Place in greased 9-in. x 5-in. x 3-in. loaf pans. Cover and let rise until doubled,

about 30 minutes. Bake at 375° for 25-30 minutes. Remove from pans to cool on wire racks. **Yield:** 2 loaves (32 slices). **Diabetic Exchanges:** One slice (prepared with margarine) equals 2 starch; also, 144 calories, 239 mg sodium, 0 cholesterol, 27 gm carbohydrate, 4 gm protein, 2 gm fat.

ZUCCHINI SANTA FE

Chopped green chilies give this summer side dish lots of zip—a popular flavor around Mom's Arizona home. It's a tasty way to use up garden vegetables.

> ✓ **This tasty dish uses less sugar, salt and fat. Recipe includes *Diabetic Exchanges*.**

- 3 cups sliced zucchini
- 1/2 cup chopped onion
- 1 tablespoon cooking oil
- 1 can (4 ounces) chopped green chilies, drained
- 1 medium tomato, chopped
- 1/2 teaspoon salt, optional
- 1/4 teaspoon pepper
- 1/4 teaspoon garlic powder
- 1/2 cup shredded cheddar *or* Monterey Jack cheese

In a large skillet, saute the zucchini and onion in oil for 3-4 minutes or until crisp-tender. Add chilies, tomato, salt if desired, pepper and garlic powder. Cook and stir for 3-4 minutes. Spoon into a serving bowl and sprinkle with cheese. **Yield:** 6 servings. **Diabetic Exchanges:** One 1/2-cup serving (prepared without salt) equals 1 vegetable, 1 fat; also, 58 calories, 60 mg sodium, 2 mg cholesterol, 5 gm carbohydrate, 3 gm protein, 3 gm fat.

MOM'S STRAWBERRY SHORTCAKE

When I was growing up, Mom sometimes experimented with different dessert recipes, but this tried-and-true spongy shortcake was always great just the way it was. It melted in my mouth!

- 2 eggs
- 1-1/2 cups sugar, *divided*
- 1 cup all-purpose flour
- 1 teaspoon baking powder
- 1/4 teaspoon salt
- 1/2 cup milk
- 1 tablespoon butter *or* margarine
- 1 teaspoon vanilla extract
- 1 to 1-1/2 quarts fresh strawberries, sliced

Whipped cream
Mint leaves, optional

In a mixing bowl, beat eggs on medium speed for 3 minutes. Gradually add 1 cup sugar, beating until thick and lemon-colored. Combine flour, baking powder and salt; beat into the egg mixture. Heat milk and butter just until butter begins to melt. Beat into batter with vanilla (batter will be thin). Pour into a greased 8-in. square baking pan. Bake at 350° for 25 minutes or until a wooden pick inserted near the center comes out clean. Cool for at least 10 minutes. Just before serving, cut cake into serving-size pieces; cut each slice in half horizontally. Combine strawberries and remaining sugar. Spoon strawberries between cake layers and over the top of each serving. Top with whipped cream; garnish with mint leaves if desired. **Yield:** 9 servings.

When stewing over what to make for dinner these days, this country cook fondly remembers her mom's heartwarming meal.

"MY 10 brothers and sisters and I grew up with cold Minnesota winters," recalls Anne Heinonen of Howell, Michigan. "One of my fondest memories is coming in from the frigid walk from the school bus stop to the comforting aroma of my mother's cooking.

"Mom, Lorraine Torola (above), is known for her Old-Fashioned Beef Stew, which she made often to warm us up. She never uses a recipe, but after numerous requests from my seven sisters and me, she finally wrote one down. I still think it tastes best served at her table.

"To go with the stew, Dad pitched in and made the flavorful Flat Bread. It was an easy job for his big, strong hands.

"Mom's Glass Bowl Salad moved quickly around the table. We loved the tasty combination of creamy and crunchy ingredients.

"Her delectable Ice Cream Sundae Dessert is still one of my favorites. It makes me think of special occasions since that's when Mom always served it.

"Now I make this meal for my husband and our 12 children. Mom and I hope you enjoy it, too!"

PICTURED AT LEFT: Old-Fashioned Beef Stew, Glass Bowl Salad, Dad's Flat Bread and Ice Cream Sundae Dessert (recipes are on the next page).

per and salt; bring to a boil. Reduce heat; cover and simmer for 2 hours. Add vegetables; cover and simmer for 30 minutes or until meat and vegetables are tender. Combine flour, browning sauce and cold water. Stir into stew; bring to a boil, stirring constantly. Boil for 1 minute. **Yield:** 8 servings.

GLASS BOWL SALAD

Crisp refreshing ingredients topped with a creamy dressing and crumbled bacon assured there'd be no leftovers when this salad bowl made its way around the table.

> 1 medium head iceberg lettuce, shredded
> 1/2 cup chopped celery
> 1 cup shredded carrots
> 1 package (10 ounces) frozen peas, thawed
> 5 green onions, sliced
> 1 medium green pepper, chopped
> 1 cup mayonnaise
> 2/3 cup sour cream
> 6 bacon strips, cooked and crumbled

In a 3-qt. clear glass serving bowl, layer the first six ingredients in order given. Combine mayonnaise and sour cream until smooth; spread evenly over salad. Cover and chill overnight. Sprinkle with bacon just before serving. **Yield:** 8-10 servings.

OLD-FASHIONED BEEF STEW

This hearty beef stew has a garden full of flavor with vegetables like cabbage, rutabaga and carrots. Mom knew this main dish is one that would suit us 11 kids. When all of us were home, she'd throw in extra vegetables to stretch it.

> 1 boneless chuck roast (2 pounds), cut into 1/2-inch cubes
> 1 tablespoon cooking oil
> 1 large onion, chopped
> 4 cups water
> 1 teaspoon seasoned salt
> 1/2 teaspoon pepper
> 2 to 3 teaspoons salt
> 5 to 6 medium potatoes, peeled and cut into 1/2-inch cubes
> 5 medium carrots, cut into 1/4-inch slices
> 1 medium rutabaga, peeled and cut into 1/2-inch cubes
> 1 cup sliced celery (1/2-inch pieces)
> 1/2 medium head cabbage, finely sliced
> 1/3 cup all-purpose flour
> 1 cup cold water
> 2 teaspoons browning sauce

In a Dutch oven over medium-high heat, brown meat in oil. Add onion, water, seasoned salt, pep-

DAD'S FLAT BREAD

While Mom was busy with the rest of the meal, Dad helped by making this flat bread. There's no mistaking that this flavorful bread is homemade. It has a wonderful texture and lovely golden color.

✓ **This tasty dish uses less sugar, salt and fat. Recipe includes *Diabetic Exchanges.***

   1 package (1/4 ounce) active dry yeast
   2 cups warm water (110° to 115°), ***divided***
1/3 cup sugar
   2 tablespoons vegetable oil
   1 tablespoon salt
1/2 cup rye *or* whole wheat flour
5-1/2 to 6 cups all-purpose flour

In a large mixing bowl, dissolve yeast in 1/2 cup water. Add sugar, oil, salt, rye or whole wheat flour, 3 cups all-purpose flour and remaining water; beat until smooth. Add enough remaining flour to form a soft dough. Turn onto a floured board; knead until smooth and elastic, about 6-8 minutes. Place in a greased bowl, turning once to grease top. Cover and let rise in a warm place until doubled, about 1 hour. Punch dough down. Divide in half. On a greased baking sheet, flatten each half to 1-in. thickness. Pierce each loaf several times with a fork. Cover and let rise in a warm place until nearly doubled, about 30 minutes. Bake at 375° for 25-30 minutes or until golden brown. **Yield:** 2 loaves (32 slices). **Diabetic Exchanges:** One slice equals 1-1/2 starch; also, 116 calories, 220 mg sodium, 0 cholesterol, 23 gm carbohydrate, 3 gm protein, 1 gm fat.

ICE CREAM SUNDAE DESSERT

We kids couldn't wait to dig into this tempting ice cream dessert. It's cool and smooth, with a ribbon of fudge inside. Whenever I make it for my family, I think of Mom.

   2 cups (12 ounces) semisweet chocolate chips
   1 can (12 ounces) evaporated milk
1/2 teaspoon salt
   1 package (12 ounces) vanilla wafers, crushed
1/2 cup butter *or* margarine, melted
   2 quarts vanilla ice cream *or* flavor of your choice, softened

In a saucepan over medium heat, melt chocolate chips with milk and salt; cook and stir until thickened, about 25 minutes. Remove from the heat; set aside. Combine the wafer crumbs and butter; set aside 1 cup. Press remaining crumbs into a greased 13-in. x 9-in. x 2-in. pan. Chill 10-15 minutes. Pour chocolate over crumbs. Cover and freeze for 20-25 minutes or until firm. Spread ice cream over chocolate. Sprinkle with reserved crumbs. Freeze at least 2 hours before serving. **Yield:** 12-16 servings.

Garnish with Flair
Try grating a chocolate candy bar over the top of this Ice Cream Sundae Dessert. It's a quick and easy way to decorate. Plus it's pretty and tasty, too.

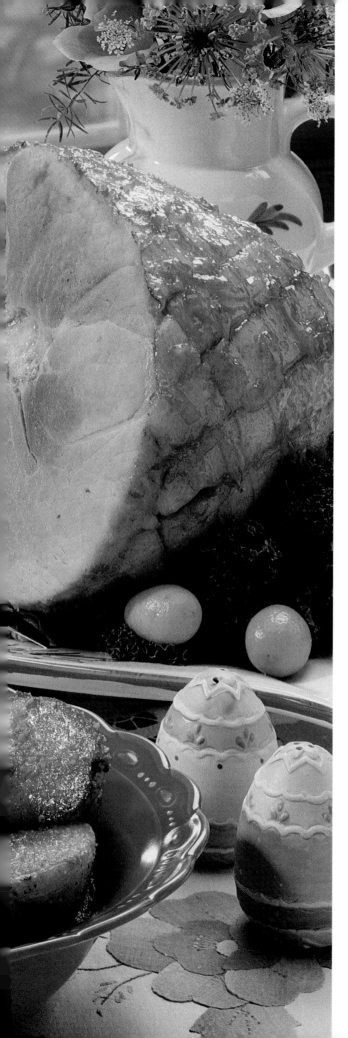

Every Easter, this beautifully baked ham would appear on the table along with scrumptious side dishes and tasty candies.

"MY SISTER and I well remember the Orange-Glazed Ham Mom served for Easter dinner," says field editor Ruth Seitz of Columbus Junction, Iowa. "She'd put it in the oven in the morning, and the sweet aroma filled the house even before we left for church.

"Mom (Naomi King, above) basted the ham with the glaze when we returned home. It made a beautiful and tasty main dish.

"Along with the ham, Mom's Parmesan Baked Potatoes were so delicious. And we even liked to eat broccoli and cauliflower when Mom served them in her Fresh Vegetable Salad.

"For us girls, the end of the meal was most special. That's when we'd hunt for Mom's wonderful home-made Chocolate Easter Eggs!

"Mom passed along her love of cooking to us, my two daughters and my four granddaughters. Even after she was living at a nursing home, Mom was always sharing her recipes, which she could recite by heart. She would be thrilled if this meal were to become a holiday tradition at your house, too."

PICTURED AT LEFT: Orange-Glazed Ham, Parmesan Baked Potatoes, Fresh Vegetable Salad and Chocolate Easter Eggs (recipes are on the next page).

Tater Tip

When purchasing potatoes, don't pick ones that are soft or have excessive cuts, cracks, bruises or discoloration. If you have to use green potatoes, peel away the green. When a potato is more than half green, throw it out.

PARMESAN BAKED POTATOES

It always amazed me that this simple recipe could make potatoes that taste so good. Mom liked to make them for Easter since they were more special than ordinary baked potatoes.

> **6 tablespoons butter *or* margarine, melted**
> **3 tablespoons grated Parmesan cheese**
> **8 medium unpeeled red potatoes (about 2-3/4 pounds), halved lengthwise**

Pour butter into a 13-in. x 9-in. x 2-in. baking pan. Sprinkle Parmesan cheese over butter. Place potatoes with cut side down over cheese. Bake, uncovered, at 400° for 40-45 minutes or until tender. **Yield:** 8 servings.

FRESH VEGETABLE SALAD

It was such a treat to have a crisp, garden-fresh salad back when Mom didn't have much room in our little icebox to keep produce chilled. This salad is as colorful and festive as it is refreshing.

> **2 cups broccoli florets**
> **2 cups cauliflowerets**
> **1/2 cup chopped celery**

ORANGE-GLAZED HAM

This delicious ham looked like a sparkling jewel on the table when my mom served it for Easter dinner. The flavor of the spice rub penetrates through every tender slice. Even its enticing aroma while baking can't match the wonderful taste.

> **1 fully cooked bone-in ham (6 to 8 pounds)**
> **1 tablespoon ground mustard**
> **1 teaspoon ground allspice**
> **3/4 cup orange marmalade**
> **Kumquats and kale, optional**

Score the ham. Combine mustard and allspice; rub over ham. Place on a rack in a shallow baking pan. Bake, uncovered, at 325° for 2 to 2-1/2 hours or until a meat thermometer reads 140°. Spread top of ham with marmalade during the last hour of baking. Baste occasionally. Garnish with kumquats and kale if desired. **Yield:** 12-16 servings.

1/2 cup chopped green pepper
1/2 cup chopped onion
1/4 cup grated carrot
1 cup mayonnaise *or* salad dressing
1/4 cup sugar
3 tablespoons grated Parmesan cheese
2 bacon strips, cooked and crumbled

Toss vegetables in a large salad bowl. In a small bowl, combine mayonnaise, sugar and Parmesan cheese; pour over vegetables and toss to coat. Cover and chill. Sprinkle with bacon just before serving. **Yield:** 8 servings.

CHOCOLATE EASTER EGGS

No store-bought Easter candy can compare to Mom's homemade chocolate-covered eggs. The heavenly centers have peanut butter, coconut and walnuts. These rich candies just melt in your mouth.

3/4 cup chunky peanut butter
1/4 cup butter *or* margarine, softened
1 cup flaked coconut
1/2 cup finely chopped walnuts
1-1/2 to 2 cups confectioners' sugar, *divided*

2 cups (12 ounces) semisweet chocolate chips
2 tablespoons shortening

In a mixing bowl, cream peanut butter and butter until well mixed. Fold in coconut, nuts and 1 cup sugar; mix well. Sprinkle some of the remaining sugar on a board. Turn peanut butter mixture onto board; knead in enough of the remaining sugar until mixture holds its shape when formed. Shape into small egg-shaped pieces. Cover and chill for 1 hour. In a double boiler over hot water, melt chocolate chips and shortening, stirring until smooth. Dip eggs; place on waxed paper to harden. Chill. **Yield:** 2 dozen.

Extra-Special Candies
Instead of dipping these Chocolate Easter Eggs in regular semisweet chocolate chips, use raspberry-flavored semisweet chocolate chips. Folks will love them!

A love of cooking—and of each other's company—led to some special moments in the kitchen for mother-and-daughter duo.

"MY MOM is a terrific cook who has inspired me to love working in the kitchen, too," relates 15-year-old Gina Squires of Salem, Oregon.

"Ever since I was little, I've enjoyed being with Mom (Shirlee, above) when she's cooking. Over the years, she's patiently shared her skills with me. Now I enjoy making and serving complete meals for her, Dad, my older sister and brother-in-law.

"Mom's Lasagna dinner has always been my favorite. For as long as I can remember, she has served her hearty lasagna with crisp Three-Green Salad and zesty homemade Italian dressing...plus Cheesy Garlic Bread—I can never eat just one slice of that!

"For dessert, Fluffy Pineapple Torte is a light treat that's a nice balance to this meaty main course—the perfect end to this satisfying meal.

"I think Mom and I make a great team in the kitchen these days. We're excited to share our special meal with you. We hope your family will enjoy this memorable down-home menu as much as ours does."

PICTURED AT LEFT: Mom's Lasagna, Three-Green Salad, Cheesy Garlic Bread and Fluffy Pineapple Torte (recipes are on the next page.)

MOM'S LASAGNA

We can hardly wait to dig into this cheesy, meaty lasagna. It smells great when baking and tastes even better! Watching Mom carefully make this wonderful main dish and hearing the raves she gets inspired me to learn to cook.

- 1/2 **pound ground beef**
- 1/2 **pound bulk Italian sausage**
- 1 **large onion, chopped**
- 3 **garlic cloves, minced**
- 1 **can (28 ounces) crushed tomatoes, undrained**
- 1 **can (6 ounces) tomato paste**
- 1-1/2 **cups water**
- 1 **cup salsa**
- 2 **teaspoons sugar**
- 1 **to 2 teaspoons chili powder**
- 1 **teaspoon fennel seed**
- 1 **teaspoon dried oregano**
- 1 **teaspoon dried basil**
- 9 **lasagna noodles**
- 1 **carton (16 ounces) cottage cheese**
- 4 **cups (1 pound) shredded mozzarella cheese**
- 3/4 **cup grated Parmesan cheese**

In a large kettle or Dutch oven, cook beef, sausage and onion until the meat is browned and onion is tender; drain. Stir in the next 10 ingredients. Simmer, uncovered, for 3 hours, stirring occasionally. Meanwhile, cook lasagna noodles according to package directions; drain and rinse in cold water. In a greased 13-in. x 9-in. x 2-in. baking dish, layer a third of the noodles and meat sauce, half of the cottage cheese, a third of the mozzarella and a third of the Parmesan. Repeat layers. Top with remaining noodles, meat sauce, mozzarella and Parmesan. Cover and bake at 350° for 45 minutes; uncover and bake for 20 minutes. Let stand 20 minutes before cutting. **Yield:** 12 servings.

THREE-GREEN SALAD
(Also pictured on front cover)

For a crisp, refreshing side dish, this tasty salad can't be beat. The bold flavor and crunch really wake up your taste buds. It goes perfectly with lasagna.

- 4 **cups torn iceberg lettuce**
- 4 **cups torn leaf lettuce**
- 4 **cups torn fresh spinach**
- 1 **medium cucumber, sliced**
- 2 **carrots, sliced**
- 2 **celery ribs, sliced**
- 6 **broccoli florets, sliced**
- 3 **cauliflowerets, sliced**
- 6 **radishes, sliced**
- 4 **green onions, sliced**
- 5 **fresh mushrooms, sliced**

ITALIAN DRESSING:
- 2/3 **cup olive *or* vegetable oil**
- 1/4 **cup plus 2 tablespoons red wine vinegar**

2 tablespoons grated Parmesan cheese
1 teaspoon sugar
1 to 2 garlic cloves, minced
1/4 teaspoon dried oregano
1/4 teaspoon dried basil
Pinch salt and pepper

In a large salad bowl, toss the greens and vegetables. Cover and chill. Combine all dressing ingredients in a blender; process for 30 seconds. Pour into a jar with tight-fitting lid; chill for at least 30 minutes. Shake dressing before serving; pour desired amount over salad and toss. **Yield:** 12 servings (about 1 cup dressing).

Celery Storage

To help keep celery crisp longer, remove it from its original packaging as soon as you buy it. Wrap the ribs in paper towel, then in aluminum foil.

CHEESY GARLIC BREAD

Some garlic breads taste more like buttered toast. Not this one—the fresh garlic flavor really comes through. Parmesan cheese on top turns golden brown in the broiler. I enjoy the crunch of the crisp crust.

1/2 cup butter *or* margarine, softened
4 garlic cloves, minced
1/4 teaspoon dried oregano
1 loaf (1 pound) French bread, halved lengthwise
3 tablespoons grated Parmesan cheese

In a small bowl, combine the butter, garlic and oregano; spread on cut sides of bread. Sprinkle with Parmesan cheese. Place on an ungreased baking sheet. Broil for 3 minutes or until golden brown. Slice and serve hot. **Yield:** 12 servings.

FLUFFY PINEAPPLE TORTE

This fluffy dessert is so good after a hearty meal because even a big slice is as light as a feather. The cream cheese-pineapple combination makes it irresistible.

1-1/2 cups graham cracker crumbs
1/4 cup butter *or* margarine, melted
2 tablespoons sugar
FILLING:
1 can (12 ounces) evaporated milk
1 package (3 ounces) lemon gelatin
1 cup boiling water
1 package (8 ounces) cream cheese, softened
1/2 cup sugar
1 can (8 ounces) crushed pineapple, drained
1 cup chopped walnuts, *divided*

Combine crumbs, butter and sugar; press into the bottom of a 13-in. x 9-in. x 2-in. baking dish. Bake at 325° for 10 minutes; cool. Pour evaporated milk into a metal mixing bowl; add the beaters. Cover and chill for at least 2 hours. Meanwhile, in a small bowl, dissolve gelatin in water; chill until syrupy, about 1-1/2 hours. Remove milk from refrigerator and beat until stiff peaks form. In a large mixing bowl, beat cream cheese and sugar until smooth. Add gelatin; mix well. Stir in pineapple and 3/4 cup walnuts. Fold in milk. Pour over crust. Chill for at least 3 hours or overnight. Sprinkle remaining walnuts over the top before filling is completely firm. **Yield:** 12 servings.

This cook's mother proved that the best way to show folks you care is by showering them with love and good food.

"MOTHER taught me the value of sitting down with those who are dear for hot home-cooked meals and warm conversation," relates Nancy Duty of Jacksonville, Florida. Nancy spent hours cooking from scratch with her mom, Nancy Herring (above).

"She wasn't always vocal about her feelings, but Mother's love for family and friends shone through in the foods she prepared and served with such care.

"Her savory Pork Chop Casserole is a mouth-watering dish. We enjoy the rich sauce and golden fried onion rings on top.

"The flavorful dressing made with garlic and honey clings beautifully to the lettuce in her Greens with Vinaigrette. And my sisters and I were always glad to see refreshing Raspberry Congealed Salad on the table.

"Mama's Spice Cake, with its luscious cream cheese frosting, was one my grandmother used to make. Mother re-created this dessert from memory." Adds Nancy, "Mother would be so pleased if you enjoy making and serving this meal as much as she did."

PICTURED AT LEFT: Pork Chop Casserole, Raspberry Congealed Salad, Greens with Vinaigrette and Mama's Spice Cake (recipes are on the next page).

RASPBERRY CONGEALED SALAD

My sisters and I especially enjoyed Mom's cool tangy side dish, which looks so lovely on the table. The pineapple and raspberries are a delectable duo, and pecans add a hearty crunch.

  1 can (8 ounces) crushed pineapple
  1 package (10 ounces) frozen unsweetened
     raspberries, thawed
  1 package (3 ounces) raspberry gelatin
  1 cup applesauce
1/4 cup coarsely chopped pecans
Mayonnaise, optional

Drain pineapple and raspberries, reserving juices. Place fruit in a large bowl; set aside. Add enough water to the juice to measure 1 cup. Pour into a saucepan; bring to a boil. Remove from the heat; stir in gelatin until dissolved. Pour over fruit mixture. Add the applesauce and pecans. Pour into a 1-qt. bowl. Chill until set. Spoon into individual dessert dishes; top with a dollop of mayonnaise if desired. **Yield:** 6 servings.

PORK CHOP CASSEROLE

One bite of these tender pork chops smothered in a creamy sauce and we could taste the care Mother put into her cooking. She was happy to share the recipe with guests who requested it after trying this delicious dish at our house.

3/4 cup all-purpose flour
  1 teaspoon salt
1/2 teaspoon pepper
  6 pork chops (3/4 to 1 inch thick)
  2 tablespoons cooking oil
  1 can (10-3/4 ounces) condensed cream of
     mushroom soup, undiluted
2/3 cup chicken broth
1/2 teaspoon ground ginger
1/4 teaspoon dried rosemary, crushed
  1 cup (8 ounces) sour cream, *divided*
  1 can (2.8 ounces) french-fried onions,
     divided

In a shallow bowl, combine the flour, salt and pepper; dredge pork chops. Heat oil in a large skillet; cook pork chops for 4-5 minutes per side or until browned. Place in a single layer in an ungreased 13-in. x 9-in. x 2-in. baking dish. Combine soup, broth, ginger, rosemary and 1/2 cup sour cream; pour over chops. Sprinkle with half of the onions. Cover and bake at 350° for 45-50 minutes. Stir remaining sour cream into sauce. Top chops with remaining onions. Return to the oven, uncovered, for 10 minutes. **Yield:** 6 servings.

Stop Garlic from Sprouting

If your garlic cloves start to sprout, cut the cloves in half and remove the green sprout in the middle. This cuts down on the bitter taste.

GREENS WITH VINAIGRETTE

This colorful salad topped with a sweet and savory dressing is a refreshing addition to any meal. It's a perfect example of how Mother could turn even simple ingredients into something special.

- 6 cups torn romaine
- 1 cup sliced radishes
- 1/3 cup olive *or* vegetable oil
- 1/4 cup honey
- 2 teaspoons white wine vinegar
- 1-1/2 teaspoons lemon juice
- 1 teaspoon Dijon mustard
- 1 teaspoon poppy seeds
- 2 garlic cloves, minced
- 1 drop hot pepper sauce

Pinch sugar
Salt and pepper to taste

In a large bowl, combine the romaine and radishes. Combine the remaining ingredients in a jar with tight-fitting lid and shake well. Just before serving, pour vinaigrette over salad and toss gently. **Yield:** 6 servings (about 2/3 cup vinaigrette).

MAMA'S SPICE CAKE

Whenever I get a craving for a tasty old-fashioned treat, I make this cake. Great cooks in my family have been baking it for generations, and their families have been enjoying the wonderful spice flavor and rich frosting.

1-1/2 cups sugar
  3/4 cup butter *or* margarine

- 1 cup water
- 1 cup raisins, chopped
- 1 teaspoon ground cinnamon
- 1/2 teaspoon ground allspice
- 1/4 teaspoon ground cloves
- 1/4 teaspoon ground nutmeg
- 4 eggs, *separated*
- 3 cups all-purpose flour
- 1 tablespoon baking powder
- 1/2 teaspoon salt
- 1/4 teaspoon baking soda
- 3/4 cup chopped pecans

CREAM CHEESE FROSTING:
- 1 package (8 ounces) cream cheese, softened
- 1/4 cup butter *or* margarine, softened
- 1 teaspoon vanilla extract

Pinch salt
- 4 cups confectioners' sugar

Additional chopped pecans, optional

In a saucepan, combine the first eight ingredients; heat slowly, stirring until butter melts. Remove from the heat; cool. In a large mixing bowl, beat egg yolks lightly; gradually stir in spice mixture. Combine flour, baking powder, salt, baking soda and pecans; stir into spice mixture. Beat egg whites until soft peaks form; fold into the batter. Pour into two greased and floured 9-in. round cake pans. Bake at 325° for 35-40 minutes or until a wooden pick inserted near the center comes out clean. Cool in pans 5 minutes before removing to a wire rack; cool completely. For frosting, beat cream cheese and butter in a mixing bowl until smooth. Add vanilla and salt. Beat in sugar until smooth and fluffy. Frost cake. Garnish with pecans if desired. Store in the refrigerator. **Yield:** 12-16 servings.

When she was a newlywed, this reader cured homesickness with a hearty helping of Mom's traditional German fare.

"I WAS just 18 when I married and came to America from Germany," relates Karin Cousineau of Burlington, North Carolina.

"Since it was my first time away from my family, I was very homesick. One thing I found that helped to ease my longing for home and my mother (Annelies Hupfeld, above) was to cook some of her special Sunday dinners.

"My favorite has always been her tender, flavorful Beef Rouladen, Spiced Red Cabbage, fluffy Potato Dumplings and delicious Apple Date Crisp.

"My parents had to rebuild after World War II. Our family was quite poor, so we grew most of our food in our large garden. Since we had lots of fresh vegetables on hand, Mom made mostly soup.

"My father worked out of town during the week. On Sunday, when we were all together, Mom would prepare a truly great meal with meat. My older brother and I couldn't wait—we were so tired of vegetable soup!

"My parents still live in Germany. Mom is proud to share these wonderful family recipes."

PICTURED AT LEFT: Beef Rouladen, Potato Dumplings, Spiced Red Cabbage and Apple Date Crisp (recipes are on the next page).

BEEF ROULADEN

Our family was poor when I was growing up in Germany, so we ate garden vegetables for many weekday meals. When Mother made meat for a Sunday dinner, it was a terrific treat. My favorite is this tender beef dish, which gets great flavor from Dijon mustard.

- 1/4 cup Dijon mustard
- 8 slices top round steak, 1/4 inch thick (about 2 pounds)
- Salt and pepper to taste
- 8 bacon strips
- 1 large onion, cut into thin wedges
- 3 tablespoons cooking oil
- 3 cups beef broth
- 1/3 cup all-purpose flour
- 1/2 cup water
- Chopped fresh parsley, optional

Lightly spread mustard on each slice of steak; sprinkle with salt and pepper. Place 1 bacon strip and a few onion wedges on each slice; roll up and secure with wooden picks. Brown in a skillet in oil; drain. Add broth; bring to a boil. Reduce heat; cover and simmer for 1-1/2 hours or until meat is tender. Remove meat and keep warm. Combine flour and water until smooth; stir into broth. Bring to a boil, stirring constantly until thickened and bubbly. Remove wooden picks from meat and return to gravy; heat through. Sprinkle with parsley if desired. **Yield:** 8 servings.

POTATO DUMPLINGS

These moist dumplings are an extra-special way to serve potatoes. The bread centers add a comforting touch, and the potato taste really comes through. They go so well with the Beef Rouladen and gravy.

- 5 to 6 medium potatoes
- 5 tablespoons all-purpose flour
- 1 egg, beaten
- 1-1/2 teaspoons salt
- 1/4 teaspoon ground nutmeg
- 2 slices white bread, toasted
- 1/3 cup mashed potato flakes, optional
- Melted butter *or* margarine and toasted bread crumbs, optional

Cook potatoes in salted water just until tender; drain. Refrigerate for 2 hours or overnight. Peel and grate potatoes. In a bowl, combine the flour, egg, salt and nutmeg. Add potatoes and mix until a stiff batter is formed, adding additional flour if necessary. Slice toasted bread into 24 squares, 1/2 in. each; shape 2 tablespoons of the potato mixture around two bread squares, forming a 2-in. ball. In a large kettle, bring salted water to a boil; add the test dumpling. Reduce heat; cover and simmer for 15-20 minutes or until dumpling is no longer sticky in the center. If test dumpling falls apart during cooking, add the mashed potato flakes to the batter. Let batter sit for 5 minutes; form remaining dumplings. Add to boiling water; return to a boil and follow the same cooking procedure. Remove dumplings with a slotted spoon to a serving bowl. If desired, drizzle with butter and sprinkle with crumbs. **Yield:** 6-8 servings.

SPICED RED CABBAGE

When it comes to vegetable dishes, this one is at the top of my list. The wonderful sweet-sour aroma and taste remind me of home. Plus, it looks so pretty on the table.

✓ **This tasty dish uses less sugar, salt and fat. Recipe includes *Diabetic Exchanges*.**

1/2 medium head red cabbage, diced
  1 tablespoon vegetable oil
1/2 cup chopped onion
  1 medium tart apple, quartered
  3 tablespoons tarragon *or* red wine vinegar
  1 tablespoon sugar
  1 bay leaf
  1 teaspoon salt, optional
1/4 teaspoon pepper
1/8 teaspoon ground cloves

Place cabbage in a large kettle of boiling salted water; boil for 1 minute. Drain. Return to kettle; stir in remaining ingredients. Cover and simmer for 1 hour or until cabbage is tender. Remove bay leaf. **Yield:** 6 servings. **Diabetic Exchanges:** One 1/2-cup serving (prepared without salt) equals 2 vegetable, 1/2 fat; also, 78 calories, 23 mg sodium, 0 cholesterol, 14 gm carbohydrate, 2 gm protein, 3 gm fat.

APPLE DATE CRISP

My mother loves to make this old-fashioned dessert, and my family and I love to eat it. Each serving is chock-full of apple slices, nuts and chewy dates. When the weather is cold, I love to warm up with this dessert.

  8 cups sliced peeled tart apples
  2 cups chopped dates
2/3 cup packed brown sugar
1/2 cup all-purpose flour
  1 teaspoon ground cinnamon
1/3 cup butter *or* margarine
  1 cup chopped nuts
Additional apple slices, optional

Combine the apples and dates in an ungreased 13-in. x 9-in. x 2-in. baking dish. In a small bowl, combine sugar, flour and cinnamon; cut in butter until crumbly. Add nuts; sprinkle over apples and dates. Bake at 375° for 35-40 minutes or until the apples are tender. Serve warm. Garnish with apple slices if desired. **Yield:** 6-8 servings.

Editors' Meals

Taste of Home magazine is edited by 1,000 cooks across North America. On the following pages, you'll "meet" some of those editors who share a family-favorite meal.

Pairing up on preparation, this cooking couple turns out memorable meals like the bountiful barbecue supper they share here.

By Anne and Jesse Foust, Bluefield, West Virginia

TWO is never too many cooks in our kitchen! Married 38 years, we share a special interest in recipes and food. It's been a tasty tie that binds.

Anne: In the early years of our marriage and as we raised our five children, Jesse helped with the cooking. He has a knack of knowing what to add to make a good dish taste even better.

Jesse: I learned to cook in the Navy while stationed at Moffitt Field Naval Air Station near San Francisco. There, I did a little of everything, from running a grill to serving on the "mess line". Cooking for a few thousand was a formidable task, to say the least!

Over the years, I've refined my cooking skills in our own kitchen. I'm always on the lookout for good food that's easy to fix.

We've served this special barbecue supper at many casual get-togethers with family and friends. With its wonderful aroma and slightly smoky taste, Shredded Barbecued Beef always wins raves. I adapted the recipe from one I'd seen, adjusting ingredients to make the sauce just right for our tastes.

Anne: Old-Fashioned Baked Beans are the kind of down-home food I grew up on in Kentucky. Hearty and savory, the beans go hand in hand with the barbecue.

Two heads are better than one for menu planning… and four hands make chores, like peeling the hard-cooked eggs for our Best Deviled Eggs, go more quickly.

Jesse: Besides serving it often at home, we frequently take a big dish of colorful Picnic Slaw by request to potluck dinners. It complements so many foods.

Anne: I'm the dessert-maker in the family. Folks have said my Peanut Butter Cream Pie is a perfect ending for this meal.

Anne: We hope you like our recipes and will prepare the meal or one or two of our dishes sometime soon.

Jesse: Yes, do try them! I'm sure there are others of you who have strengthened your family ties by sharing the role of "cook"!

PICTURED AT LEFT: Shredded Barbecued Beef, Old-Fashioned Baked Beans, Best Deviled Eggs, Picnic Slaw and Peanut Butter Cream Pie (recipes are on the next page).

SHREDDED BARBECUED BEEF

Once family and friends have dug into this tender and tangy barbecued beef, you'll be making it again and again. It takes a little time to prepare, but it's well worth the effort for a picnic or dinner anytime.

>   1 boneless beef chuck roast (about 4 pounds)
>   3 tablespoons cooking oil, *divided*
>   2 large onions, chopped
>   1 cup ketchup
>   1 cup beef broth
> 2/3 cup chili sauce
> 1/4 cup cider vinegar
> 1/4 cup packed brown sugar
>   3 tablespoons Worcestershire sauce
>   2 tablespoons prepared mustard
>   2 tablespoons molasses
>   2 tablespoons lemon juice
>   1 teaspoon salt
> 1/4 teaspoon cayenne pepper
> 1/8 teaspoon pepper
>   1 tablespoon liquid smoke, optional
>   12 to 16 kaiser rolls *or* hamburger buns

In a Dutch oven, brown roast on all sides in 1 tablespoon of oil. Meanwhile, in a large saucepan, saute onions in remaining oil until tender. Add remaining ingredients except rolls; bring to a boil. Reduce heat; simmer, uncovered, for 15 minutes, stirring occasionally. Pour over roast. Cover and bake at 325° for 2 hours; turn the roast and bake for 2 more hours or until meat is very tender. Remove roast; shred with a fork and return to sauce. Serve on rolls. **Yield:** 12-16 servings.

OLD-FASHIONED BAKED BEANS

These hearty beans are a super side dish for a casual meal. The ingredients blend perfectly for a wonderful from-scratch taste.

>   1 pound dry navy beans
> 1-1/2 teaspoons salt
>   4 quarts cold water, *divided*
>   1 cup chopped red onion
> 1/2 cup molasses
>   6 bacon strips, cooked and crumbled
> 1/4 cup packed brown sugar
>   1 teaspoon ground mustard
> 1/4 teaspoon pepper

In a large saucepan, bring beans, salt and 2 qts. water to a boil; boil for 2 minutes. Remove from the heat; let stand for 1 hour. Drain beans and discard liquid. Return beans to pan. Cover with remaining water; bring to a boil. Reduce heat; cover and simmer for 1-1/2 to 2 hours or until beans are tender. Drain, reserving liquid. In a greased 2-1/2-qt. baking dish, combine beans, 1 cup liquid, onion, molasses, bacon, brown sugar, mustard and pepper. Cover and bake at 325° for 3 to 3-1/2 hours or until beans are as thick as desired, stirring occasionally. Add more of the reserved cooking liquid if needed. **Yield:** 12-16 servings.

BEST DEVILED EGGS
(Pictured on page 182)

Herbs lend a nice zest to these pick-up-and-eat accompaniments to our easy menu.

>   12 hard-cooked eggs
> 1/2 cup mayonnaise

1 teaspoon dried parsley flakes
1/2 teaspoon dried chives
1/2 teaspoon ground mustard
1/2 teaspoon dill weed
1/4 teaspoon salt
1/4 teaspoon paprika
1/8 teaspoon pepper
1/8 teaspoon garlic powder
2 tablespoons milk
Fresh parsley and additional paprika

Slice eggs in half lengthwise; remove yolks and set whites aside. In a small bowl, mash yolks. Add the next 10 ingredients; mix well. Evenly fill the whites. Garnish with parsley and paprika. **Yield:** 2 dozen.

PICNIC SLAW

Everyone loves this festive, colorful coleslaw. It not only looks good, it tastes great, too. Crisp vegetables covered with a light creamy dressing make a refreshing side dish you'll be proud to serve.

1 medium head cabbage, shredded
1 large carrot, shredded
1 medium green pepper, julienned
1 medium sweet red pepper, julienned
1 medium onion, finely chopped
1/3 cup sliced green onions
1/4 cup chopped fresh parsley
DRESSING:
1/4 cup milk
1/4 cup buttermilk
1/2 cup mayonnaise
1/3 cup sugar
2 tablespoons lemon juice
1 tablespoon vinegar
1/2 teaspoon salt
1/2 teaspoon celery seed
Dash pepper

In a large bowl, combine the first seven ingredients. Combine dressing ingredients in a blender; process until smooth. Pour over vegetables; toss to coat. Cover and refrigerate overnight. Stir before serving. **Yield:** 12-16 servings.

PEANUT BUTTER CREAM PIE

During the warm months, it's nice to have a fluffy, no-bake dessert that's a snap to make. Packed with peanut flavor, this pie gets gobbled up even after a big meal!

1 package (8 ounces) cream cheese, softened
3/4 cup confectioners' sugar
1/2 cup creamy peanut butter
6 tablespoons milk
1 carton (8 ounces) frozen whipped topping, thawed
1 graham cracker crust (9 inches)
1/4 cup chopped peanuts

In a mixing bowl, beat cream cheese until fluffy. Add sugar and peanut butter; mix well. Gradually add the milk. Fold in whipped topping; spoon into the crust. Sprinkle with peanuts. Chill overnight. **Yield:** 6-8 servings.

Upper Crust

If you have chocolate lovers in your family, use a chocolate crumb crust in the Peanut Butter Cream Pie instead of the standard graham cracker crust. It's a simply delicious substitution.

This busy grandma with decades of cooking experience—at home and at a family restaurant—still loves to plan menus.

By Adeline Piscitelli, Sayreville, New Jersey

PREPARING a whole meal from scratch has long been one of my greatest pleasures.

Some cooks may specialize in making main dishes, desserts or salads, but I like every part of selecting recipes that work well together and then fixing a complete dinner.

My parents came to the U.S. from Poland, so many of my recipes, like the Paprika Chicken I'm sharing here, reflect that heritage.

This main dish was featured at the restaurant my late husband, Nick, and I operated for 11 years. It appealed to folks of many backgrounds, including some Hungarians who came in especially for this dish.

Asparagus with Pimientos is a really simple side dish. When fresh asparagus is available, it speaks for itself. The pimientos are basically for color—I always try to present something that looks appetizing—while the Parmesan delicately complements the asparagus.

Honey Corn Bread, still warm from the oven, adds to this meal's appeal. This bread is very moist, slightly sweet and has a nice texture. It comes recommended by my 10 grandchildren.

I consider a meal unfinished without dessert. Slices of Apple Cheesecake bring my menu to a lip-smacking conclusion...and you'll be pleasantly surprised at how easy this unbaked treat is to prepare.

Following my husband's death 15 years ago, I sold the restaurant. But it didn't take long for me to realize how much I missed feeding folks. So I got a job cooking for four priests at their rectory in the next town.

I still do a little catering for family parties and church functions, but I'm taking it easier now.

Looking back on the many years I've enjoyed cooking and the thousands of recipes I've prepared gives me great satisfaction. All along, I have loved pleasing people with flavorful food I've fixed from scratch using fresh, quality ingredients.

PICTURED AT LEFT: Paprika Chicken, Asparagus with Pimientos, Honey Corn Bread and Apple Cheesecake (recipes are on the next page).

Bring to a boil; cook and stir for 1 minute or until thickened. Stir in tomato paste, paprika, salt and pepper. Return chicken to pan; bring to a boil. Reduce heat; cover and simmer for 60-70 minutes or until chicken juices run clear. Remove chicken to a platter of noodles; keep warm. Add sour cream to sauce; stir until smooth (do not boil). Spoon over chicken and noodles. **Yield:** 4-6 servings.

Asparagus Pointers

When buying asparagus, look for stalks that are brittle enough to snap and fairly uniform in circumference. The tips should be tightly closed.

PAPRIKA CHICKEN

My family has always enjoyed this dish. Mushrooms and red and green peppers add color and flavor to the chicken pieces in a creamy paprika sauce. Served over noodles, it looks and tastes delicious.

> 1 broiler/fryer chicken (3-1/2 to 4 pounds), cut up
> 1 tablespoon cooking oil
> 1 tablespoon butter *or* margarine
> 1 cup sliced fresh mushrooms
> 1 cup diced onion
> 1 cup diced green pepper
> 1 cup diced sweet red pepper
> 3 tablespoons all-purpose flour
> 1 can (14-1/2 ounces) chicken broth
> 1 tablespoon tomato paste
> 1 tablespoon paprika
> 1 to 1-1/2 teaspoons salt
> 1/2 teaspoon pepper
> Hot cooked noodles
> 1/4 cup sour cream

In a Dutch oven over medium heat, brown chicken in oil and butter; remove chicken. Discard all but 3 tablespoons drippings. Saute mushrooms, onion and peppers in the drippings until crisp-tender, about 2-3 minutes. Stir in the flour until smooth. Gradually add broth, stirring constantly.

ASPARAGUS WITH PIMIENTOS

This lovely, simple-to-prepare side dish highlights the asparagus rather than hiding it. The delicate topping of Parmesan cheese and bread crumbs complements the asparagus flavor and looks impressive.

> 1 pound fresh asparagus, trimmed
> 1/4 cup dry bread crumbs
> 3 tablespoons butter *or* margarine
> 2 tablespoons grated Parmesan cheese
> 2 tablespoons chopped pimientos

In a saucepan over medium heat, cook asparagus in boiling salted water until tender, about 8 minutes. Meanwhile, in a skillet, brown bread crumbs in butter. Drain asparagus; place in a serving dish. Sprinkle with crumbs, cheese and pimientos. **Yield:** 4-6 servings.

HONEY CORN BREAD

It's a pleasure to serve this moist corn bread to family and guests. Honey gives it a slightly sweet taste. Most people find it's difficult to eat just one piece.

    1 cup all-purpose flour
    1 cup yellow cornmeal
  1/4 cup sugar
    1 tablespoon baking powder
  1/2 teaspoon salt
    2 eggs
    1 cup whipping cream
  1/4 cup vegetable oil
  1/4 cup honey

In a bowl, combine flour, cornmeal, sugar, baking powder and salt. In a small mixing bowl, beat the eggs. Add cream, oil and honey; beat well. Stir into the dry ingredients just until moistened. Pour into a greased 9-in. square baking pan. Bake at 400° for 20-25 minutes or until a wooden pick inserted in the center comes out clean. **Yield:** 9 servings.

APPLE CHEESECAKE

After a big meal, this fluffy no-bake cheesecake with its deliciously different applesauce and peanut topping really hits the spot. It needs no crust, and the light cheese layer is smooth and creamy.

    2 envelopes unflavored gelatin
  1/3 cup cold water

1-3/4 cups apple juice
  1/2 cup sugar
    3 egg yolks, beaten
    3 packages (8 ounces *each*) cream cheese, softened
  1/2 teaspoon ground cinnamon
  1/4 teaspoon ground nutmeg
    1 cup whipping cream, whipped
TOPPING:
  1/2 cup chopped dry roasted peanuts
    2 tablespoons butter *or* margarine
    1 cup applesauce
  1/3 cup packed brown sugar
  1/4 teaspoon ground cinnamon
Additional whipped cream, cinnamon and peanuts, optional

In a small bowl, soften gelatin in water; let stand for 2 minutes. In a saucepan over medium heat, cook and stir apple juice, sugar, egg yolks and gelatin mixture until gelatin is dissolved. Cool to room temperature. In a large mixing bowl, beat the cream cheese, cinnamon and nutmeg until smooth. Gradually beat in gelatin mixture until smooth. Chill until slightly thickened, about 20 minutes. Fold in cream. Pour into an ungreased 9-in. springform pan. Chill 4 hours or overnight. In a saucepan over medium heat, brown peanuts in butter for 2 minutes. Add applesauce, brown sugar and cinnamon; cook and stir for 5 minutes. Cool. Spread over top of cheesecake. If desired, garnish with whipped cream, cinnamon and peanuts. **Yield:** 12-16 servings.

Christmas Eve dinner is a delicious tradition for this reader as she celebrates in her gaily trimmed Victorian home.

By Dorothy Anderson, Ottawa, Kansas

GOOD FARE, fellowship and tradition all play a part in our holiday meals—especially at Christmas!

Our wonderful Victorian home, built in the 1800's, lends itself to family occasions. My husband, Charles, and I have spent the last 20 years refurbishing and re-decorating it.

Holiday decorating begins in October, when we set up miniature villages filled with homes and scenes that remind us of our childhood. Later come decorations that reflect our Scandinavian heritage, a collection of finely crafted Santas and a treasured Nativity—an important reminder of the true meaning of Christmas.

Following Christmas Eve candlelight service, we return home for a celebration meal and gift exchange. The atmosphere of a meal is very important to me, and I enjoy tying together the many elements of our home, the table presentation and the food.

On that special night, we begin with assorted appetizers and Wassail Punch. The wonderful cinnamon, spice and fruit aroma of this punch fills the house and adds to the festive atmosphere.

I've served Rice-Stuffed Cornish Hens for several years now after deciding they'd be a nice change from turkey or ham. Plus, the entree's English origins complement our Victorian surroundings.

Charles' aunt, Eleanor Johnson, shared the Easy Berry Relish recipe. Ginger ale and raspberry gelatin combine flavorfully with tart cranberries.

Fancy Brussels Sprouts get added flavor and texture from an unexpected ingredient—water chestnuts.

Noel Ice Cream Cups are a refreshing finish. This easy Italian-style "tortoni" ice cream includes red and green maraschino cherries, and I add colorful M&M candies, which the grandchildren love.

The dessert can be made well in advance and frozen, an important benefit during the busy holidays.

I hope you'll enjoy my recipes and find joy in the Christmas season with your dear ones and traditions.

PICTURED AT LEFT: Wassail Punch, Rice-Stuffed Cornish Hens, Easy Berry Relish, Fancy Brussels Sprouts and Noel Ice Cream Cups (recipes are on the next page).

WASSAIL PUNCH

(Pictured on page 190)

Cloves and cinnamon dress up a blend of fruit juices for special occasions.

> 2 quarts apple cider
> 2 cups orange juice
> 2 cups pineapple juice
> 1/2 cup lemon juice
> 1/2 cup sugar
> 12 whole cloves
> 4 cinnamon sticks (3 to 4 inches)
> Orange slices and additional cloves, optional

In a large kettle, bring the first seven ingredients to a boil. Reduce heat; simmer for 10-15 minutes. Remove cinnamon and cloves. Serve warm. If desired, stud orange slices with cloves and float in punch bowl. (Be sure bowl is safe for hot liquid.) **Yield:** about 3-1/2 quarts.

EASY BERRY RELISH

This flavorful relish will catch your eye and entice your taste buds. It adds color, too. Guests will be impressed.

> 1 package (12 ounces) fresh *or* frozen
>   cranberries
> 2-1/2 cups sugar
> 1-2/3 cups ginger ale
> 1/3 cup lemon juice
> 1 package (3 ounces) raspberry gelatin

In a saucepan, combine the first four ingredients. Cook over medium heat until the berries pop, about 15 minutes. Remove from the heat; stir in gelatin until dissolved. Pour into serving bowl. Chill overnight. **Yield:** 5 cups.

RICE-STUFFED CORNISH HENS

These moist golden hens are a tradition at our house on Christmas Eve. We think the spiced rice stuffing with cinnamon, sweet raisins and honey goes so well with the birds and makes the meal a special one.

> 3/4 cup chopped onion
> 3/4 cup chopped celery
> 1/2 cup butter *or* margarine, **divided**
> 3 cups cooked rice
> 3/4 cup raisins
> 1/3 cup chopped walnuts
> 3 tablespoons honey
> 2 tablespoons lemon juice
> 3/4 teaspoon ground cinnamon
> 1/2 teaspoon salt
> 1/8 teaspoon pepper
> 6 Cornish game hens (about 20 ounces *each*)

In a skillet, saute onion and celery in 3 tablespoons butter until tender; remove from the heat. Add rice, raisins, walnuts, honey, lemon juice, cinnamon, salt and pepper; mix well. Stuff hens. Place on a rack in a large shallow baking pan. Soften the remaining butter; rub over skins. Bake, uncovered, at 375° for 1 hour or until the juices run clear. **Yield:** 6 servings.

FANCY BRUSSELS SPROUTS

This is a simple and tasty way to dress up brussels sprouts for the holidays. The parsley, sugar and crisp water chestnuts make the sprouts fresh tasting and festive looking.

✓ **This tasty dish uses less sugar, salt and fat. Recipe includes *Diabetic Exchanges*.**

    1 **cup water**
1/4 **cup minced fresh parsley**
    1 **teaspoon sugar**
1/2 **teaspoon salt, optional**
    2 **pints fresh brussels sprouts, halved *or* 2 packages (10 ounces *each*) frozen brussels sprouts, thawed**
    1 **can (8 ounces) water chestnuts, drained and diced**
    1 **tablespoon butter *or* margarine**

In a saucepan over medium heat, bring water, parsley, sugar and salt to a boil. Add brussels sprouts. Cover and simmer for 6-8 minutes or until tender; drain. Add water chestnuts and butter; heat through. **Yield:** 6 servings. **Diabetic Exchanges:** One serving (prepared with margarine and without salt) equals 2 vegetable, 1/2 fat; also, 67 calories, 34 mg sodium, 0 cholesterol, 11 gm carbohydrate, 3 gm protein, 2 gm fat.

NOEL ICE CREAM CUPS

Each year, our family enjoys a dessert that's much more fun than the typical pies and cakes. With refreshing ice cream chock-full of holiday ingredients like nuts, cherries and candies, these treats are a delightful end to a perfect meal.

    1 **quart vanilla ice cream, softened**
1/4 **cup chopped pecans, toasted**
    2 **tablespoons *each* chopped red and green maraschino cherries**
    1 **teaspoon vanilla extract**
1/2 **teaspoon almond extract**
1/2 **cup M&M's**
Additional M&M's, chopped

In a medium bowl, combine the ice cream, pecans, cherries and extracts; mix well. Fold in M&M's. Spoon into paper-lined muffin cups and freeze for at least 30 minutes. Sprinkle with chopped M&M's. **Yield:** 8-10 servings. **Variations:** Substitute chocolate ice cream (or any other family favorite) for the vanilla ice cream. Make this dessert a year-round treat by substituting chopped cream-filled chocolate sandwich cookies for the red and green maraschino cherries.

> ### Selecting Sprouts
> Brussels sprouts should be purchased when they're firm and compact. Avoid large, old-looking sprouts because their flavor will be bitter. The smaller bright green varieties will be the sweetest.

A proud pork producer and enthusiastic cook, this reader plans a flavorful meal around her versatile farm product.

By Patricia Staudt, Marble Rock, Iowa

RAISED on a farm and now married to a farmer, I draw on a heritage of good country cooking! It's reflected in this dinner I like to fix for my family.

We live on Dennis' family's farm in northeast Iowa near Marble Rock, where we grow grain and raise hogs with his two brothers. Our state leads the nation in pork production, and I've gotten many delicious recipes from our Iowa Pork Producers Association.

One family favorite is Italian Meat Loaves. Made with economical lean ground pork and Italian seasonings, these individual loaves are simple to prepare.

Tangy Coleslaw, which has a pleasant sweet/sour dressing, is my mom's recipe. Whenever I make it, I recall her shredding a firm head of cabbage and cutting up onions, carrots and peppers from her garden.

My sister introduced me to Oatmeal Dinner Rolls. Their fluffy, light texture and oat taste are terrific. (I also use this dough to make cinnamon rolls.)

Both the rolls and meat loaves freeze well, so you can make them ahead when you're planning a party.

I discovered the recipe for Peanut Butter Bars in a church cookbook. The combination of peanut butter, chocolate chips and oatmeal is irresistible.

These bars can be dressed up for festive occasions by substituting colored icing for the peanut butter frosting. I drizzle them with pastel colors for Easter…red, white and blue for the Fourth of July…and orange and chocolate for Halloween.

Often when I'm cooking and canning, I remember my childhood 4-H projects. Now I'm beginning my second year as a 4-H leader with my own daughters experimenting in the kitchen.

All the dishes featured here are also excellent to carry to a potluck. We attend many functions at our church, where I'm a lector and Sunday school teacher.

I hope you enjoy this menu that's so popular at our house. If you like meals that are homey but easy to prepare, you should find it satisfying.

PICTURED AT LEFT: Italian Meat Loaves, Tangy Coleslaw, Oatmeal Dinner Rolls and Peanut Butter Bars (recipes are on the next page).

ITALIAN MEAT LOAVES

We raise hogs, so pork is something I cook with a lot. These miniature meat loaves made with ground pork and Italian herbs are full of flavor. Our children especially like the topping of ketchup and Parmesan cheese.

>   2 eggs, beaten
>   3/4 cup cracker *or* bread crumbs
>   1/2 cup milk
>   1/2 cup plus 2 tablespoons grated Parmesan
>   cheese, *divided*
>   1/4 cup finely chopped onion
>   1 teaspoon Worcestershire sauce
>   1 teaspoon garlic salt
>   1 teaspoon Italian seasoning, *divided*
>   2 pounds ground pork
>   1/4 cup ketchup

In a large bowl, combine eggs, crumbs, milk, 1/2 cup cheese, onion, Worcestershire sauce, garlic salt and 1/2 teaspoon Italian seasoning. Add pork and mix well. Shape into 10 individual loaves; place on a rack in a greased large shallow baking pan. Spread ketchup over loaves; sprinkle with remaining cheese and Italian seasoning. Bake at 350° for 45-55 minutes or until no pink remains. **Yield:** 10 servings.

TANGY COLESLAW

If you've been searching for the perfect coleslaw, give this one a try! It has a terrific crunch, and the simple dressing is sweet and tangy all in one. This is a great way to get your family to eat cabbage. We love it.

>   1/2 large head cabbage, shredded
>   2 large carrots, shredded
>   1/2 cup finely chopped green pepper
>   2 tablespoons finely chopped onion
> DRESSING:
>   1/4 cup sugar

3 tablespoons vinegar
2 tablespoons vegetable oil
1 teaspoon celery seed
1/2 teaspoon salt

In a large bowl, combine cabbage, carrots, green pepper and onion. In a jar with tight-fitting lid, combine dressing ingredients; shake well. Pour over cabbage mixture and toss. Cover and chill 4 hours before serving. **Yield:** 10 servings.

OATMEAL DINNER ROLLS

These fluffy rolls go perfectly with any meal. They have a delicious homemade flavor that's irresistible. They're not hard to make and they bake up nice and high.

✓ **This tasty dish uses less sugar, salt and fat. Recipe includes *Diabetic Exchanges*.**

2 cups water
1 cup quick-cooking oats
3 tablespoons butter *or* margarine
1 package (1/4 ounce) active dry yeast
1/3 cup warm water (110° to 115°)
1/3 cup packed brown sugar
1 tablespoon sugar
1-1/2 teaspoons salt
4-3/4 to 5-1/4 cups all-purpose flour

In a saucepan, bring water to a boil; add oats and butter. Cook and stir for 1 minute. Remove from the heat; cool to lukewarm. In a mixing bowl, dissolve yeast in warm water. Add the oat mixture, sugars, salt and 4 cups of flour; beat until smooth. Add enough remaining flour to form a soft dough. Turn onto a floured board; knead until smooth and elastic, about 6-8 minutes. Place in a greased bowl, turning once to grease top. Cover and let rise in a warm place until doubled, about 1 hour. Punch dough down; allow to rest for 10 minutes.

Shape into 18 balls. Place in two greased 9-in. round baking pans. Cover and let rise until doubled, about 45 minutes. Bake at 350° for 20-25 minutes or until golden brown. Remove from pan to wire racks. **Yield:** 1-1/2 dozen. **Diabetic Exchanges:** One roll (prepared with margarine) equals 2 starch, 1/2 fat; also, 180 calories, 212 mg sodium, 0 cholesterol, 34 gm carbohydrate, 4 gm protein, 2 gm fat.

PEANUT BUTTER BARS

These bars are a big hit with kids of all ages. Since I always have these basic ingredients on hand, I can whip up a batch anytime.

1/2 cup butter *or* margarine, softened
1/2 cup sugar
1/2 cup packed brown sugar
1/2 cup creamy peanut butter
1 egg, beaten
1 teaspoon vanilla extract
1 cup all-purpose flour
1/2 cup quick-cooking oats
1 teaspoon baking soda
1/4 teaspoon salt
1 cup (6 ounces) semisweet chocolate chips
ICING:
1/2 cup confectioners' sugar
2 tablespoons creamy peanut butter
2 tablespoons milk

In a mixing bowl, cream butter, sugars and peanut butter. Add egg and vanilla; mix well. Combine the flour, oats, baking soda and salt; stir into the creamed mixture. Spread into a greased 13-in. x 9-in. x 2-in. baking pan. Sprinkle with chocolate chips. Bake at 350° for 20-25 minutes or until lightly browned. Cool 10 minutes. Combine icing ingredients; drizzle over bars. **Yield:** 3-4 dozen.

This Midwestern cook grills up a casual supper and mingles with guests when the backyard deck becomes her fresh-air kitchen.

By Nancy Johnson, Connersville, Indiana

"DINNER on the deck" is a favorite way for my husband, John, and me to entertain our family and friends on a nice summer evening.

There's nothing like the aroma of good food cooking on the grill to enhance everyone's appetite...and the setting is so pleasant and peaceful, looking out over our perennial gardens toward rolling fields.

Since I enjoy visiting with our guests even during the meal preparation, I've come up with a no-fuss menu that lets me do so.

On a balmy evening, folks often arrive thirsty! So we start them sipping refreshing Fruit Juice Cooler that combines peach, orange, grapefruit and lemon flavors with mineral water.

After we get the grill going on the deck, the Vegetable Kabobs are put on first. (Meantime, I start the rice cooking on my stovetop inside.) You can vary which vegetables to use according to whatever your garden is yielding or what is in season at the market.

Sesame Ginger Chicken is fast and flavorful. The honey-ginger basting sauce gives this recipe its character. You'll find the chicken breasts cook in just minutes alongside the vegetables.

Since they're so good served fresh and warm, I make the Soft Breadsticks shortly before the party starts.

Don't overlook the opportunity to "cook out" dessert when you plan a deck or backyard party. My Grilled Peaches with Berry Sauce are a simple but elegant finish. I make the sauce ahead and keep it chilled.

This meal is so tasty and satisfying that your guests may not even be able to guess that it's also quite low in fat!

While we make the most of our Midwest winter, I'm always yearning for the warmer weather when I can get into the garden, clean off the deck furniture and invite friends and family to come out for a casual outdoor meal.

I think you will be pleased at how easy it is to prepare a delicious summer "dinner on the deck".

PICTURED AT LEFT: Fruit Juice Cooler, Sesame Ginger Chicken, Vegetable Kabobs with Rice, Soft Breadsticks, Grilled Peaches with Berry Sauce (recipes on next page).

1/2 cup orange juice
1/4 cup grapefruit juice
2 tablespoons lemon juice
1 can (12 ounces) seltzer water *or* sparkling mineral water, chilled

Combine juices in a 1-qt. pitcher; chill. Just before serving, stir in seltzer or mineral water. Serve over ice. **Yield:** 4 servings (about 1 quart).

SESAME GINGER CHICKEN

Why grill plain chicken breasts when a simple ginger-honey basting sauce can make them extra special? This tempting chicken is a wonderful summer main dish since it's quick and light. We love it.

2 tablespoons soy sauce
2 tablespoons honey
1 tablespoon sesame seeds toasted
1/2 teaspoon ground ginger
4 boneless skinless chicken breast halves
2 green onions with tops, cut into thin strips

In a small bowl, combine the first four ingredients; set aside. Pound the chicken breasts to 1/4-in. thickness. Grill over medium-hot coals, turning and basting frequently with soy sauce mixture, for 8 minutes or until juices run clear. Garnish with green onions. **Yield:** 4 servings.

FRUIT JUICE COOLER
(Pictured on page 198)

Be sure to mix up enough of this sparkling beverage so you can offer your guests a second glass to enjoy with the meal.

1-1/2 cups peach nectar

VEGETABLE KABOBS WITH RICE

My husband and I like gardening, and these kabobs are a fun way to enjoy our fresh vegetables. They're so easy to make and they can grill right along with the main course.

✓ **This tasty dish uses less sugar, salt and fat. Recipe includes *Diabetic Exchanges.***

1/2 cup Italian salad dressing
1 tablespoon minced fresh parsley
1 teaspoon dried basil
2 medium yellow squash, cut into 1-inch pieces
8 small boiling onions, peeled
8 cherry tomatoes
8 medium fresh mushrooms
2 cups hot cooked rice

In a small bowl, combine dressing, parsley and basil. Alternate the vegetables on eight skewers. Place on a grill rack over medium-hot coals. Baste with dressing mixture and turn frequently for 15 minutes or until vegetables are tender. To serve, place 1/2 cup rice on each plate and top with two kabobs. **Yield:** 4 servings. **Diabetic Exchanges:** One serving (prepared with fat-free dressing; rice prepared without added salt) equals 2 vegetable, 1-1/2 starch; also, 171 calories, 70 mg sodium, 0 cholesterol, 38 gm carbohydrate, 5 gm protein, trace fat.

SOFT BREADSTICKS

I've been making these tasty breadsticks that go with almost any meal for years. Since they use ingredients like flour, sugar, baking powder and milk, it's convenient and inexpensive to mix up a batch.

1-1/4 **cups all-purpose flour**
   2 **teaspoons sugar**
1-1/2 **teaspoons baking powder**
  1/2 **teaspoon salt**
  2/3 **cup milk**
   3 **tablespoons butter** *or* **margarine, melted**
   2 **teaspoons sesame seeds**

In a small bowl, combine flour, sugar, baking powder and salt. Gradually add milk and stir to form a soft dough. Turn onto a floured surface, knead gently 3-4 times. Roll into a 10-in. x 5-in. x 1/2-in. rectangle; cut into 12 breadsticks. Place butter in a 13-in. x 9-in. x 2-in. baking pan. Place breadsticks in the butter and turn to coat. Sprinkle with sesame seeds. Bake at 450° for 14-18 minutes or until golden brown. Serve warm. **Yield:** 1 dozen.

GRILLED PEACHES WITH BERRY SAUCE

This unusual dessert is as pretty as it is delicious. Topped with brown sugar and cinnamon, the peaches come off the grill sweet and spicy. The raspberry sauce adds a refreshing touch.

  1/2 **of a 10-ounce package frozen raspberries in syrup, slightly thawed**
1-1/2 **teaspoons lemon juice**
   2 **medium fresh peaches, peeled and halved**
   5 **teaspoons brown sugar**
  1/4 **teaspoon ground cinnamon**
  1/2 **teaspoon vanilla extract**
   1 **teaspoon butter** *or* **margarine**

In a blender or food processor, process raspberries and lemon juice until pureed. Strain and discard seeds. Cover and chill. Place peach halves, cut side up, on a large piece of heavy-duty foil (about 18 in. x 12 in.). Combine brown sugar and cinnamon; sprinkle into peach centers. Sprinkle with vanilla; dot with butter. Fold foil over peaches and seal. Grill over medium-hot coals for 15 minutes or until heated through. To serve, spoon the raspberry sauce over peaches. **Yield:** 4 servings.

This grateful cook stirs up fond memories as she prepares Thanksgiving dinner using recipes that reflect her heritage, church and community ties.

By Denise Goedeken, Platte Center, Nebraska

I HAVE my two German grandmothers to thank for the showpiece of my family's Thanksgiving dinner—Roast Goose with Apple-Raisin Stuffing.

My maternal Grandma Kant lived to be 99 years old, and even in her later years, nothing delighted her more than to sit down to a holiday meal of roast goose or duck. I think this goes back to the 1930's, when she was raising a family and wouldn't have dreamed of purchasing a turkey for a meal when she raised geese or ducks and had them running in the yard.

Memories of Thanksgiving at my paternal Grandma Bakenhus' house include eating plenty of her wonderful apple-raisin stuffing. I think the apples and raisins are an especially good flavor complement to waterfowl.

My cousins and I liked Grandma's stuffing so much we once had a contest to see who could eat the most! I can personally vouch for this recipe being passed down in my dad's family for at least 40 years, and Dad says Grandma served it long before that.

Scalloped Onions and Peas has a more recent origin. Years ago, I was looking for a vegetable to serve for company, when I came across this recipe in a small cookbook my employer—Nebraska Public Power District in Columbus—issued. It passed the "taste test" and has been part of my collection of favorites since then.

Festive Cranberry Salad conveniently calls for a can of cranberry sauce. Plus, it can be prepared a few days in advance and then frozen. I found it in a "working woman's cookbook" put together by the Columbus Chapter of the American Business Women's Association.

The Pumpkin Pie Squares recipe came from our Christ Lutheran Church cookbook. With no crust to roll, it's a real time- and energy-saver for me.

Major cooking events at our house are centered around holidays and birthdays. And it doesn't really matter what the menu is—everything just seems to taste better with family gathered 'round.

PICTURED AT LEFT. Roast Goose with Apple-Raisin Stuffing, Scalloped Onions and Peas, Festive Cranberry Salad and Pumpkin Pie Squares (recipes are on the next page).

ROAST GOOSE WITH APPLE-RAISIN STUFFING

A tempting Thanksgiving goose is a family tradition I've kept up. Paired with moist, lightly sweet apple-raisin stuffing, it's a special main dish that makes us count our blessings.

    1 goose (10 to 12 pounds)
    1 cup chopped celery
    1 cup chopped onion
    2 tablespoons butter *or* margarine
    3 cups chopped peeled apples
    2 cups raisins
    8 cups cubed day-old white bread
    2 to 3 tablespoons sugar
    1 teaspoon salt
    2 eggs
 1/2 cup apple cider
 1/2 cup water

Sprinkle the inside of the goose with salt. Prick skin well; set aside. In a skillet, saute celery and onion in butter; transfer to a large bowl. Add apples, raisins, bread, sugar and salt. In a small bowl, beat eggs, cider and water. Pour over bread mixture and toss lightly. Stuff into goose. Place with breast side up on a rack in a large shallow roasting pan. Bake, uncovered, at 350° for 3 to 3-1/2 hours or until a meat thermometer reads 185°. Drain fat from pan as it accumulates. Remove all dressing. **Yield:** 8-10 servings.

SCALLOPED ONIONS AND PEAS

With tasty peas and onions smothered in a creamy sauce, this is an irresistible side dish that gets passed around until the bowl is empty. We especially like the crunch of the almonds and the flavor from the Parmesan cheese.

 1/4 cup butter *or* margarine
    3 tablespoons all-purpose flour
 1/2 teaspoon ground mustard
 1/2 teaspoon salt
1-1/2 cups milk
    1 teaspoon Worcestershire sauce
    3 jars (15 ounces *each*) white onions, drained
    1 package (10 ounces) frozen peas
 1/2 cup sliced blanched almonds
    3 tablespoons grated Parmesan cheese
Paprika

In a saucepan over medium heat, melt butter. Stir in flour, mustard and salt; cook and stir until bubbly. Stir in milk and Worcestershire sauce; cook and stir until thickened, about 2 minutes. Gently stir in onions, peas and almonds. Pour into an ungreased 2-qt. baking dish. Sprinkle with Parmesan and paprika. Cover and bake at 350° for 30 minutes. **Yield:** 8-10 servings.

FESTIVE CRANBERRY SALAD

This cool tangy salad always prompts recipe requests. It must be the combination of tart cranberries, sweet pineapple and pecans blended together in a fluffy base. I appreciate how easy it is to prepare.

    1 can (14 ounces) sweetened condensed milk
    1/4 cup lemon juice
    1 can (20 ounces) crushed pineapple, drained
    1 can (16 ounces) whole-berry cranberry
        sauce
    2 cups miniature marshmallows
    1/2 cup chopped pecans
    Red food coloring, optional
    1 carton (8 ounces) frozen whipped
        topping, thawed

In a bowl, combine milk and lemon juice; mix well. Stir in pineapple, cranberry sauce, marshmallows, pecans and food coloring if desired. Fold in whipped topping. Spoon into a 13-in. x 9-in. x 2-in. baking dish. Freeze until firm, 4 hours or overnight. Cut into squares. **Yield:** 12-16 servings.

PUMPKIN PIE SQUARES

I have to confess that rolling out a pie crust is not something I particularly enjoy. This dessert has all the spicy pumpkin goodness of the traditional pie without

the fuss of a pastry crust. The first time my husband and two daughters tried it, they thought it was delicious!

    1 cup all-purpose flour
    1/2 cup quick-cooking oats
    1/2 cup packed brown sugar
    1/2 cup butter *or* margarine
FILLING:
    2 cans (15 ounces *each*) pumpkin
    2 cans (12 ounces *each*) evaporated milk
    4 eggs
 1-1/2 cups sugar
    2 teaspoons ground cinnamon
    1 teaspoon ground ginger
    1/2 teaspoon ground cloves
    1 teaspoon salt
TOPPING:
    1/2 cup packed brown sugar
    1/2 cup chopped pecans
    2 tablespoons butter *or* margarine, softened

Combine the first four ingredients until crumbly; press into a greased 13-in. x 9-in. x 2-in. baking pan. Bake at 350° for 20 minutes or until golden brown. Meanwhile, beat filling ingredients in a mixing bowl until smooth; pour over crust. Bake for 45 minutes. Combine brown sugar, pecans and butter; sprinkle over the top. Bake 15-20 minutes longer or until a knife inserted near the center comes out clean. Cool. Store in the refrigerator. **Yield:** 16-20 servings.

Meals in Minutes

Mix and match these recipes to make countless meals you can take from start to serving in 30 minutes or less.

SPENDING TIME in the kitchen preparing an elaborate meal is a joyful task for those who love to cook. But some days you need to pull together a satisfying meal in just minutes.

The complete-meal menu here is made up of family favorites from three great cooks. You can have everything in this tasty meal ready to serve in about 30 minutes.

● Hearty Reuben Salad, shared by Mrs. Paul Tremblay of Fort Wayne, Indiana, is a unique, flavorful dish that tastes very much like the sandwich for which it was named.

● Herbed French Bread comes from Karen Paumen of Buffalo, Minnesota. "It's made of a tasty mix of ingredients from several recipes my daughter and I combined. Plus, it's easy to prepare," Karen reports.

● Chocolate Caramel Sundaes are a delightful way to end a quick-to-fix meal. The recipe for this simple yet irresistible dessert was sent by Pat Yaeger of Naples, Florida.

Speedy Spread That Satisfies

HEARTY REUBEN SALAD

  4 cups torn iceberg lettuce
  1 can (16 ounces) sauerkraut, rinsed and drained
  1 cup cubed Swiss cheese
  2 packages (2-1/2 ounces *each*) sliced corned beef, chopped
  2 tablespoons chopped fresh parsley
1/4 to **1/2** cup Thousand Island salad dressing
1/2 cup rye croutons
  4 hard-cooked eggs, quartered

In a large salad bowl or shallow platter, toss lettuce, sauerkraut, cheese, corned beef and parsley. Drizzle with dressing. Garnish with croutons and eggs. Serve immediately. **Yield:** 4 servings.

HERBED FRENCH BREAD

1/4 cup butter *or* margarine
  2 tablespoons olive *or* vegetable oil
  1 garlic clove, minced
  3 tablespoons grated Parmesan cheese
  2 tablespoons chopped fresh chives
  1 teaspoon Dijon mustard
  1 loaf (8 ounces) French bread, cut into 1/2-inch slices

Melt butter in a saucepan. Add oil and garlic; saute until garlic is tender. Remove from the heat; stir in Parmesan, chives and mustard. Cool for 5 minutes or until creamy. Spread on one side of each slice of bread. Place with buttered side up on an ungreased baking sheet. Bake at 400° for 6-8 minutes or broil 2-3 minutes or until lightly browned. **Yield:** 4-6 servings.

CHOCOLATE CARAMEL SUNDAES

  1 package (10 ounces) Milk Duds
1/4 cup milk
Vanilla *or* coffee-flavored ice cream

In a saucepan over medium heat, cook and stir Milk Duds and milk until smooth. Serve warm over ice cream. Refrigerate leftovers. **Yield:** 1 cup sauce.

A Quick and Tasty Way To Start the Day

COOKING UP a big hearty breakfast for your brood is a great way to help them start their day off right. But there are some days when time is short or you and your family just want to be able to make the most of a beautiful morning. On those days, a fast-to-fix delicious breakfast will help your family get going in no time.

The complete-meal menu here is made up of favorites from three great cooks. You can have everything ready to serve in about half an hour!

● Breakfast Burritos are a fun and filling way to serve scrambled eggs, and the zippy flavor will wake up your taste buds, assures Brenda Spann of Granger, Indiana, who shares her recipe.

● Potatoes O'Brien comes from Nila Towler of Baird, Texas. "I usually serve these colorful potatoes for breakfast," notes Nila. "But they're great as a tasty potato side dish for just about any meal. My family often asks me to prepare them instead of regular fried potatoes."

● Lemon Blueberry Biscuits are easy to make and a treat to eat. Kristin Dallum of Vancouver, Washington says she got the recipe from her mother, who's a wonderful baker.

BREAKFAST BURRITOS

    1 pound bulk pork sausage
    1 small onion, chopped
1/2 green pepper, chopped
    1 can (4 ounces) mushroom stems and pieces, drained
    8 flour tortillas (7 inches), warmed
    6 eggs, beaten
    1 cup (4 ounces) shredded cheddar cheese
Salsa, optional

In a skillet, brown sausage. Drain, discarding all but 2 tablespoons drippings. Add onion, green pepper and mushrooms; saute until tender. Meanwhile, in another skillet or in the microwave, scramble the eggs. Place an equal amount of sausage mixture on each tortilla; cover with an equal amount of eggs and 2 tablespoons of cheese. Fold bottom of tortilla over filling and roll up. Serve with salsa if desired. **Yield:** 4 servings.

POTATOES O'BRIEN

1/2 cup chopped onion
1/2 cup chopped green pepper
1/2 cup chopped sweet red pepper
    4 medium red potatoes, cubed
    3 tablespoons cooking oil
1/4 cup beef broth
1/2 teaspoon Worcestershire sauce
    1 teaspoon salt

In a skillet over medium heat, saute the onion, peppers and potatoes in oil for 4 minutes. Combine broth, Worcestershire sauce and salt; pour over vegetables. Cover and cook for 10 minutes or until potatoes are tender, stirring occasionally. Uncover and cook until liquid is absorbed, about 3 minutes. **Yield:** 4 servings.

LEMON BLUEBERRY BISCUITS

    2 cups all-purpose flour
1/3 cup sugar
    2 teaspoons baking powder
1/2 teaspoon baking soda
1/4 teaspoon salt
    1 carton (8 ounces) lemon yogurt
    1 egg, lightly beaten
1/4 cup butter *or* margarine, melted
    1 teaspoon grated lemon peel
    1 cup fresh or frozen blueberries
GLAZE:
1/2 cup confectioners' sugar
    1 tablespoon lemon juice
1/2 teaspoon grated lemon peel

In a large bowl, combine dry ingredients. Combine yogurt, egg, butter and lemon peel; stir into dry ingredients just until moistened. Fold in blueberries. Drop by tablespoonfuls onto a greased baking sheet. Bake at 400° for 15-18 minutes or until lightly browned. Combine glaze ingredients; drizzle over warm biscuits. **Yield:** 1 dozen.

Savory Skillet Supper That's Ready in a Snap

WHEN cooler days signal the start of the busy pre-holiday season, even dedicated cooks can't always spend much time in the kitchen. Hearty, fast-to-fix meals come in handy then.

The complete-meal menu here from four great cooks can be ready to serve in just 30 minutes!

• Sausage Skillet Supper is a simple and satisfying main dish and a favorite of Mildred Sherrer's family in Bay City, Texas.

• Honey Poppy Seed Dressing, sent by Michelle Bentley of Niceville, Florida, is a light, refreshing way to dress up a plain lettuce salad.

• Lemon Garlic Bread has a deliciously different hint of lemon. Adeline Piscitelli of Sayreville, New Jersey shares the recipe.

• Speedy Rice Pudding has rich, old-fashioned flavor, but it's quick to make, assures great-grandmother Ann Vershowske of West Allis, Wisconsin.

SAUSAGE SKILLET SUPPER

    1 pound bulk pork sausage
    1 can (14-1/2 ounces) stewed tomatoes, undrained
    1 can (16 ounces) kidney beans, rinsed and drained
    1 cup uncooked long grain rice
    1 cup water
  2/3 cup picante sauce *or* salsa

In a medium skillet, cook and crumble sausage; drain. Add remaining ingredients; bring to a boil. Reduce heat; cover and simmer for 20-25 minutes or until rice is tender. **Yield:** 6-8 servings.

HONEY POPPY SEED DRESSING

  1/3 cup vegetable oil
  1/4 cup honey
    2 tablespoons cider vinegar
    2 teaspoons poppy seeds
  1/2 teaspoon salt

In a small bowl or jar with tight-fitting lid, combine all ingredients; mix or shake well. Serve over a green salad or fresh fruit. Store in the refrigerator. **Yield:** about 2/3 cup.

LEMON GARLIC BREAD

    1 loaf (1 pound) French bread
  1/2 cup butter *or* margarine, melted
    2 tablespoons grated Parmesan cheese
    4 teaspoons lemon juice
    1 tablespoon grated lemon peel
    1 garlic clove, minced
  1/4 teaspoon pepper

Cut bread diagonally into 1-in. slices. Combine remaining ingredients; brush over cut sides of bread. Wrap loaf in foil. Bake at 400° for 15-20 minutes or until heated through. **Yield:** 8-10 servings.

SPEEDY RICE PUDDING

    4 cups milk
    1 egg, beaten
    1 package (3 ounces) cook-and-serve vanilla pudding mix
    1 cup uncooked instant rice
  1/4 cup raisins
  1/4 teaspoon ground cinnamon
  1/8 teaspoon ground nutmeg

In a saucepan, combine milk, egg and pudding mix. Add rice and raisins. Bring to a boil over medium heat, stirring constantly. Remove from the heat; cool for 5 minutes, stirring twice. Pour into dessert dishes or a serving bowl. Serve immediately or cover with plastic wrap and refrigerate. Sprinkle with cinnamon and nutmeg. **Yield:** 8-10 servings.

Eggspert Advice

If a recipe calls for eggs to be at room temperature before mixing with other ingredients, remove the eggs from the refrigerator no more than 30 minutes before using to avoid bacteria growth.

Fast 'n' Flavorful Mexican Fare

QUICK TACO PLATTER

2 pounds ground beef
2 cans (15 ounces *each*) tomato sauce
2 envelopes taco seasoning mix
Tortilla *or* corn chips
Shredded lettuce, chopped tomato, chopped
  onion and shredded cheddar cheese

In a skillet, cook the beef until browned; drain. Stir in tomato sauce and taco seasoning; simmer for 15 minutes, stirring occasionally. Cover a serving platter with chips; top with lettuce. Layer with beef mixture, tomato, onion and cheese. **Yield:** 6-8 servings.

MEXICAN RICE

✓ This tasty dish uses less sugar, salt and fat.
  Recipe includes *Diabetic Exchanges.*

1-1/2 cups water
    1 cup salsa
    2 chicken bouillon cubes
    2 cups uncooked instant rice

In a saucepan over medium heat, bring water, salsa and bouillon to a boil. Stir in rice; remove from the heat. Cover and let stand 6-8 minutes or until liquid is absorbed. Fluff with a fork. **Yield:** 6-8 servings. **Diabetic Exchanges:** One 1/2-cup serving (prepared with low-sodium bouillon) equals 1 starch; also, 89 calories, 207 mg sodium, 0 cholesterol, 19 gm carbohydrate, 2 gm protein, 0 fat.

CHOCOLATE ICEBOX COOKIES

2 cups (12 ounces) semisweet chocolate
  chips, melted
4 cups cornflakes, crushed
1/2 cup chopped dates
1/2 cup chopped pecans

Combine all ingredients in a large bowl. Drop by tablespoonfuls onto waxed paper-lined baking sheets. Chill until firm, about 15-20 minutes. **Yield:** about 4 dozen.

IT'S GREAT when a meal your whole family enjoys is also quick and easy to prepare.

The complete-meal menu here is made up of family favorites from three great cooks. You can have everything ready to serve in about 30 minutes.

● Quick Taco Platter comes from Celia Rixman of Sylmar, California. "This fast-to-fix main dish is like a huge taco salad," Celia reports. "Even the kids love it."

● Mexican Rice, shared by Pattie Hess, Grabill, Indiana, is a zippy, flavorful south-of-the-border side dish. "My family always requests this rice when I'm making a Mexican dinner," Pattie relates.

● Chocolate Icebox Cookies are a simple treat with rich chocolate flavor and a nice crunch, assures Mary Neville of Fredericktown, Missouri.

Warm-Weather Meal With Mouth-Watering Appeal

WHETHER you're working in the garden or relaxing in the shade, summer tempts even the most avid cooks to spend more time outdoors and less in the kitchen. Since fresh air builds hearty appetites, what you will surely need is a fast-to-fix, nutritious meal that satisfies.

The complete-meal menu here is made up of favorites from three great cooks. You can sit down to eat in about 30 minutes!

● Garbanzo Cucumber Salad is shared by Sharon Semph of Victorville, California. "This crisp, refreshing salad is great for a barbecue or potluck," Sharon suggests.

● Tasty Turkey Sub makes a delicious warm-weather main dish, says Steven Scott of Cameron, West Virginia, who sent the recipe.

● Orange Sauce for Angel Food Cake comes from Karen Bourne of Magrath, Alberta. It's a tasty way to end a summer meal—without turning on the oven.

GARBANZO CUCUMBER SALAD

✓ **This tasty dish uses less sugar, salt and fat. Recipe includes *Diabetic Exchanges*.**

- 1 can (15 ounces) garbanzo beans, rinsed and drained
- 1 medium cucumber, sliced and quartered
- 1/2 cup sliced ripe olives
- 1/3 cup chopped red onion
- 1/4 cup minced fresh parsley
- 3 tablespoons vegetable oil
- 3 tablespoons red wine vinegar
- 1 tablespoon sugar
- 1 tablespoon fresh lemon juice
- 2 garlic cloves, minced
- 1/2 teaspoon grated lemon peel
- 1/4 teaspoon salt, optional
- 1/8 teaspoon pepper

In a medium bowl, combine beans, cucumber, olives, onion and parsley. In a jar with tight-fitting lid, combine remaining ingredients; shake well. Pour over vegetables and toss. Serve immediately or chill up to 24 hours. **Yield:** 8 servings. **Diabetic Exchanges:** One 1/2-cup serving (prepared without salt) equals 1-1/2 fat, 1 starch; also, 145 calories, 251 mg sodium, 0 cholesterol, 18 gm carbohydrate, 4 gm protein, 8 gm fat.

TASTY TURKEY SUB

- 1 loaf (1 pound) French bread
- 1/3 cup blue cheese salad dressing
- 1/3 cup mayonnaise
- 2 tablespoons Dijon mustard
- 1 pound cooked turkey, thinly sliced
- 12 bacon strips, cooked and drained
- 1 avocado, thinly sliced
- 6 tomato slices (1/4 inch thick)

Shredded lettuce

Halve bread lengthwise. Spread blue cheese dressing on cut side of top of bread. Combine mayonnaise and mustard; spread on cut side of bottom of bread. Layer with turkey, bacon, avocado, tomato and lettuce. Cover with top half of bread. Serve immediately. **Yield:** 6 servings.

ORANGE SAUCE FOR ANGEL FOOD CAKE

- 1-1/4 cups water
- 1 can (6 ounces) frozen orange juice concentrate, thawed
- 1 package (3.4 ounces) instant vanilla pudding mix
- 1 cup whipped topping
- 1 prepared angel food cake, sliced

In a mixing bowl, combine water, orange juice concentrate and pudding. Beat on low until mixed; beat on high for 2 minutes. Whisk in whipped topping. Spoon over cake slices. Store leftovers in the refrigerator. **Yield:** 2-3/4 cups sauce.

No-Fry Bacon

As an alternative to frying bacon, lay the strips on a jelly roll pan and bake at 350° for about 30 minutes. Prepared this way, bacon comes out crisp and flat. Plus, the pan cleans easily, and there's no stovetop splattering.

Family-Pleasing Feast Cooks Up in a Flash

IF THE HUSTLE and bustle of the holidays keeps your time in the kitchen to a minimum, a satisfying quick meal may be the perfect gift to give yourself and your family!

The complete-meal menu here is made up of favorite recipes shared by three great cooks. You can have everything ready to serve in about 30 minutes.

● Microwave Parmesan Chicken comes from Ruth Andrewson of Leavenworth, Washington. She says, "The golden coating over moist chicken makes people think you fussed."

● Festive Green Beans can't be beat for a vegetable dish that sports the colors of the season and gets people coming back for seconds, assures Frances Janssen of Canyon Lake, Texas, who notes that this is a side dish her whole family enjoys. Made with Mexican-style stewed tomatoes or salsa, it has zip.

● Cookies in a Jiffy are from Clara Hielkema of Wyoming, Michigan. She reports you'll be amazed and delighted at how quickly you can whip up a batch of homemade cookies.

MICROWAVE PARMESAN CHICKEN

1/4 cup butter *or* margarine
3/4 cup crushed butter-flavored crackers
1/2 cup grated Parmesan cheese
  1 tablespoon dried minced onion
  1 tablespoon dried parsley flakes
1/2 teaspoon garlic powder
1/8 teaspoon pepper
  1 broiler-fryer chicken (2-1/2 to 3 pounds), cut up

Melt butter in a 13-in. x 9-in. x 2-in. microwave-safe baking dish. In a shallow bowl, combine the next six ingredients. Dredge chicken in butter, then in crumb mixture. Place chicken in the baking dish, with skin side up and thick edges toward the outside. Sprinkle with remaining crumb mixture. Microwave on high for 20-25 minutes or until juices run clear and chicken is no longer pink, rotating dish occasionally. **Yield:** 4-6 servings. **Editor's Note:** This recipe was tested using a 700-watt microwave.

FESTIVE GREEN BEANS

✓ **This tasty dish uses less sugar, salt and fat. Recipe includes *Diabetic Exchanges*.**

  1 pound fresh green beans *or* 1 can (16 ounces) green beans, drained
1/2 cup water
1/2 teaspoon salt, optional
1/4 teaspoon pepper
1/2 teaspoon garlic powder
3/4 cup Mexican stewed tomatoes *or* chunky salsa

Cut beans into 2-in. pieces; place in a saucepan. Add water and salt if desired; bring to a boil. Reduce heat and simmer for 15 minutes or until tender; drain. Add pepper, garlic powder and tomatoes; heat through. **Yield:** 6 servings. **Diabetic Exchanges:** One 1/2-cup serving (prepared with fresh beans and salsa and without salt) equals 1-1/2 vegetable; also, 35 calories, 225 mg sodium, 0 cholesterol, 8 gm carbohydrate, 1 gm protein, trace fat.

COOKIES IN A JIFFY

  1 package (9 ounces) yellow cake mix
2/3 cup quick-cooking oats
1/2 cup butter *or* margarine, melted
  1 egg
1/2 cup red and green Holiday M&M's *or* butterscotch chips

In a mixing bowl, beat the first four ingredients. Stir in the M&M's or chips. Drop by tablespoonfuls 2 in. apart onto ungreased baking sheets. Bake at 375° for 10-12 minutes or until lightly browned. Remove to wire racks to cool. **Yield**: 2 dozen.

Extraordinary Beans

If you want to put some zip into an ordinary can of green beans, try adding a few shakes of seasoning salt and a couple drops of liquid smoke.

Enjoy Seasonal Meals in Minutes... Year-Round!

The 12 time-saving menus on the following pages were created by the Taste of Home staff with your hectic schedule in mind. These meals will keep you satisfied the whole year through.

DURING the course of the year, there are some days when you can take plenty of time to prepare a delicious meal for your family. But then there are days when so much is happening you can't be sure whether you're coming or going.

The 12 meals (36 recipes in all) on the following pages were created and kitchen-tested by the staff of *Taste of Home* with those hectic days in mind—and specific seasons of the year in mind as well. Each takes 30 minutes or less to prepare.

You'll be ready for the "wearin' of the green" when you serve your family tasty "Corned Beef and Cabbage Sandwiches", "Spinach Potato Soup" and "Shamrock Sundaes" (all recipes found on pages 226 and 227).

When it's time to fire up the grill, sizzling "Garlic Grilled Steaks" along with colorful "Zesty Vegetable Skewers" and creamy "Cheesecake Dip" (recipes on pages 232 and 233) make a great summertime meal. And you can welcome your brood in from those cool, crisp autumn days with a steaming bowl of "Pronto Chili", "Cornmeal Cheddar Biscuits" and "Peanut Butter Tarts" (recipes on pages 240 and 241).

You can even mix and match the recipes to create your own savory seasonal meals. So, with the 12 mouth-watering meals on the next few pages plus your own creations, the possibilities for year-round fast and flavorful menus are endless.

A Winning Winter Dinner

AFTER PLAYING in a winter wonderland, your family will build up big appetites. Made with hearty ingredients, sizzling Skillet Beef Stew—like the individual portion shown at right—and fresh-from-the-oven Parmesan Garlic Bread are guaranteed to chase away Jack Frost in a hurry! For a sweet finale to this satisfying meal, why not serve Quick Fruit Crisp and mugs of hot cocoa?

SKILLET BEEF STEW

Think you can't prepare a hot and hearty stew in under 30 minutes? Well you can! This super stew recipe uses frozen vegetables and prepared gravy, plus it cooks on the stove, so you can serve up steaming bowlsful in no time.

- 1 pound sirloin steak
- 2 tablespoons cooking oil
- 1 bag (16 ounces) frozen vegetables for stew
- 1 jar (12 ounces) beef gravy
- 2 tablespoons Worcestershire sauce
- 1/2 teaspoon dried thyme
- 1/4 teaspoon pepper
- 1/4 teaspoon garlic powder

Cut steak into 2-in. x 1/4-in. strips. Heat oil in a large skillet; brown meat over medium-high heat for 5 minutes or until no longer pink. Drain if necessary. Stir in remaining ingredients; bring to a boil. Reduce heat; cover and simmer for 15 minutes or until heated through. **Yield:** 4 servings.

PARMESAN GARLIC BREAD

Dress up ordinary French bread by topping it with butter, Parmesan cheese and seasonings. It's a quick side dish that will complement the beef stew or most any meal. But don't expect leftovers...your family will have a hard time stopping at just one slice!

- 1/4 cup butter *or* margarine, softened
- 1/4 cup olive *or* vegetable oil
- 1/4 cup grated Parmesan cheese

- 2 garlic cloves
- 4 sprigs fresh parsley
- 1/2 teaspoon lemon-pepper seasoning
- 1 small loaf (8 ounces) French bread

In a mixing bowl or food processor, blend butter, oil and Parmesan cheese. Add garlic, parsley and lemon pepper; mix or process until smooth. Slice the bread on the diagonal but not all the way through, leaving slices attached at the bottom. Spread butter mixture on one side of each slice and over the top. Wrap in foil and bake at 400° for 15-20 minutes. **Yield:** 4 servings.

QUICK FRUIT CRISP

Fruit crisps often take time to prepare, what with slicing the fruit and baking in the oven. But this quick and easy dessert uses canned pie filling and is cooked in a skillet! Serve it alone or with a scoop of ice cream.

1 can (21 ounces) peach, apple *or* cherry pie filling
1 tablespoon lemon juice
1 cup Fruit & Fibre cereal
1 tablespoon butter *or* margarine
1 tablespoon sugar
1/4 teaspoon ground cinnamon
Vanilla ice cream, optional

In a medium skillet, heat pie filling and lemon juice over medium heat for 5 minutes or until bubbly, stirring occasionally. Meanwhile, place cereal in a resealable plastic bag; crush slightly with a rolling pin. In a small skillet, melt butter. Stir in cereal, sugar and cinnamon; cook and stir for 2-3 minutes. Sprinkle over the fruit mixture. Serve warm with ice cream if desired. **Yield:** 4 servings.

Valentine's Day Delights

SHOW YOUR LOVED ONES you care by preparing a festive meal that comes straight from the heart! Your family will be pleasantly surprised when they find tender chicken starring in Cheesy Chicken Pizza. It's also packed with tasty toppings, like cheese, onions and peppers. Italian Salad—featuring homemade dressing and your favorite greens—adds plenty of "zip" to the meal. For a special dessert, why not whip up chocolaty Mint Truffles? They're fancy yet fast, and they'll be gobbled up before you know it.

CHEESY CHICKEN PIZZA

Why pop a frozen pizza in the oven when you can serve your family generous slices of this fast and flavorful pizza pie? Chicken provides a unique change of pace from the usual beef or pepperoni...and it pairs nicely with the onion, peppers and cheese.

- 1 tube (10 ounces) refrigerated pizza crust dough
- 1 can (8 ounces) pizza sauce
- 1/2 cup diced cooked chicken
- 1 small onion, sliced
- 1/4 cup sliced green pepper
- 1/4 cup sliced sweet red pepper
- 1 cup (4 ounces) shredded cheddar cheese
- 1 cup (4 ounces) shredded mozzarella cheese

Unroll pizza crust onto a greased baking sheet; form into a heart shape or a 12-in. circle. Spread with pizza sauce. Top with the chicken, onion and peppers. Sprinkle with cheeses. Bake on lowest rack at 425° for 16-20 minutes or until crust is dark golden brown. **Yield:** 4 servings.

ITALIAN SALAD

Salad's never been speedier than this! Gather up a few greens and vegetables, then make your own dressing by mixing together a mere five ingredients you most likely have right on hand.

- **1/4 cup olive *or* vegetable oil**

- 1/4 cup red wine vinegar
- 1/2 teaspoon Italian seasoning
- 1/4 teaspoon salt
- 1/4 teaspoon coarsely ground black pepper

Romaine *or* other lettuce
Tomatoes, mushrooms, cucumber, olives *and/or* other vegetables of choice
Shredded Parmesan cheese, optional

In a jar with tight-fitting lid, combine the oil, vinegar, Italian seasoning, salt and pepper; shake well. In a large bowl, combine lettuce and vegetables. Add the dressing and Parmesan cheese if desired; toss to coat. **Yield:** 1/2 cup dressing.

MINT TRUFFLES

These chocolaty candies have such an appealing look and sweet flavor, it's hard to believe they take only minutes to prepare. They're the perfect thing to serve for both everyday treats and special-occasion desserts.

1 cup (6 ounces) milk chocolate chips
3/4 cup whipped topping
1/4 teaspoon peppermint extract
2 tablespoons baking cocoa

In a small saucepan, melt chocolate chips over low heat. Place in a mixing bowl and allow to cool to lukewarm, about 7 minutes. Beat in whipped topping and extract. Place in freezer for 15 minutes or until firm enough to form into balls. Shape into 1-in. balls. Roll in cocoa. Store in a covered container in the refrigerator. **Yield:** about 1 dozen.

Salad in a Snap

Speed up salad making by washing, drying and cutting all ingredients as soon as you have them in the kitchen. Then store in a plastic bag. At mealtime, just pull out the bag and make the salad.

Leprechaun's Lunch

EVEN eyes that aren't Irish will be smiling when they behold this bountiful meal. Corned Beef and Cabbage Sandwiches tastefully combine creamy cabbage and tender corned beef. And folks will be delighted to see a bit o' the green when you serve them some hearty Spinach Potato Soup. Extra-easy Shamrock Sundaes—with mint ice cream and homemade chocolate sauce—and a refreshing beverage top off the meal tastily.

CORNED BEEF AND CABBAGE SANDWICHES

You don't have to wait for St. Patrick's Day to serve these festive sandwiches. Your family is sure to enjoy the flavorful combination of cabbage and corned beef piled high on a hard roll anytime of year.

      1/3 cup mayonnaise
        1 tablespoon vinegar
      1/4 teaspoon ground mustard
      1/4 teaspoon celery seed
      1/4 teaspoon pepper
  1-1/2 cups thinly shredded raw cabbage
        4 kaiser *or* hard rolls, split
      3/4 to 1 pound fully cooked corned beef, sliced

In a bowl, combine mayonnaise, vinegar, mustard, celery seed and pepper until smooth. Stir in cabbage and mix well. Spoon onto the bottom halves of rolls. Cover with corned beef; replace tops of rolls. Serve immediately. **Yield:** 4 servings.

Some Souper Storage Ideas

Before freezing homemade soup, refrigerate it until the fat rises to the surface. Skim off the fat and discard any bones.

To store individual servings from a big batch of soup, line several bowls with plastic wrap, pour in the soup and freeze. Once frozen, the soup can be popped out of the bowls and stored in large freezer bags. This also makes a nice gift for an ill friend or someone living alone.

SPINACH POTATO SOUP

When your clan is hungry, hot and hearty soup surely fills the bill...not to mention stomachs! You'll find the spinach in this recipe makes this soup more colorful than ordinary potato soup.

        2 cups cubed peeled potatoes (1/2-inch pieces)
  1-1/2 cups water
        1 tablespoon dried minced onion
        1 teaspoon instant chicken bouillon granules
      1/2 teaspoon garlic salt
        1 cup thinly sliced fresh *or* chopped frozen spinach

1 cup whipping cream
1/4 teaspoon ground nutmeg

In a saucepan, combine the potatoes, water, onion and bouillon; bring to a boil. Cook until potatoes are tender, about 10 minutes. Add the remaining ingredients and cook until spinach is tender and heated through. **Yield:** 4 servings.

SHAMROCK SUNDAES

If your family loves ice cream (and whose doesn't?), you'll probably serve these simple-to-make sun- *daes—with their from-scratch chocolate sauce—often.*

1/4 cup butter *or* margarine
1 square (1 ounce) unsweetened chocolate
1 cup sugar
1/3 cup half-and-half cream
1/4 cup corn syrup
1/2 teaspoon vanilla extract
Mint ice cream

In a saucepan, melt butter and chocolate over low heat. Add sugar, cream and corn syrup; bring to a boil, stirring constantly. Boil for 1 minute. Remove from the heat and stir in vanilla. Serve warm or cool over ice cream. **Yield:** about 1-2/3 cups chocolate sauce.

Easy Easter Entree

HOLIDAYS are a wonderful time to get together with family and friends to share a meal, and Easter's no exception. But when hectic weekdays and weekends keep you hopping, you'll reach for these mouthwatering recipes often. Apricot Ham Steak turns leftover Easter ham into a wonderfully different main course. And for an easy alternative to the apricot glaze in this recipe, see the tip at the bottom of page 229. Hot-off-the-griddle Potato Pancakes and some fresh green beans really round out the meal. For dessert, there's nothing better than a deliciously creamy Easy Rice Pudding.

APRICOT HAM STEAK

Ham is a versatile main menu item that's a standby with all country cooks. One of the best and easiest ways to serve ham slices is topped off with a slightly sweet glaze, like this apricot version. The mouth-watering flavor can't be beat.

> **4 slices fully cooked ham (1/2 inch thick)**
> **2 tablespoons butter *or* margarine, *divided***
> **1/2 cup apricot preserves**
> **1 tablespoon cider vinegar**
> **1/4 teaspoon ground ginger**

Dash salt
Hot cooked green beans, optional

In a skillet, saute ham slices in 1 tablespoon of butter until lightly browned, turning once. Meanwhile, in a saucepan or microwave-safe bowl, combine the preserves, vinegar, ginger, salt and remaining butter; heat through. Serve ham with the apricot sauce and green beans if desired. **Yield:** 4 servings.

POTATO PANCAKES

Preparing traditional potato pancakes can be a time-consuming process...so you'll really relish this recipe. That's because there's no need to grate potatoes. By using frozen hash browns, these "spud-tacular" palate-pleasing pancakes are ready in a hurry!

> **4 cups frozen shredded hash browns**
> **1/2 cup finely chopped onion**

> **1/4 cup minced fresh parsley**
> **2 tablespoons milk**
> **2 eggs, beaten**
> **1/4 cup all-purpose flour**
> **1 teaspoon salt**

Cooking oil

Place hash browns in a strainer and rinse with cold water until thawed. Drain thoroughly; transfer to a large bowl. Add onion, parsley, milk, eggs, flour and salt; mix well. In a skillet over medium heat, heat 1/4 in. of oil. Drop batter by 1/4 cupfuls into hot oil. Fry until golden brown on both sides. Drain on paper towels. **Yield:** 4 servings.

EASY RICE PUDDING

Rice pudding has been a family favorite for generations, both because of its fantastic flavor and ease of preparation. Your family will love this pudding's creamy texture, and you will love its fast-to-fix convenience.

- 4 cups milk
- 1 package (3 ounces) cook-and-serve vanilla pudding mix
- 1 cup instant rice
- 1 egg, beaten
- 1/4 teaspoon ground cinnamon
- 1/4 teaspoon vanilla extract

In a saucepan, combine the first five ingredients; bring to a full boil, stirring constantly. Remove from the heat and stir in vanilla. Cool for 5 minutes, stirring twice. Spoon into individual serving dishes. Serve warm or chill until serving. **Yield:** 4 servings.

Likable Leftovers
If you're looking for an easy glaze to keep on hand, small amounts of jelly left in jars can be combined, melted and used as a glaze for ham.

Springtime Specialties

IT'S SPRING! Serve up a garden-fresh goody like Sesame Asparagus. Your family will love its slightly crunchy texture. Served with parsley buttered new potatoes, Chicken with Dilly Ham Sauce has a tangy breading and savory sauce that's perfect for entertaining…or everyday meals. And impress guests with generous slices of No-Bake Chocolate Torte…it's a no-fuss favorite with lots of flavor!

CHICKEN WITH DILLY HAM SAUCE

Whether you're preparing a weekday meal or entertaining weekend company, this delicious chicken dish is sure to please. The mustard adds a little "zip", and the ham sauce is a tasty way to top it off.

    1/2 cup seasoned dry bread crumbs
    1/2 cup grated Parmesan cheese, *divided*
      4 boneless skinless chicken breast halves
    1/3 cup Dijon mustard
    1/2 cup julienned fully cooked ham (1/4
          pound)
      2 tablespoons butter *or* margarine
      2 tablespoons all-purpose flour
      1 cup whipping cream
    1/2 teaspoon dill weed
Parsley buttered potatoes, optional

In a shallow dish, combine the bread crumbs and 1/4 cup of the Parmesan cheese; set aside. Pound each chicken breast to 1/4-in. thickness. Brush both sides with mustard; coat evenly with crumb mixture. Place in a greased 13-in. x 9-in. x 2-in. baking pan. Bake, uncovered, at 425° for 15 minutes or until juices run clear. Meanwhile, in a saucepan, saute ham in butter for 2 minutes. Stir in flour until smooth and bubbly. Add cream, dill and remaining Parmesan; cook and stir until thickened and bubbly. Spoon over chicken. Serve with parsley buttered potatoes if desired. **Yield:** 4 servings.

SESAME ASPARAGUS

If you're looking for a unique way to serve asparagus, you'll want to try this tasty dish. Garlic, butter and

chicken broth enhance the delicate flavor of fresh young asparagus in this quick and easy recipe. And sesame seeds add just the right amount of "crunch".

      1 pound fresh asparagus, cut into
          1-1/2-inch pieces (4 cups)
      1 garlic clove, minced
      2 tablespoons butter *or* margarine
    1/2 cup chicken broth
      1 tablespoon sesame seeds, toasted

In a skillet over medium-high heat, saute the asparagus and garlic in butter for 2 minutes. Stir in broth; bring to a boil. Reduce heat; cover and simmer for 5-6 minutes or until asparagus is crisp-tender. Remove to a serving dish with a slotted spoon; sprinkle with sesame seeds. Serve immediately. **Yield:** 4 servings.

NO-BAKE CHOCOLATE TORTE

Here's a delightful dessert that only looks like you fussed all day. With its attractive appearance and wonderful taste, no one will know that you saved time by spreading an easy-to-prepare frosting on a store-bought pound cake.

- **1 frozen pound cake (10-3/4 ounces), thawed**
- **2 cups whipping cream**
- **6 tablespoons confectioners' sugar**
- **6 tablespoons baking cocoa**
- **1/2 teaspoon almond extract**
- **1/2 cup sliced almonds, toasted, optional**

Slice pound cake lengthwise into three layers and set aside. In a mixing bowl, beat the cream until soft peaks form. Gradually add sugar and cocoa, beat-ing until stiff peaks form. Stir in extract. Frost between cake layers and stack on a serving plate; frost top and sides. Garnish with almonds if desired. Chill at least 15 minutes. Refrigerate any leftovers. **Yield:** 4-6 servings.

Almond Joys

To blanch almonds, cover shelled nuts with boiling water and let stand 3 to 5 minutes. Drain and slide the skins off. Dry on paper towels.

To toast almonds, spread shelled nuts in a shallow baking pan. Place in a cold oven; toast at 350° for 8 to 12 minutes for whole almonds, stirring occasionally. Remove from pan to cool.

Cookout Classics

SUMMERTIME…and the cooking is easy! Just fire up the grill for a good old-fashioned barbecue featuring sizzling Garlic Grilled Steaks. With a tangy marinade and assortment of fresh produce, Zesty Vegetable Skewers are sure to disappear in a hurry. Cool and creamy Cheesecake Dip for sweet strawberries provides a perfectly happy ending to this flavorful fare.

GARLIC GRILLED STEAKS

For a mouth-watering change of taste at your next barbecue, take steak to new flavor heights by basting your choice of cuts with a great garlicky blend that requires no more than minutes to fix.

      10 garlic cloves
  1-1/2 teaspoons salt
       2 tablespoons olive *or* vegetable oil
       1 tablespoon lemon juice
       2 teaspoons Worcestershire sauce
    1/2 teaspoon pepper
       4 New York strip *or* rib eye steaks
          (8 ounces and 1-1/4 inches thick)

In a small bowl, mash garlic with salt to form a paste. Add the oil, lemon juice, Worcestershire sauce and pepper; mix well. Grill the steaks over medium-hot coals, turning once and brushing with garlic mixture during the last few minutes of cooking. Allow approximately 11-12 minutes for rare, 13-14 minutes for medium and 15-16 minutes for well-done. **Yield:** 4 servings.

ZESTY VEGETABLE SKEWERS

Grilling is a delightful way of preparing the season's freshest produce. The zesty Italian marinade adds just the right amount of spice to the appealing assortment of vegetables.

      1 garlic clove
      1 teaspoon salt
    1/3 cup olive *or* vegetable oil
      3 tablespoons lemon juice
      1 teaspoon Italian seasoning

    1/4 teaspoon pepper
      8 medium fresh mushrooms
      2 small zucchini, sliced 1/2 inch thick
      2 small onions, cut into sixths
      8 cherry tomatoes
      4 wooden skewers (10 inches)

In a small bowl, mash garlic with salt to form a paste. Stir in oil, lemon juice, Italian seasoning and pepper. Thread vegetables alternately onto skewers; place in a shallow baking pan. Pour garlic mixture over kabobs; let stand for 15 minutes. Grill for 10-15 minutes, turning frequently, or until vegetables are just tender. **Yield:** 4 servings.

CHEESECAKE DIP

When you're in the mood for something sweet, but you want to keep it light, this simple dip really hits the spot. Dipping fresh plump strawberries in the cool and creamy concoction is a fun and delicious way to eat dessert.

> 4 ounces cream cheese, softened
> 1/3 cup sour cream
> 3 tablespoons confectioners' sugar
> 1 tablespoon milk
> 1/4 teaspoon almond extract
> 1 pint fresh strawberries

1/4 cup graham cracker crumbs

In a mixing bowl, beat cream cheese until smooth. Add the sour cream, sugar, milk and extract; mix until smooth. Transfer to a serving bowl. Place the strawberries and crumbs in separate serving bowls. Dip strawberries into cheesecake mixture, then into crumbs. **Yield:** about 1 cup.

Avoid a Sticky Situation
To keep your meat from sticking on the grill, brush the grill's grid surface with vegetable oil.

July Fourth Favorites

YOU'RE BOUND TO CREATE fireworks when you present these favorites at your Independence Day picnic, especially when hearty helpings of a Turkey Hero are the main feature. Summertime Pasta Salad gets a new twist with its combination of frozen vegetables and salad dressings. And for the finale, get in the spirit with a Red, White and Blue Dessert of angel food cake and berries.

TURKEY HERO

Who says sandwiches have to be boring? Here, a special cream cheese and ranch dressing spread adds zest to the hearty turkey, cheese and vegetables. Get set to slice up second helpings!

> 1 package (3 ounces) cream cheese, softened
> 2 tablespoons ranch salad dressing
> 1 teaspoon poppy seeds
> Pinch garlic powder
> 1 loaf (1 pound) French bread, split lengthwise
> Shredded lettuce
> 3/4 pound thinly sliced cooked turkey
> 1/4 pound thinly sliced Swiss cheese
> 2 medium tomatoes, sliced

In a small mixing bowl, beat the first four ingredients until smooth. Spread on both cut surfaces of bread. Layer lettuce, turkey, cheese and tomatoes on bottom half of bread. Top with the other half. Cut into serving-size pieces. **Yield:** 6 servings.

SUMMERTIME PASTA SALAD

Nothing says summer quite like a cool pasta salad with loads of vegetables! Best of all, this recipe calls for frozen vegetables, so it's perfect when you don't have time to slice and dice fresh produce.

> 2-1/2 cups uncooked spiral pasta
> 1 package (10 ounces) frozen mixed vegetables
> 2/3 cup ranch salad dressing

> 1/3 cup Italian salad dressing
> 1/2 teaspoon dill weed
> 1/2 teaspoon garlic salt
> 2 small tomatoes, diced

In a large kettle, cook pasta according to package directions. Place frozen vegetables in a strainer. Pour cooked pasta and water over vegetables to thaw; rinse and drain well. In a small bowl or jar with tight-fitting lid, combine salad dressings, dill and garlic salt until smooth. Place pasta mixture in a large bowl. Add tomatoes and dressing; stir gently to coat. **Yield:** 6 servings.

RED, WHITE AND BLUE DESSERT

Beat the summer heat with this light and refreshing dessert. No one will be able to resist sweet raspberries and blueberries atop moist angel food cake.

- 1 cup fresh raspberries
- 1 cup fresh blueberries
- 1/4 cup sugar
- 1/2 teaspoon almond extract
- 6 slices angel food cake

Combine raspberries and blueberries in a bowl. Sprinkle with sugar and extract; toss gently. Place cake on dessert plates and top with berry mixture. **Yield:** 6 servings.

Be Kind to Your Cake

If the top of your angel food cake burns before the rest of the cake is done, use an oven thermometer to make sure your oven is not baking at a higher temperature than you set it. Also, place the pan on the lowest rack to allow sufficient air circulation over the top of the cake.

Harvest of Goodness

YOU'VE WORKED HARD in your garden all summer, and now it's time to reap the rewards with a bountiful dinner. Herbs and fresh peppers add a palate-pleasing touch to Chunky Spaghetti Sauce. Your family will never tire of zucchini when they sample Zesty Zucchini. Then cool off with a slice of Refreshing Lemon Pie and a glass of iced tea.

CHUNKY SPAGHETTI SAUCE

When your hungry clan requests, "Spaghetti, please!", you'll be happy to oblige with this simple savory sauce. It proves appetizingly that homemade spaghetti sauce doesn't have to simmer all day in order to be hearty and delicious.

> 1 **pound bulk Italian sausage**
> 1 **to 2 medium green peppers, julienned**
> 1/2 **medium onion, chopped**
> 1 **garlic clove, minced**
> 2 **cans (14-1/2 ounces *each*) Italian stewed tomatoes**
> 1/4 **cup tomato paste**
> 1-1/2 **teaspoons minced fresh oregano *or* 1/2 teaspoon dried oregano**
> 1-1/2 **teaspoons minced fresh basil *or* 1/2 teaspoon dried basil**
>
> **Hot cooked pasta**

Brown sausage in a large saucepan; drain. Add green peppers, onion and garlic; cook until tender, about 5 minutes. Add tomatoes, tomato paste, oregano and basil; simmer, uncovered, for 10-15 minutes. Serve over pasta. **Yield:** 4 servings.

ZESTY ZUCCHINI

Here's a great way to use up an often overabundant vegetable. Perfect for potlucks and everyday dinners, it's sure to become a recipe you reach for frequently.

> 1/3 **cup vegetable oil**
> 1/4 **cup white wine vinegar**
> 1 **tablespoon minced fresh basil *or* 1 teaspoon dried basil**

> 1/2 **teaspoon salt**
> 1/4 **teaspoon pepper**
> 1/4 **teaspoon garlic powder**
> 2 **to 3 medium zucchini, sliced**

In a large bowl, whisk together the first six ingredients. Add zucchini and toss. Chill until ready to serve. **Yield:** 4 servings.

REFRESHING LEMON PIE

Have little time on your hands, but your family still expects dessert with dinner? This easy-as-pie recipe pro-

vides a refreshingly simple solution. You'll appreciate the short list of ingredients—and the even shorter preparation time! Your family will love the cool lemony flavor of this pie.

> 1 can (14 ounces) sweetened condensed milk
> 1/2 cup lemon juice
> 1 tablespoon grated lemon peel
> 2 to 3 drops yellow food coloring, optional
> 1 carton (8 ounces) frozen whipped topping, thawed
> 1 graham cracker crust (9 inches)

Mint leaves and lemon peel strips, optional

In a bowl, combine milk, lemon juice, grated lemon peel and food coloring if desired; mix until smooth (mixture will begin to thicken). Fold in whipped topping; spoon into crust. Chill until ready to serve. If desired, garnish with mint leaves and lemon peel strips. Refrigerate leftovers. **Yield:** 6-8 servings.

A Zest for Lemons

Lemon zest is the outer peel or rind of the lemon. To remove it, peel thin strips with a small sharp knife, being careful not to include the white membrane, and mince firmly.

Mmmm-
Morning Meal

NOTHING STARTS your day off right like a down-home country breakfast featuring a Fluffy Harvest Omelet that's chock-full of fresh vegetables and cheese. Your family will be delighted when you serve their favorite fruit in Honey Fruit Cups. And Simple Pecan Rolls use prepackaged buns so they bake up to a sweet and sticky golden brown in just minutes.

FLUFFY HARVEST OMELET

With its mushrooms, zucchini and tomato sauce, this hearty omelet isn't just for breakfast. Your family will savor it as a change-of-pace lunch or dinner, too.

    6 eggs, *separated*
1/4 teaspoon salt
1/4 cup light cream
1/4 cup grated Parmesan cheese
1/4 teaspoon pepper
    2 tablespoons butter *or* **margarine**
    1 can (15 ounces) chunky Italian tomato
       sauce
    1 cup cubed fresh zucchini
3/4 cup sliced fresh mushrooms
    1 cup (4 ounces) shredded mozzarella
       cheese

In a large mixing bowl, beat egg whites until soft peaks form. Add salt; continue beating until stiff peaks form. In a small mixing bowl, beat the egg yolks, cream, Parmesan cheese and pepper until foamy. Gently fold into the egg whites. Melt butter in a 10-in. ovenproof skillet; add egg mixture. Cook over medium-low heat for 8 minutes or until bottom is golden brown. Place skillet in a 350° oven for 10 minutes or until top is golden brown. Meanwhile, combine the tomato sauce, zucchini and mushrooms in a small saucepan. Cook, uncovered, until zucchini is tender, about 10 minutes. Sprinkle mozzarella cheese over omelet; fold in half and top with tomato sauce. **Yield:** 4 servings.

Basil Makes It Better
Basil adds great flavor to scrambled eggs, salads and buttered noodles.

HONEY FRUIT CUPS

For a naturally sweet addition to your meal, combine your family's favorite fruits and top with a refreshing honey-yogurt sauce. It'll disappear fast!

    4 cups cut-up fresh fruit (pears, apples,
       bananas, grapes, etc.)
    1 carton (6 ounces) mandarin orange,
       vanilla *or* **lemon yogurt**
    1 tablespoon honey
1/2 teaspoon grated orange peel
1/4 teaspoon almond extract

Divide fruit among individual serving bowls. Combine yogurt, honey, orange peel and extract; spoon over the fruit. **Yield:** 4 servings.

SIMPLE PECAN ROLLS

There's no letting the dough rise overnight with these delightful cinnamon pecan rolls...all you need is a package of ready-made rolls. It can stay your secret that these sticky treats weren't made from scratch!

- 1/2 cup butter *or* margarine, softened
- 1/2 cup packed brown sugar
- 1/2 teaspoon ground cinnamon
- 3/4 cup pecan halves
- 1 package (12 count) brown-and-serve rolls

In a mixing bowl, beat butter, brown sugar and cinnamon until well blended. Spread in the bottom of a 9-in. round baking pan. Top with pecans. Place rolls upside down over pecans. Bake at 450° for 8-10 minutes or until golden. Immediately turn onto a serving platter. Serve warm. **Yield:** 4-6 servings.

Spooktacular Menu

AUTUMN brings with it cool, crisp days, and there's no better way to take the chill out of your family's bones than to have them sit down to a steaming-hot bowl of Pronto Chili loaded with meat, vegetables …and flavor! Cornmeal Cheddar Biscuits are a perfect complement to this hearty chili, and because no rolling or cutting is required, you can have fresh-from-the-oven goodness in no time. And while your family is busy "goblin" up those deliciously satisfying dishes, individual Peanut Butter Tarts can be chilling in the meantime.

PRONTO CHILI

Your busy schedule doesn't always allow you to simmer chili all day long on the stove. But you don't have to wait until the weekend to make some. This chili can be made in a flash and is easily doubled or tripled to satisfy any famished family.

- 1 **pound ground beef**
- 1 **medium onion, chopped**
- 1 **medium green pepper, chopped**
- 2 to 3 **teaspoons chili powder**
- 1 **teaspoon ground cumin**
- 1 **teaspoon salt**
- 1 **can (14-1/2 ounces) Mexican stewed tomatoes**
- 1 **can (15-3/4 ounces) chili beans in gravy**
- 1 **cup frozen corn**

Shredded cheddar cheese, optional

In a 2-qt. saucepan, cook beef, onion and green pepper until the meat is browned and the vegetables are tender. Drain. Add the next six ingredients; cover and simmer for 20 minutes. Sprinkle individual servings with cheese if desired. **Yield:** 6 servings.

CORNMEAL CHEDDAR BISCUITS

Unlike traditional biscuits, this cheesy cornmeal version lets you drop them from a spoon…so there's no mess and no fuss…and no precious time wasted! Serve them fresh-from-the-oven with chili or your favorite soup or stew.

- 1-1/2 **cups all-purpose flour**
- 1/2 **cup yellow cornmeal**
- 2 **teaspoons sugar**
- 1 **tablespoon baking powder**
- 1/4 to 1/2 **teaspoon salt**
- 1/2 **cup butter *or* margarine**
- 1/2 **cup shredded cheddar cheese**
- 1 **cup milk**

In a bowl, combine dry ingredients; cut in butter until crumbly. Stir in cheese and milk just until moistened. Drop by 1/4 cupfuls onto an ungreased baking sheet. Bake at 450° for 12-15 minutes or until light golden brown. Serve warm. **Yield:** 1 dozen.

PEANUT BUTTER TARTS

These tiny tarts taste delicious and are a fun and easy way to round out a meal. Children especially like having their own "little pie" to help decorate. Make these goodies throughout the year with an assortment of favorite candies. These tarts will surely become a big part of your recipe collection because they're so convenient—they chill while you're enjoying the rest of your meal.

- 1 cup peanut butter chips
- 1 tablespoon vegetable oil
- 1 package (3.9 ounces) instant chocolate pudding mix
- 1-3/4 cups cold milk
- 1 package (6 count) individual graham cracker tart shells

Whipped topping
Halloween candy, sprinkles *and/or* cake decorations

In the top of a double boiler over simmering water, melt chips with oil, stirring until smooth. Remove top pan from water and cool for 5 minutes. Meanwhile, in a bowl, whisk pudding and milk until thick. Fold in peanut butter mixture. Spoon into tart shells. Chill for 15 minutes. Top with a dollop of whipped topping and decorate as desired. **Yield:** 6 servings.

Make It 'Turkey Day'...Any Day

YOU'LL be showered with "Thanks!" when you serve this succulent speedy supper. Herb-Glazed Turkey Slices let you enjoy wonderful fowl without preparing the whole turkey. For lighter side dishes that are full of flavor, try Rice Pilaf and your favorite vegetables, like carrots and brussels sprouts. Pumpkin Mousse is as easy as pie to prepare...and tastes even better.

HERB-GLAZED TURKEY SLICES

In the mood for a taste of turkey, but don't have time to prepare a whole bird? Here's the perfect solution! These savory slices—and easy-to-prepare herb glaze—offer the goodness of turkey in a hurry.

> 1 package (about 1-1/4 pounds) turkey breast slices (1/4 inch thick)
> 1 tablespoon cooking oil
> 1/2 cup chicken broth
> 1/2 cup apple juice
> 1 tablespoon honey
> 1 tablespoon Dijon mustard
> 1/2 teaspoon salt
> 1/4 teaspoon *each* dried basil, rosemary and garlic powder
> 1 tablespoon cornstarch
> 1 tablespoon water

Hot cooked brussels sprouts and carrots, optional

In a large skillet, brown turkey slices in oil. Combine broth, apple juice, honey, mustard, salt, basil, rosemary and garlic powder; pour over turkey. Cover and simmer for 8 minutes or until the turkey is no longer pink. Mix the cornstarch and water; stir into skillet. Cook and stir until thickened and bubbly. Serve with brussels sprouts and carrots if desired. **Yield:** 4 servings.

Look, Ma! No Hands!

The next time you're struggling to fill a storage bag, try this easy method. Line a tall drinking glass with the bag, and fold the top of the bag over the rim of the glass. With the glass holding the bag, your hands are free to fill it.

RICE PILAF

Onion soup mix and frozen peas really "rev up" your rice in this recipe. This side dish is a nice alternative to potatoes and complements turkey or any main course.

> 1 cup uncooked long grain rice
> 1 tablespoon cooking oil
> 1-1/2 to 2 tablespoons dry onion soup mix
> 1/4 teaspoon pepper
> 1-2/3 cups boiling water
> 1 cup frozen peas

In a large skillet, brown rice in oil, stirring constantly. Blend in soup mix and pepper. Stir in water; bring to a boil. Reduce heat; cover and simmer for 15 minutes or until the rice is tender. Stir

in peas. Cover and cook for 5 minutes. Serve immediately. **Yield:** 4 servings.

PUMPKIN MOUSSE

If you've had your fill of pumpkin pie, this cool and creamy mousse is just right for you. Its light and fluffy texture won't make you feel "stuffed" after your favorite turkey dinner.

    1 package (8 ounces) cream cheese,
       softened
  1/4 cup sugar
    1 can (16 ounces) pumpkin

    1 package (3.4 ounces) instant vanilla
       pudding mix
    2 teaspoons pumpkin pie spice
    1 cup cold milk
    1 carton (4 ounces) frozen whipped
       topping, thawed
   24 gingersnaps

In a mixing bowl, beat cream cheese and sugar until smooth. Beat in pumpkin. Add pudding mix and pie spice; mix well. Gradually beat in milk. Fold in whipped topping. Spoon about 1/4 cup each into serving dishes. Crumble 2 gingersnaps over each. Divide remaining pumpkin mixture among dishes. Garnish with a whole gingersnap. Chill until ready to serve. Refrigerate leftovers. **Yield:** 8 servings.

Hurry-up Holiday Meal

THE HUSTLE AND BUSTLE of the holidays can keep any busy cook out of the kitchen. So why not present your hungry clan with this fast and festive meal highlighting Pork with Mushroom Sauce? Deliciously cheesy Topped Taters are made extra-easy by using leftover spuds. With their cool minty flavor, Peppermint Parfaits are the perfect ending to your favorite meals…anytime of year!

PORK WITH MUSHROOM SAUCE

Treat your family to a festive meal of pork tenderloin without spending hours in the kitchen. It's easy enough to prepare for weekday dinners and impressive enough to serve on special occasions.

```
    1  pork tenderloin (about 1 pound)
    3  tablespoons butter or margarine
1/2  teaspoon dried thyme
1/2  teaspoon salt
1/4  teaspoon pepper
    1  cup sliced fresh mushrooms
    1  small onion, sliced
2/3  cup milk
    1  tablespoon Dijon mustard
1-1/2  teaspoons cornstarch
```

Cut tenderloin crosswise into fourths. Slice each piece in half but do not cut all the way through; open and flatten each piece. Melt butter in a large skillet; add pork. Combine thyme, salt and pepper; sprinkle half over the meat. Cook 3-4 minutes per side. Add mushrooms and onion. Cook and stir until vegetables are almost tender and pork is no longer pink. Remove meat to a platter and keep warm. Combine milk, mustard, cornstarch and the remaining thyme mixture; stir into the vegetables. Bring to a boil; cook and stir for 2 minutes. Spoon over pork and serve immediately. **Yield:** 4 servings.

TOPPED TATERS

Leftover mashed potatoes don't have to be plain and boring. Simply stir in sour cream and onions and top

with cheese for a creative new way to serve taters.

```
    3  cups leftover mashed potatoes
3/4  cup sour cream, divided
    3  tablespoons sliced green onions with tops,
         divided
1/4 to 1/2  teaspoon garlic salt
1/2  cup shredded cheddar cheese
```

Combine the potatoes, 1/4 cup of sour cream, 1 tablespoon green onions and the garlic salt; mix well. Spoon into a greased 1-qt. baking dish. Cover and bake at 350° for 20 minutes. Uncover; spread with the remaining sour cream. Sprinkle with the cheese and remaining onions. Return to the oven for 5 minutes or until the cheese melts. **Yield:** 4 servings.

PEPPERMINT PARFAITS

Nothing is as pleasing to your palate after a satisfying meal like mint. These easy-to-prepare peppermint parfaits are the perfect way to end any meal.

    24 large marshmallows
   1/2 cup milk
     1 teaspoon vanilla extract
Pinch salt
   1/4 teaspoon peppermint extract
     5 to 8 drops red food coloring
     2 cups whipped topping
Crushed chocolate wafers

In a saucepan over low heat, melt marshmallows with milk. Remove from the heat; stir in vanilla, salt, extract and food coloring. Chill for 10 minutes; fold in whipped topping. Spoon into individual dishes. Chill until ready to serve. Garnish with chocolate wafers. **Yield:** 4 servings.

Splendid Spuds

To make mashed potatoes hold their shape when topping a casserole or shepherd's pie, thicken them by beating in an egg yolk or two instead of milk.

Instead of adding whole milk to mashed potatoes, reserve some of the water used to boil the potatoes and mix in powdered milk. This retains the nutrients (and potato flavor) in the water...and it's economical, too.

Meals on a Budget

These economical dinners deliciously prove you don't have to sacrifice taste or quality to feed your family for just pennies a person.

Feed Your Family for 64¢ a Plate!

THE FRUGAL—yet flavorful—meal here goes to show you can make your bunch a terrific lunch without feeling a financial crunch. The three great cooks who sent the recipes for this meal estimate a total cost of just 64¢ per setting (which includes two cookies per person).

Double-Decker Cheese Melt, shared by Leslie Eisenbraun of Columbiana, Ohio, is a recipe that's easy to make and deliciously different. "Whenever I serve these tasty sandwiches, my family looks for more," remarks Leslie.

Turkey Noodle Soup, from Margaret Shauers of Great Bend, Kansas, is hearty and flavorful. Margaret remarks, "I use leftover turkey and the carcass to prepare this soup—a little goes a long way."

An inexpensive meal can still include dessert, assures Dottie LaPierre of Woburn, Massachusetts, who shares the recipe for simple Sugar 'n' Spice Cookies. Says Dottie, "These sweet and tart cookies are a treat."

DOUBLE-DECKER CHEESE MELT

   1 **cup (4 ounces) shredded cheddar cheese**
1/4 **cup butter *or* margarine, softened**
   1 **egg**
1/2 **teaspoon garlic salt**
1/2 **teaspoon onion salt**
   6 **slices white bread**
Paprika, optional

In a food processor, blend cheese and butter. Add egg, garlic salt and onion salt; process for 1 minute or until creamy. Spread 2 tablespoons on each slice of bread. Stack two slices of bread, cheese side up, for each sandwich; sprinkle with paprika if desired. Cut sandwiches in half diagonally. Place on an ungreased baking sheet. Bake at 400° for 10-15 minutes or until golden and bubbly. **Yield:** 6 servings.

TURKEY NOODLE SOUP

   9 **cups homemade turkey *or* chicken broth**
   4 **medium carrots, shredded**
   3 **celery ribs, sliced**
   1 **medium onion, chopped**
   1 **teaspoon rubbed sage**
1/2 **teaspoon pepper**
   3 **whole cloves**
   1 **bay leaf**
   2 **cups diced cooked turkey**
   1 **cup uncooked macaroni**
1/4 **cup chopped fresh parsley**

In a large kettle or Dutch oven, combine the first six ingredients. Tie cloves and bay leaf in a cheesecloth bag and add to kettle; bring to a boil. Reduce heat; cover and simmer for 1 hour. Add the turkey, macaroni and parsley; cover and simmer for 15-20 minutes or until macaroni is tender and soup is heated through. Discard spice bag. **Yield:** 6 servings (3 quarts).

SUGAR 'N' SPICE COOKIES

   3/4 **cup shortening**
     1 **cup sugar**
     1 **egg**
   1/4 **cup molasses**
     2 **cups all-purpose flour**
     1 **teaspoon baking soda**
1-1/2 **teaspoons ground ginger**
     1 **teaspoon ground cinnamon**
   3/4 **teaspoon ground cloves**
   1/2 **teaspoon salt**
LEMON FROSTING:
     2 **cups confectioners' sugar**
     3 **tablespoons butter *or* margarine, softened**
     1 **teaspoon grated lemon peel**
     3 **to 4 tablespoons lemon juice**

In a mixing bowl, cream shortening and sugar. Add egg; mix well. Beat in molasses. Combine dry ingredients; add to creamed mixture and mix well. Drop by rounded teaspoonfuls onto greased baking sheets. Bake at 350° for 8-10 minutes. Remove to wire racks; cool. For frosting, cream sugar, butter and lemon peel in a mixing bowl. Gradually add lemon juice, beating until frosting reaches desired spreading consistency. Frost cookies. **Yield:** about 4-1/2 dozen.

Feed Your Family for $1.04 a Plate!

IT LOOKS like a million dollars. But this hearty meal is another mouth-watering example of the fact that with the right combination of ingredients you don't have to give up fully enjoying food to eat inexpensively.

Three wonderful cooks show how easy it is to put together a low-budget menu perfect to serve family or guests for just $1.04 per setting.

Lemony Salmon Patties is an impressive main dish from Lorice Britt of Severn, North Carolina. "With the tasty salmon and zippy sauce, my family finds this delicious," Lorice assures.

Zucchini Pancakes are shared by Charlotte Goldberg of Honey Grove, Pennsylvania. "They're very tasty and easy to make," remarks Charlotte. "And they're a nice change of pace from potato pancakes."

For a sweet, old-fashioned dessert, try Apple Brown Betty from Florence Palmer of Marshall, Illinois. Florence says she can whip up this tasty treat in no time. And she asserts, "It costs little to prepare, but it's big on flavor."

LEMONY SALMON PATTIES

1 can (14-3/4 ounces) pink salmon, drained, skin and bones removed
3/4 cup milk
1 cup soft bread crumbs
1 egg, beaten
1 tablespoon chopped fresh parsley
1 teaspoon minced onion
1/2 teaspoon Worcestershire sauce
1/4 teaspoon salt
1/8 teaspoon pepper
LEMON SAUCE:
2 tablespoons butter *or* margarine
4 teaspoons all-purpose flour
3/4 cup milk
2 tablespoons lemon juice
1/4 teaspoon salt
1/8 to 1/4 teaspoon cayenne pepper

Combine the first nine ingredients; mix well. Spoon into eight greased muffin cups, using 1/4 cup in each. Bake at 350° for 45 minutes or until browned. Meanwhile, melt butter in a saucepan; stir in the flour to form a smooth paste. Gradually stir in milk; bring to a boil over medium heat, stirring constantly. Cook for 2 minutes or until thickened. Remove from the heat; stir in lemon juice, salt and cayenne. Serve over patties. **Yield:** 4 servings.

ZUCCHINI PANCAKES

1-1/2 cups shredded zucchini
1 egg, lightly beaten
2 tablespoons biscuit/baking mix
3 tablespoons grated Parmesan cheese
Dash pepper
1 tablespoon cooking oil

In a bowl, combine zucchini, egg, biscuit mix, cheese and pepper. Heat oil in a skillet over medium heat; drop batter by 1/4 cupfuls and flatten. Fry until golden brown; turn and cook the other side. **Yield:** 4 servings.

APPLE BROWN BETTY

4 slices white bread, toasted
3 cups sliced peeled baking apples
1/2 cup sugar
1/2 cup packed brown sugar
1 teaspoon ground cinnamon
1/4 cup butter *or* margarine, melted
1/2 cup half-and-half cream

Tear toast into bite-size pieces; place in a greased 1-1/2-qt. casserole. Top with apples. Combine sugars and cinnamon; sprinkle over apples. Drizzle with butter. Cover and bake at 350° for 1 hour, stirring after 30 minutes. Serve warm with cream. **Yield:** 4 servings.

Don't Stop Me Now

To avoid having to stop in the middle of a recipe and unscrew the cap on a bottle of cooking oil, keep the oil in a handy plastic squeeze bottle like the kind used for ketchup in restaurants.

Feed Your Family for $1.15 a Plate!

IF THE HOLIDAYS stretch the family budget, it's a great time to make a penny-pinching meal everyone will love. The enjoyably economical feast here is from three great cooks. The total cost is estimated at just $1.15 per setting.

Pork Stroganoff is a creamy, comforting main dish from Janice Mitchell of Aurora, Colorado.

Broccoli in Herbed Butter, shared by Norma Apel of Dubuque, Iowa, dresses up a plain vegetable.

Dill Biscuits are quick to prepare and easy on your pocketbook, assures Marcille Meyer of Battle Creek, Nebraska.

PORK STROGANOFF

✓ **This tasty dish uses less sugar, salt and fat. Recipe includes *Diabetic Exchanges*.**

1-1/2 **pounds pork stew meat, cut into 1-1/2-inch cubes**
1-1/2 **cups water, *divided***
  1 **teaspoon instant chicken bouillon granules**
  2 **teaspoons paprika**
  1 **cup chopped onion**
  1 **garlic clove, minced**
  1 **tablespoon cornstarch**
  3/4 **cup sour cream**
  2 **tablespoons snipped fresh parsley**
  1 **package (12 ounces) noodles, cooked and drained**

In a saucepan coated with nonstick cooking spray, brown pork; drain. Remove meat and set aside. In the same pan, bring 1-1/4 cups water, bouillon and paprika to a boil. Add pork, onion and garlic. Reduce heat; cover and simmer 45 minutes or until meat is tender. Combine cornstarch and remaining water; gradually add to pan, stirring constantly. Bring to a boil; cook and stir 2 minutes or until thickened. Remove from heat; stir in sour cream and parsley. Serve over noodles. **Yield:** 6 servings. **Diabetic Exchanges:** One serving (prepared with low-sodium bouillon and light sour cream and without noodles) equals 4 lean meat, 1/2 starch; also, 251 calories, 99 mg sodium, 76 mg cholesterol, 8 gm carbohydrate, 30 gm protein, 12 gm fat.

BROCCOLI IN HERBED BUTTER

✓ **This tasty dish uses less sugar, salt and fat. Recipe includes *Diabetic Exchanges*.**

  1 **pound fresh broccoli, cut into spears**
  2 **tablespoons butter *or* margarine**
1-1/2 **teaspoons lemon juice**
1-1/2 **teaspoons finely chopped onion**
  1/4 **teaspoon salt, optional**
  1/8 **teaspoon *each* dried thyme, marjoram and savory**

Cook broccoli until crisp-tender. Melt butter; add lemon juice, onion, salt if desired and herbs. Drain broccoli and place in a serving dish. Add butter mixture; stir to coat. **Yield:** 6 servings. **Diabetic Exchanges:** One serving (prepared with margarine and without salt) equals 1 fat, 1/2 vegetable; also, 51 calories, 42 mg sodium, 0 cholesterol, 3 gm carbohydrate, 2 gm protein, 4 gm fat.

DILL BISCUITS

  1/4 **cup butter *or* margarine, melted**
  1 **tablespoon finely chopped onion**
  1 **teaspoon dill weed**
  1 **tube (10 ounces) refrigerated buttermilk biscuits**

In a bowl, combine butter, onion and dill. Cut biscuits in half lengthwise; toss in the butter mixture. Arrange in a single layer in an ungreased 9-in. square baking pan. Bake at 450° for 8-10 minutes. **Yield:** 6 servings.

Fresh and Flavorful

To keep fresh parsley in the refrigerator for several weeks, wash the entire bunch in warm water, shake off all excess moisture, wrap in paper towel and seal in a plastic bag.

Feed Your Family for $1.18 a Plate!

HERE'S another meal that will make everybody happy—you…your family…and your household budget manager!

Three creative cooks show how easy it is to put together a low-budget menu for just $1.18 per setting (which includes two slices of bread per person).

Spaghetti with Homemade Turkey Sausage is a savory, satisfying main dish with rich flavor from Shirley Goodson of West Allis, Wisconsin.

Sesame French Bread bakes into crunchy golden loaves, according to Peggy Van Arsdale of Trenton, New Jersey, who shares her recipe.

Squash and Pepper Saute, from June Formanek of Belle Plaine, Iowa, is tasty and beautiful, plus it's a great way to use your zucchini harvest.

SPAGHETTI WITH HOMEMADE TURKEY SAUSAGE

- **1 pound ground turkey**
- **1 teaspoon fennel seed, crushed**
- **1 teaspoon water**
- **1/2 teaspoon salt**
- **1/2 teaspoon pepper**
- **1 jar (27 ounces) spaghetti sauce**
- **12 ounces spaghetti, cooked and drained**

In a bowl, combine turkey, fennel seed, water, salt and pepper. Refrigerate overnight. Crumble into bite-size pieces; cook in a skillet over medium heat until no pink remains. Add spaghetti sauce and heat through. Serve over hot spaghetti. **Yield:** 6 servings.

SESAME FRENCH BREAD

- **2 packages (1/4 ounce *each*) active dry yeast**
- **2-1/2 cups warm water (110° to 115°)**
- **2 tablespoons sugar**
- **2 tablespoons vegetable oil**
- **2 teaspoons salt**
- **6 to 6-1/2 cups all-purpose flour**
- **Cornmeal**

- **1 egg white**
- **1 tablespoon water**
- **2 tablespoons sesame seeds**

In a large mixing bowl, dissolve yeast in warm water. Add sugar, oil, salt and 4 cups of flour; beat until smooth. Add enough remaining flour to form a soft dough. Turn onto a floured board; knead until smooth and elastic, about 6-8 minutes. Place in a greased bowl, turning once to grease top. Cover and let rise in a warm place until doubled, about 1 hour. Punch dough down. Divide in half. Roll each half into a 15-in. x 10-in. rectangle. Roll up from a long side; seal well. Place with seam side down on a greased baking sheet sprinkled with cornmeal. Beat egg white and water; brush over loaves. Sprinkle with sesame seeds. Cover with plastic wrap sprayed with nonstick cooking spray; let rise until nearly doubled, about 30 minutes. With a very sharp knife, make four shallow diagonal cuts across top. Bake at 400° for 25 minutes or until lightly browned. Remove from pan and cool on a wire rack. **Yield:** 2 loaves.

SQUASH AND PEPPER SAUTE

- **2 medium yellow squash, sliced**
- **2 medium zucchini, sliced**
- **1 medium sweet red pepper, julienned**
- **1/4 cup olive *or* vegetable oil**
- **1 envelope (.7 ounce) Italian salad dressing mix**
- **3 tablespoons red wine vinegar**

In a skillet over medium-high, stir-fry the vegetables in oil until crisp-tender, about 3-4 minutes. Sprinkle with salad dressing mix; toss. Stir in vinegar; mix well. **Yield:** 6 servings.

Just Like the Real Thing

When using ground turkey in pasta dishes, add about a teaspoon of fennel seed per pound of meat as you brown it. This will make the turkey taste like sausage.

Feed Your Family for 98¢ a Plate!

USING RECIPES that call for ground beef is one of the most economical ways to cook. And there's nothing more fun and flavorful than a juicy hamburger. But instead of preparing the same old burger, how about trying this mouth-watering version?

This deliciously different meal was put together by three great cooks who estimate the total cost at just 98¢ per setting.

Chili Burgers are hearty, zippy sandwiches shared by Dolores Skrout of Summerhill, Pennsylvania. These burgers are definitely a crowd pleaser. "People are pleasantly surprised to find beans in this recipe," Dolores notes.

Garden Potato Salad puts a fresh-tasting spin on traditional potato salad. "This zesty side dish disappears quickly," says Caroline Weese of Greybull, Wyoming.

Hot Apple Sundaes make a comforting dessert. The orange flavor complements the light cinnamon-apple taste. These sundaes are a perfect way to round out your penny-pinching menu, assures Betty Matthews of South Haven, Michigan.

CHILI BURGERS

  1 **pound ground beef**
  1 **can (15 to 16 ounces) kidney beans, rinsed and drained**
  1 **can (10-3/4 ounces) condensed tomato soup, undiluted**
  1 **cup chopped celery**
1/2 **cup chopped green pepper**
1/2 **cup chopped onion**
1/4 **cup ketchup**
  1 **tablespoon brown sugar**
  1 **teaspoon chili powder**
1/2 **teaspoon ground mustard**
1/2 **teaspoon salt**
1/4 **teaspoon pepper**
1/8 **teaspoon cayenne pepper**
1/8 **teaspoon garlic powder**
 12 **hamburger buns, split**

In a saucepan over medium heat, brown beef; drain. Add beans, soup, celery, green pepper, onion, ketchup, brown sugar and seasonings; bring to a boil. Reduce heat; cover and simmer for 30-40 minutes or until vegetables are tender. Serve on buns. **Yield:** 12 servings.

GARDEN POTATO SALAD

1-1/2 **pounds red potatoes, quartered**
  3/4 **pound fresh green beans, halved**
   10 **cherry tomatoes, halved**
    1 **small onion, chopped**
DRESSING:
  1/2 **cup olive *or* vegetable oil**
  1/4 **cup cider vinegar**
    2 **tablespoons lemon juice**
    2 **tablespoons Dijon mustard**
    2 **teaspoons dried basil**
    2 **garlic cloves, minced**
1-1/4 **teaspoons sugar**
  1/4 **teaspoon hot pepper sauce**

Cook potatoes in boiling salted water for 8 minutes. Add beans; return to a boil. Cook for 5 minutes or until the beans are crisp-tender and the potatoes are just tender; drain and cool. Place in a large bowl; add the tomatoes and onion. Combine dressing ingredients; pour over the salad and toss. Refrigerate. **Yield:** 12 servings.

HOT APPLE SUNDAES

    1 **cup sugar**
    1 **cup orange juice**
  1/2 **cup lemon juice**
  1/2 **teaspoon ground cinnamon**
   10 **cups sliced peeled apples**
1-1/2 **quarts vanilla ice cream**

In a saucepan over medium heat, bring sugar, juices and cinnamon to a boil. Reduce heat; simmer, uncovered, for 5 minutes. Add apples and return to a boil. Reduce heat; cover and simmer for 15 minutes or until the apples are tender. Serve warm over ice cream. Sprinkle with cinnamon if desired. **Yield:** 12 servings (5 cups topping).

Feed Your Family for 79¢ a Plate!

HOW MUCH does a meal that includes a main dish…soup…*and* bread cost? With this one, a lot less than you probably think. The total cost for the following meal is estimated at just 79¢ per setting—and that includes two slices of bread per person.

Fresh from the garden, Creamy Tomato Soup is from Sue Gronholz of Columbus, Wisconsin. "I can a lot of tomato juice, which makes this recipe even more economical," Sue notes. "My husband really enjoys this soup, so I like to pack it in his lunch."

From Essex Junction, Vermont, Jackie Gavin sends her favorite recipe for delicious Oatmeal Wheat Bread. "My mother taught me to make this bread when I was 10 years old," she remembers. "And of the many kinds of breads I've baked over the years, this one is my favorite. It tastes marvelous *and* it's good for you!"

Tuna Pasta Salad is a tasty main dish shared by Pat Kordas of Nutley, New Jersey. "Mustard and dill really enhance the flavor of this simple salad," Pat says.

CREAMY TOMATO SOUP

  2 **tablespoons all-purpose flour**
  1 **tablespoon sugar**
  2 **cups milk,** *divided*
  4 **cups tomato juice, heated**
Chopped fresh parsley

In a large saucepan, combine flour, sugar and 1/4 cup milk; stir until smooth. Add remaining milk. Bring to a boil over medium heat, stirring constantly. Cook and stir for 2 minutes or until thickened. Slowly stir in hot tomato juice until blended. Sprinkle with parsley. **Yield:** 4 servings.

OATMEAL WHEAT BREAD

✓ This tasty dish uses less sugar, salt and fat.
   Recipe includes *Diabetic Exchanges*.

1-3/4 **cups boiling water**
  1 **cup quick-cooking oats**
1/2 **cup molasses**
1/4 **cup shortening**
1/4 **cup orange juice**
1-1/2 **teaspoons salt**
  2 **packages (1/4 ounce** *each***) active dry yeast**
1/2 **cup warm water (110° to 115°)**
2-1/2 **cups whole wheat flour**
  3 **to 3-1/2 cups all-purpose flour**
Melted butter *or* **margarine**

In a large mixing bowl, combine boiling water, oats, molasses, shortening, orange juice and salt; let stand until warm (110°-115°). In a small bowl, dissolve yeast in warm water; add to oat mixture. Add whole wheat flour and beat until smooth. Add enough all-purpose flour to form a soft dough. Turn onto a floured board; knead until smooth and elastic, about 6-8 minutes. Place in a greased bowl, turning once to grease top. Cover and let rise in a warm place until doubled, about 1 hour. Punch dough down. Shape into two loaves; place in greased 8-in. x 4-in. x 2-in. loaf pans. Cover and let rise until doubled, about 45 minutes. Bake at 350° for 40 minutes. Remove from pans; brush with butter. Cool on wire racks. **Yield:** 2 loaves (32 slices). **Diabetic Exchanges:** One slice (prepared with margarine) equals 1-1/2 starch; also, 121 calories, 110 mg sodium, 0 cholesterol, 23 gm carbohydrate, 3 gm protein, 2 gm fat.

TUNA PASTA SALAD

  1 **package (7 ounces) small shell pasta, cooked and drained**
  1 **can (6 ounces) tuna, drained and flaked**
  1 **large carrot, shredded**
1/4 **cup chopped onion**
3/4 **cup mayonnaise**
1/4 **cup milk**
  1 **tablespoon lemon juice**
  2 **teaspoons prepared mustard**
  1 **teaspoon dill weed**
1/2 **teaspoon salt**
1/8 **teaspoon pepper**

In a large salad bowl, combine pasta, tuna, carrot and onion. Combine remaining ingredients; whisk until smooth. Pour over pasta mixture and toss to coat. Cover and refrigerate for 1-2 hours. **Yield:** 4 servings.

Getting in the Theme of Things

*These fun and festive meals
—featuring theme-related menus,
decorating ideas and activities—will
make your get-togethers extra special.
Party planning couldn't be easier!*

Chubby 'teddy bears' and fun finger foods delight hibernating youngsters.

By Annette Ellyson, Carolina, West Virginia

In the middle of winter, if your "cubs" get bored with hibernation, just grin and "bear" it—with a teddy bear party!

Daughters Rachel, 6, and Leah, 3—not to mention me!—found it the perfect way to beat the blahs. We made invitations using teddy bear cookie cutters as patterns, tracing the shapes onto folded construction paper so they'd open like a card. Besides including the usual party details, we asked each guest to bring a favorite teddy bear.

My child-friendly menu for this whimsical event included Chicken Nuggets, Teddy Bear Rolls and Valentine Cutouts, plus "cubcakes" and a sparkling berry punch.

Quick and easy Chicken Nuggets are always a hit with kids. The coating is flavorful but not too spicy.

I remember my mom making Teddy Bear Rolls for me when I was a girl, and it's a tradition I enjoy passing on to my daughters. I always give each of them a portion of dough to shape.

If you're in a hurry, you can use hot roll mix instead of mixing the dough from scratch. The easy-to-make honey butter included with my recipe is delicious with the tiny teddy breads.

I'm often asked to share my secret for shaping Valentine Cutouts so perfectly. It's actually easy. Instead of using cookie cutters, I coat a mini heart pan with nonstick cooking spray and fill it with the gelatin mixture. After the hearts are set, they simply slide out.

For dessert, bake your favorite cupcakes, frost them with white icing and sprinkle with coconut. Then add a chocolate peppermint patty and three brown M&M's to the center to create "bear paws".

For our party table, we used a red tablecloth with a lace overlay and red heart doilies as place mats. Heart-shaped confetti (made with a heart paper punch) was strewn over the table.

Our favorite stuffed bears served as a focal point amid Victorian boxes, tins, flowers and heart-shaped trinkets. Tiny baskets brimming with chocolate hearts and teddy bear-shaped graham crackers were the favors.

Theme-related activities included a bear hunt, musical bears (musical chairs) and a reading of *Goldilocks and the Three Bears*. Lots of bear hugs at the end of the party assured me that our young guests had enjoyed themselves.

This theme could easily be adapted for a birthday or Valentine's Day party. Whatever the occasion, you can be certain that your guests will have a "beary" good time!

CHICKEN NUGGETS

I like to make these golden chicken nuggets because they're so quick and easy and the whole family loves them. The seasoning can also be used on chicken breast halves to make great sandwiches.

  1 cup all-purpose flour
  4 teaspoons seasoned salt
  1 teaspoon paprika
  1 teaspoon poultry seasoning
  1 teaspoon ground mustard
1/2 teaspoon pepper
  8 boneless skinless chicken breast halves
1/4 cup vegetable *or* olive oil

In a resealable plastic bag, combine the first six ingredients. Pound chicken to 1/2-in. thickness and cut into 1-1/2-in. pieces. Place chicken pieces, a few at a time, into bag and shake to coat. Heat oil in a skillet; cook chicken, turning frequently, until browned and juices run clear, about 6-8 minutes. **Yield:** 8-10 servings.

TEDDY BEAR ROLLS

When planning the menu for this "Teddy Bear" party, I just had to include these delectable rolls and the homemade honey butter. Their oven-fresh goodness appeals to the kid in all of us.

  2 packages (1/4 ounce *each*) active dry yeast
  1 cup warm water (110° to 115°)
  1 cup warm milk (110° to 115°)
  2 tablespoons sugar
  2 tablespoons vegetable oil
  1 egg
  1 teaspoon salt
5-1/2 to 6-1/2 cups all-purpose flour
Raisins (2 for each roll)
White frosting
HONEY BUTTER:
  1 cup butter *or* margarine, softened
  1/4 cup honey
  1/4 cup confectioners' sugar

In a mixing bowl, dissolve yeast in water. Add the milk, sugar, oil, egg, salt and 4 cups flour; beat until smooth. Add enough remaining flour to form a soft dough. Turn onto a floured board; knead until smooth and elastic, about 6-8 minutes. Place in a greased bowl, turning once to grease top. Cover and let rise in a warm place until doubled, about 1 hour. Punch dough down. For each bear, shape a 2-in. ball for the body. Add a 1-1/4-in. ball for the head and six 1/2-in. balls for the ears, arms and legs. Place 2 in. apart on greased baking sheets. Cover and let rise until doubled, about 20 minutes. Bake at 400° for 17 minutes or until golden brown. Cool on wire racks. Add raisins for eyes, anchoring with a dab of frosting. Add a frosting smile. In another mixing bowl, beat honey butter ingredients until fluffy. Chill; serve with rolls. **Yield:** about 10 rolls (1-1/4 cups butter).

VALENTINE CUTOUTS

Cool, fruity and creamy, these gelatin treats are richer than plain gelatin and cut easily into whatever shape you'd like. They're a fun finger food that works for any holiday or theme.

  2 packages (6 ounces *each*) cherry *or* raspberry gelatin
2-1/2 cups boiling water
  1 cup cold milk
  1 package (3.4 ounces) instant vanilla pudding mix

In a bowl, dissolve gelatin in water; set aside for 30 minutes. In a small bowl, whisk milk and pudding mix until smooth, about 1 minute. Quickly pour into gelatin; whisk until well blended. Pour into an oiled 13-in. x 9-in. x 2-in. dish. Chill until set. Cut into cubes or use a heart-shaped cookie cutter. **Yield:** 8-10 servings.

Backyard citrus harvest adds sunny zest to her Thanksgiving table.

By Zita Wilensky, North Miami, Florida

Seldom do I prepare a special dinner without some theme to it—even for a holiday like Thanksgiving that has its own traditional foods and colors. Oranges from our own backyard provided the ingredients for this meal that celebrates our area's sweet, juicy citrus crop.

When relatives arrived for our holiday celebration, we all toasted the occasion with a sparkling "mimosa" beverage made with freshly squeezed orange juice before I brought on the festive feast. A menu printed on orange or yellow paper whetted everyone's appetite.

Presenting the Turkey with Orange-Honey Glaze was a pleasure. The recipe originated with my mother, who came to the U.S. from Hungary. Native dishes she fixed were often sweet or sweet-tart.

Golden brown and full of flavor, this turkey is roasted with an orange in the cavity and basted with a sauce made with orange marmalade and orange juice.

Another family favorite I served—Onion Orange Salad—is a refreshing medley I made up to enter in a recipe contest, something I often do. It features fresh orange slices tossed with mixed greens, blue cheese, slivered almonds and red onion rings, and the dressing calls for orange juice.

To complement the poultry, I came up with Orange Rice Medley, a pretty pilaf that includes mandarin oranges. They aren't produced locally, but they fit in fine to liven up this side dish and add to its eye appeal.

Orange-Buttered Peas added another appetizing hue to foods we passed. Grated orange peel and a little marmalade were the qualifying ingredients.

Orange was primary among the autumn colors for the table setting. On a solid orange cloth, I set a terracotta turkey container filled with fruits, berries and grapes, plus a basket of Indian corn, mini-pumpkins and squash between tall spiral candles in my favorite glass holders.

I found large dinner-sized paper napkins with a Thanksgiving design and filled little plastic pumpkins with individual servings of cranberry relish.

While this meal made a big impression, it is really

264

quite simple to make, which is great for the cook! Sharing the festive foods with those near and dear was fun for me, too.

TURKEY WITH ORANGE-HONEY GLAZE

A tangy fresh-tasting glaze over a savory golden roast turkey makes for a memorable holiday main dish.

- 2 teaspoons rubbed sage
- 2 teaspoons salt
- 1/2 teaspoon pepper
- Pinch dried thyme
- 1 turkey (18 to 20 pounds)
- 1 small orange, peeled and halved
- 1/4 cup butter *or* margarine, melted
- 1/3 cup orange juice
- 1/3 cup orange marmalade
- 1-1/2 teaspoons honey
- Pinch ground cinnamon

In a small bowl, combine sage, salt, pepper and thyme; mix well. Rub 2 teaspoons inside the turkey; set the remainder aside. Place orange inside turkey. Skewer openings; tie drumsticks together. Place on a rack in a roasting pan. Combine remaining sage mixture with butter; brush over turkey. Bake, uncovered, at 325° for 5-1/2 hours or until a meat thermometer reads 170°, basting every 30 minutes. When turkey begins to brown, cover lightly with foil. In a saucepan, combine remaining ingredients; bring to a boil. Reduce heat; simmer, uncovered, for 15-20 minutes or until slightly thickened, stirring occasionally. Brush over turkey. Continue to bake, uncovered, 30 minutes to 1 hour longer or until thermometer reads 185°, brushing with glaze occasionally. Remove from the oven; cover and let stand 20 minutes before carving. Thicken pan juices for gravy if desired. **Yield:** 16-18 servings.

ONION ORANGE SALAD

Tongues tingle after tasting all the bold flavors in this delightful salad. It's an eye-catching dish.

- 1/3 cup olive *or* vegetable oil
- 1/4 cup orange juice
- 3 tablespoons vinegar
- 1 garlic clove, minced
- 1 teaspoon minced fresh parsley
- 1/4 teaspoon salt
- Dash pepper

- 8 cups torn spinach *or* mixed greens
- 3 medium oranges, peeled and sliced
- 1 cup sliced red onion
- 1/2 cup crumbled blue cheese
- 1/4 cup slivered almonds, toasted

In a small bowl, whisk the first seven ingredients. On a serving platter or individual plates, arrange greens, oranges and onion. Drizzle with dressing. Sprinkle with cheese and almonds. **Yield:** 6-8 servings.

ORANGE RICE MEDLEY

This side dish looks so pretty with the colorful chopped green and red peppers and orange slices tucked in with the rice.

- 1/2 cup chopped onion
- 1/2 cup chopped green pepper
- 1/2 cup chopped sweet red pepper
- 2 teaspoons olive or vegetable oil
- 1 cup uncooked long grain rice
- 1-1/2 cups chicken broth
- 1/2 cup orange juice
- 1/4 teaspoon salt
- Dash pepper
- 1 can (11 ounces) mandarin oranges, drained and coarsely chopped

In a saucepan over medium heat, saute onion and peppers in oil until tender. Add rice; stir until lightly browned. Add broth, orange juice, salt and pepper; bring to a boil. Reduce heat; cover and simmer for 15-20 minutes or until liquid is absorbed. Stir in oranges. **Yield:** 6-8 servings.

ORANGE-BUTTERED PEAS

Fresh mushrooms sauteed in a tangy orange-butter sauce give peas a new and interesting twist.

- 3 tablespoons orange marmalade
- 2 tablespoons butter *or* margarine
- 1 tablespoon grated orange peel
- 1/2 cup sliced fresh mushrooms
- 1 package (16 ounces) frozen peas
- Salt and pepper to taste

In a saucepan over medium heat, combine marmalade, butter and orange peel. Add mushrooms; cook and stir until tender. Cook peas according to package directions; drain. Add mushroom mixture and toss. Season with salt and pepper. **Yield:** 6-8 servings.

Yippee!
Food and fun at cowboy-style celebration honor country bride-to-be.

By Sandra Thorn, Sonora, California

When I learned that a good friend was planning a Western-style wedding, I gave her a bridal shower with plenty of cowboy flavor. What fun it was to come up with Western decorations and a menu!

I decorated the front door with a cowboy hat, and in the entryway I put a saddle, rope, bridle and horse collar on a sawhorse. After all the guests arrived, we sang a little song I'd made up especially for guest-of-honor Deanna.

To the tune of *Home on the Range*, the chorus was "Home, home on the ranch, where there's love for

Deanna and Dave...there's candlelit dinners, where they both come out winners, love is the present they gave."

A special keepsake gift from the group was a decorative wooden rolling pin, which hangs on the wall in a holder made from horseshoes. During the party, each of us signed the rolling pin and added a few sage words of marital advice. (I provided a pen with indelible ink for this autograph session.)

My buffet table was covered with a patchwork gingham cloth on which I grouped cactus plants, cowboy boots, canning jars filled with colorful dry beans, and some cute stuffed cowgirl dolls. A basket held individual gingham bags filled with Trail Mix, which were given to guests as favors.

All the food was served on tin pie plates. Serving pieces included kettles, baskets and tin cans and sifters. A black cast-iron kettle held the Molasses Baked Beans. (This dish always tastes better if made the day before.) Cheesy Corn Bread, baked in cactus-shaped molds, was a big hit, and zippy Stuffed Jalapenos disappeared quickly, too, as guests helped themselves to the "grub".

Chips and salsa, a few other favorite finger foods and fresh strawberry shortcake rounded out the menu.

STUFFED JALAPENOS

Cool cream cheese contrasts nicely with slightly spicy peppers in this simple recipe.

- **2 jars (11-1/2 ounces *each*) whole jalapeno peppers, drained**
- **1 package (8 ounces) cream cheese, softened**

Cut a slit along one side of each pepper. Remove seeds; rinse and dry. Fill the inside of each with about 2 teaspoons of cream cheese. **Yield:** about 20 appetizers.

MOLASSES BAKED BEANS

These hearty from-scratch baked beans taste like they were simmered over an open fire. Their sweet and zippy flavor is as big as the great outdoors. No matter what kind of meal you're "rustling up", this satisfying side dish is certain to please.

- **2 pounds dry navy beans**
- **5 quarts water, *divided***
- **1 can (28 ounces) diced tomatoes, undrained**
- **1-1/2 cups ketchup**
- **1 cup butter *or* margarine, melted**
- **2 large onions, quartered**
- **1/2 cup packed brown sugar**
- **1/2 cup molasses**
- **1 tablespoon salt**
- **1 tablespoon liquid smoke *or* barbecue sauce**

Place beans and 2-1/2 qts. water in a 6-qt. Dutch oven; bring to a boil and boil for 2 minutes. Remove from the heat; soak for 1 hour. Drain and rinse beans; return to pan with remaining water. Bring to a boil. Reduce heat; cover and simmer for 1 hour or until beans are tender. Drain, reserv-

ing cooking liquid. Return beans to pan; add remaining ingredients and mix well. Cover and bake at 350° for 2 to 2-1/2 hours or until beans reach desired consistency, stirring occasionally. Add some of the reserved cooking liquid if too thick. **Yield:** 16-20 servings.

TRAIL MIX

With nuts, raisins, M&M's and coconut, this is a super snack. In small gingham bags, it made wonderful party favors for each guest at the cowboy-theme wedding shower I hosted. This mix is a tasty treat anytime.

- **2 pounds dry roasted peanuts**
- **2 pounds cashews**
- **1 pound raisins**
- **1 pound M&M's**
- **1/2 pound flaked coconut**

Combine all ingredients in a large bowl. Store in an airtight container. **Yield:** 6 quarts.

CHEESY CORN BREAD

What could be more fun for a Southwestern or a cowboy theme party than corn bread shaped like cactus? Cheddar cheese mixed in makes it even more special.

- **4 cups all-purpose flour**
- **2 cups yellow cornmeal**
- **2/3 cup sugar**
- **3 tablespoons baking powder**
- **1 tablespoon salt**
- **1 cup shortening**
- **3 cups milk**
- **4 eggs, beaten**
- **1/2 cup finely shredded cheddar cheese**

In a large bowl, combine the first five ingredients; cut in shortening until the mixture resembles coarse crumbs. In a small bowl, combine milk and eggs; stir into dry ingredients just until blended. Pour into a greased 13-in. x 9-in. x 2-in. baking pan. Sprinkle with cheese. Bake at 400° for 25 minutes or until golden brown. Cut into squares. **Yield:** 16-20 servings. **Editor's Note:** To make cactus-shaped corn bread, fill well-greased cactus molds almost full. Sprinkle each with 1 teaspoon cheese. Bake at 400° for 13-15 minutes or until golden brown. Molds are available from Lodge Manufacturing Company, Customer Service, P.O. Box 380, South Pittsburg TN 37380; 1-423/837-7181.

Savory soup simmers while hostess and guests are out caroling merrily.

By Mary Anne McWhirter, Pearland, Texas

What better way to celebrate the wonderful music of the Christmas season than with a caroling party?

This simple theme gathering provided a great way to get together with friends—and we all enjoyed sharing Christmas greetings in song with neighbors and some other special folks in our community.

Blank pages from a student sheet music notebook were so appropriate for making the party invitations. I drew musical notes to accent the basic information of date and time and added a food-related request: Since our supper would feature "Bring an Ingredient" Soup, each guest should contribute a fresh vegetable, meat or garnish.

These ingredients could include diced green pepper, tomatoes, carrots and mushrooms, or meatballs or cubed cooked chicken to add to the soup.

I also asked that some guests bring toppings like shredded cheddar cheese, sour cream, parsley, croutons or popcorn. This "add-to-it" soup gave me the perfect answer for "What can I bring?", a common question among our friends.

As guests arrived, I gave each a paper sack I'd stenciled with a Christmas tree. Inside they found an inexpensive flashlight and the music we'd sing during the evening.

While I put the soup on and invited them to stir in any ingredients that should simmer in the broth I'd prepared, we practiced the songs.

Then off we went, joyfully caroling door-to-door!

Back home later, we gathered around the table I'd decorated with baskets of greenery, musical instruments and sheet music. If you don't have a real trumpet or French horn available, you likely can find smaller decorative replicas.

My Christmas dishes added color to the setting. If you don't have any, look for colorful holiday paper plates to use with your bowls. I served cold beverages in soft drink bottles sprayed with Christmas tree flocking and tied with a festive ribbon.

Then we ladled out the hearty, flavorful soup and everyone helped themselves to the buffet of garnishes.

Warm bread and Christmas Crunch Salad (a colorful, crispy blend of vegetables you can make ahead) rounded out the casual menu.

Everyone was glad they'd saved room for a big slice of my easy, elegant Cherry Cream Torte. This pretty and delicious treat makes a big impression without being a lot of fuss for the cook.

Our evening began and ended on a high note with everyone agreeing the caroling party was especially in tune with this joyous season. I'm hoping it might be a theme that strikes a chord with you!

"BRING AN INGREDIENT" SOUP

A steaming bowl of soup is just the thing to take the chill off a cold winter evening spent caroling. Asking each guest to bring an ingredient adds to the fun and means less fuss for you.

> 4 cups thinly sliced onions
> 1 garlic clove, minced
> 3 tablespoons butter *or* margarine
> 3 tablespoons all-purpose flour
> 6 cans (14-1/2 ounces *each*) beef broth
> 2 cups tomato puree
> 1 tablespoon red wine vinegar
> 1 tablespoon Worcestershire sauce
> 1 tablespoon sugar
> 1/2 teaspoon *each* dried oregano, tarragon, ground cumin, salt and pepper
> 1/4 to 1/2 teaspoon hot pepper sauce

VEGETABLES (choose two or three):
> 1-1/2 cups *each* diced green pepper, tomato *or* carrots
> 2 cups sliced fresh mushrooms

MEATS (choose two):
> 3 cups cooked mini meatballs
> 3 cups cubed cooked chicken
> 3 cups diced fully cooked ham
> 1 package (10 ounces) smoked kielbasa, sliced and browned

GARNISHES (choose three or four):
Shredded cheddar cheese, garbanzo beans, sour cream, chopped fresh parsley, croutons *or* popcorn

In a large Dutch oven, saute the onions and garlic in butter until tender. Stir in flour and blend well. Add broth, puree, vinegar and seasonings; mix well. Bring to a boil; reduce heat and simmer for 40 minutes. Add two or three vegetables; simmer for 30 minutes or until tender. Add two meats; heat through. Garnish as desired. **Yield:** 16-18 servings (4-1/2 quarts).

CHRISTMAS CRUNCH SALAD

With its creamy dressing and colorful vegetables, this salad is both lovely and refreshing. Make it before you head out caroling, and when you return, guests' compliments will be music to your ears.

> 4 cups fresh broccoli florets (about 3/4 pound)
> 4 cups fresh cauliflowerets (about 3/4 pound)
> 1 medium red onion, chopped
> 2 cups cherry tomatoes, halved

DRESSING:
> 1 cup mayonnaise
> 1/2 cup sour cream
> 1 to 2 tablespoons sugar
> 1 tablespoon vinegar

Salt and pepper to taste

In a large salad bowl, combine vegetables. Whisk the dressing ingredients until smooth; pour over vegetables and toss to coat. Cover and chill for at least 2 hours. **Yield:** 16-18 servings.

CHERRY CREAM TORTE

When you set this gorgeous dessert on the table, your guests will sing your praises. You're the only one who has to know how simple it is to prepare.

> 2 packages (3 ounces *each*) lady fingers
> 2 tablespoons white grape *or* apple juice
> 1 package (8 ounces) cream cheese, softened
> 2/3 cup sugar
> 1 teaspoon almond extract, *divided*
> 2 cups whipping cream, whipped
> 1 can (21 ounces) cherry pie filling

Toasted sliced almonds and additional whipped cream, optional

Split lady fingers lengthwise; brush with juice. Place a layer of lady fingers around the sides and over the bottom of a lightly greased 9-in. springform pan. In a mixing bowl, beat cream cheese until smooth; add sugar and 1/2 teaspoon extract. Beat on medium for 1 minute. Fold in whipped cream. Spread half over crust. Arrange remaining lady fingers in a spoke-like fashion. Spread evenly with the remaining cream cheese mixture. Cover and chill overnight. Combine the pie filling and remaining extract; spread over the cream cheese layer. Refrigerate for at least 2 hours. To serve, remove sides of pan. Garnish with almonds and whipped cream if desired. **Yield:** 16-18 servings.

Feather your nest for a fanciful, gals-only 'Hen Party' brunch.

By Gayle Grigg, Phoenix, Arizona

The old expression "hen party" found its way into the conversation as my mom, Liz Richards, and I planned a ladies-only gathering…and we decided it would make a fun theme for the brunch.

Soon ideas began to hatch! We mailed egg-shaped invitations (cut from poster board) with this little verse: *You're invited to a "Hen Party"—We're going to have some fun! Wear country clothes and add a smile—Good food will make your day worthwhile!*

Checkered tablecloths and bandanna-print napkins lent a cheerful country look to the party scene. Hen-shaped centerpieces were cut from white poster board and decorated with construction-paper beaks, combs and wattles.

We pasted two hen cutouts together with a wooden tongue depressor between and stuck each hen into a foam base. (You could use fabric or ceramic hens instead if you have them.)

"Straw" around the hens was raffia (found at craft stores). We scattered real eggshells around each nest.

The day of the party, we decked our front door with a "Welcome to the Henhouse" sign. Greeting guests, we let each choose a red or blue bandanna to put around her neck. After everyone was seated, we drew numbers for the door prize—a dozen eggs, of course!

Our main entree was Sausage and Egg Casserole, one of those great dishes you can put together the day before, refrigerate overnight and bake for the meal.

"Chicken Little" Cinnamon Rolls went well with the casserole. These delicious raised rolls start with convenient frozen bread dough, so even if you're not a veteran yeast baker, your guests will think otherwise!

Orange Cream Fruit Salad made a colorful and refreshing accompaniment. This medley of fruit with creamy dressing is delightful for brunch, but Mom and I often fix it as a side dish with other meals as well.

For dessert, we made "chick cookies"—using a basic sugar cookie recipe, a chick-shaped cutter, yellow colored sugar and blue decorator's gel (see a plateful in photo at left).

Our sunny theme and tasty late-morning meal prompted happy "clucking" and corny "yolks" from our guests, along with plenty of sincere compliments for the food and fun. We're happy to share this theme, hoping some of you might scramble your ideas with ours and plan a Hen Party of your own.

SAUSAGE AND EGG CASSEROLE

For the perfect combination of eggs, sausage, bread and cheese, this is the dish to try. My mom and I like it because it bakes up tender and golden, slices beautifully and goes over well whenever we serve it.

- 1 pound bulk pork sausage
- 6 eggs
- 2 cups milk
- 1 teaspoon salt
- 1 teaspoon ground mustard
- 6 slices white bread, cut into 1/2-inch cubes
- 1 cup (4 ounces) shredded cheddar cheese

In a skillet, brown and crumble sausage; drain and set aside. In a large bowl, beat eggs; add milk, salt and mustard. Stir in bread cubes, cheese and sausage. Pour into a greased 11-in. x 7-in. x 2-in. baking dish. Cover and refrigerate for 8 hours or overnight. Remove from the refrigerator 30 minutes before baking. Bake, uncovered, at 350° for 40 minutes or until a knife inserted near the center comes out clean. **Yield:** 8-10 servings.

Keep Farm-Fresh Flavor

Eggs stay fresher longer and pick up fewer refrigerator odors if they're kept on the shelf in their carton rather than in the egg holders on the door.

"CHICKEN LITTLE" CINNAMON ROLLS

The delectable homemade taste of these cinnamon rolls brings raves when Mom and I serve them to friends and family. With raisins and a light lemon glaze, these rolls are perfect for a special brunch.

- 1 loaf (1 pound) frozen bread dough, thawed
- 3 tablespoons butter *or* margarine, melted
- 1/3 cup sugar
- 2 teaspoons ground cinnamon
- 1 teaspoon grated lemon peel
- 1/2 cup raisins

GLAZE:
- 1/2 cup confectioners' sugar
- 2 tablespoons lemon juice

On a lightly floured surface, roll the dough into a 14-in. x 10-in. rectangle. Brush with butter. Combine the sugar, cinnamon and lemon peel; sprinkle evenly over butter. Sprinkle with raisins. Starting from a long side, roll dough up tightly. Seal seams. Slice into 12 rolls; place in a greased 11-in. x 7-in. x 2-in. baking pan. Cover and let rise until doubled, about 45 minutes. Bake at 350° for 25-30 minutes or until golden brown. Cool for 10 minutes. Combine the glaze ingredients; brush over rolls. **Yield:** 1 dozen.

ORANGE CREAM FRUIT SALAD

Creamy, tangy dressing over a refreshing combination of fruits makes this salad taste so good. Our guests especially enjoyed the surprising orange flavor.

- 1 can (20 ounces) pineapple tidbits, drained
- 1 can (16 ounces) peach slices, drained
- 1 can (11 ounces) mandarin oranges, drained
- 2 medium firm bananas, sliced
- 1 medium apple, chopped
- 1 package (3.4 ounces) instant vanilla pudding mix
- 1-1/2 cups milk
- 1/3 cup frozen orange juice concentrate
- 3/4 cup sour cream

In a large salad bowl, combine fruits; set aside. In a small mixing bowl, beat pudding mix, milk and orange juice concentrate for 2 minutes. Add sour cream; mix well. Spoon over fruit; toss to coat. Cover and refrigerate for 2 hours. **Yield:** 8-10 servings.

Gardening gal's idea for birthday party gets two (green) thumbs up!

By Kimberly Speta, Kennedy, New York

When our daughter, Nicole, wanted to celebrate her 14th birthday with a "growing-up" party, we didn't look any further than the garden for inspiration!

Nicole had spent the summer before tending her uncle's vegetable patch, so we planned a "Garden's Bounty Party" theme.

Fresh dill, zucchini, carrots and beets—*real* fruits of Nicole's labor—were featured in the meal, which harvested happy memories for everyone.

DILLED CHICKEN SALAD

I harvest a bushel of recipe requests whenever I serve this hearty, fresh-tasting salad.

> 1 package (16 ounces) spiral pasta, cooked and drained
> 2 cups cubed cooked chicken
> 1 cup chopped celery
> 1/3 cup chopped onion
> 1 package (10 ounces) frozen peas, thawed

DRESSING:
> 1 envelope (1 ounce) ranch salad dressing mix
> 2 cups (16 ounces) sour cream

> 1 cup mayonnaise
> 1 cup milk
> 3 tablespoons minced fresh dill *or* 1 tablespoon dill weed
> 1/2 teaspoon garlic salt

In a large bowl, combine the first five ingredients; mix well. Combine dressing ingredients; whisk until smooth. Pour over salad; toss to coat. Cover and refrigerate for at least 2 hours. **Yield:** 10-12 servings. **Editor's Note:** If using a terra-cotta or clay bowl for serving this salad as shown in the photo, line it with plastic wrap or aluminum foil, or use a plastic bowl that looks like terra-cotta.

ITALIAN ZUCCHINI CASSEROLE

Compliments crop up as fast as zucchini vines when folks sample this casserole.

> 3 medium zucchini, sliced (about 6-1/2 cups)
> 3 tablespoons olive *or* vegetable oil, *divided*
> 1 medium onion, sliced
> 1 garlic clove, minced
> 1 can (28 ounces) diced tomatoes, undrained

1 tablespoon minced fresh basil *or* 1 teaspoon dried basil
1-1/2 teaspoons minced fresh oregano *or* 1/2 teaspoon dried oregano
1/2 teaspoon garlic salt
1/4 teaspoon pepper
1-1/2 cups dry instant stuffing mix
1/2 cup grated Parmesan cheese
3/4 cup shredded mozzarella cheese

In a large skillet, cook zucchini in 1 tablespoon oil until tender, about 5-6 minutes; drain and set aside. In the same skillet, saute the onion and garlic in remaining oil for 1 minute. Add tomatoes, basil, oregano, garlic salt and pepper; simmer, uncovered, for 10 minutes. Remove from the heat; gently stir in zucchini. Place in an ungreased 13-in. x 9-in. x 2-in. baking dish. Top with stuffing mix; sprinkle with Parmesan cheese. Cover and bake at 350° for 20 minutes. Uncover and sprinkle with mozzarella cheese. Return to the oven for 10 minutes or until golden. **Yield:** 6-8 servings.

GARDEN PATCH CAKE

This moist cake deliciously combines shredded zucchini, carrots and beets with chocolate chips.

1 cup vegetable oil
3 eggs
1-1/2 cups sugar
1 teaspoon vanilla extract
2 cups all-purpose flour
2 teaspoons baking powder
1-1/2 teaspoons ground cinnamon
1/4 teaspoon salt
1 cup finely shredded carrots
1 cup finely shredded zucchini
1/2 cup finely shredded beets
1-1/2 cups semisweet chocolate chips
FROSTING:
2 packages (3 ounces *each*) cream cheese, softened
1/2 cup butter *or* margarine, softened
2 teaspoons vanilla extract
4-1/2 cups confectioners' sugar

In a large mixing bowl, beat oil, eggs, sugar and vanilla. Combine flour, baking powder, cinnamon and salt; add to egg mixture and mix well. Stir in vegetables. Add chips and mix well. Pour into a greased and floured 13-in. x 9-in. x 2-in. baking pan. Bake at 350° for 35-40 minutes or until a wooden pick inserted near the center comes out clean. Cool 15 minutes; remove from pan to a wire rack to cool completely. For frosting, beat cream cheese, butter and vanilla until light and fluffy. Gradually beat in confectioners' sugar until smooth. Spread over cake. Store in the refrigerator. **Yield:** 12-16 servings.

CAKE DECORATING

3/4 cup shortening
1 teaspoon vanilla extract
1/2 teaspoon almond extract
Pinch salt
3 to 3-1/2 cups confectioners' sugar
2 tablespoons milk
7 wooden craft *or* Popsicle sticks (4-1/2 inches)
1/2 teaspoon baking cocoa
Red, yellow, orange and green liquid *or* paste food coloring
Pastry tips—#5 and #10 round, #67 leaf and #20 star
5 pastry bags *or* small heavy-duty resealable plastic bags

In a mixing bowl, cream shortening, extracts and salt. Gradually beat in sugar alternately with milk until smooth and stiff. Cover with a wet paper towel and plastic wrap until ready to use.

To make trellis: Lay 5 craft or Popsicle sticks on a sheet of waxed paper with 1/4 in. between bottom of sticks (ends that are inserted into cake) and 1/2 in. between tops. Spread back side of remaining sticks with frosting; position across 5 sticks 1 in. and 2 in. down from top. Allow to dry, about 1 hour. Press bottom of sticks into upper left corner of cake.

To make garden patch: Using a toothpick, mark a 5-1/2-in. x 3-1/2-in. patch in lower right corner. Lightly sprinkle with cocoa; gently press into cake.

To make vegetables and border: Cut a small hole in corner of a pastry or plastic bag; insert #10 round tip. Combine 1/4 cup frosting and red food coloring; fill bag. Holding bag straight up and down, form 8-10 tomatoes in front of the trellis. Prepare another bag, inserting #5 round tip. Combine 1/4 cup frosting and yellow food coloring; fill bag. Using the same procedure, form rows of small dots to create kernels of 8-10 ears of corn in upper right corner. Wash #10 tip and insert into a third bag. Combine 1/2 cup frosting and orange food coloring; fill bag. Using the same procedure, form 3 rows of 4 carrots on the garden patch.

Add green food coloring to remaining frosting. Prepare a fourth bag, inserting leaf tip; fill with some of the frosting. Form husks on edges of ears of corn; add stems and leaves to tomatoes and carrots. Add vines to trellis. Prepare a fifth bag, inserting the star tip; fill with remaining green frosting. Form a border around base and upper edge of cake.

Cooking for One or Two

Don't sacrifice quality or taste when cooking for one or two people. Just turn to these perfectly portioned main dishes, side dishes, desserts and more.

Singling Out Good Food

WITH the hectic days and hurried nights around Christmas, why not present yourself with this fast, festive dinner?

Chicken Monterey lets you prepare a single serving of your favorite poultry. Then tastefully top it off with homemade No-Cook Cranberry Relish. Mashed Potato for One is a just-the-right-size recipe you'll likely reach for throughout the year. Don't forget to add a side of your favorite vegetables.

You'll find more singular sensations on the following four pages.

CHICKEN MONTEREY
(Pictured at left)

Being single, I buy chicken when it's on sale and freeze the breasts individually. Then I can use them one at a time for delicious recipes like this.

—Melanie DuLac
Northboro, Massachusetts

  1 **boneless skinless chicken breast half**
Dash salt and pepper
  1/2 **teaspoon chopped fresh parsley**
  1/8 **teaspoon dried tarragon**
  1 **ounce Monterey Jack *or* cheddar cheese (cut into a 2-1/2- x 1/2-inch stick)**
  2 **tablespoons all-purpose flour**
  1 **egg, beaten**
  2 **tablespoons seasoned *or* plain dry bread crumbs**
  1 **tablespoon butter *or* margarine**
  1 **tablespoon cooking oil**

Pound chicken to 1/4-in. thickness. Season the inside with salt, pepper, parsley and tarragon. Place cheese in the center and fold chicken around it. Roll in flour; dip into egg, then roll in crumbs. Place chicken, seam side down, on a plate; refrigerate for 30 minutes. In a skillet, saute chicken in butter and oil until golden. Place in a small shallow baking dish. Bake, uncovered, at 375° for 15 minutes or until juices run clear. **Yield:** 1 serving.

NO-COOK CRANBERRY RELISH
(Pictured at left)

This relish is a tangy addition served with chicken or ham and makes a plate look so pretty! It's so important to do something nice for yourself, and a good meal is an easy way to do that.

—Eleanor Slimak
Chicago, Illinois

  1/2 **cup fresh *or* frozen cranberries**
  1/4 **medium orange, peeled**
  1 **tablespoon sugar**

In a blender or food processor, process all ingredients until coarsely chopped. Cover and chill for 30 minutes or until ready to serve. **Yield:** 1 serving.

MASHED POTATO FOR ONE
(Pictured at left)

With two dance classes, bowling and crafting each week, this easy recipe is perfect when I need an out-of-the-ordinary side dish but have little time.

—Winifred Chesborough
Truth or Consequences, New Mexico

✓ **This tasty dish uses less sugar, salt and fat. Recipe includes *Diabetic Exchanges*.**

  1 **medium potato, peeled and cooked**
  2 **tablespoons milk**
  1 **tablespoon cream cheese, softened**
  1 **teaspoon butter *or* margarine**
  1/4 **teaspoon salt, optional**
  1/8 **teaspoon snipped fresh dill *or* pinch dill weed**
Dash pepper

In a small bowl, mash all ingredients until smooth. Spoon into a small microwave-safe dish. Cook on high for 1 minute or until heated through. **Yield:** 1 serving. **Diabetic Exchanges:** One serving (prepared with skim milk, margarine and light cream cheese and without salt) equals 1-1/2 starch, 1 fat; also, 163 calories, 134 mg sodium, 9 mg cholesterol, 22 gm carbohydrate, 5 gm protein, 6 gm fat.

Eat Your Vegetables

Buy bags of individually frozen vegetables and remove only as much as needed at a time.

Try tossing your favorite plain vegetables with herbs and seasonings or bottled salad dressings. It's deliciously different.

WHETHER served as a hearty lunch or light dinner, the classic combination of soup, salad and bread is sure to please folks who are cooking for themselves. And with these perfectly portioned recipes, you won't have to hassle with leftovers!

Stash away the bulky soup kettle and reach for Peasant Soup for One. It simmers in a saucepan in a matter of minutes. Of course, if you care to serve this soup to a larger crowd, the ingredients can easily be increased.

Most salads don't keep very long in the refrigerator. So why bother making a full-size recipe that will only go to waste? Apple Ham Salad makes just the right amount and uses everyday ingredients. And the tasty dressing makes this salad a special single-serving dish.

Scaling down muffin recipes can be tricky business. You'll come to rely on this recipe for two Sunny Cornmeal Muffins. Now you won't have to make a big batch when cooking for one. Plus, this pair of muffins is perfect alongside the soup and salad.

PEASANT SOUP FOR ONE
(Pictured at left)

In the mood for soup? There's no need to open a can when it's so easy to simmer up a bowl of this soup. I first had this at a favorite restaurant. When it was removed from the menu, I duplicated it at home using herbs from my garden.
—Kay Harris
Amarillo, Texas

✓ **This tasty dish uses less sugar, salt and fat.**
Recipe includes *Diabetic Exchanges*.

  1 **boneless skinless chicken breast half**
    (4 ounces), cubed
1/4 **cup chopped onion**
  1 **small potato, cubed**
  1 **small carrot, sliced**
  1 **cup chicken broth**
  1 **garlic clove, minced**
1/4 **teaspoon dried tarragon, crushed**
1/8 **teaspoon salt, optional**
Dash pepper
  2 **teaspoons chopped fresh parsley**

Coat a saucepan with nonstick cooking spray; brown chicken over medium-high heat. Add the next eight ingredients; bring to a boil. Reduce heat. Cover and simmer for 20-25 minutes or until vegetables are tender. Sprinkle with parsley. **Yield:** 1 serving. **Diabetic Exchanges:** One serving (prepared with fat-free low-sodium broth and without salt) equals 3 very lean meat, 2 vegetable, 1-1/2 starch; also, 280 calories, 95 mg sodium, 73 mg cholesterol, 31 gm carbohydrate, 31 gm protein, 3 gm fat.

APPLE HAM SALAD
(Pictured at left)

With precooked ham, chopped apples and celery, this refreshing salad is crisp and hearty. —Ruth Stekert
Manheim, Pennsylvania

✓ **This tasty dish uses less sugar, salt and fat.**
Recipe includes *Diabetic Exchanges*.

  2 **tablespoons mayonnaise**
1/4 **teaspoon prepared mustard**
1/2 **teaspoon honey**
1/2 **teaspoon lemon juice**
Dash ground cloves
1/2 **cup julienned fully cooked ham**
  1 **small apple, diced**
  1 **celery rib, sliced**
Lettuce leaves, optional
1/4 **teaspoon sesame seeds, toasted**

In a bowl, blend the first five ingredients. Stir in ham, apple and celery. Cover and refrigerate for 1 hour. Serve on a bed of lettuce if desired. Sprinkle with sesame seeds. **Yield:** 1 serving. **Diabetic Exchanges:** One serving (prepared with fat-free mayonnaise) equals 3 lean meat, 1-1/2 fruit; also, 253 calories, 328 mg sodium, 48 mg cholesterol, 25 gm carbohydrate, 22 gm protein, 8 gm fat.

SUNNY CORNMEAL MUFFINS
(Pictured at left)

Most muffin recipes make such a big batch that I can't possibly eat them all before they go bad. So I was thrilled to find this recipe. —Lethea Weber
Newport, Arkansas

1/4 **cup biscuit/baking mix**
1/4 **cup yellow cornmeal**
  1 **tablespoon sugar**
1/4 **cup milk**
  1 **egg, beaten**
  2 **teaspoons vegetable oil**

In a small bowl, combine the baking mix, cornmeal and sugar. Combine milk, egg and oil; stir into dry ingredients just until moistened (batter will be thin). Pour into two greased 6-oz. ovenproof custard cups. Bake at 400° for 15-18 minutes or until golden brown. **Yield:** 2 muffins. **Editor's Note:** Muffins may be baked in a muffin pan; fill empty cups halfway with water.

THESE economical specialties lend themselves wonderfully to dining alone. Plus, they're quick to prepare.

You don't have to break the bank to prepare a meat-and-potatoes meal like Hobo Dinner.

Egg and Tomato Salad gets its zest from a flavorful dressing made with everyday ingredients.

Individual Apple Crisp makes an ordinary fruit extraordinary. Give leftover meat a lift by adding it to a fast, flavorful Quesadilla.

HOBO DINNER

(Pictured at left)

Dining alone has its benefits…I can cook what I like! This is a favorite.
—Pat Walter
Pine Island, Minnesota

✓ **This tasty dish uses less sugar, salt and fat. Recipe includes *Diabetic Exchanges*.**

- **1/4 pound ground beef**
- **1 potato, sliced**
- **1 carrot, sliced**
- **2 tablespoons chopped onion**
- **1 sheet heavy-duty aluminum foil (18 inches x 13 inches)**

Salt and pepper to taste

Shape beef into a patty; place in the center of foil with potato, carrot and onion. Sprinkle with salt if desired and pepper. Fold foil over and seal well; place on a baking sheet. Bake at 350° for 45 minutes. Open foil carefully. **Yield:** 1 serving. **Diabetic Exchanges:** One serving (prepared with extra-lean ground beef and without salt) equals 3 meat, 1-1/2 starch, 1 vegetable; also, 371 calories, 81 mg sodium, 82 mg cholesterol, 28 gm carbohydrate, 28 gm protein, 16 gm fat.

EGG AND TOMATO SALAD

(Pictured at left)

I often need to prepare a salad just for myself. And when I want a change from ordinary greens, this is the recipe I reach for.
—Joan Schroeder
Pinedale, Wyoming

- **1 small tomato, thinly sliced**
- **1 hard-cooked egg, sliced**

Leaf lettuce

- **2 tablespoons olive *or* vegetable oil**
- **4 teaspoons lemon juice**
- **1/2 teaspoon sugar**
- **1/4 teaspoon seasoned salt**
- **1/4 teaspoon ground mustard**

- **1/8 to 1/4 teaspoon salt**
- **1/8 teaspoon pepper**
- **2 drops hot pepper sauce**

On a salad plate or in a bowl, alternate tomato and egg slices on lettuce. In a small bowl, whisk remaining ingredients until smooth. Pour over salad and serve immediately. **Yield:** 1 serving.

INDIVIDUAL APPLE CRISP

(Pictured at left)

This single-serving dessert that doesn't leave leftovers is a fitting finale to all meals.
—Lethea Weber
Newport, Arkansas

- **1 small apple, peeled and sliced**
- **1 tablespoon all-purpose flour**
- **1 tablespoon brown sugar**
- **1 tablespoon quick-cooking oats**
- **1/8 teaspoon ground cinnamon**

Dash ground nutmeg
Dash salt

- **1 tablespoon cold butter *or* margarine**

Place apple in a small greased baking dish. In a small bowl, combine the dry ingredients; cut in butter until crumbly. Sprinkle over apple. Bake, uncovered, at 375° for 30-35 minutes or until apple is tender. **Yield:** 1 serving.

QUESADILLA

I often make this quesadilla just for myself. It's a snap to prepare.
—Amber Waddell
Grand Rapids, Michigan

- **1 to 2 teaspoons cooking oil**
- **2 flour tortillas (6 inches)**
- **1/2 cup shredded cheddar cheese, *divided***
- **1/2 cup cubed cooked chicken, turkey, pork *or* beef**
- **1/4 cup sliced fresh mushrooms**
- **1/2 cup shredded Monterey Jack cheese, *divided***

Sour cream and salsa, optional

Heat oil in a nonstick skillet; add one tortilla. Layer with half the cheddar cheese, all of the chicken and mushrooms and half the Monterey Jack cheese. Top with the second tortilla. Cover and heat until cheese melts and bottom tortilla is crisp and golden brown. Turn over; sprinkle remaining cheese on top. Cook until bottom tortilla is crisp and golden brown and cheese is melted. Cut into wedges; serve with sour cream and salsa if desired. **Yield:** 1 serving.

Cooking for 'Just the Two of Us'

YOU DON'T have to stop dishing up old-fashioned Sunday dinners even though you're cooking for two instead of 12!

Tender, moist Swiss Steak for Two is an old-time favorite that appeals to all. And don't serve boxed scalloped potatoes when you can easily prepare the homemade Creamy Scalloped Potatoes also featured here. You'll both agree they're irresistible.

Baked Peaches conveniently calls for canned fruit, so you can serve this simply delicious dessert throughout the year…even when peaches aren't in season. It's a fresh finale to a down-home dinner.

The following four pages present more delightful dishes for two.

SWISS STEAK FOR TWO

Even though I'm a widow, I still cook for two since I frequently have a friend or grandchild join me for lunch or dinner. This is a hearty main dish that gets great flavor and color from tomatoes, green pepper and onion.
—Mildred Stubbs
Hamlet, North Carolina

- 2 tablespoons all-purpose flour
- 3/4 teaspoon salt, *divided*
- 1/4 teaspoon pepper
- 3/4 pound boneless round steak (1/2 inch thick)
- 1 tablespoon cooking oil
- 1 can (8 ounces) stewed tomatoes
- 1 medium green pepper, sliced
- 1 medium onion, sliced

In a resealable plastic bag, combine flour, 1/4 teaspoon salt and pepper. Cut steak into two pieces; place in bag and shake to coat. In a skillet over medium heat, brown steak in oil. Add tomatoes. Reduce heat; cover and simmer for 40 minutes. Add green pepper, onion and remaining salt. Cover and simmer until meat is tender, about 30 minutes. **Yield:** 2 servings.

CREAMY SCALLOPED POTATOES

Here's a rich, comforting side dish that bakes up golden brown. It's a wonderful recipe for the colder months. I often serve these potatoes with my Swiss Steak (recipe above).
—Mildred Stubbs

- 2 tablespoons butter *or* margarine
- 2 tablespoons all-purpose flour
- 1/2 teaspoon salt
- 1/8 teaspoon pepper
- 1-1/2 cups milk
- 2 large potatoes, peeled and thinly sliced
- 2 tablespoons finely chopped onion

In a small saucepan over low heat, melt butter. Stir in flour, salt and pepper until smooth and bubbly. Gradually add milk, stirring constantly. Bring to a boil; boil for 2 minutes. Remove from the heat. In a greased 1-qt. baking dish, layer half of the potatoes. Add the onion and half of the sauce. Top with remaining potatoes and sauce. Cover and bake at 350° for 35-40 minutes or until potatoes are tender. **Yield:** 2 servings.

BAKED PEACHES

For a dressed-up dessert without the fuss, try these baked peaches. This easy recipe makes a special treat that's different and delicious.
—Mildred Stubbs

- 4 canned peach halves, drained
- 2 tablespoons chopped walnuts
- 2 tablespoons brown sugar
- 1/2 teaspoon grated orange peel
- 1/8 teaspoon ground allspice
- Ice cream, optional

Place peaches with cut side up in a 1-qt. baking dish. In a small bowl, combine walnuts, brown sugar, orange peel and allspice; sprinkle over peaches. Bake, uncovered, at 350° for 20 minutes. Serve warm, topped with ice cream if desired. **Yield:** 2 servings.

Table for Two

Setting the table for two can be fun! Look for "white sales" and seasonal closeouts and pick up a variety of colorful placemats and napkins.

An inexpensive bouquet of fresh flowers livens up the table with little fuss.

Take in a new view! When serving more elegant fare, move to the dining room. Or head outdoors for casual dining.

AS a couple of these mouth-watering ideas deliciously prove, farm-fresh eggs make any main meal memorable, especially featured at breakfast. They're inexpensive, readily available and easy to keep on hand. And because they come in their own individual "packages", they can serve a handful or a whole crowd!

Thanks to a taste-tempting combination of flavors, ordinary eggs get some sparking up in Chili Omelet and Zesty Poached Eggs.

A hearty helping of Breakfast Potatoes really rounds out a morning meal. And no breakfast would be complete without hot-off-the-griddle Pancakes for Two topped with rich syrup.

PANCAKES FOR TWO
(Pictured at left)

These light and fluffy pancakes are perfectly portioned for two, so there's no need to worry about what to do with leftover batter. For a special taste treat, I like to prepare them with blueberries. —Annemarie Pietila
Farmington Hills, Michigan

1-1/4 cups all-purpose flour
1 tablespoon sugar
1 teaspoon baking powder
1/2 teaspoon baking soda
1/2 teaspoon salt
1-1/4 cups buttermilk
2 tablespoons vegetable oil
1 egg, beaten
1 cup fresh *or* frozen blueberries, optional

In a bowl, combine flour, sugar, baking powder, baking soda and salt. Combine buttermilk, oil and egg; stir into dry ingredients and mix well. Fold in blueberries if desired. Pour batter by 1/4 cupfuls onto a lightly greased hot griddle; turn when bubbles form on top of pancakes. Cook until second side is golden brown. **Yield:** about 8 pancakes.

ZESTY POACHED EGGS
(Pictured at left)

My husband and I have two young daughters, but we often eat breakfast before they get up. This meal is one of our favorite "breakfasts for two". It's tasty and fun and looks great on the table. —Kathy Scott
Hemingford, Nebraska

4 eggs, poached
2 slices whole wheat bread, toasted
1/4 cup Cheese Whiz, melted
1/4 cup salsa

Place two eggs on each slice of toast. Top with cheese sauce and salsa. Serve immediately. **Yield:** 2 servings.

CHILI OMELET

This omelet, stuffed with cheese, olives and sour cream and topped with zippy taco sauce, is easy to prepare. It makes a wonderfully filling main dish that's great for breakfast, lunch or supper. —Pamela Immekus
Sullivan, Missouri

4 eggs
1/2 cup shredded cheddar cheese
1/4 cup sliced ripe olives
1/4 cup canned chopped green chilies
1/8 teaspoon salt
Dash pepper
2 tablespoons butter *or* margarine
3 tablespoons sour cream
3 tablespoons taco sauce

In a small bowl, beat eggs. Add cheese, olives, chilies, salt and pepper. In a 10-in. skillet, heat the butter until it sizzles; turn pan to coat. Add egg mixture; cook over medium heat. As eggs set, lift eggs, letting the uncooked portion flow underneath. When eggs are set, spoon sour cream across center; fold in half. Transfer to a warm plate; top with taco sauce. Serve immediately. **Yield:** 2 servings.

BREAKFAST POTATOES

These cheesy, hearty potatoes are a super morning side dish. Because they take no time to fix, I prepare them often for me and my husband. They go great with just about any type of entree. —Judy Dupree
Thief River Falls, Minnesota

2 medium potatoes, peeled and sliced
1/4 cup sliced onion
1/4 teaspoon salt
1/8 teaspoon pepper
1/4 teaspoon garlic salt
1/4 cup shredded cheddar cheese

Coat a 9-in. microwave-safe plate with nonstick cooking spray. Arrange potato and onion slices on plate; sprinkle with seasonings. Cover and microwave on high for 5 minutes. Sprinkle with cheese. Cover and microwave on high for 4-5 minutes or until potatoes are tender. **Yield:** 2 servings.
Editor's Note: This recipe was tested in a 700-watt microwave.

JUST BECAUSE you're planning meals for two doesn't mean you always have to rely on prepackaged foods to put them together.

The lighter fare featured here shows that cooking from scratch lets you control your sugar, salt and fat intake. Plus, it's more economical than purchasing prepared foods.

Baked Fish and Roasted Potatoes were specifically developed for folks on restricted diets. But they're guaranteed to please all palates. And Special Citrus Salad is loaded with oranges, grapefruit, cucumber, onion and tomato. So it's naturally good for you.

BAKED FISH
(Pictured at left)

I created this quick recipe after enjoying a seafood dish with Parmesan cheese sprinkled on top at a restaurant. The cheese added extra zip and gave me the idea to try the fish at home. —*Lynn Mathieu*
Great Mills, Maryland

✓ **This tasty dish uses less sugar, salt and fat. Recipe includes** *Diabetic Exchanges*.

1/2 **pound panfish fillets (perch, trout** *or* **whitefish)**
4 **teaspoons grated Parmesan cheese**
1/2 **teaspoon dill weed**

Place fish in a 10-in. pie plate that has been coated with nonstick cooking spray. Sprinkle with Parmesan cheese and dill. Bake, uncovered, at 350° for 8-10 minutes or until fish flakes easily with a fork. **Yield:** 2 servings. **Diabetic Exchanges:** One serving (prepared with perch) equals 3 very lean meat; also, 119 calories, 131 mg sodium, 104 mg cholesterol, 0 carbohydrate, 23 gm protein, 2 gm fat.

ROASTED POTATOES
(Pictured at left)

I like trying out new recipes on my boyfriend, and he's always willing to taste-test. The lemon juice and thyme give these golden potatoes fabulous flavor.
—*Sally Sue Campbell*
Greenville, Tennessee

✓ **This tasty dish uses less sugar, salt and fat. Recipe includes** *Diabetic Exchanges*.

2 **tablespoons lemon juice**
4 **teaspoons olive** *or* **vegetable oil**
1/2 **teaspoon dried thyme**

1/2 **teaspoon garlic salt**
1/8 **teaspoon pepper**
6 **small red potatoes (about 1 pound), quartered**

In a medium bowl, combine lemon juice, oil, thyme, garlic salt and pepper. Add potatoes; toss to coat. Place in an 8-in. square baking dish that has been coated with nonstick cooking spray. Bake, uncovered, at 450° for 40 minutes or until potatoes are tender, stirring occasionally. **Yield:** 2 servings. **Diabetic Exchanges:** One serving equals 2 fat, 1 starch; also, 173 calories, 335 mg sodium, 0 cholesterol, 22 gm carbohydrate, 2 gm protein, 9 gm fat.

SPECIAL CITRUS SALAD
(Pictured at left)

An easy tangy dressing makes this salad taste as impressive as it looks. —*Janice Ubaldi*
Petaluma, California

1 **can (11 ounces) mandarin oranges**
1/4 **cup minced fresh parsley**
3 **tablespoons French** *or* **Italian salad dressing**
1 **teaspoon dried basil**
1 **teaspoon lemon juice**
1/2 **teaspoon brown sugar**
1/4 **teaspoon pepper**
Pinch dried tarragon
Leaf lettuce, optional
1/2 **grapefruit, peeled and sectioned**
1/2 **small cucumber, sliced**
1/2 **small red onion, sliced**
1 **small tomato, sliced**

Drain juice from oranges into a small bowl; set oranges aside. To the juice, add the parsley, salad dressing, basil, lemon juice, brown sugar, pepper and tarragon; mix well. Line individual salad plates with lettuce if desired; arrange oranges, grapefruit, cucumber, onion and tomato on lettuce. Serve with dressing. **Yield:** 2 servings.

Splendid Seafood

Store-bought frozen fish should be wrapped tightly with no air in the packaging. Purchase fillets that are individually frozen so you can remove from your freezer the exact amount you need.

Leftover cooked fish should be tightly covered and refrigerated no more than 1 to 2 days.

Cooking for a Crowd

Whether you're planning a menu for 20 or 200, you'll appreciate these large-quantity recipes. They come from experienced cooks, so they're guaranteed to be real potluck pleasers!

PICTURED AT LEFT: Potluck Spareribs, Cherry Pudding Cake, Ham 'n' Cheese Potato Salad and Layered Spinach Salad (recipes are on the next page).

POTLUCK SPARERIBS

(Pictured on page 288)

These ribs are perfect for a potluck...I never have leftovers. I've been planning meals since I was 13. Now I love cooking for my family. —Sheri Kirkman
Lancaster, New York

> 6 pounds pork spareribs
> 1-1/2 cups ketchup
> 3/4 cup packed brown sugar
> 1/2 cup vinegar
> 1/2 cup honey
> 1/3 cup soy sauce
> 1-1/2 teaspoons ground ginger
> 1 teaspoon salt
> 3/4 teaspoon ground mustard
> 1/2 teaspoon garlic powder
> 1/4 teaspoon pepper

Cut ribs into serving-size pieces; place with the meaty side up on racks in two greased 13-in. x 9-in. x 2-in. baking pans. Cover tightly with foil. Bake at 350° for 1-1/4 hours or until meat is tender. Drain; remove racks and return ribs to pans. Combine remaining ingredients; pour over ribs. Return to the oven, uncovered, for 35 minutes or until sauce coats ribs, basting occasionally. Ribs can also be grilled over medium-hot coals for the last 35 minutes instead of baking. **Yield:** 12 servings.

HAM 'N' CHEESE POTATO SALAD

(Pictured on page 288)

This is one potato salad that's hearty enough to be a main dish. My family especially likes to take it along when we go on picnics. —Tamara Sellman
Barrington, Illinois

> 2-1/2 to 3 pounds red potatoes
> 1 cup mayonnaise
> 1/2 cup sour cream
> 2 tablespoons Dijon mustard
> 1 teaspoon celery seed
> 1/2 teaspoon salt
> 1/4 teaspoon pepper
> 8 ounces cheddar cheese, cubed
> 8 ounces Monterey Jack cheese, cubed
> 2 cups diced fully cooked ham
> 3/4 cup chopped fresh tomatoes
> 1/4 cup sliced green onions
> 1/4 cup minced fresh parsley

In a saucepan, cook potatoes in boiling salted water until tender; drain and cool. Meanwhile, in a large salad bowl, combine mayonnaise, sour cream, mustard, celery seed, salt and pepper; mix well. Cut potatoes into cubes. Add to mayonnaise mixture and toss to coat. Add remaining ingredients; mix well. Cover and refrigerate for at least 2 hours. **Yield:** 16-20 servings.

LAYERED SPINACH SALAD

(Pictured on page 288)

When this dish goes on a buffet, it's a real eye-catcher with its colorful layers. People enjoy the unique addition of cheese tortellini. This salad always goes fast! —Lori Cumberledge
Pasadena, Maryland

> ✓ This tasty dish uses less sugar, salt and fat.
> Recipe includes *Diabetic Exchanges*.

> 1 package (9 ounces) refrigerated cheese tortellini
> 2 cups shredded red cabbage
> 6 cups torn fresh spinach
> 2 cups cherry tomatoes, halved
> 1/2 cup sliced green onions
> 1 bottle (8 ounces) ranch salad dressing
> 8 bacon strips, cooked and crumbled, optional

Cook tortellini according to package directions. Drain and rinse with cold water; set aside. In a large glass bowl, layer cabbage, spinach, tortellini, tomatoes and onions. Pour dressing over top; sprinkle with bacon if desired. Cover and refrigerate for at least 1 hour. **Yield:** 10 servings. **Diabetic Exchanges:** One 1-cup serving (prepared with low-fat salad dressing and without bacon) equals 1 starch, 1 vegetable, 1 fat; also, 159 calories, 350 mg sodium, 14 mg cholesterol, 16 gm carbohydrate, 6 gm protein, 8 gm fat.

CHERRY PUDDING CAKE

(Pictured on page 288)

A cross between a cake and a cobbler, this pudding is a hit whenever I make it to share at a potluck. My family insists I make an extra batch to leave at home. A neighbor shared the recipe over 30 years ago. —Brenda Parker
Kalamazoo, Michigan

> 2 cups all-purpose flour
> 2-1/2 cups sugar, *divided*

4 teaspoons baking powder
1 cup milk
2 tablespoons vegetable oil
2 cans (14-1/2 ounces *each*) water-packed pitted tart red cherries, well drained
2 to 3 drops red food coloring, optional
1/8 teaspoon almond extract
Whipped cream *or* ice cream, optional

In a mixing bowl, combine flour, 1 cup of sugar, baking powder, milk and oil; pour into a greased shallow 3-qt. baking dish. In a bowl, combine cherries, food coloring if desired, extract and remaining sugar; spoon over batter. Bake at 375° for 40-45 minutes or until a wooden pick inserted in the cake portion comes out clean. Serve warm with whipped cream or ice cream if desired. **Yield:** 10-12 servings.

PIZZA CASSEROLE

My husband, Mark, and I host Wednesday night dinners at our church. It's a fun way to help others and to experiment with different recipes. No matter how many times I prepare it, this remains a favorite.
—Becky Carnell
Rowlett, Texas

4 pounds spaghetti, broken into 2-inch pieces
5 to 7 quarts prepared spaghetti sauce
3 to 4 pounds sliced pepperoni
3 pounds shredded mozzarella cheese

Cook spaghetti according to package directions; drain. In six greased 13-in. x 9-in. x 2-in. baking dishes, layer equal amounts of spaghetti, sauce and pepperoni. Bake, uncovered, at 350° for 30 minutes. Sprinkle with cheese; bake 15 minutes longer. **Yield:** 50-60 servings.

CHOCOLATE CHIP COOKIE MIX

These are the perfect cookies when cooking for a crowd because the mix can be prepared and stored for months. Also, you can bake a couple batches of cookies at a time and freeze.
—Helen Woronik
Salem, Connecticut

COOKIE MIX:
9 cups all-purpose flour
4 teaspoons baking soda
2 teaspoons salt
3 cups packed brown sugar

3 cups sugar
4 cups shortening
COOKIES:
6 cups Cookie Mix (above)
1 teaspoon vanilla extract
2 eggs, beaten
2 cups (12 ounces) semisweet chocolate chips

Thoroughly combine dry ingredients; cut in shortening until crumbly. Store in an airtight container in a cool dry place up to 6 months. **Yield:** 18 cups of mix (3 batches of cookies). **To make cookies:** Combine mix, vanilla and eggs; mix well. Fold in chocolate chips. Drop by tablespoonfuls 2 in. apart onto greased baking sheets. Bake at 375° for 10-12 minutes or until golden brown. Remove from pans to cool on wire racks. **Yield:** about 5 dozen per batch.

FRUITED CHICKEN SALAD

Grapes, mandarin oranges and pineapple chunks add fruity goodness and color to this hearty main-dish salad. It's perfect for a large luncheon.
—Marion Baker
Sun Lakes, Arizona

2 cans (20 ounces *each*) pineapple chunks
20 cups cubed cooked chicken
12 cups cooked rice
8 cups seedless green grape halves
4 cups sliced celery
4 cans (15 ounces *each*) mandarin oranges, drained
4 cans (8 ounces *each*) sliced water chestnuts, drained and halved
4 cups mayonnaise *or* salad dressing
7 tablespoons frozen orange juice concentrate
1 to 2 tablespoons salt
1 teaspoon pepper
4 cups slivered almonds, toasted

Drain the pineapple, reserving 2 tablespoons of juice. Combine pineapple and the next six ingredients. Combine mayonnaise, concentrate, salt, pepper and the reserved pineapple juice until smooth; toss with chicken mixture. Chill several hours or overnight. Add almonds just before serving. **Yield:** 40-50 servings.

Proven Potluck Tip
Make holiday cutout cookies ahead and freeze without frosting. Before a get-together, thaw and frost. They taste fresh-baked.

FARMER'S STRATA
(Pictured at left)

For an inexpensive and easy-to-prepare dish, try this hearty casserole. You can assemble it ahead and bake it just before leaving for a potluck. People go back for seconds since it includes tasty basic ingredients like bacon, cheese and potatoes.
—Pat Kuether
Westminster, Colorado

  1 pound sliced bacon, cut into 1/2-inch pieces
  2 cups chopped fully cooked ham
  1 small onion, chopped
10 slices white bread, cubed
  1 cup cubed cooked potatoes
  3 cups (12 ounces) shredded cheddar cheese
  8 eggs
  3 cups milk
  1 tablespoon Worcestershire sauce
  1 teaspoon ground mustard
Pinch salt and pepper

In a skillet, cook bacon until crisp; add ham and onion. Cook and stir until onion is tender; drain. In a greased 13-in. x 9-in. x 2-in. baking dish, layer half the bread cubes, potatoes and cheese. Top with all of the bacon mixture. Repeat layers of bread, potatoes and cheese. In a bowl, beat the eggs; add milk, Worcestershire sauce, mustard, salt and pepper. Pour over all. Cover and chill overnight. Remove from refrigerator 30 minutes before baking. Bake, uncovered, at 325° for 65-70 minutes or until a knife inserted near the center comes out clean. **Yield:** 12-16 servings.

BREAKFAST SAUSAGE BREAD
(Pictured at left)

Any time we take this savory, satisfying bread to a potluck, it goes over very well. We never bring any home. My husband generally makes this bread and prides himself on the beautiful golden loaves.
—Shirley Caldwell
Northwood, Ohio

2 loaves (1 pound *each*) frozen white bread dough, thawed

PICTURED AT LEFT: Farmer's Strata, Breakfast Sausage Bread, Cherry-Cheese Cake (recipes on this page) and Cranberry Crumble Coffee Cake (recipe on page 294).

1/2 pound mild pork sausage
1/2 pound hot pork sausage
1-1/2 cups diced fresh mushrooms
1/2 cup chopped onion
  3 eggs
2-1/2 cups (10 ounces) shredded mozzarella cheese
  1 teaspoon dried basil
  1 teaspoon dried parsley flakes
  1 teaspoon dried rosemary, crushed
  1 teaspoon garlic powder

Allow dough to rise until nearly doubled. Meanwhile, in a skillet over medium heat, cook and crumble sausage. Add mushrooms and onion. Cook and stir until the sausage is browned and vegetables are tender; drain. Cool. Beat 1 egg; set aside. To sausage mixture, add 2 eggs, cheese and seasonings; mix well. Roll each loaf of dough into a 16-in. x 12-in. rectangle. Spread half the sausage mixture on each loaf to within 1 in. of edges. Roll up jelly-roll style, starting at a narrow end; seal edges. Place on a greased baking sheet. Bake at 350° for 25 minutes; brush with beaten egg. Bake 5-10 minutes more or until golden brown. Serve warm. **Yield:** 2 loaves.

CHERRY-CHEESE CAKE
(Pictured at left)

This dessert is simple to make but looks so beautiful on the buffet. I appreciate easy recipes like this that have impressive results. Since it makes two pans, everyone can save room for a creamy, fruity piece or two. For a little variety, substitute apple or blueberry pie filling for the cherry filling.
—Marilyn Hillam
Brigham City, Utah

1 package (18-1/4 ounces) white cake mix
2 packages (8 ounces *each*) cream cheese, softened
4 cups confectioners' sugar
1 pint whipping cream, whipped
2 cans (21 ounces *each*) cherry pie filling

Prepare cake mix according to package directions. Pour into two greased 13-in. x 9-in. x 2-in. baking pans. Bake at 350° for 20 minutes or until a wooden pick inserted near the center comes out clean. Cool. In a mixing bowl, beat the cream cheese and sugar until fluffy; fold in the whipped cream. Spread over each cake. Top with pie filling. Chill for 4 hours or overnight. **Yield:** 24-30 servings.

CRANBERRY CRUMBLE COFFEE CAKE

(Pictured on page 292)

People are delighted to find the cranberry sauce swirled inside this tempting coffee cake. With the crumble topping, moist cake and tangy filling, it won't last long!
—Jeani Robinson
Weirton, West Virginia

  1/4 cup chopped almonds
    1 cup sugar
  1/2 cup butter *or* margarine, softened
    1 teaspoon vanilla extract
    2 eggs
    2 cups all-purpose flour
1-1/4 teaspoons baking powder
  1/2 teaspoon baking soda
  1/4 teaspoon salt
    1 cup (8 ounces) sour cream
    1 cup whole-berry cranberry sauce
TOPPING:
  1/4 cup all-purpose flour
  1/4 cup sugar
  1/4 cup chopped almonds
  1/4 teaspoon vanilla extract
    2 tablespoons cold butter *or* margarine

Sprinkle almonds over the bottom of a greased 9-in. springform pan; set aside. In a mixing bowl, cream the sugar, butter and vanilla; beat on medium for 1-2 minutes. Add eggs, one at a time, beating well after each. Combine dry ingredients; add to batter alternately with sour cream. Mix well. Spread 3 cups over almonds. Spoon cranberry sauce over batter. Top with remaining batter. For topping, combine flour, sugar, almonds and vanilla; cut in butter until crumbly. Sprinkle over batter. Bake at 350° for 70-75 minutes or until a wooden pick inserted near the center comes out clean. Cool in pan on a wire rack for 15 minutes; remove sides of pan. Serve warm. **Yield:** 12 servings.

HOT TURKEY SANDWICHES

Twice a week for 20 years, I've prepared meals for our church community. These deliciously down-home turkey sandwiches are always on the menu.
—Mollie Flack
Copper Center, Alaska

    8 quarts turkey *or* chicken broth
    2 tablespoons onion powder
    4 teaspoons garlic powder
    4 teaspoons salt

    2 teaspoons pepper
    2 cups cornstarch
    2 cups cold water
    2 cups half-and-half cream
    2 teaspoons browning sauce
  40 large slices roast turkey breast (about 6-1/2 pounds cooked turkey)
  40 slices bread
    7 quarts hot mashed potatoes (about 45 medium potatoes)

In a large kettle, bring broth and seasonings to a boil. Combine cornstarch and water; gradually add to boiling broth. Cook and stir for 2 minutes. Add cream and browning sauce. Place each slice of turkey on a slice of bread; top with a spoonful of mashed potatoes. Cover with gravy. **Yield:** 20 servings.

OVEN SCRAMBLED EGGS

I cook for a youth camp during the summer, so I've grown accustomed to preparing large quantities of food. This fluffy egg recipe was originally handed down to me by a previous cook. I made a few alterations and came up with this easy-to-make version.
—Terry Bringhurst
Berlin, New Jersey

    2 cups butter *or* margarine, melted
 100 eggs, beaten
    3 tablespoons salt
2-1/2 quarts milk

Divide butter among four 13-in. x 9-in. x 2-in. baking dishes. Combine eggs and salt; mix well. Gradually stir in milk. Pour evenly into baking dishes. Bake, uncovered, at 350° for 10 minutes; stir. Bake 10-15 minutes more or until eggs are set. Serve immediately. **Yield:** 100 servings.

RAISIN SAUCE FOR BAKED HAM

Here's a recipe I discovered in my mother's recipe collection. It's a thick, flavorful old-fashioned sauce that's perfect any time of year.
—Cheryl Holland
Ortonville, Michigan

  12 cups packed brown sugar
  3/4 cup ground mustard
  3/4 cup all-purpose flour
    6 cups raisins
    6 cups vinegar
6-1/2 quarts water

In a Dutch oven, combine brown sugar, mustard and flour; mix well. Fold in the raisins. Stir in vinegar and water; bring to a boil. Reduce heat; simmer, uncovered, for 2 to 2-1/2 hours or until mixture is like syrup, stirring occasionally. Serve over hot baked ham slices. **Yield:** 100 servings.

CHEERY CHERRY PUNCH

Whenever I need to quench the thirst of a hungry horde, this is the recipe I reach for. It's a refreshing beverage that nicely complements a variety of meals.
—*Florence Grewe*
Long Prairie, Minnesota

  3 **packages (3 ounces *each*) cherry gelatin**
  2 **to 3 cups sugar**
  6 **cups boiling water**
  1 **can (46 ounces) unsweetened pineapple juice**
  1 **can (12 ounces) frozen orange juice concentrate, thawed**
  1 **can (12 ounces) frozen lemonade concentrate, thawed**
  1 **gallon cold water**
  2 **bottles (2 liters *each*) ginger ale**

Dissolve gelatin and sugar in boiling water. Add pineapple juice, concentrates and cold water; mix well. Freeze. Just before serving, add ginger ale and mix well. **Yield:** 60 (4-ounce) servings.

BUSHEL OF COOKIES

This recipe turns out what seems like a bushelful of cookies—that's probably how it got its name. But watch out! They disappear fast in a crowd. The flavor of the raisins and pecans comes through in every bite, and the butterscotch chips add a deliciously distinctive taste.
—*Martha Schwartz*
Jackson, Ohio

  2 **pounds raisins**
  1 **pound pecans**
  5 **cups butter *or* margarine, softened**
11 **cups sugar**
12 **eggs**
  1 **cup maple syrup**
  1 **quart milk**
1/4 **cup vanilla extract**
12 **cups quick-cooking oats**
21 **cups all-purpose flour**

1/4 **cup baking powder**
1/4 **cup baking soda**
  2 **teaspoons salt**
  2 **packages (12 ounces *each*) butterscotch chips**

Grind or finely chop raisins and pecans; set aside. In a mixing bowl, cream butter and sugar. Add eggs, a few at a time, mixing well after each. Add syrup, milk and vanilla; mix well. Stir in oats, raisins and pecans. Combine flour, baking powder, baking soda and salt; stir into oat mixture. Fold in chips. Cover and chill for 2 hours. Drop by rounded tablespoonfuls 2 in. apart onto greased baking sheets. Bake at 350° for 15 minutes. **Yield:** about 24 dozen.

SPICY HASH BROWNS

These easy hash browns really rise to the occasion at any breakfast gathering. They're group-approved specialties that are guaranteed to please.
—*Mike Marratzo*
Florence, Alabama

  25 **pounds potatoes, peeled**
2-1/2 **pounds fully cooked ham, diced**
2-1/2 **pounds onions, chopped**
2-1/2 **pounds green peppers, chopped**
  1/2 **pound fresh jalapeno peppers, chopped**
   1 **cup butter *or* margarine, *divided***
   2 **jars (4 ounces *each*) pimientos, drained and chopped**
  10 **teaspoons salt**
   5 **teaspoons pepper**
2-1/2 **teaspoons cayenne pepper**
2-1/2 **teaspoons paprika**
   2 **pounds (8 cups) shredded cheddar cheese**

Cook potatoes in water until just tender; drain. Chill several hours or overnight; grate into a large bowl. Saute ham, onions and peppers in 1/4 cup butter until tender. Cool 10 minutes; add to potatoes. Add pimientos and seasonings; mix well. On a griddle, cook potatoes in remaining butter until browned; turn over and cook the second side until browned. Place half of the potatoes on a platter; top with cheese and remaining potatoes. **Yield:** 90-100 servings.

> ### *Proven Potluck Tip*
> To keep salad greens cold and crisp on the way to a party, add a cup of frozen peas to the salad and cover tightly.

BASIL BEAN SALAD
(Pictured at left)

I included garbanzo beans in a recipe for three-bean salad for taste and color. It's now a family favorite.
—Ruth Ann Ramuscak
Merrillville, Indiana

1 can (15 to 16 ounces) kidney beans, rinsed and drained
1 can (15 ounces) garbanzo beans, rinsed and drained
1 can (14-1/2 ounces) wax beans, drained
1 can (14-1/2 ounces) cut green beans, drained
1 medium green pepper, thinly sliced
1 medium onion, thinly sliced
1/2 cup white wine vinegar
1/2 cup vegetable oil
6 tablespoons sugar
1 tablespoon minced fresh basil *or* 1 teaspoon dried basil
3/4 teaspoon ground mustard
3/4 to 1 teaspoon salt

In a large bowl, combine beans, green pepper and onion. In a small bowl, combine vinegar, oil, sugar, basil, mustard and salt. Pour over bean mixture; toss to coat. Chill for several hours or overnight. **Yield:** 10-12 servings.

SANDWICH FOR 12
(Pictured at left)

This sandwich makes a fun supper, and it's also a great way to feed your bunch lunch. *—Melissa Collier*
Wichita Falls, Texas

1/2 cup old-fashioned oats
1/2 cup boiling water
2 tablespoons butter *or* margarine
1 package (16 ounces) hot roll mix
3/4 cup warm water (110° to 115°)
2 eggs, beaten
1 tablespoon dried minced onion
TOPPING:
1 egg
1 teaspoon garlic salt
1 tablespoon dried minced onion
1 tablespoon sesame seeds

PICTURED AT LEFT: Basil Bean Salad, Sandwich for 12, Tropical Slush (recipes on this page) and Coconut Crunch Delight (recipe on page 298).

FILLING:
1/2 cup mayonnaise
4 teaspoons prepared mustard
1/2 teaspoon prepared horseradish
Lettuce leaves
8 ounces thinly sliced fully cooked ham
8 ounces thinly sliced cooked turkey
1 medium green pepper, thinly sliced
1 medium onion, thinly sliced
6 ounces thinly sliced Swiss cheese
2 large tomatoes, thinly sliced

In a large bowl, combine oats, boiling water and butter; let stand for 5 minutes. Meanwhile, dissolve yeast from hot roll mix in warm water. Add to the oat mixture with eggs and onion. Add flour mixture from hot roll mix; stir well (do not knead). Spread dough into a 10-in. circle on a well-greased pizza pan. Cover with plastic wrap coated with non-stick cooking spray; let rise in a warm place until doubled, about 45 minutes. Beat egg and garlic salt; brush gently over dough. Sprinkle with onion and sesame seeds. Bake at 350° for 25-30 minutes or until golden brown. Remove from pan; cool on a wire rack. Split lengthwise. Combine mayonnaise, mustard and horseradish; spread over cut sides of loaf. Layer with remaining filling ingredients. Cut into wedges. **Yield:** 12 servings.

TROPICAL SLUSH
(Pictured at left)

I first tried this refreshing beverage at a church reception. It's perfect for any type of party.
—Hollis Mattson
Brush Prairie, Washington

6 cups water, *divided*
5 medium ripe bananas
2 cups sugar
2 cans (12 ounces *each*) frozen orange juice concentrate, thawed
1 can (12 ounces) frozen lemonade concentrate, thawed
1 can (46 ounces) unsweetened pineapple juice
3 bottles (2 liters *each*) lemon-lime soda

In a blender container, process 1 cup of water, bananas and sugar until smooth. Pour into a large container; add the concentrates, pineapple juice and remaining water. Cover and freeze. Remove from freezer 2 hours before serving. Just before serving, break up and mash mixture with a potato masher. Stir in soda. **Yield:** 40-50 servings (about 11 quarts).

COCONUT CRUNCH DELIGHT

(Pictured on page 296)

I tasted this light dessert 7 years ago at a potluck and got the recipe from my mom's dear friend. It's a terrific way to end a heavy meal. —Debby Chiorino
Oxnard, California

1/2 cup butter *or* margarine, melted
1 cup all-purpose flour
1-1/4 cups flaked coconut
1/4 cup packed brown sugar
1 cup slivered almonds
1 package (3.4 ounces) instant vanilla pudding mix
1 package (3.4 ounces) instant coconut cream pudding mix
2-2/3 cups cold milk
2 cups whipped topping
Fresh strawberries, optional

In a bowl, combine the first five ingredients; press lightly into a greased 13-in. x 9-in. x 2-in. baking pan. Bake at 350° for 25-30 minutes or until golden brown, stirring every 10 minutes to form coarse crumbs. Cool. Divide crumb mixture in half; press half into the same baking pan. In a mixing bowl, beat pudding mixes and milk. Fold in whipped topping; spoon over the crust. Top with remaining crumb mixture. Cover and refrigerate overnight. Garnish with strawberries if desired. **Yield:** 12-16 servings.

BARBECUED PORK SANDWICHES

(Pictured at right)

When our office held a bridal shower for a co-worker, we presented the future bride with a collection of our favorite recipes. I included this one. It's a nice alternative to a typical ground beef barbecue.
—Karla Labby
Otsego, Michigan

2 boneless pork loin roasts (2-1/2 to 3 pounds *each*)
1 cup water
2 teaspoons salt
2 cups ketchup
2 cups diced celery
1/3 cup steak sauce
1/4 cup packed brown sugar
1/4 cup vinegar
2 teaspoons lemon juice
20 to 25 hamburger buns

Place roasts in an 8-qt. Dutch oven; add water and salt. Cover and cook on medium-low heat

PICTURED AT RIGHT: Barbecued Pork Sandwiches, Warm Cabbage Slaw, German Potato Salad and Caramel Nut Bars (recipes on these pages).

for 2-1/2 hours or until meat is tender. Remove roasts and shred with a fork; set aside. Skim fat from cooking liquid and discard. Drain all but 1 cup cooking liquid. Add meat, ketchup, celery, steak sauce, brown sugar, vinegar and lemon juice. Cover and cook over medium-low heat for 1-1/2 hours. Serve on buns. **Yield:** 20-25 servings.

WARM CABBAGE SLAW

(Pictured at right)

For a deliciously different dish to pass, try this cabbage. It cooks up tender yet still refreshingly crisp, and the almonds add flavor and crunch. —Mary Crigler
Fayette, Missouri

16 cups thinly sliced cabbage (about 3 pounds)
2 garlic cloves, minced
1/4 cup vegetable *or* olive oil
1/2 cup sliced green onions
2 tablespoons cornstarch
1/3 cup water
4 teaspoons soy sauce
1 teaspoon salt
1/4 cup slivered almonds, toasted

In a 5-qt. Dutch oven, combine cabbage, garlic and oil; cook over low heat for 3-4 minutes, tossing lightly. Cover and cook for 4-5 minutes or until cabbage is crisp-tender. Add onions. Combine cornstarch, water, soy sauce and salt; mix well. Pour over cabbage; toss lightly. Cook and stir for 2-3 minutes or until mixture thickens. Place in a serving bowl; top with almonds. Serve warm. **Yield:** 12-16 servings.

GERMAN POTATO SALAD

(Pictured above right)

A dear German friend gave me this recipe. I take this satisfying salad to many gatherings. The seasonings give traditional potato salad enticing flavor.
—Donna Cline
Pensacola, Kansas

12 medium potatoes
12 bacon strips

1-1/2 cups chopped onion
1/4 cup all-purpose flour
1/4 cup sugar
1 tablespoon salt
1 teaspoon celery seed
1 teaspoon ground mustard
Pinch pepper
1-1/2 cups water
3/4 cup vinegar
Chopped fresh parsley

In a saucepan, cook potatoes until just tender; drain. Peel and slice into a large bowl; set aside. In a skillet, cook bacon until crisp. Remove bacon to paper towels; discard all but 1/3 cup of drippings. Saute onion in drippings until tender. Stir in the next six ingredients. Gradually stir in water and vinegar; bring to a boil, stirring constantly. Cook and stir 2 minutes more. Pour over potatoes. Crumble bacon and gently stir into potatoes. Sprinkle with parsley. **Yield:** 12-14 servings.

Proven Potluck Tip
Bring corn on the cob, hot and ready to eat, to your next party. Just boil the corn before leaving, wrap in aluminum foil and stack in a thermal chest.

CARAMEL NUT BARS
(Pictured above)

No one can resist these chewy caramel and chocolate bars with a delightful oat crust and topping. They're perfect for a potluck since a little goes a long way.
—Pat Hills
South Dayton, New York

1 cup quick-cooking oats
1 cup packed brown sugar
1 cup all-purpose flour
3/4 cup butter *or* margarine, melted
1/2 teaspoon baking soda
1/4 teaspoon salt
1 package (14 ounces) caramels
1/3 cup milk
1 cup (6 ounces) semisweet chocolate chips
1/2 cup chopped walnuts

Combine the first six ingredients; sprinkle 1 cup into a greased 13-in. x 9-in. x 2-in. baking pan (do not press). Bake at 350° for 10 minutes. In the top of a double boiler over boiling water, cook and stir caramels and milk until caramels are melted. Pour over crust. Top with chocolate chips and nuts. Sprinkle with remaining oat mixture. Bake at 350° for 10 minutes. Cool on a wire rack. Refrigerate to set the caramel. **Yield:** 3 dozen.

PIZZA MEATBALLS

(Pictured above)

With mozzarella cheese inside, these tender meatballs taste almost like pizza. Young and old alike love them, so I can make them for any occasion.

—Kim Kanatzar
Blue Springs, Missouri

2 **pounds ground beef**
2 **cups seasoned bread crumbs**
1 **cup milk**
1/4 **cup dried minced onion**
2 **teaspoons garlic salt**
1/4 **teaspoon pepper**

1 **block (8 ounces) mozzarella cheese**
1/3 **cup all-purpose flour**
1/4 **cup cooking oil**
2 **jars (28 ounces** *each***) pizza sauce**

In a bowl, combine the first six ingredients just until mixed. Shape into 48 small meatballs. Cut mozzarella into 48 cubes, 1/2 in. each; push a cube into the center of each meatball, covering the cheese completely with meat. Roll lightly in flour. In a large skillet, cook the meatballs in oil until browned; drain. Add pizza sauce; bring to a boil. Reduce heat; cover and simmer for 25-30 minutes or until meatballs are no longer pink. Serve over pasta or rice, in buns or as an appetizer. **Yield:** 4 dozen.

PICTURED AT LEFT: Pizza Meatballs, Layered Basil Salad and Bake-Sale Lemon Bars (recipes on these pages).

LAYERED BASIL SALAD
(Pictured at left)

The basil in the dressing makes this salad stand out from the usual layered ones. The colorful ingredients look beautiful and taste wonderful together. It's especially impressive on a potluck buffet.
—Marcy Cella
L'Anse, Michigan

  4 cups torn assorted salad greens
  4 medium carrots, julienned
1-1/2 cups cooked macaroni shells
  2 cups frozen peas, thawed
  1 medium red onion, diced
  3/4 pound fully cooked ham, cubed
  1/3 cup shredded Swiss cheese
  1/3 cup shredded cheddar cheese
DRESSING:
  1 cup mayonnaise
  1/2 cup sour cream
  2 teaspoons Dijon mustard
1-1/2 teaspoons chopped fresh basil *or* 1/2
      teaspoon dried basil
  1/2 teaspoon salt
  1/4 teaspoon pepper
  2 hard-cooked eggs, cut into wedges,
      optional

In a 3-1/2-qt. glass bowl, layer greens, carrots, macaroni, peas, onion, ham and cheeses. In a small bowl, combine the first six dressing ingredients; spread over salad. Garnish with eggs if desired. Cover and chill for several hours. **Yield:** 12-14 servings.

BAKE-SALE LEMON BARS
(Pictured above left)

The recipe for these tangy bars comes from my cousin Bernice, a farmer's wife famous for cooking up feasts. This mouth-watering dessert is perfect year-round. It's also a best-seller at church mission sales.
—Mildred Keller
Rockford, Illinois

1-1/2 cups all-purpose flour
  2/3 cup confectioners' sugar
  3/4 cup butter *or* margarine, softened
  3 eggs, lightly beaten
1-1/2 cups sugar

  3 tablespoons all-purpose flour
  1/4 cup lemon juice
Additional confectioners' sugar

Combine flour, sugar and butter; pat into a greased 13-in. x 9-in. x 2-in. baking pan. Bake at 350° for 20 minutes. Meanwhile, in a bowl, whisk eggs, sugar, flour and lemon juice until frothy; pour over the hot crust. Bake at 350° for 20-25 minutes or until light golden brown. Cool on a wire rack. Dust with confectioners' sugar. Cut into squares. **Yield:** 3-4 dozen.

VEGETABLE CHEESE SALAD

Here's a satisfying salad that's garden-fresh. It stars three delicious cheeses and refreshing vegetables like crisp cucumber, bell peppers and juicy tomatoes. This unique salad makes a nice light lunch or super side dish.
—Shary Geidner
Clear Lake, Iowa

  3 cups shredded cheese: cheddar, Monterey
      Jack *and/or* mozzarella
  1 medium cucumber, chopped
  1 medium tomato, seeded and chopped
  1 green onion, thinly sliced
  1/2 cup chopped green pepper
  1/2 cup chopped sweet red pepper
  1/2 cup sour cream
  1/4 cup mayonnaise
  1 tablespoon lemon juice
  1 tablespoon lime juice
  1 garlic clove, minced
  1/2 teaspoon Dijon mustard
  1/2 teaspoon dried basil
  1/2 teaspoon dried marjoram
  1/2 teaspoon paprika
  1/2 teaspoon sugar
Lettuce, optional

In a bowl, combine cheeses, cucumber, tomato, onion and peppers. In a small bowl, combine sour cream, mayonnaise, lemon and lime juice, garlic, mustard and seasonings; mix well. Pour over salad and toss to coat. Chill for 1 hour. Serve in a lettuce-lined bowl if desired. **Yield:** 16 servings.

Proven Potluck Tip

Afraid to lose a cherished bowl or plate you take to a potluck? Look for pretty, inexpensive dishes at thrift stores and rummage sales.

CHICKEN SALAD FOR 50

When this was served at a women's luncheon, there were lots of recipe requests. The creamy dressing, grapes and cashews make it extra special.

—*Florence Vold*
Story City, Iowa

- 9 cups diced cooked chicken
- 9 cups cooked mini shell macaroni
- 8 cups diced celery
- 8 cups seedless green grape halves
- 18 hard-cooked eggs, diced
- 2 cans (20 ounces *each*) pineapple tidbits, drained

DRESSING:
- 1 quart mayonnaise
- 2 cups (16 ounces) sour cream
- 2 cups whipped topping
- 1/4 cup lemon juice
- 1/4 cup sugar
- 1-1/2 teaspoons salt
- 2 cups cashew pieces

In a large bowl, combine the first six ingredients. Combine the first six dressing ingredients and whisk until smooth. Pour over salad; toss to coat. Chill at least 1 hour. Fold in cashews just before serving. **Yield:** 50 (1-cup) servings.

OATMEAL RAISIN BARS

These bars are so popular with my family that I have to hide them if they're bound for a buffet! I got the recipe from a farm wife with growing boys. I always make plenty, because even this big batch disappears quickly around our house. —*Annie Beiler*
Leola, Pennsylvania

- 9-1/2 cups crisp rice cereal
- 5 cups quick-cooking oats
- 2 cups (12 ounces) semisweet chocolate chips
- 1-1/2 cups raisins
- 1 cup chopped peanuts
- 1-1/2 pounds marshmallows
- 1/4 cup butter *or* margarine
- 1/2 cup honey
- 1/4 cup vegetable oil
- 1/4 cup peanut butter

In a large bowl, combine the first five ingredients; set aside. In a large saucepan over low heat, cook and stir marshmallows and butter until smooth. Add honey, oil and peanut butter; mix well. Pour over cereal mixture; toss to coat. Pour into two

greased 13-in. x 9-in. x 2-in. baking pans; press firmly and evenly. Cool. **Yield:** 3 dozen.

CHUNKY TURKEY CHILI

When I needed a hearty dish for a benefit cook-off at work, I decided on this recipe but substituted ground turkey for the beef. Everyone raved about the delicious flavor, and many people requested the recipe.

—*Judith Southcombe*
Aurora, Colorado

- 5 pounds ground turkey
- 6 cups chopped celery
- 2 medium green peppers, chopped
- 2 large onions, chopped
- 2 cans (28 ounces *each*) crushed tomatoes
- 2 cups water
- 2 envelopes (1-3/4 ounces *each*) chili seasoning mix
- 1 to 2 tablespoons chili powder
- 2 cans (15 to 16 ounces *each*) kidney beans, rinsed and drained

In a Dutch oven over medium heat, brown turkey; drain. Add celery, peppers and onions; cook and stir for 5 minutes. Add the next four ingredients; bring to a boil. Reduce heat; cover and simmer for 2 hours. Add beans; heat through. **Yield:** 24 (1-cup) servings.

PICNIC HOT DOGS

Kids of all ages will have a hard time eating just one of these hot dogs. The tempting ground beef sauce makes them especially fun and flavorful.

—*Helen Thomas*
Ravenswood, West Virginia

- 10 pounds ground beef
- 5 cups chopped onions
- 2 medium green peppers, chopped
- 1 gallon tomato juice
- 1/2 gallon tomato paste
- 2-1/2 cups chopped celery
- 1/3 cup dried parsley flakes
- 3 tablespoons salt
- 1/4 cup sugar
- 1 tablespoon pepper
- 1 tablespoon dried oregano
- 1-1/2 teaspoons garlic powder
- 145 hot dogs and buns

In a large kettle, brown beef; drain. Add the next 11 ingredients; bring to a boil. Reduce heat; cover and simmer for 4 hours, stirring occasionally. Heat the hot dogs; place in buns and top each with about 1/4 cup sauce. **Yield:** 145 servings (about 8 quarts sauce).

BUFFET RICE SALAD

This is a lovely dish that combines common ingredients in an interesting and flavorful way. I'm regularly requested to bring this salad to potlucks.
—Dixie Terry
Marion, Illinois

    4 pounds uncooked long grain rice
    1 quart mayonnaise
    2 cups minced onion
    2 cups French salad dressing
1/2 cup prepared mustard
    4 teaspoons salt
    1 teaspoon pepper
    6 pounds cubed fully cooked ham
   36 hard-cooked eggs, chopped
    8 cups (2 pounds) shredded cheddar cheese
    6 cups thinly sliced celery
    4 cups sweet pickle relish
    2 cups diced pimientos, drained

Cook rice according to package directions. Combine the mayonnaise, onion, dressing, mustard, salt and pepper; add to hot rice and mix well. Cool to room temperature. Fold in ham, eggs, cheese, celery, relish and pimientos; mix well. Chill for 2-3 hours. **Yield:** 80 (1-cup) servings.

GLAZED CARROTS FOR A CROWD

Whenever our church group plans a gathering, I'm undoubtedly asked to bring these carrots. I never complain because I enjoy them as much as everyone else!
—Bonnie Milner
DeRidder, Louisiana

    3 cups sugar
    1 cup light corn syrup
1/2 cup butter (no substitutes)
1/4 cup orange juice concentrate
    1 teaspoon salt
    2 cans (No. 10 size) baby carrots, drained
      or 12 pounds medium carrots, sliced and cooked

In a large saucepan, combine the first five ingredients; bring to a boil over medium heat. Boil for 5 minutes, stirring occasionally. Place carrots in

two 13-in. x 9-in. x 2-in. baking pans; pour sugar mixture over carrots. Bake, uncovered, at 350° for 30-40 minutes or until heated through. **Yield:** 45 servings.

BROCCOLI CAULIFLOWER SALAD

For a crunchy side dish, why not try this salad? With crisp vegetables and crumbled bacon, this salad's a popular one at fund-raiser dinners. *—Janet Les*
Chilliwack, British Columbia

    5 pounds broccoli, cut into florets
    5 pounds cauliflower, cut into florets
1-2/3 cups thinly sliced green onions
    6 cups mayonnaise
  1/3 cup sugar
    3 tablespoons vinegar
2-1/2 pounds sliced bacon, cooked and crumbled
1-1/2 pounds cheddar cheese, cubed

In a large bowl, combine broccoli, cauliflower and onions. Combine mayonnaise, sugar and vinegar; pour over vegetables 1 hour before serving. Chill. Just before serving, add bacon and cheese; toss. **Yield:** 100 (1/2-cup) servings.

MOLDED CRANBERRY SALAD

For 75 years, our parish, Christ Church, has served special luncheons. This fresh and fruity salad is one of my favorite recipes when cooking for a large group.
—Shea Szachara
Binghamton, New York

   10 packages (6 ounces *each*) strawberry gelatin
    5 quarts boiling water
   10 cans (16 ounces *each*) whole-berry cranberry sauce
    5 cups cold water
    5 cans (20 ounces *each)* crushed pineapple, undrained
    5 cans (15 ounces *each*) mandarin oranges, drained

Dissolve gelatin in boiling water. Break up and stir in cranberry sauce; mix well. Stir in cold water; mix well. Chill until partially set. Fold in pineapple with liquid and oranges. Coat five 13-in. x 9-in. x 2-in. pans with nonstick cooking spray; pour about 11-1/2 cups gelatin mixture into each. Chill until firm, about 4 hours. **Yield:** 100 servings.

SCALLOPED CARROTS

After my mother passed away, I found this recipe of hers. It's a crowd-pleasing side dish with a comforting sauce and a pretty, golden crumb topping.
—Cheryl Holland
Ortonville, Michigan

- 1-1/2 **cups butter** *or* **margarine**
- 1-1/2 **cups all-purpose flour**
- 3 **quarts milk**
- 1/2 **cup lemon juice**
- 4 **teaspoons celery salt**
- 2 **teaspoons salt**
- 2 **teaspoons pepper**
- 6 **pounds carrots, diced and cooked**
- 2-1/2 **pounds shredded cheddar cheese**
- 6 **cups crushed butter-flavored crackers**

In a saucepan over medium heat, cook and stir butter and flour until smooth and bubbly, about 2 minutes. Gradually add milk and lemon juice; cook and stir until thickened. Add celery salt, salt and pepper; mix well. Remove from the heat. In four greased 2-1/2-qt. baking dishes, layer half of the carrots, sauce, cheese and crackers. Repeat layers. Bake, uncovered, at 350° for 45-50 minutes or until top is golden brown. Serve immediately. **Yield:** 50 servings.

DILLY ROLLS

These versatile rolls are great served warm alongside any dinner. My family even enjoys the rolls after they're cool, stuffed with filling like egg salad or ham salad, so I always make a big batch. *—Mary Bickel*
Terre Haute, Indiana

✓ **This tasty dish uses less sugar, salt and fat.**
   Recipe includes *Diabetic Exchanges.*

- 2 **cups (16 ounces) small curd cottage cheese**
- 2 **tablespoons butter** *or* **margarine**
- 2 **packages (1/4 ounce** *each***) active dry yeast**
- 1/2 **cup warm water (110° to 115°)**
- 2 **eggs** *or* **egg substitute equivalent**
- 1/4 **cup sugar**
- 2 **tablespoons dried minced onion**
- 1 **to 2 tablespoons dill weed**
- 1 **tablespoon salt**
- 1/2 **teaspoon baking soda**
- 4-1/2 **to 5 cups all-purpose flour**

In a large saucepan over medium heat, cook cottage cheese and butter until butter is melted. Cool to 110° to 115°. In a large mixing bowl, dissolve yeast in wa-

PICTURED AT RIGHT: Wild Rice Salad, Potluck Chicken Casserole and Cranberry Cake (recipes on these pages).

ter. Add eggs, sugar, onion, dill, salt, baking soda and cottage cheese mixture. Add 3 cups flour; beat until smooth. Add enough remaining flour to form a soft dough. Turn onto a floured board; knead until smooth and elastic, about 6-8 minutes. Place in a greased bowl, turning once to grease top. Cover and let rise in a warm place until doubled, about 1 hour. Punch dough down. Form into 24 balls; place in a greased 13-in. x 9-in. x 2-in. baking pan that has been sprayed with nonstick cooking spray. Cover and let rise until doubled, about 45 minutes. Bake at 350° for 20-25 minutes. **Yield:** 2 dozen. **Diabetic Exchanges:** One roll (prepared with margarine and egg substitute) equals 1-1/2 starch, 1/2 fat; also, 125 calories, 383 mg sodium, 3 mg cholesterol, 20 gm carbohydrate, 5 gm protein, 3 gm fat.

WILD RICE SALAD
(Pictured at right)

Since cranberries grow well in this area, I love to use the dried variety to give recipes like this hearty salad color and tang. Visitors love it. *—Lyn Graebert*
Park Falls, Wisconsin

✓ **This tasty dish uses less sugar, salt and fat.**
   Recipe includes *Diabetic Exchanges.*

- 4 **cups cooked wild rice**
- 1 **can (8 ounces) sliced water chestnuts, drained and chopped**
- 1/2 **cup thinly sliced celery**
- 1/2 **cup chopped green pepper**
- 1/2 **cup frozen peas, thawed**
- 1/2 **cup dried cranberries**
- 1/4 **cup thinly sliced green onions**
- 1/4 **cup minced fresh parsley**
- 1/3 **cup cranberry juice**
- 1/3 **cup vinegar**
- 2 **teaspoons olive** *or* **vegetable oil**
- 3/4 **teaspoon dried basil**
- 3/4 **teaspoon sugar**
- 3/4 **teaspoon salt, optional**
- 1/4 **teaspoon pepper**
- 1/2 **cup chopped pecans, optional**

In a large bowl, combine the first eight ingredients. In a small bowl, combine cranberry juice, vinegar, oil, basil, sugar, salt if desired and pepper; mix well. Pour over rice mixture and toss to coat. Refrigerate overnight. Just before serving, stir in

pecans if desired. **Yield:** 12 servings. **Diabetic Exchanges:** One 1/2-cup serving (prepared without salt and pecans, and with rice that was cooked without salted water) equals 1 starch, 1 vegetable; also, 114 calories, 18 mg sodium, 0 cholesterol, 24 gm carbohydrate, 3 gm protein, 1 gm fat.

POTLUCK CHICKEN CASSEROLE
(Pictured above)

With its down-home flavor, rich sauce and golden topping, folks go back for seconds of this casserole.
—*Ruth Andrewson*
Leavenworth, Washington

- 1/2 cup chopped fresh mushrooms
- 3 tablespoons finely chopped onion
- 2 garlic cloves, minced
- 4 tablespoons butter *or* margarine, *divided*
- 3 tablespoons all-purpose flour
- 1-1/4 cups milk
- 3/4 cup mayonnaise
- 4 cups cubed cooked chicken
- 3 cups cooked long grain rice
- 1 cup chopped celery
- 1 cup frozen peas, thawed
- 1 jar (2 ounces) diced pimientos, drained
- 2 teaspoons lemon juice
- 1 teaspoon salt
- 1/2 teaspoon pepper
- 3/4 cup coarsely crushed cornflakes

In a saucepan over medium heat, saute mushrooms, onion and garlic in 3 tablespoons butter until tender. Stir in flour until thoroughly combined. Gradually add milk; bring to a boil. Cook and stir for 2 minutes or until thickened and bubbly. Remove from the heat; stir in mayonnaise until smooth. Add chicken, rice, celery, peas, pimientos, lemon juice, salt and pepper; mix well. Spoon into an ungreased 13-in. x 9-in. x 2-in. baking dish. Melt remaining butter; toss with cornflakes. Sprinkle over casserole. Bake, uncovered, at 350° for 30-35 minutes or until bubbly. **Yield:** 8-10 servings.

CRANBERRY CAKE
(Pictured above)

You can't beat this cake to showcase true fall flavor. The ruby cranberries stay bright and beautiful and their tartness is irresistible. —*Marilyn Paradis*
Woodburn, Oregon

- 3 eggs
- 2 cups sugar
- 3/4 cup butter *or* margarine, softened
- 1 teaspoon almond extract
- 2 cups all-purpose flour
- 2-1/2 cups fresh *or* frozen cranberries, thawed
- 2/3 cup chopped pecans
- Whipped cream, optional

In a mixing bowl, beat eggs with sugar until slightly thickened and light in color, about 5 minutes. Add butter and extract; beat 2 minutes. Stir in flour just until combined. Stir in cranberries and pecans. Spread in a greased 13-in. x 9-in. x 2-in. baking pan. Bake at 350° for 45-50 minutes or until a wooden pick inserted near the center comes out clean. Serve with whipped cream if desired. **Yield:** 16-20 servings.

General Recipe Index

This handy index lists every recipe by food category and/or major ingredient, so you can easily locate recipes.

APPETIZERS & SNACKS

Cold Appetizers
Best Deviled Eggs, 184
Stuffed Jalapenos, 267

Dips
Creamy Taco Dip, 13
Low-Fat Bean Dip, 13
Lunch-Box Apple Dip, 16
Picadillo Dip, 9
Pretzels with Cheese Dip, 9
Strawberry Yogurt Dip, 11
Veggie Christmas Tree, 8
Veggie Dill Dip, 11

Hot Appetizers
Appetizer Meatballs, 12
Garlic-Parmesan Crisps, 10
Golden Chicken Nuggets, 12
Herbed Garlic Toast, 8
Honey-Mustard Turkey Meatballs, 11
Mozzarella Puffs, 16
Peanut Butter Puffs, 15
Pronto Mini Pizzas, 14
Shrimp and Cheddar Snacks, 13

Snack Mixes
Cajun Popcorn, 12
Crunchy Italian Mix, 12
Popcorn Snacks, 15
Sweet Potato Chips, 10
Sweet Snack Mix, 14
Trail Mix, 267
White Chocolate Party Mix, 10
Zesty Snack Mix, 16

Spreads
Braunschweiger Spread, 15
Chutney Cracker Spread, 13
Creamy Chicken Spread, 14
Creamy Egg Spread, 12
Cucumber Dill Spread, 11
Hearty Cheese Spread, 10
Pecan-Date Cheese Ball, 15
Pineapple Cream Cheese Spread, 10
Salmon Party Spread, 8
Tuna Snack Spread, 15
Wade's Shrimp Spread, 16

APPLES
A.M. Delight Muffins, 99
All-Day Apple Butter, 112
Almond-Apple Stuffed Turkey, 87
Apple Beet Salad, 28
Apple Brown Betty, 251
Apple Cheesecake, 189
Apple Date Crisp, 179
Apple Ham Salad, 279
Apple Orange Bread, 98
Apple Pie Filling, 137
Baked Apples in Caramel Cream, 150
Blue-Ribbon Apple Cake, 149
Bumbleberry Pie, 148
Cinnamon Apple Refresher, 17
Double Apple Salad, 29
Easy Apple Crisp, 134
Hot Apple Sundaes, 257
Individual Apple Crisp, 281
Lunch-Box Apple Dip, 16
Peachy Applesauce Salad, 25
Perfect Apple Pie, 152
Roast Goose with Apple-Raisin
   Stuffing, 204
Southern Ambrosia Apple Pie, 142
Spiced Red Cabbage, 179

APRICOTS
Apricot Ham Steak, 228
Apricot Muffins, 101
Apricot Rice Custard, 151

ASPARAGUS
Asparagus Chicken Chowder, 35
Asparagus with Pimientos, 188
Beef and Asparagus Stir-Fry, 93
Creamy Asparagus and Carrots, 54
Oven-Baked Asparagus, 61
Sesame Asparagus, 230
Spring Breakfast Strata, 76
Wild Asparagus Salad, 23

BACON & CANADIAN BACON
Big Sandwich, 38
Dilly Turkey Melt, 32
Farmer's Strata, 293
Hearty Chicken Club, 36
Mom's Easy Bean Bake, 58
Old-Fashioned Baked Beans, 184
Tasty Turkey Sub, 217
Wilted Lettuce, 21

BANANAS
Banana Crumb Muffins, 96
Banana Oatmeal Cookies, 124
Tropical Slush, 297

BARLEY
Barley and Corn Casserole, 60
Barley-Stuffed Peppers, 75
Beef Barley Soup, 47
Mushroom Barley Soup, 41
Vegetable Barley Soup, 44

BARS & BROWNIES
Bake-Sale Lemon Bars, 301
Black Walnut Brownies, 121
Caramel Nut Bars, 299
Cupcake Brownies, 127
Fudge Brownies, 116
Harvest Pumpkin Brownies, 125
Mocha Brownies, 120
Oatmeal Raisin Bars, 302
Peanut Butter Bars, 197
Rich Chocolate Brownies, 119
S'mores Bars, 127
Snack Bars, 116
Spiderweb Brownies, 128

BEANS

Baked Beans
Molasses Baked Beans, 267
Mom's Easy Bean Bake, 58
Old-Fashioned Baked Beans, 184

Canned Beans
Basil Bean Salad, 297
Bean Soup with Dumplings, 48
Black Bean and Corn Salad, 24
Garbanzo Cucumber Salad, 217
Hearty Ribs and Beans, 91
Kielbasa and Beans, 69
Low-Fat Bean Dip, 13
Red Beans and Sausage, 81
Three-Bean Salad, 27

Dried Beans
Ham and Bean Soup, 43
Lucky Bean Soup, 46
Navy Bean Stew, 86

Green Beans
Festive Green Beans, 219
Garlicky Green Beans, 57
Green Bean Sesame Salad, 20
Herbed Green Beans, 58
Marinated Garden Platter, 26
Tangy Green Bean Casserole, 61

BEEF *(also see Corned Beef and Ground Beef)*

Main Dishes
Beef and Asparagus Stir-Fry, 93
Beef Rouladen, 178
Bohemian Beef Dinner, 65
Country-Fried Steaks, 89
Fabulous Fajitas, 87
Garlic Grilled Steaks, 232
Grilled Fajitas, 78
Herbed Pot Roast, 71
Marinated Sirloin Steak, 66
Oven Swiss Steak, 66
Party Beef Casserole, 65

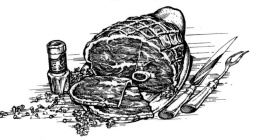

Hot Tuna Sandwiches, 34
Mashed Potato for One, 277
Microwave Parmesan Chicken, 219

MUFFINS
A.M. Delight Muffins, 99
Apricot Muffins, 101
Banana Crumb Muffins, 96
Chocolate Chip Mini-Muffins, 103
Ham and Cheese Muffins, 104
Rhubarb Nut Muffins, 101
Sunny Cornmeal Muffins, 279

MUSHROOMS
Baked Mushroom Rice, 55
Chicken Mushroom Stew, 78
Country Mushroom Soup, 42
Cream of Mushroom Soup, 39
Mushroom Barley Soup, 41
Mushroom Beef Patties, 82
Mushroom Cheese Stromboli, 44
Mushroom Lamb Chops, 73
Mushroom Spaghetti Sauce, 68
Pork with Mushroom Sauce, 244

MUSTARD
Honey-Mustard Turkey Meatballs, 11
Pheasant in Mustard Sauce, 72

NUTS
Almond Cranberry Tart, 147
Almond Dream, 17
Almond Rhubarb Coffee Cake, 100
Almond-Apple Stuffed Turkey, 87
Black Walnut Brownies, 121
Caramel Nut Bars, 299
Cranberry Nut Dessert, 137
Cream Filberts, 118
Hazelnut Crunchers, 117
Hickory Nut Cake, 152
Honey Pecan Snaps, 127
Jeweled Cookies, 117
Nutty Chicken Pita Sandwiches, 38
Peanut Cookies, 126
Pecan-Date Cheese Ball, 15
Pineapple Nut Bread, 100
Pistachio Chip Cookies, 128
Rhubarb Nut Muffins, 101
Simple Pecan Rolls, 239
Sweet Snack Mix, 14
Trail Mix, 267
White Chocolate Party Mix, 10
Zesty Snack Mix, 16

OATS
Banana Oatmeal Cookies, 124

Bushel of Cookies, 295
Cookies in a Jiffy, 219
Fruitcake Cookies, 122
Oatmeal Dinner Rolls, 197
Oatmeal Raisin Bars, 302
Oatmeal Wheat Bread, 259
Snack Bars, 116
Toasted Coconut Cookies, 116

ONIONS
Four-Onion Soup, 40
Marinated Vidalia Onions, 21
Onion Orange Salad, 265
Orange Onion Chicken, 76
Scalloped Onions and Peas, 204
Vidalia Onion Soup, 48

ORANGE
Apple Orange Bread, 98
Citrus Mint Punch, 8
Diabetic Orange Cookies, 126
Eggnog Molded Salad, 24
Onion Orange Salad, 265
Orange-Buttered Peas, 265
Orange Charlotte, 136
Orange Cream Fruit Salad, 271
Orange-Glazed Ham, 166
Orange Knots, 98
Orange Onion Chicken, 76
Orange Rice Medley, 265
Orange Sauce for Angel Food Cake, 217
Turkey with Orange-Honey Glaze, 265

PANCAKES & FRENCH TOAST
Blueberry French Toast, 90
Blueberry Sour Cream Pancakes, 85
Multigrain Pancakes, 75
Pancakes for Two, 285

PASTA & NOODLES (also see Spaghetti)
Antipasto Salad, 28
Beet Macaroni Salad, 26
Chicken Salad for 50, 302
Dilled Chicken Salad, 272
Garlic Pasta, 58
Layered Basil Salad, 301
Layered Spinach Salad, 290
Mom's Lasagna, 170
Pizza Casserole, 291
Pork Stroganoff, 253
Spinach Pasta Sauce, 83
Summertime Pasta Salad, 234
Tuna Pasta Salad, 259
Turkey Noodle Soup, 249
Turkey Pasta Supreme, 74
Turkey Primavera, 90
Zesty Vegetable Beef Soup, 49

PEACHES
Baked Peaches, 283
Cherry-Peach Dumplings, 139
Grilled Peaches with Berry Sauce, 201

Peachy Applesauce Salad, 25

PEANUT BUTTER
Chocolate Easter Eggs, 167
Chocolate Peanut Butter Cookies, 128
Peanut Butter Bars, 197
Peanut Butter Cream Pie, 185
Peanut Butter Puffs, 15
Peanut Butter Tarts, 241
Quick Ghost Cookies, 124
Sweet Snack Mix, 14

PEAS
Hearty Split Pea Soup, 38
Orange-Buttered Peas, 265
Peas and Carrots with Mint, 57
Scalloped Onions and Peas, 204
Split Pea Soup, 45

PEPPERS
Barley-Stuffed Peppers, 75
Calico Rice, 58
Grilled Fajitas, 78
Pepper Steak, 68
Rice-Stuffed Peppers, 86
Squash and Pepper Saute, 255
Stuffed Pepper Soup, 41
Sweet Pepper Relish, 113
Swiss Steak for Two, 283
Tomato Pepper Steak, 88
Zesty Stuffed Peppers, 82

PIES & TARTS
Almond Cranberry Tart, 147
Apple Pie Filling, 137
Berry Best Fried Pies, 147
Berry Tarts, 146
Blueberry Cream Pie, 150
Brownie Pie, 136
Bumbleberry Pie, 148
Buttermilk Pie, 133
Concord Grape Pie, 138
Crustless Pumpkin Pie, 146
Fresh Raspberry Pie, 153
Glazed Pineapple Pie, 140
Peanut Butter Cream Pie, 185
Peanut Butter Tarts, 241
Perfect Apple Pie, 152
Plum Pie, 132
Raisin Butterscotch Pie, 151
Refreshing Lemon Pie, 236
Southern Ambrosia Apple Pie, 142
Vanilla Cream Fruit Tart, 135

PINEAPPLE
Aloha Burgers, 51
Fluffy Pineapple Torte, 171

Issue-by-Issue Index

Do you have a favorite dish from a specific Taste of Home issue but can't recall the recipe's actual name? You'll easily find it in this categorized listing of recipes by issue.

Black Bean and Corn Salad, 24
Fresh Vegetable Salad, 166
German Potato Salad, 298
Hearty Reuben Salad, 209
Lemon Rice Salad, 26
Turkey Fruit Salad, 21
Wild Asparagus Salad, 23

SANDWICHES
Aloha Burgers, 51
Barbecued Pork Sandwiches, 298
Dilly Roast Beef Sandwich, 39
Hot Tuna Sandwiches, 34
Mushroom Cheese Stromboli, 44

SIDE DISHES
Au Gratin Carrots, 58
Breakfast Potatoes, 285
Cranberry Wild Rice Pilaf, 59
Creamy Asparagus and Carrots, 54
Mom's Easy Bean Bake, 58
Parmesan Baked Potatoes, 166
Rice Croquettes, 54
Spicy Hash Browns, 295
Tangy Coleslaw, 196
Three-Rice Pilaf, 54
Valentine Cutouts, 263
Warm Cabbage Slaw, 298
Zucchini Pancakes, 251

SOUPS
Bachelor Chili, 31
Bean Soup with Dumplings, 48
Ham and Bean Soup, 43
Italian Chicken Soup, 40
Sausage Kale Soup, 49
Sizzling Rice Soup, 42
Split Pea Soup, 45

APRIL/MAY

APPETIZERS & SNACKS
Chutney Cracker Spread, 13
Creamy Chicken Spread, 14
Low-Fat Bean Dip, 13
Pretzels with Cheese Dip, 9
Zesty Snack Mix, 16

BREADS & ROLLS
Almond Rhubarb Coffee Cake, 100
Cheesy Garlic Bread, 171
"Chicken Little" Cinnamon Rolls, 271
Golden Raisin Buns, 102
Honey Corn Bread, 189
Oatmeal Wheat Bread, 259
Sour Cream 'n' Chive Biscuits, 98

CONDIMENTS
Ranch-Style Dressing, 109
Rhubarb Relish, 109
Rhubarb-Strawberry Sauce, 108

COOKIES
Banana Oatmeal Cookies, 124
Chocolate Chip Cookie Mix, 291
Chocolate Icebox Cookies, 215
Diabetic Orange Cookies, 126

Slice-and-Bake Cookies, 126
Soft Lemonade Cookies, 120

DESSERTS (*also see Cookies*)
Apple Cheesecake, 189
Buttermilk Pie, 133
Cherry Pudding Cake, 290
Coconut Layer Cake, 143
Fluffy Pineapple Torte, 171
Go Anywhere Rhubarb Squares, 138
Rhubarb Raisin Crisp, 132
Southern Shortcake, 146
Spiced Pineapple Upside-Down Cake, 139

MAIN DISHES
Amy's Green Eggs and Ham, 66
Braised Lamb Shanks, 80
Deluxe Ham Omelet, 80
Easy Taco Casserole, 80
Egg Pizzas, 72
Huevos Rancheros, 67
Mom's Lasagna, 170
Mushroom Lamb Chops, 73
Mushroom Spaghetti Sauce, 68
Old-Fashioned Lamb Stew, 72
Paprika Chicken, 188
Pheasant in Mustard Sauce, 72
Pizza Casserole, 291
Potluck Spareribs, 290
Quick Taco Platter, 215
Red Beans and Sausage, 81
Roast Lamb with Plum Sauce, 80
Sausage and Egg Casserole, 271
Spring Breakfast Strata, 76
Tangy Beef Stroganoff, 71

MUFFINS
Apricot Muffins, 101
Banana Crumb Muffins, 96
Chocolate Chip Mini-Muffins, 103
Ham and Cheese Muffins, 104
Rhubarb Nut Muffins, 101
Sunny Cornmeal Muffins, 279

SALADS
Antipasto Salad, 28
Apple Ham Salad, 279
Fruited Chicken Salad, 291
Ham 'n' Cheese Potato Salad, 290
Layered Spinach Salad, 290
Marinated Vidalia Onions, 21
Orange Cream Fruit Salad, 271
Salmon-Stuffed Tomatoes, 22
Strawberry Gelatin Salad, 24
Three-Green Salad, 170
Tuna Pasta Salad, 259

SANDWICHES
Baked Southwest Sandwiches, 34
Barbecued Hot Dogs, 50
Big Sandwich, 38
Dilly Turkey Melt, 32
French Dip, 43
Grilled Ham and Egg Salad Sandwiches, 46
Hearty Chicken Club, 36
Italian Sloppy Joes, 44
Nutty Chicken Pita Sandwiches, 38
Poor Boy Sandwich, 42
Salmon-Salad Sandwiches, 41

Sausage-Stuffed Loaf, 36
Tuna Burgers, 48

SIDE DISHES
Asparagus with Pimientos, 188
Basil Spaetzle, 57
Mexican Rice, 215
Oven-Baked Asparagus, 61
Potato-Spinach Casserole, 56

SOUPS
Chilled Sorrel Soup, 36
Creamy Tomato Soup, 259
Peasant Soup for One, 279
Vidalia Onion Soup, 48

JUNE/JULY

APPETIZERS & SNACKS
Cajun Popcorn, 12
Cucumber Dill Spread, 11
Herbed Garlic Toast, 8
Mozzarella Puffs, 16
Stuffed Jalapenos, 267
Trail Mix, 267
Tuna Snack Spread, 15
Veggie Dill Dip, 11

BEVERAGES
Almond Dream, 17
Blackberry Breeze, 17
Blackberry Fizz, 9
Cinnamon Apple Refresher, 17
Citrus Mint Punch, 8
Fruit Juice Cooler, 200
Lemon Cranberry Cider Tea, 17
Raspberry Lemon Smoothie, 17
Warm Tea Punch, 17

BREADS
Blueberry Streusel Coffee Cake, 97
Cheesy Corn Bread, 267
Lemon Blueberry Biscuits, 211
Sesame French Bread, 255
Soft Breadsticks, 201

CONDIMENTS
Crisp Sweet Relish, 111
Easy Salsa, 108
Four-Berry Spread, 109
Poppy Seed Parmesan Salad Dressing, 108
Strawberry Salsa, 110
Three-Hour Refrigerator Pickles, 113

COOKIES & BARS
Bake-Sale Lemon Bars, 301
Chocolate Peanut Butter Cookies, 128
Peanut Cookies, 126
Toasted Coconut Cookies, 116

DESSERTS (*also see Cookies & Bars and Pies*)
Berry Tarts, 146
Chocolate Eclairs, 141
Chocolate Mousse with Strawberries, 135
Cookies-and-Cream Cake, 134
Grilled Peaches with Berry Sauce, 201
Lemon Whirligigs with Raspberries, 149
Mama's Spice Cake, 175
Raspberry Ribbon Cheesecake, 144

Diabetic Recipes Index

*Refer to this index when you're looking for a recipe that uses less
sugar, salt and fat and that includes Diabetic Exchanges. These good-for-you
recipes are conveniently marked with this check ✓ throughout the book.*

The Cook's Quick Reference

From the *Taste of Home* Test Kitchens

Substitutions & Equivalents

Cooking Terms

Guide to Cooking with Popular Herbs

Substitutions & Equivalents

Equivalent Measures

3 teaspoons	=	1 tablespoon	16 tablespoons	=	1 cup
4 tablespoons	=	1/4 cup	2 cups	=	1 pint
5-1/3 tablespoons	=	1/3 cup	4 cups	=	1 quart
8 tablespoons	=	1/2 cup	4 quarts	=	1 gallon

Food Equivalents

Grains

Macaroni	1 cup (3-1/2 ounces) uncooked	=	2-1/2 cups cooked
Noodles, Medium	3 cups (4 ounces) uncooked	=	4 cups cooked
Popcorn	1/3 to 1/2 cup unpopped	=	8 cups popped
Rice, Long Grain	1 cup uncooked	=	3 cups cooked
Rice, Quick-Cooking	1 cup uncooked	=	2 cups cooked
Spaghetti	8 ounces uncooked	=	4 cups cooked

Crumbs

Bread	1 slice	=	3/4 cup soft crumbs; 1/4 cup fine, dry
Graham Crackers	7 squares	=	1/2 cup finely crushed
Rich Round Crackers	12 crackers	=	1/2 cup finely crushed
Saltine Crackers	14 crackers	=	1/2 cup finely crushed

Fruits

Bananas	1 medium	=	1/3 cup mashed
Lemons	1 medium	=	3 tablespoons juice, or 2 teaspoons grated peel
Limes	1 medium	=	2 tablespoons juice, or 1-1/2 teaspoons grated peel
Oranges	1 medium	=	1/4 to 1/3 cup juice, or 4 teaspoons grated peel

Vegetables

Cabbage	1 head	=	5 cups shredded	Green Pepper	1 large	=	1 cup chopped
Carrots	1 pound	=	3 cups shredded	Mushrooms	1/2 pound	=	3 cups sliced
Celery	1 rib	=	1/2 cup chopped	Onions	1 medium	=	1/2 cup chopped
Corn	1 ear fresh	=	2/3 cup kernels	Potatoes	3 medium	=	2 cups cubed

Nuts

Almonds	1 pound	=	3 cups chopped	Pecan Halves	1 pound	=	4-1/2 cups chopped
Ground Nuts	3-3/4 ounces	=	1 cup	Walnuts	1 pound	=	3-3/4 cups chopped

Easy Substitutions

When you need...		Use...
Baking Powder	1 teaspoon	1/2 teaspoon cream of tartar + 1/4 teaspoon baking soda
Buttermilk	1 cup	1 tablespoon lemon juice or vinegar + enough milk to measure 1 cup (let stand 5 minutes before using)
Cornstarch	1 tablespoon	2 tablespoons flour
Honey	1 cup	1-1/4 cups sugar + 1/4 cup liquid
Light Cream	1 cup	1 tablespoon melted butter + enough whole milk to measure 1 cup
Onion	1 small, chopped (1/3 cup)	1 teaspoon onion powder or 1 tablespoon dried minced onion
Tomato Juice	1 cup	1/2 cup tomato sauce + 1/2 cup water
Tomato Sauce	2 cups	3/4 cup tomato paste + 1 cup water
Unsweetened Chocolate	1 square (1 ounce)	3 tablespoons cocoa + 1 tablespoon shortening or oil
Whole Milk	1 cup	1/2 cup evaporated milk + 1/2 cup water

Cooking Terms

HERE'S a quick reference for some of those cooking terms used in *Taste of Home* recipes:

Baste—To moisten food with melted butter, pan drippings, marinades or other liquid to add more flavor and juiciness.

Beat—A rapid movement to combine ingredients using a fork, spoon, wire whisk or electric mixer.

Blend—To combine ingredients until *just* mixed.

Boil—To heat liquids until bubbles form that cannot be "stirred down". In the case of water, the temperature will reach 212°.

Bone—To remove all meat from the bone before cooking.

Cream—To beat ingredients together to a smooth consistency, usually in the case of butter and sugar for baking.

Dash—A small amount of seasoning, less than 1/8 teaspoon. If using a shaker, a dash would comprise a quick flip of the container.

Dredge—To coat foods with flour or other dry ingredients. Most often done with pot roasts and stew meat before browning.

Fold—To incorporate several ingredients by careful and gentle turning with a spatula. Used generally with beaten egg whites or whipped cream when mixing into the rest of the ingredients to keep the batter light.

Julienne—To cut foods into long thin strips much like matchsticks. Used most often for salads and stir-fry dishes.

Mince—To cut into very fine pieces. Used often for onion or fresh parsley.

Parboil—To cook partially, usually used in the case of chicken, sausages and vegetables.

Partially set—Describes the consistency of gelatin after it has been chilled for a small amount of time. Mixture should resemble the consistency of egg whites.

Puree—To process foods to a smooth mixture. Can be prepared in an electric blender, food processor, food mill or sieve.

Saute—To fry quickly in a small amount of fat, stirring almost constantly. Most often done with onions, mushrooms and other chopped vegetables.

Score—To cut slits partway through the outer surface of foods. Often used with ham or flank steak.

Stir-Fry—To cook meats and/or vegetables with a constant stirring motion in a small amount of oil in a wok or skillet over high heat.

Guide to Cooking with Popular Herbs

HERB	APPETIZERS SALADS	BREADS/EGGS SAUCES/CHEESE	VEGETABLES PASTA	MEAT POULTRY	FISH SHELLFISH
BASIL	Green, Potato & Tomato Salads, Salad Dressings, Stewed Fruit	Breads, Fondue & Egg Dishes, Dips, Marinades, Sauces	Mushrooms, Tomatoes, Squash, Pasta, Bland Vegetables	Broiled, Roast Meat & Poultry Pies, Stews, Stuffing	Baked, Broiled & Poached Fish, Shellfish
BAY LEAF	Seafood Cocktail, Seafood Salad, Tomato Aspic, Stewed Fruit	Egg Dishes, Gravies, Marinades, Sauces	Dried Bean Dishes, Beets, Carrots, Onions, Potatoes, Rice, Squash	Corned Beef, Tongue Meat & Poultry Stews	Poached Fish, Shellfish, Fish Stews
CHIVES	Mixed Vegetable, Green, Potato & Tomato Salads, Salad Dressings	Egg & Cheese Dishes, Cream Cheese, Cottage Cheese, Gravies, Sauces	Hot Vegetables, Potatoes	Broiled Poultry, Rissoles, Poultry & Meat Pies, Stews, Casseroles	Baked Fish, Fish Casseroles, Fish Stews, Shellfish
DILL	Seafood Cocktail, Green, Potato & Tomato Salads, Salad Dressings	Breads, Egg & Cheese Dishes, Cream Cheese, Fish & Meat Sauces	Beans, Beets, Cabbage, Carrots, Cauliflower, Peas, Squash, Tomatoes	Beef, Veal Roasts, Lamb, Steaks, Chops, Stews, Roast & Creamed Poultry	Baked, Broiled, Poached & Stuffed Fish, Shellfish
GARLIC	All Salads, Salad Dressings	Fondue, Poultry Sauces, Fish & Meat Marinades	Beans, Eggplant, Potatoes, Rice, Tomatoes	Roast Meats, Meat & Poultry Pies, Hamburgers, Casseroles, Stews	Broiled Fish, Shellfish, Fish Stews, Casseroles
MARJORAM	Seafood Cocktail, Green, Poultry & Seafood Salads	Breads, Cheese Spreads, Egg & Cheese Dishes, Gravies, Sauces	Carrots, Eggplant, Peas, Onions, Potatoes, Dried Bean Dishes, Spinach	Roast Meats & Poultry, Meat & Poultry Pies, Stews & Casseroles	Baked, Broiled & Stuffed Fish, Shellfish
MUSTARD	Fresh Green Salads, Prepared Meat, Macaroni & Potato Salads, Salad Dressings	Biscuits, Egg & Cheese Dishes, Sauces	Baked Beans, Cabbage, Eggplant, Squash, Dried Beans, Mushrooms, Pasta	Chops, Steaks, Ham, Pork, Poultry, Cold Meats	Shellfish
OREGANO	Green, Poultry & Seafood Salads	Breads, Egg & Cheese Dishes, Meat, Poultry & Vegetable Sauces	Artichokes, Cabbage, Eggplant, Squash, Dried Beans, Mushrooms, Pasta	Broiled, Roast Meats, Meat & Poultry Pies, Stews, Casseroles	Baked, Broiled & Poached Fish, Shellfish
PARSLEY	Green, Potato, Seafood & Vegetable Salads	Biscuits, Breads, Egg & Cheese Dishes, Gravies, Sauces	Asparagus, Beets, Eggplant, Squash, Dried Beans, Mushrooms, Pasta	Meat Loaf, Meat & Poultry Pies, Stews & Casseroles, Stuffing	Fish Stews, Stuffed Fish
ROSEMARY	Fruit Cocktail, Fruit & Green Salads	Biscuits, Egg Dishes, Herb Butter, Cream Cheese, Marinades, Sauces	Beans, Broccoli, Peas, Cauliflower, Mushrooms, Baked Potatoes, Parsnips	Roast Meat, Poultry & Meat Pies, Stews & Casseroles, Stuffing	Stuffed Fish, Shellfish
SAGE		Breads, Fondue, Egg & Cheese Dishes, Spreads, Gravies, Sauces	Beans, Beets, Onions, Peas, Spinach, Squash, Tomatoes	Roast Meat, Poultry, Meat Loaf, Stews, Stuffing	Baked, Poached & Stuffed Fish
TARRAGON	Seafood Cocktail, Avocado Salads (all), Salad Dressings	Cheese Spreads, Marinades, Sauces, Egg Dishes	Asparagus, Beans, Beets, Carrots, Mushrooms, Peas, Squash, Spinach	Steaks, Poultry, Roast Meats, Casseroles & Stews	Baked, Broiled & Poached Fish, Shellfish
THYME	Seafood Cocktail, Green, Poultry, Seafood & Vegetable Salads	Biscuits, Breads, Egg & Cheese Dishes, Sauces, Spreads	Beets, Carrots, Mushrooms, Onions, Peas, Eggplant, Spinach, Potatoes	Roast Meat, Poultry & Meat Loaf, Meat & Poultry Pies, Stews & Casseroles	Baked, Broiled & Stuffed Fish, Shellfish, Fish Stews